"I've never had quite the response to a literary biography that I've had to this one. As told by Leavell, the story of Marianne Moore's psychological entrapment by her mother is the stuff of a monumental novel or play or opera."　　　　　—Bruce Bawer, *The New Criterion*

"At the heart of Linda Leavell's revealing, respectful biography is a 'tyrannical love' . . . Leavell wields her wealth of material with great tact and conviction of the depth of love and understanding between Marianne and her mother."

　　　　　—Lucy Daniel, *The Sunday Telegraph* (five out of five stars)

"Leavell's skillful interpretations of both poems and often cryptic family letters yield a remarkably clear and sympathetic analysis of the internal forces that brought Moore's talents to the fore and made the crafting of poetry 'the only outlet for her individuality and ambition.'"

　　　　　—Megan Marshall, *The Washington Post*

"A modernist master comes to vibrant life in Linda Leavell's *Holding On Upside Down*."　　　　　—Megan O'Grady, Vogue.com

"Linda Leavell's fine new biography is the first life of Moore to be done with the blessing of Moore's executors . . . [and] the first . . . to characterize her mother unequivocally as a lesbian."

　　　　　—Dan Chiasson, *The New Yorker*

"With a Moorish blend of precisely chosen details, high ethical standards, and love, [Linda Leavell] rescues Moore from invisibility and restores her to the forefront of modernist poetry."

　　　　　—Meg Schoerke, *The Hudson Review*

"Leavell writes very well indeed about a woman who found the metaphors to talk about a most unconventional childhood while observing and testing and questioning convention."

　　　　　—Hilton Als, *Page-Turner* (blog), *The New Yorker*

"Marianne Moore is a 'poet of paradoxes,' Leavell asserts at the outset of this superb, recalibrating biography . . . Like a sculptor working in clay, Leavell steadily builds up contour and texture as she portrays Moore as a poet of 'sly wit' and 'undetected but stormy passion.'"
—Donna Seaman, *Booklist* (starred review)

"[*Holding On Upside Down* is] deliberate and sensitive—'creeping slowly as with meditated stealth,' in Moore's words—capable of containing her many contradictions, most notably her desires for recognition and privacy."   —Parul Sehgal, *Book forum*

"This first authorised biography is notably level-headed and clear, with much new information about Moore's family and early life, health, finances and the father she never knew. With permission to quote from the archive, . . . Leavell is able to provide a deeper psychological study of this 'wonderful, amazing and delightful creature,' as Elizabeth Bishop called her."   —Jane Rye, *The Spectator*

"*Holding On Upside Down* goes a long way toward restoring Moore's place as a cornerstone of modern American poetry."
—Bruce Jacobs, *Shelf Awareness*

"*Holding On Upside Down* is an essential addition to the canon of literary biography."   —Patrick James Dunagan, *Rain Taxi Review of Books*

"Finally, Marianne Moore has a biography that does justice to the richness, complexity, and significance of her writing career . . . *Holding On Upside Down* combines the grace, humor, and compelling story line one expects in good fiction with the detail of formidable scholarship, definitively deconstructing myths about Moore that have prevented too many readers and scholars from expending the effort required to deal seriously with her work . . . Whether you are interested in a good summer read or in taking notes on Leavell's scholarly excavations, you will like this book. It is a magnificent biography."
—Cristanne Miller, *Modernism/modernity*

"In this well-researched biography, Moore emerges as a poet of freedom with a passionate inner life."   —*Publishers Weekly*

HOLDING
ON
UPSIDE
DOWN

Farrar, Straus and Giroux

New York

HOLDING

ON

UPSIDE

DOWN

The Life

and Work of

MARIANNE

MOORE

LINDA

LEAVELL

Farrar, Straus and Giroux
18 West 18th Street, New York 10011

Printed in the United States of America
First edition, 2013

Owing to limitations of space, all acknowledgments for permission to
reprint previously published material can be found on page 457.

Library of Congress Cataloging-in-Publication Data
Leavell, Linda, 1954–
    Holding on upside down : the life and work of Marianne Moore / Linda
Leavell. — First edition.
        pages   cm
    Includes bibliographical references and index.
    ISBN 978-0-374-10729-1 (hardcover)
    1. Moore, Marianne, 1887–1972.   I. Title.

PS3525.O5616 Z6857 2013
811'.52—dc23
[B]
                                                                2013006521

Designed by Jonathan D. Lippincott

Farrar, Straus and Giroux books may be purchased for educational, business, or
promotional use. For information on bulk purchases, please contact the Macmillan
Corporate and Premium Sales Department at 1-800-221-7945, extension 5442, or
write to specialmarkets@macmillan.com.

www.fsgbooks.com
www.twitter.com/fsgbooks • www.facebook.com/fsgbooks

1   3   5   7   9   10   8   6   4   2

to Brooks

One's life has taught one something, and I think it is "arrogant" to decree that it should not teach others something.

—Marianne Moore, 1938

Contents

Preface

G reatly beloved yet little understood, highly esteemed yet barely known outside of English departments, Marianne Moore is a poet of paradoxes. She was generous to a fault in answering queries and granting interviews, yet she revealed her deepest feelings to no one. Although she left to posterity an archive that chronicles virtually every week of her life, the archive reveals little about her private thoughts, emotions, fears, and aspirations. She had lifelong, deeply devoted friendships—including those with T. S. Eliot, Ezra Pound, Elizabeth Bishop, and other well-known writers—but she never married and apparently never fell in love. "No poet has been so chaste," wrote the critic R. P. Blackmur in 1935. Her literary maiden-aunt persona won many fans in the 1950s and '60s. But for too long since then the perceived chasteness in her art and life has all but dehumanized her in the public imagination.

From the time her poems first received notice, critics were divided on the question of feeling in her work. Mark Van Doren, Louis Untermeyer, and other leading critics of the 1920s called her poetry haughty, needlessly obscure, and devoid of emotion. But all the poet-critics whom we now consider important—T. S. Eliot, Ezra Pound, H.D. (Hilda Doolittle), William Carlos Williams, and later Wallace Stevens—praised her in superlatives. From 1915, when her poems first attracted their attention, until 1925, when she won the prestigious Dial Award and assumed editorship of *The Dial*, they thought her the finest poet writing in America. They admired especially the subtlety of feeling in her work and her startling diction. "With Miss Moore a word is a word most," wrote Williams, "when it is separated out by science, treated with acid to remove the smudges, washed, dried, and placed right side up on a clean surface."

The one point upon which both her detractors and admirers agreed is that her readership would never be large. Van Doren placed her among the "insufferable high brows" while Eliot said her poetry was "too good . . . to be appreciated anywhere." No one, least of all the poet herself, could have predicted that three decades later, at the age of sixty-two, she would launch a career as a celebrity and public poet. *Vogue, Harper's Bazaar*, and *Ladies' Home Journal* published her poems; *McCall's* paid her a thousand dollars for an interview. Macmillan and then Viking issued new books of her poems as fast as she could produce them. Her readings on college campuses drew crowds to rival those of Robert Frost and Dylan Thomas. On her eightieth birthday in 1967, she appeared on *Today* and a few months later on *The Tonight Show*. She threw out the first pitch to open the 1968 season in Yankee Stadium and was recognized everywhere for her tricorne hat and cape. She was widely hailed as America's most distinguished living poet.

While her new books of the late 1950s and '60s received glowing reviews from poets as diverse as James Dickey and John Ashbery, public life took a toll on her poetry. Instead of spending months on a single poem, as she often did earlier in her career, she wrote quickly and prolifically. She wrote primarily for a listening audience or for a specific publication or event. Ever more fluid and technically proficient, her late poems lose the verve of her earlier work; they charm rather than disarm the reader. *The Complete Poems of Marianne Moore*, published to much fanfare on her eightieth birthday, omitted nearly half the poems she published before 1951 and included virtually all those she published afterward. This far-from-complete collection distorted her oeuvre and framed her reputation for decades to come.

Meanwhile during the 1960s and '70s young people were discovering the poetry of Allen Ginsberg, Sylvia Plath, Anne Sexton, and other consciousness-raising taboo breakers. To readers captivated by such voices, the witty ironies of Marianne Moore came to seem irrelevant and her elderly quirkiness embarrassing. Identity politics in the 1970s called upon women to express raw anger and honest sexuality. Rather than celebrating Moore's success as a woman poet, the new generation of feminists accused her of repressing her sexuality in order to achieve that success.

For more than a decade after her death in 1972, Moore's poetry languished in obscurity. Serious readers never doubted her prominence among America's major modernists, but she became more than ever a poet's poet, unread by all but the elite. As identity politics loosened its grip in the late 1980s and '90s, academics began turning their attention to women poets who did not necessarily fit the post–World War II feminist paradigm. Graduate students were advised to take another look at Marianne Moore. Those who investigated the Moore archives in Philadelphia and who sought out her early poems in rare-book rooms discovered a poet quite different from the media darling who still lingered in the public imagination. Dissertations and monographs about Moore's feminism and her contribution to modernism proliferated.

As more professors began teaching her poetry, anthologies expanded their selections of her work and substituted her early, difficult poems for the later, more accessible ones. In contrast to the anti-Semitism that was taking its toll on the reputations of Pound and Eliot, Moore's politics began to seem remarkably prescient. Her poetry pled for multicultural tolerance and endorsed biodiversity many decades before these issues grabbed our national attention. Her posthumously published *Complete Prose* and *Selected Letters* along with new editions of her poems have provided today's readers a more complete view of her achievements than did her *Complete Poems*. Yet the woman behind those achievements remains as elusive as ever.

"Moore's poems are famously unforthcoming," wrote Brad Leithauser in a 2004 book review, "you can study them for years and derive little sense of her family, friendships, jobs, and littler sense still of the nature of any balked hopes and private losses."

It is not Moore's dearth of feeling but rather its depths, she claimed, that make her poems unaccommodating. "Feeling at its deepest—as we all have reason to know—tends to be inarticulate. If it does manage to be articulate, it is likely to seem overcondensed, so that the author is resisted as being enigmatic or disobliging or arrogant." Yet expressing her feelings in enigmatic, overcondensed poetry became for Marianne Moore a means of survival. From the time she was twenty-three until her mother's death when Marianne was almost sixty, the two women lived together and were rarely apart for even one night. Mary Warner Moore did all of the housekeeping and mostly supported her daughter's literary ambitions. She was the first reader of everything that Marianne wrote, and she served as a trusted assistant during the four years that Marianne edited *The Dial*. The two were genuinely devoted to each other and enjoyed each other's company—while the mother exacted from her adult daughter the emotional subservience of a young child. Marianne had no place to hide—except in her poems.

Her many poems about obscure, and often armored, animals are both studies in the art of survival and acts of survival themselves. As impersonal and unforthcoming as they might seem, these poems reveal much, I have found, about the poet's interior life. Marianne always defended her mother to outsiders. She told an interviewer in the 1950s that her mother was "the least possessive of beings," yet said in a later interview, without mentioning her mother, that she felt herself to be "a case of arrested emotional development." Her poetry includes many images of confinement, such as "the sea in a chasm, struggling to be / free and unable to be." And it rails against greed, tyranny, egotism, and all forms of possessiveness. Her heroes are nocturnal, unassuming, solitary creatures. They survive by fortitude and nonviolent resistance.

As constraining as Mary's love was, Marianne found in that love the artistic space she needed. As she wrote about the eggs of an obsessive mother in "The Paper Nautilus," she was "hindered to succeed." Not only did she insist to her friends that living with her mother provided the ideal environment in which to work, she proved it. With literally no "room of her own," she wrote poetry that stands at the forefront of American modernism.

Living within the narrow confines of her mother's love, Marianne Moore came to identify with the oppressed and marginalized. She valued individual freedom and autonomy above all else and knew from experience the difficulty of achieving them. "Politically I cannot contemplate anything but freedom for all races and persons," she wrote. Sweeping generalizations of any kind were for her a form of tyranny, and she repeatedly warned against typecasting or lazy first impressions. Those who make the effort to be precise and to recognize nuances of individuality she praised as heroes. The cry for freedom in her domestic life becomes in her poetry a political imperative.

I knew Marianne Moore's name before I knew that of almost any other poet. The eighty-year-old celebrity read at the University of Texas when I was thirteen, and two of my friends were driven a hundred miles to hear her. The next time her name caught my attention, I was researching an honors thesis on William Carlos Williams. I learned from his autobiography that he and Moore formed part of the circle of artists who clustered in Greenwich Village tearooms and art galleries during the years before World War I. "We'd have arguments over cubism which would fill an afternoon," recalled Williams. "There was a comparable whipping up of interest in the structure of the poem. It seemed daring to omit capitals at the head of each poetic line. Rhyme went by the board. We were, in short, 'rebels,' and were so treated." That poets, painters, sculptors, and photographers knew one another, launched magazines together, and drew inspiration from one another fascinated me. I wanted to know as much about their world as I possibly could.

Marianne Moore's place in this world was the focus of my research in 1984, when I first investigated her archive at the Rosenbach Museum & Library in Philadelphia. I found long, vividly detailed letters about Moore's first visit to Alfred Stieglitz's influential 291 gallery, snippets of conversation from subsequent Village gatherings, and numerous reviews she saved of the famous 1913 Armory Show, which introduced cubism and fauvism to the American public. My findings at the Rosenbach and my growing appreciation for Moore's enigmatic poetry convinced me that she understood the questions posed by modern art as few writers of the time did and that she responded to those questions in ingenious ways. I began to understand why her better-known contemporaries held her in such awe. This was the subject of my first book, *Marianne Moore and the Visual Arts: Prismatic Color.*

When Marianne's elder brother, Warner, left home for college in 1904, the Moore family threesome began a voluminous correspondence that would last for most of their lives. While searching in these letters for Moore's encounters with the visual arts, I became enthralled with the family's private language and the complexities of their relationships. They called one another names such as Fangs, Biter, and Baby Fawn, and they used a private vocabulary that often baffled me. The world they shared seemed as idyllic to me as that of *The Wind in the Willows*, a book all three adults loved. After they read it in 1914, Marianne adopted the character of Rat, the "scribbler of verses," for herself. Mary, her mother, became the home-loving Mole, and Warner, the distinguished Mr. Badger. Not only did I recognize in the family letters the verbal wit and playful obscurity of Moore's poetry, but I found myself envious of the family's closeness. The private language and mythology both reinforced their bonds of affection and excluded outsiders. But the more I read, the more I began to sense something lurking in this family idyll that was both less innocent and more interesting.

Contrary to the common perception that Moore led a chaste and cloistered life—a view she tried to foster—these letters reveal a family dynamic that was both familiar to me and strange. The value the Moores placed upon education and their high moral purpose were familiar. But not the animal names, the subterfuge, and the extraordinary agility with words—nor the absent father, the lesbian mother, the feminist upbringing, and the fierce opposition to most heterosexual unions. "Sometimes I think 'If I could just present [Thomas] Hardy with our life story,'" Marianne's mother once mused, "'he might have a ready-made story needing no adjustings or additions.'" I found a drama in these letters quite different from the narrative of Moore's first biography, which focused on the "external facts" of her life.

The first few weeks of a National Endowment for the Humanities seminar on literary biography (conducted by N. John Hall at the CUNY Graduate Center in 1998) convinced me to attempt a biography of Moore. But knowing that her family had denied the previous biographer permission to quote from her archive, I did not want to proceed if they would stand in my way. I was advised to write to Marianne Craig Moore, the poet's niece and literary executor, and request a meeting. She called me immediately upon receiving my letter and offered to come to New York with her sister Sallie the following week. To my great surprise, they told me over lunch that they had been looking for a biographer and had been waiting for the right person to step forward. I had hoped for cooperation at best and found myself interviewing for my dream job.

In the course of our three-hour conversation, I warned them that the Marianne Moore who emerged from my pages might not resemble the aunt they knew. Sallie Moore nodded appreciatively and told me she hoped I would bring imagination as well as scholarship to the task. On the basis of my first book and our meeting that day, I was granted the full support of the estate. The Moores made it clear that they wanted me to have the freedom to tell my story as I pleased. The whole family has been remarkably magnanimous ever since, even when my findings surprised them and contradicted what they had always believed to be true. I was shown documents that no one outside the family had seen. These documents, especially a large cache of letters about Moore's father, filled a major gap in her history.

The great majority of my conclusions, however, are drawn from archives that have been available to scholars since the poet's death in 1972. I knew when I began the project that my greatest challenge as Moore's biographer was not accumulating the facts—though that would take time—so much as gleaning from the abundance of facts a compelling story. But eight years and six hundred draft pages into the project, I realized that while I had come to know Mary and Warner rather well, I still knew little about Marianne. She was the least engaging character in the family drama I was piecing together. Why did she stay with her mother rather than making the break into adulthood as Warner did? And why did she appear to share her mother's genteel pieties at the same time that she joined a group of artists whose sole purpose was to overthrow them? Most important, where out of the profusion of words that make up her archive—some thirty-five thousand letters as well as manuscripts, notebooks, and photographs—could I find answers to these questions?

I was not much better off than the biographers who begin with a paucity of facts, I realized, and would have to pay close attention, as they do, to circumstantial evidence. Marianne remained angry for three years after Warner announced his intention to marry Constance Eustis, an intelligent and spirited young woman. But she shared her feelings with no one. To Mary she presented only a "little narrow white face with a monk-like severity." To Warner she wrote brief, newsy letters. The long, playful letters she was not writing revealed more about her feelings than the letters she wrote. While learning to read my subject's silences, I cut my draft by nearly half and rewrote the book. The best record of her inner life, I discovered, was in her poems.

Although Moore's poetry does not invite biographical interpretation, it does offer excellent advice to the biographer. As an expert herself in assembling facts and quotations, she taught me the difference between "relentless accuracy"—which demands hard work, imagination, and respect for human dignity—and what she called "the haggish, uncompanionable drawl of certitude."

Marianne Moore stands with Emily Dickinson and Elizabeth Bishop, her famous protégée, as one of America's greatest women poets. And she stands alongside Eliot, Pound, Stevens, and Williams as one of our great modernists. She deserves to be more widely known, if for no other reason, because her work epitomized what other modernists aspired to. Eliot and Williams found little to like in each other's work and yet both nearly idolized Moore's. She did not just break with the past but responded in imaginative ways to the questions modernism posed.

Like the iridescent surfaces and shifting perspectives to which she was drawn, her poetry can seem puritanical to one reader and postmodern to another. And while she often took political positions that are labeled conservative, she was arguably the most liberal-minded of the modernists. She herself eschewed such labels and asked her readers to do so. With distinctive phrases such as "certain Ming products" and "miniature cavalcades of chlorophylless fungi," she undercuts aesthetic hierarchies and reveals the poetry in America's "business documents and school-books." With her startling precision and unsettling wit, she invites us to view the world with what she regards as a characteristically American mind, one that is "incapable of a shut door in any direction."

Linda Leavell
Fayetteville, Arkansas
July 2012

Family Tree

CRAIGS

William Craig (1794–1855) m. Mary Vance Watson (1797–1878)
  John Watson Craig (1830–1908) m. Caroline Crossan
    nine children
  Hugh Boyd Craig (1831–1904) m. Martha Orr
    Mary Watson Craig "Cousin Mary" (1862–1955) m. Ira Hayes
                  Shoemaker
    John Orr Craig (1865–1942) m. Elizabeth Brewer
      Sue Brewer Craig m. Ralph Stauffer
        Ralph Stanley Stauffer (b. 1925)
        John Craig Stauffer (b. 1926) m. Phyllis Schilt
          three children
        Martha Craig Stauffer (b. 1934)
      Mary Watson Craig m. Clifford Heindel
        Clifford Craig Heindel (b. 1939)
  Mary Craig (1833–1893) "Grandma" m. George Eyster
    Jennie Eyster (1859–1877)
    Sallie Eyster (1860–1881)
  Jennie Craig (1835–1863) m. John Riddle Warner
    Mary Warner (1862–1947) m. John Milton Moore
      John Warner Moore (1886–1974) [see Moores]
      Marianne Craig Moore (1887–1972)
  William Henry Craig (1837–1899) m. Sarah Ellen Keyser
    two children
  David Vance Craig (1841–1878) m. Louisa J. Reed
    four children

MOORES

Levi Moore (1793–1865) m. Amanda Gunn (1793–1888)
  William McKendrie Moore (1815–1902) m. Elizabeth Frances
                  Smith (1826–1904)
    Louisiana Margaret Moore (1848–1934) m. James Wood Ricker
      Margaret Ricker (b. 1871)
      Will Ricker (b. 1873)

Carl Ricker (b. 1876)
May Ricker (1878–1950)
Elizabeth Ricker (b. 1880)
Mary Elizabeth Moore (1850–1931)
Virginia Sarah Moore (1853–1920) m. Elisha Barton Greene III
    nine children
Elizabeth Florence Moore (1856–1929) m. Richard R. Peebles
    seven children
John Milton Moore (1858–1925) m. Mary Warner
    John Warner Moore (1886–1974) m. Constance Eustis
        Mary Markwick "Mark" Moore (1919–2010) m. John Reeves
        Sarah Eustis "Sallie" Moore (1921–2007)
        Marianne Craig "Bee" Moore (b. 1923)
        John Warner Moore, Jr. (b. 1926), m. Virginia H. Smith
            John Warner Moore III (1956–1991)
            David Markwick Moore (b. 1962) m. Elizabeth McCabe
                three children
            James McWilliams Moore (b. 1972)
    Marianne Craig Moore (1887–1972)
Enos Levi Moore (1860–1932) m. Helen "Nellie" Robinson
Anna Lora Moore (1863–1865)
Milton Moore (1819–1855) m. Hannah Weller
Maria Moore (1822–1894) m. Solomon McCall
Enos Bascomb Moore (1823–1906) m. (a) Maria Pratt (b) Mary
                                    Ellen Switzer
    six children
Lora Moore (1827–1844)
Samuel Gunn Moore (1833–1911) m. Isabella Flanders
    five children
Mary Ellen Moore (1837–1862)

HOLDING
ON
UPSIDE
DOWN

1

Sojourn in the Whale

December 1915

On the first of December 1915, Marianne Moore made her way down Fifth Avenue in search of a now famous address. This was not her first trip to New York, but it was her first venture into the city unescorted. Many visitors at the time were unnerved by the blare of motorcars and the crush of pedestrians, the incessant motion of the city. But while Marianne compared herself half jokingly to Jonah in Nineveh and his "Sojourn in the Whale," the city thrilled her. She had gained a sense of independence while navigating Philadelphia on her own during college, and the brisk morning air brought back that rush of freedom.

Her venture began that morning at the YWCA Training Center, a recently refurbished mansion on East Fifty-second Street. She was staying there as the guest of two sisters, family friends, who hoped that she would find the mission of the YWCA as captivating as they did. For her first two days in New York, she dutifully attended training sessions with them.

A snapshot taken before they left home shows the three women standing next to a horse-drawn buggy. Marianne is modeling her new "Airedale coat," as she called it. Her chin tucked under, she peers at the camera from beneath her most brilliant feature—the thick auburn braid wound many times about her head. Her shirtwaist blouse with a tie at the neck and her ankle-length gored skirt make her look crisply professional like her traveling companions.

It was not, however, enthusiasm for the YWCA that brought the aspiring poet from Carlisle, Pennsylvania, to New York. As soon as she could politely break free, she headed straight for 291 Fifth Avenue. Six years earlier she had jotted the address in her notebook when a college acquaintance told her about Alfred Stieglitz and showed her his magazine *Camera Work*.

Although Marianne had read avidly about new directions in the arts during the intervening years and knew all about the controversial Armory Show of 1913, she read little in that time about Stieglitz or his influential gallery. Yet 291, as the gallery was called, had quietly introduced Picasso, Matisse, and other leaders of the Parisian avant-garde to New York well before the Armory Show brought them to the attention of a broader public. The gallery did not advertise or accept commissions. Its purpose rather was to open possibilities for what art might be. Alongside lavish reproductions of photographs and drawings, *Camera Work* published articles assessing what was "modern" in art. And 291 was as much a gathering place for experimental painters, photographers, and writers as it was an exhibition space. Its regulars used words such as *honesty, freedom, enthusiasm,* and *individuality* to describe the *spirit* of the place.

When Marianne arrived at her destination, a Caribbean elevator man who had himself contributed to *Camera Work* took her to the fourth floor. She expected to find a photography studio but instead crossed the threshold of American modernism into a modest exhibition room, fifteen feet square. A green burlap curtain covered the bottom half of the walls, and a large copper bowl gathered light in the center of the room. On the gray walls above the curtain hung the brightly colored, cubist-inspired paintings of Oscar Bluemner, an architect.

What impressed Marianne that morning even more than the room or the paintings was Alfred Stieglitz himself. Old enough to be her father, he had a commanding white mustache and thick, disheveled hair. He repeatedly adjusted his pince-nez as he talked.

"Mr. Stieglitz was exceedingly unemotional and friendly," Marianne recalled of this first meeting, "and finally after telling me how he was hated, said I might come back and look at some of the things standing with their faces to the wall in a back room." The exhibition room had no heat; and so, having determined that Miss Moore was the kind of visitor he liked, Stieglitz invited her to the back room, where the stove was.

He showed her works by Picasso and Picabia and by several of his American protégés, including John Marin and Marsden Hartley. (A month later he could have shown her the work of a new discovery, Georgia O'Keeffe.) He invited her to return before she left New York in case he had new things to show her and also suggested she stop by the Modern Gallery on her way back to the Training Center. There she saw recent issues of *Camera Work* and an exhibit of Van Goghs.

Little did Marianne imagine that the next winter she would herself become a regular at 291 or that within a decade she would edit an arts magazine much like *Camera Work*. For now the YWCA seemed a far more likely option for a twenty-eight-year-old woman such as herself. In college she was drawn to writers now associated with modernism— Robert Browning, W. B. Yeats, and especially Henry James—and she demonstrated a prescient distaste for sentimentality. But as of 1909, when she graduated, there was no modern movement in literature with which to identify. Living in Carlisle over the next six years, she read everything she could find about contemporary art, theater, music, and literature. And with nary an acceptance nor a word of encouragement for the first five of those years, she sent her cryptic, hard-edged poems to magazines such as *The Century* and *The Atlantic Monthly*.

Then in 1912 Ezra Pound, H.D., and Richard Aldington launched a new movement in poetry. Calling themselves Imagists, they rejected florid metaphor and conventional meter in favor of their own elliptical, haiku-like verses. Reading about the Imagists, Marianne learned the names of several experimental magazines and sent her work to *The Masses* in New York, *Poetry* in Chicago, and *The Egoist* in London even before seeing the magazines themselves. Immediately she began to receive the encouragement she had long sought. In the spring of

1915 her first published poems appeared simultaneously in *Poetry* and *The Egoist*.

When H.D. recognized Marianne's name in *The Egoist*, she wrote to identify herself as a Bryn Mawr classmate, Hilda Doolittle, and as Mrs. Richard Aldington. Marianne's poems were the finest that she and Aldington, who was poetry editor for *The Egoist*, had seen from America, H.D. said, and she urged Marianne to come to London. Yet as much as Marianne longed to accept the invitation, she could not consider leaving her mother even for a summer.

Just a few months after receiving H.D.'s letter, she received one from Alfred Kreymborg accepting several of her poems for *Others*, the magazine that he edited out of his Greenwich Village apartment. He called her poems "'an amazing output and absolutely original' if with his 'uneddicated consciousness' he might judge'" and encouraged her to come to New York. The *Others* contributors often met, he said, to socialize and talk about poetry. Thus, when Mary Hall Cowdrey and her sister Ruth invited Marianne and her mother to go to New York, Marianne leaped at the chance. The Moores could not at the time afford clothes for both to go, and so the mother refused the invitation for herself but splurged on a new coat for her daughter.

At four o'clock on the same day Marianne first visited 291, she returned to the YWCA Training Center to find Kreymborg waiting for her, as planned. She had feared he might be one of the "literary monstrosities, long-haired, speaking a lingo, etc." that she had read about, but the young man she met was "quiet, dignified, dry, unpuffed up, very deliberate and kind." "I was never so surprised to see anyone," she said afterward. Kreymborg was in turn surprised by Marianne. He later described her as "an astonishing person."

Speaking softly but seamlessly with a hint of Missouri in her vowels, she asked Kreymborg all about the New York artists and writers of whom she had read. When she asked about Floyd Dell, editor of *The Masses*, Kreymborg said he "couldn't live with him." But Marcel Duchamp, whose *Nude Descending a Staircase* had gained such notoriety at the Armory Show, was "a lovely fellow." When Kreymborg asked if she had mentioned his name to Stieglitz, she said, "No, I didn't know he knew . . . you or any of the men who are interested in poetry."

Kreymborg was such a 291 devotee that he wanted to create a gathering of poets and artists along with his magazine. The previous summer he had launched *Others* at an artists' colony near Grantwood, New Jersey, where the contributors often congregated for Sunday-afternoon picnics. With the onset of winter he moved to 29 Bank Street, where he both published *Others* and continued to host parties. Was there, Marianne inquired, to be such a party while she was there? He was not sure, since both he and his wife had been sick. But he invited her home to supper if she would be willing to accompany him on an errand on the way.

On their way to the Village, Marianne encountered her first actual bohemian. Kreymborg took her to the Madison Avenue studio of Adolf Wolff, a sculptor, poet, and anarchist who had recently been released from the political prison on Blackwell's Island. He first appeared leaning over the banister wearing a "blouse," Marianne thought, and after they climbed four flights of stairs, he greeted her "very limply." She also noted his black hair, beard, and accent. She did not say that she liked Wolff's poetry, but she admired his sculpture— "done all in right angles" yet "full of drollery and wit."

Marianne instantly felt at ease with Kreymborg and his wife, Gertrude. Neither of them smoked, she told her mother, nor did they exhibit any "bohemian fierceness." Yet Kreymborg seemed to know everyone in the New York art world, both poets and artists. When Marianne asked about Amy Lowell, he told her about Lowell's lectures to the Poetry Society, a highbrow group that met in evening dress over dinner. As for Lowell herself, she was "impossible" and "about so wide." She talked about nothing but herself and her falling out with Ezra Pound. Kreymborg did not, he confessed, like Pound's recent poetry but liked him personally. Marianne in turn told what she knew of H.D. and the other London Imagists and offered to put in a good word for *Others* with H.D. and Richard Aldington. After supper Kreymborg showed her photographs that Stieglitz had given him, portraits of literary figures and "some of the most superb pictures of snow and engines and boats that I have ever seen."

In her long account of the evening afterward, Marianne clearly wished to persuade her family of her new friends' respectability. She noted that Kreymborg wore a suit much like one of her brother's and emphasized the Kreymborgs' "silver spoons like ours" and bookshelves "full of the things we have, the Brownings in lambskin and Tennyson and Shelley." But her wall-by-wall description of the Kreymborgs' apartment indicates that she was also beginning to envision an artist's life for herself. It was possible, she saw, to live among artists and writers without adopting a bohemian lifestyle.

Shortly after her trip, she wrote "Is Your Town Nineveh?," in which she contrasts Jonah's desolation in the corrupt city of Nineveh with her own sense of freedom in New York.

Is Your Town Nineveh?

Why so desolate?
   And why multiply
      In phantasmagoria about fishes,
         What disgusts you? Could
            Not all personal upheaval in
               The name of freedom, be tabooed?

Is it Nineveh
   And are you Jonah
      In the sweltering east wind of your wishes?
         I myself, have stood
            There by the aquarium, looking
               At the Statue of Liberty.

It was the first of many poems she wrote over the course of her career about freedom, both personal and political.

After the YWCA training sessions were over and the Cowdrey sisters returned to Carlisle, Marianne remained in New York for several days. She stayed in the Village with two friends who ran Varick House, a Presbyterian boardinghouse for working girls. Both Margaret and

Laura were "in ecstasies," Marianne said, when she brought Kreymborg to Varick House to dine with them, and Margaret thought it was
"the mark of the elect" when Kreymborg, to her surprise, addressed
Marianne by her first name.

Laura was a published poet herself and the older sister of the poets
William Rose Benét and Stephen Vincent Benét. Marianne had
known Laura and William, who were slightly older than herself, since
childhood. Though she had seen little of William in recent years, he
had achieved enviable success as a poet. By the time Marianne visited
New York, he had published two volumes of poetry and had appeared
so often in *The Century* that the magazine hired him as an editor.
Laura, too, regularly appeared in magazines that rejected Marianne's
work. Even seventeen-year-old Stephen Vincent Benét had published a
collection of poems.

It was hard on Marianne that *The Masses*, known for its revolutionary
politics, accepted poems by William and Laura but rejected her own.
She had already determined by the time she went to New York that she
and William "had diverged and diverged until we had nothing in common aesthetically." Benét's poetry epitomized the conventional verse
forms and complacencies against which *Others* poets defined themselves.

Although *Poetry* had introduced Imagism two years before the first
issue of *Others* appeared, *Others* was the first of the little magazines to
devote itself exclusively to experimental poetry. Despite its small circula-
tion and as yet unknown contributors—such as T. S. Eliot, Ezra Pound,
Wallace Stevens, and William Carlos Williams—it received much attention in the press, mostly in the form of amused ridicule. "You know
that is the most modern thing in poetry," opined one of Marianne's table-
mates at Varick House, "no rhyme, no meter, no anything, just craziness."

Only a few critics, such as J. B. Kerfoot of *Life* magazine and W. S.
Braithwaite of the *Boston Evening Transcript*, took *Others* at all seriously. Kerfoot, a 291 associate, praised the "revolutionary" spirit of *Others*. "It is the expression of a democracy of feeling," he wrote, "against
an aristocracy of form."

A few days after Marianne moved her things to Varick House, she
and Laura called on William Rose Benét at *The Century*. Having recently seen the Kreymborgs' kitchen, where *Others* was published, and
the back room of 291, where *Camera Work* was published, she noted

the "light, airy, club-like" atmosphere of the *Century* reception room, where she and Laura waited for William to see them. Despite initial apprehensions on both sides, Marianne and William soon recovered their old friendliness, and it pleased Marianne that he showed as much interest as he did in *Others* and the new poetry. The notices by Kerfoot and Braithwaite, she decided, had made the conservatives nervous.

The conservatives had little to worry about. They would prevail in the popular anthologies and magazines until after World War II. Despite modernism's growing momentum over the next two decades, none of the modernists who now dominate anthologies—Eliot, Pound, Stevens, Williams, H.D., and Moore—would, for instance, win the Pulitzer Prize in poetry until Moore won it for her *Collected Poems* in 1952. Yet Stephen Vincent Benét had won it twice by then, and William Rose Benét won it as late as 1942. The Pulitzer and other accolades heaped upon Moore's *Collected Poems* in the early 1950s not only launched a new career for her as a celebrity but also ushered in the reading public's acceptance of modernist poetry.

During the course of her ten days in New York, Marianne did return to 291. Although Stieglitz had no new art to show her, he introduced her to J. B. Kerfoot, with whom Marianne held her own discussing the current state of literary criticism.

She also twice visited the Daniel Gallery, which was run by the *Others* poet Alanson Hartpence. Hartpence was "a positive dogmatist on art theory," according to Marianne, and played an important role in educating poets about modern painting. She stood her ground there, too, in assessing the current exhibit of paintings and tapestries by William and Marguerite Zorach. The Zorachs contributed poems to *Others* and later designed covers for it. They may have come to the party Kreymborg hosted in Marianne's honor, where she met several of the poets and artists who would soon form her social nexus.

What Marianne learned and saw in New York so impressed her that her work matured rapidly after she returned home. By the fall, when she was exploring New York galleries again and socializing with the *Others* group, she had developed her unique rhymed stanza, one of modern literature's most original innovations.

Over the next few years her work received praise from both sides of the Atlantic. In a 1916 review, H.D. compared her work to "light flashed from a very fine steel blade." And in 1918, after thirteen of Moore's poems appeared in an *Others* anthology, reviews by both Pound and Eliot singled out her poetry for praise. What these poet-critics chiefly admired was her bold departure from sentimentality. Appreciation for her formal innovations would come later. To Williams, who became an early friend and ardent admirer, she epitomized all that was new and vital in modern poetry—"the unbridled leap."

Marianne did not, as might be supposed from the boldness of her poetry and her conversation, return from New York and insist upon moving there. Just after Christmas her family did discuss leaving Carlisle, but there is no indication that Marianne's literary aspirations were a factor in their discussion. When an acquaintance asked if she were considering a move to New York, she replied that nothing could be further from her thoughts.

Her foremost concern at the time was to persuade her elder brother, Warner, to live with her mother and herself. He had not lived at home since he left for college eleven years earlier. Yet both children knew that their mother's deepest desire was to live out her days under the same roof with her son and daughter. Mary Warner Moore, then fifty-three, became convinced that she did not have long to live. (She would live to be eighty-five.) Marianne so feared for her mother's life that she persuaded Warner to make Mary's dream a reality. The following spring he accepted a pastorate in Chatham, New Jersey, and in August the three moved into the manse together.

One happy circumstance of this otherwise miserable experiment was Chatham's proximity to New York. An hour's train ride brought Marianne to the heart of the city.

2

A Genius for Disunion

to 1887

So intense was the mutual devotion of Mary Warner Moore and her two adult children that it bewildered and incensed outsiders. William Carlos Williams complained that Marianne's adoration of her brother and "pathological" devotion to her mother prevented her from marrying any "literary guys." Her genius, he guessed, came from her father, who was "indefinite! maybe skipped, maybe dead—never mentioned."

Even the poet's ancestors were a daily presence. Their faces hung on her walls. Their things crowded her rooms. Their voices—preserved in stories and in bundle after bundle of letters—rang in her ears. As did their silences. Scotch-Irish and clannish they called themselves. It was a family of profuse words and inauspicious marriages.

Yet readers of Moore's poetry would hardly guess that she had a family. In only one poem, "Spenser's Ireland," does she allow a family member to appear undisguised:

It was Irish;
    a match not a marriage was made
    when my great great grandmother'd said

with native genius for
disunion, "Although your suitor be
    perfection, one objection
is enough; he is not
Irish."

This great-great-grandmother, Susan Henderson, was a Scot by birth. She married an Irishman, John Riddle, against *her* parents' wishes. In 1815 they left the Riddle family home in County Monaghan and brought their large family to New York. Marianne's great-grandmother there met the objectionable suitor, an American. The Riddles then followed other Scotch Irish to Pittsburgh, where the "match" of the poem was made: Mary Riddle wed Henry Warner.

The son of a wealthy Dublin businessman, Henry Warner was as defiant a youth as his wife was compliant. At the age of twelve, he ran away from boarding school to join the navy and sailed throughout the British Empire for more than a decade. He brought to the family a love of the sea, his countrymen's gift for storytelling, and the sly wit inherited by his great-granddaughter.

Three of the couple's four children lived to pass on the "genius for disunion." The marriage of the youngest, Henry, to a tavern keeper's daughter caused his mother years of grief. So did the marriage of their daughter, Annie, to an abusive alcoholic. Only the marriage of the eldest, the poet's grandfather, received his parents' blessing. They hoped that marriage would tame the young minister, for he had had a succession of churches and fiancées before he settled in Gettysburg and began courting Jennie Craig. Although opposite in demeanor— John Riddle Warner had a fiery temper and Jennie Craig an even one—they shared a strong Christian faith and love of books. The happy union lasted three years.

It was primarily through her Craig relatives that Marianne learned about her Scotch-Irish heritage. Every summer she went with her mother and brother to Locust Hill, the Craig family homestead just north of Hagerstown, Maryland, near Welsh Run, Pennsylvania. The farm animals at Locust Hill became characters in stories that Marianne and Warner made up together, and Marianne's unpublished novel of the 1930s includes family lore that she first heard on the porch of the old farmhouse. Reminiscing about Locust Hill in 1954, Marianne wrote that "nothing will ever look as beautiful to me as the Pennsylvania corn and pumpkins and blue of the mountains."

Formed by two Appalachian ridges in the south central part of the state, Pennsylvania's Cumberland Valley extends from Hagerstown northeast through Chambersburg to Carlisle, where Marianne moved at the age of nine. During most of the twenty years that the Moores lived in Carlisle, their closest relative, Mary Craig Shoemaker, was compiling a genealogy and family history. She privately published *Five Scotch-Irish Families of the Cumberland Valley* in 1922. As Shoemaker's title makes clear, Scotch Irish was a regional as well as a family identity.

The poet's own "genius for disunion"—evident in her poetry of precise distinctions as well as in her distrust of romantic love—runs deep in her Scotch-Irish heritage. Early in the seventeenth century, King James I encouraged Protestant Scots and Englishmen to colonize northern Ireland, or Ulster. The Scottish immigrants resisted intermarriage with either the Irish natives or English colonists and thus maintained their Scottish Presbyterian identity—and reputation for clannishness—over many generations. Various religious, economic, and political factors forced waves of Scotch Irish to North America during the eighteenth century and to Pennsylvania in particular. Marianne's own ancestor, William Craig, received 150 acres from the Penns in 1739. His sons fought in the American Revolution.

Like others of Scotch-Irish descent, Shoemaker claims a significant role for her forebears in building the new nation. George Norcross, the Moores' minister in Carlisle, characterized the Scotch Irish as "strenuous asserters of civil and religious freedom . . . intelligent and patriotic . . . thrifty and hardy." "They brought to this country an indignant sense of outraged rights and persecuted piety," he said, and as followers of John Knox, they readily attached themselves to the Jeffersonian principle that "resistance to tyrants is obedience to God."

After the Easter Rising of 1916, Marianne called herself Irish rather than Scotch-Irish yet proudly identified with her ancestors. "I am Irish by descent," she told Ezra Pound, "possibly Scotch also, but

purely Celtic." Like many Americans, she supported the Irish nation-
alists who led the Easter Rising and opposed the Scotch Irish who
sided with the Crown. Her poem "Sojourn in the Whale," written in
1916, praises Ireland's ability to survive "every kind of shortage" and to
"rise automatically," like "water in motion," "when obstacles happened
to bar the path." Resistance to tyranny, in its various forms, is her
poetry's most pervasive theme.

On April 11, 1862, John Riddle Warner and Jennie Craig became parents to their first and only child, the poet's mother. Fifteen months
later Union and Confederate armies unexpectedly converged near their
Gettysburg home. Like most Gettysburg residents, Jennie and the
baby took refuge in the cellar. Reverend Warner, however, watched
the bloodiest battle of the Civil War through the trapdoor of his roof,
even when cannonballs were "whistling around in every direction."

In the weeks following the battle he tended the physical and spiritual needs of wounded soldiers from both sides, and Jennie made beds
on her floor for strangers who came to nurse the wounded. By the end
of the summer typhoid fever had spread through the region, and Jennie, whose health was fragile in any case, succumbed. She died on the
last day of September and was buried in Gettysburg's Evergreen Cemetery, within shouting distance of where Abraham Lincoln delivered
his famous address two months later. Today her arched marble head-
stone stands between two matching stones, on one side her husband's
and on the other side a single stone commemorating her daughter and
famous granddaughter.

Sightseers swarmed into Gettysburg after the battle, hungry for
eyewitness accounts such as Reverend Warner's. The battle offered
him a unique opportunity to distract himself from grief. In early 1864
he delivered a two-hour lecture called "The Three Days Battle of Gettysburg" at a church in Philadelphia. Although the church setting at first
inhibited applause, once it started, it was thunderous until the end.

John Riddle Warner spent the next six months delivering the lecture in churches and lecture halls from Baltimore to Boston. In February he addressed an audience of twenty-five hundred soldiers and
dignitaries at the Academy of Music in Philadelphia, and in May

Congress passed a resolution allowing him to speak in the House of Representatives, where the audience included President Lincoln. Invitations arrived less often after the first year, but the lecture drew crowds in Chicago and St. Louis as late as 1867. The minister friend who booked him in St. Louis arranged at the same time for him to preach in nearby Kirkwood—which resulted in Reverend Warner's accepting the pastorate at the Kirkwood Presbyterian Church the following November.

Seven decades later, when Marianne Moore gave her first public poetry reading, she felt her grandfather's fortifying presence. "Our ancestry speaks through us," she told her mother, "when we are put to the test."

Mary Warner was a beautiful child who quickly won the affection of all who knew her. Her paternal grandmother wanted to take her home to Allegheny (now part of Pittsburgh) as soon as Jennie died, but Mary lived with her aunt and uncle in Chambersburg for the next year. George and Mary Craig Eyster, Jennie Craig's sister, had two daughters a little older than Mary and provided a comfortable home for her. Although she got her share of "little whippens," she received indulgences, too, such as permission to wear a new pair of shoes to bed. All seemed content with the arrangement—except that Reverend Warner could not get his sister-in-law to write the kind of letters he craved. He had little sympathy with the demands of managing a household and three small children, and Mary Eyster's weekly notes assuring him of his daughter's good health did not suffice.

The burning of Chambersburg—and the Eysters' home—by Confederate cavalry in July 1864 provided the occasion for change he needed. In September he took Mary with him to Allegheny for two weeks' vacation and left her there with his parents when he returned to Gettysburg. Despite Mary's greater distance from him and his concerns about burdening his aging parents, he could count on vivid letters from his father and on the familiar discipline of his mother—who disapproved of children wearing new shoes to bed.

The decision did not please Mary Eyster, whose recent effort to write longer letters revealed the deep affection she and her daughters had for little Mary. She continued to press for Mary's return and over the years insisted upon seeing her, either by accompanying Reverend Warner to Allegheny or by having him bring Mary to Chambersburg.

Not only had Mary lost two mother figures before she turned three, but she also entered a more frugal existence with her grandparents than she had known before—without servants and without young playmates. She learned, however, to ask her grandfather to "bring out the moosy [music]" and to dance while he played the flageolet. From the time Mary arrived at her grandparents' home, she sat every week by her grandfather's side as he wrote a letter to her father. She soon began to "write" letters herself by scribbling lines on tiny sheets of paper that her grandfather tucked into his own letters. Life with her aging grandparents offered few amusements beyond the weekly ritual of writing letters, a ritual to which Mary attached great emotional significance for the rest of her life.

Her father came to visit twice a year, in December and August. "My own sad babyhood was kept on fire by a wild longing for my father," she recalled. Yet one morning when she saw him after his arrival late the night before, she was "horrified and cried terribly." "It is not my Pa," she cried, "take him away."

Despite his busy lecture schedule, Reverend Warner did not recover quickly from his wife's death. In 1867, when Mary was five, he moved to Kirkwood, Missouri, for its milder climate and better-educated congregation but mostly to relieve the "brown study" his relatives observed in him. Loneliness and despondency, however, continued to haunt him. He occasionally thought of bringing his daughter to live with him, but she remained in Allegheny, nursing her grandparents and keeping house for them until their deaths in 1873 and 1876. Mary was fourteen when she moved to Kirkwood, yet not even her adoring presence could lift the cloud over the pastoral study.

If he could not provide his daughter with a cheerful home, Reverend Warner did provide her with a first-class education. He had, despite his parents' limited means, graduated at the top of his class from Duquesne College (later absorbed into what is now the University of Pittsburgh) and then completed the Theological Seminary of the Associate Reformed Presbyterian Church in Allegheny. Rather than send his daughter to the local Kirkwood Seminary, where he served on the board, he sent her a short train ride away, to the highly regarded Mary Institute in St. Louis.

The Mary Institute was founded by William Greenleaf Eliot, a Unitarian minister of Reverend Warner's acquaintance, and named in memory of Dr. Eliot's beloved daughter. The founder also of Washington University, Dr. Eliot is now best remembered as T. S. Eliot's grandfather. Readers have sometimes marveled that two poets of such prominence as Eliot and Moore were born within a year of each other in the same western city. The coincidence may be at least a little explained by the value their grandfathers placed upon education and by Dr. Eliot's indirect influence on both poets.

Mary Warner attended the Mary Institute under the progressive leadership of Calvin Smith Pennell, the nephew and protégé of the famous American educator Horace Mann. Whereas Kirkwood Seminary and most other girls' schools of the time emphasized character development over academic subjects, Pennell implemented a curriculum whereby the girls had to demonstrate academic proficiency before they could advance to the next grade or receive a diploma. A report card from Mary's senior year shows that she studied reading, English literature, French, English history, history and geography, mathematics, physics, and drawing.

Mary made high marks in school and shared her father's love of books. But people who knew her as a young woman thought of her not as an intellectual like her father but as a beauty. Her friends at the Mary Institute provided her access to society in St. Louis, and the Eysters provided access to society in Philadelphia, where George Eyster served as assistant treasurer of the United States, in charge of the Philadelphia mint. Mary spent months at a time with her aunt and uncle, who had lost both of their own daughters to tuberculosis. She received the attentions of young men in Philadelphia and St. Louis, but she met her future husband through a Kirkwood family, the Rickers.

Mary became friendly with Louisiana Moore Ricker, a professional journalist and mother of five, while "Lou" was visiting her in-laws in Kirkwood. Lou was so named because she was born on a steamboat en route to Louisiana, and she had grown up on the banks of the Ohio River in Portsmouth, Ohio. During the winter of 1882–83, Mary went to visit her friend in Portsmouth and there met Lou's younger brother, John Milton Moore, the sixth of seven Moore children.

If Marianne Moore's maternal ancestors commanded a presence in her life, her paternal ones commanded an equally great absence there. Her parents separated before she was born, and she never met her father. When she was asked as a college freshman what her father did for a living, she replied that she could not remember. She never saw a picture of him until late adulthood, and she refused to answer journalists' questions about him until she was almost seventy. Her mother, rarely at a loss for words about anything, described herself as "deaf and mute" when anyone asked about her husband.

Mary's silence lasted for fifty years, from shortly after Marianne's birth in 1887 until the 1937 flood of the Ohio River aroused her concern. She asked her banker to contact the Portsmouth Moores and send them a hundred dollars. Several months later she learned through her banker that John Milton Moore had died and that his five sisters had as well.

Another five years passed before Mary wrote directly to her nieces, Elizabeth and May Ricker, the recipients of her hundred dollars, and began a regular correspondence with them. They responded warmly, sent photographs and other mementos, and put Mary in contact with other Moore cousins. Over the years these cousins wrote to Marianne and her brother, included them in family reunions, and provided reminiscences and other forms of family history.

Marianne and Warner heard vivid stories from their cousins about Captain William Moore, their paternal grandfather. He and his three brothers were riverboat men. With one brother he designed and built the steamer *Hope*, which he served as captain, and with another brother he established a foundry at Portsmouth to make steamboat boilers. He cut quite a figure in his Prince Albert coat, diamond pin, and silk top hat. A man of solitary habits and few words, Captain Moore spent most of his leisure hours in his library, reputedly one of the finest in the state. Like his poet granddaughter, he enjoyed performances of almost any kind and never missed the circus. Most impressive to his juvenile relatives was his tender regard for animals. One grandchild saw him "take a struggling fly from syrup, wash it in a teaspoon, dry it with his napkin then set it free."

By contrast, Marianne and Warner learned little from their cousins about their own father. Marianne told an interviewer in 1965 that her father and his brother were engineers, both graduates of the Stevens Institute in Hoboken, New Jersey. In fact, neither graduated. John's younger brother, Enos, entered Stevens first, and John joined him there for only one year.

The 1879 Stevens yearbook indicates that John nevertheless made an impression. He was known for his sense of humor, his devotion to the theater, and his proficiency in debate. The Moore brothers' duet of "There Is a Balm in Gilead" culminated one evening of hilarity. On another memorable evening, twenty-seven Stevens boys ferried across the river to New York to see a performance by the popular actress "Miss Lotta" Crabtree. They presented her with a basket of flowers at intermission and afterward, at Delmonico's, christened themselves "The Lotta Racket." Credit for the success of the evening was given to "the untiring zeal" of John M. Moore, the "committee of one" who made all the arrangements. His zeal and extravagance undoubtedly account for his short career at Stevens.

It is easy to imagine what John Moore saw in Mary Warner. Like Miss Lotta, she had a petite figure and a doll's face framed by curls. Mary did not think John handsome, but this mattered little to her. She liked his boyish spirit and sense of humor. When he called on her in Philadelphia during the fall of 1883, the subject of marriage had already been mentioned. The Eysters liked him, but Mary was not ecstatic over him, she told her father, and would not be brokenhearted if her father did not approve.

Reverend Warner thought highly of the Moore family but did have misgivings about John himself. John bought Mary a diamond brooch and planned a monthlong wedding trip, but he had no job at the time of the wedding. A month earlier he left his position in his father's foundry under murky circumstances. Reverend Warner did not, however, stand in the way of his daughter's happiness, as his ancestors had done. The couple were married in Kirkwood on June 4, 1885.

Reverend Warner's fears were not unfounded. To pay for the brooch and wedding trip, John Moore borrowed $1,200, using his and his brother's stock in the foundry as collateral, but he allowed the stock to be undervalued, thus threatening the financial stability of the entire business. The money lasted long enough to move himself and his bride to Newton, a suburb of Boston, where he and Enos believed they had prospects. After working in their father's foundry for years, the brothers had at last had enough of their father, the Old Gentleman, or "O.G.," as they called him, and decided to strike out on their own.

Cheerfulness prevailed in the early months of Mary's marriage. Enos lived with the newlyweds, and the brothers pored over the newspaper in search of work. But while there was much laughter among them, four months of looking brought no jobs. The country was experiencing a depression in 1885, and the brothers demanded high salaries. Mary observed how wearing the ordeal was to John, but his optimism did not falter until October.

"I am utterly helpless," he then confessed one morning. "I never knew before what '*helpless*' meant: it seems to me the Lord has made me as humble as I can get to be: I am now willing to do anything he wants me to do: I know of no earthly place to go for a situation, and my heart just sinks within me." They then prayed together, and Mary wrote her father that she felt blessed to have found "the most thoughtful, and in every way the most devoted husband that my imagination can conceive of."

A week later John Moore wrote Reverend Warner himself, apologizing for not providing better for Mary. He had had no income since April. But unlike Enos, who went out daily to look for work, John relied on prayer. Reverend Warner began supporting the young couple, as he would for the next two years. He invited them to move to Kirkwood, but they would not consider it. By Thanksgiving Enos had found a job, but John's spirits continued to plummet.

Enos quickly earned the favor of his employer and a new respect from Mary, who called him "a mechanical *genius*" with a "*remarkable* business ability." Enos wanted to invent a smokeless furnace—one that through combustion of gases would burn only a blue, hence smokeless, flame. He convinced his employer to form the Stevens Furnace Company and to employ both brothers for a handsome salary of $1,500 each.

For the first two months of 1886 Enos and John conducted their experiments with "untiring zeal," according to Mary. She describes them flying up and down stairs, back and forth between roof and cellar, clutching their wires and insulation. The brothers laughed and teased each other when their efforts failed and then went back to work. John mostly withdrew from the project in March due to a lingering cold and exhaustion. Enos persisted through the summer, making steady improvements until July, when two models proved more disappointing than ever. Enos then moved to Virginia to accept a lucrative position there.

John and Mary both feared that God was punishing the brothers for breaking the fifth commandment—honor thy father—and John began a program of earnest Bible reading. At first Mary approved. But when Reverend Warner came to Newton in August, he observed that his son-in-law could talk about nothing else and that his talk was often irrational. By January John cared for nothing except "the question of eternal salvation" and would take no action of any kind, such as finding employment, until that question could be resolved. "He talks much to me on this subject," wrote Mary, "and I must say I'm often weary and confused."

Meanwhile, on June 18, 1886, Mary delivered a son. She named him John Warner Moore after her father and called him Warner. Her mother-in-law pleaded with John to bring his family to Portsmouth, where a job was waiting at the foundry. And Reverend Warner urged them to move to Kirkwood. But John would not discuss any change whatsoever and was in such an incapacitated state, Mary told her father, that she could not bear to bring him to Kirkwood even if it meant using all of her future inheritance and going to work herself in order to support him.

Throughout the spring of 1887, Mary agonized over her own connubial responsibilities. Above all, she wished to do right by her wedding vows, even if it meant considerable sacrifice. Although John took no interest in anything except the Bible, and occasionally the baby, she assured her father that she never felt herself in danger. "He is kind and cheerful in all his treatment of me," she said, "and our attitude toward each other is pleasant, and even loving." They thus conceived a daughter.

At times Mary reasoned that the man with whom she was living was not the man she married. At other times she blamed herself. She asked God how one as prayerful as herself could make such a mistake. She concluded that it was her own blind will that deceived her, that John was the same person he had always been, and that she had thought marriage would change him. She lived with a man obsessed with the Bible, her own greatest authority, and yet marveled at "how silent the Bible is about wives ever being justified in leaving their husbands!"

Hers was not the only tragedy in the family. After suffering from a series of financial disappointments and an unspecified "affliction," George Eyster died suddenly, probably by his own hand, on the last day of 1886. Mary Eyster—having now lost her entire family—accepted Reverend Warner's invitation to move into the Kirkwood manse. She had for many years been like a mother to Mary, and after Warner's birth Mary began calling her Mother. The children would call her Grandma.

Fearing for Mary's and Warner's safety, Reverend Warner sent Mary Eyster to Newton in April 1887. Mary found her aunt much changed after her recent ordeal, and they set out a garden together, a pleasure for both women. Mary wrote her father in June that for some months she had had "vague, random thoughts" of going to Wernersville, Pennsylvania, or to Battle Creek, Michigan, for medical treatment. She thus informed him of her pregnancy. It was the cue for which Reverend Warner had been waiting.

In August he came to Newton himself. He sent Mary, Mary Eyster, and fourteen-month-old Warner off to the Battle Creek Sanitarium and stayed in Newton with his incapacitated son-in-law. Enos arrived to help divide the household goods and then took John to Portsmouth.

Though now best known for the cornflakes he invented with his brother, J. H. Kellogg was a renowned abdominal surgeon. Mary expected to stay at Battle Creek until her child could be delivered surgically. She found Dr. Kellogg and the "hygienic" staff at Battle Creek eccentric but thought the treatments "splendid." These treatments included rest, fresh air, exercise, and a vegetarian diet rich in nuts and whole grains.

"I certainly look very different from when I came," she wrote her father after ten days, "and not all the change is due to the treatment, for I'm sure that absence from those dark scenes at Newton is of great benefit physically."

Although she continued to have confidence in Dr. Kellogg's surgical ability, she did not like his policy that children be kept from their mothers (for the relaxation of the mothers). After three weeks, she decided to take Warner to Kirkwood, but she expected to return to Battle Creek for the delivery.

Mary gave birth to her daughter, without surgery or complications, at her father's home on November 15, 1887. Mary sent word of the birth to Portsmouth and received a prompt, affectionate reply from her mother-in-law. A letter from her husband, who did not yet know he had a daughter, arrived about the same time from the Cincinnati Sanitarium. It was the first letter he had written since they parted in August, and he guessed Mary knew more about what had happened to him in the intervening months than he did. He was recovering from a psychotic episode, during which he was admittedly "real crazy" for several days.

John soon returned to Portsmouth and reluctantly began work at the foundry. But his letters and normally fluid handwriting reflect an agitated mind. He wrote his wife throughout the winter, pleading for reconciliation. After he wandered away from home without apparent purpose the following summer, Enos had him committed to the state asylum in Athens. John was diagnosed, according to court records, with "delusional monomania," his delusion being "that he is appointed to find the truths of the Bible."

A few months after Marianne's birth, Mary stopped answering the letters she received from her husband and in-laws. Her father encouraged her to cut relations with them completely. Though Mary worried that it was not right to do so, she wrote her mother-in-law that her memories of Newton were so sorrowful that all she wanted was relief from them.

Two years after the separation (there was never a divorce), Reverend Warner learned through the Rickers in Kirkwood that John Moore had severed his own hand. The patient took literally Matthew 5:30: "And if thy right hand offend thee, cut it off." Reverend Warner wrote to Athens, offering to go there if needed. The asylum superintendent answered that John Moore was in good physical health and that his mental health had not changed.

"He does not deplore the accident," explained the superintendent, "thinks he has done right and that the time will come when we will think as he does . . . On all other subjects he talks sensibly and the case is one of the most interesting and peculiar I have ever seen . . . He never asks about his family and seems to be entirely absorbed in his religious duties as he has interpreted them. In my view it is useless for his wife to anticipate much improvement or a restoration to his family."

Court records indicate that in 1895 and 1896 John Moore was often granted leave for up to two months at a time. And in November 1896 he was discharged from the asylum as recovered. He returned to Portsmouth, where he would remain for thirteen years until, after a gradual decline, Enos again had John committed. The doctors who examined John this time found him well-groomed and mannerly and his "remembrance of dates and events remarkable." But John told them that Captain Moore was not his father, "that God was his father." Noting in the report that John had no insane relatives, the doctors diagnosed him with "mania on moral and religious matters." He would remain in the Athens State Hospital until his death on May 11, 1925.

Mary sometimes sent photographs of the children to Portsmouth but refused the Moores' offers of affection and financial assistance. John Moore's release from the asylum in November 1896 coincided with Mary and the children's move to Carlisle. Enos attempted to call on her in Carlisle. But Mary sent ten-year-old Warner to the train station to meet his uncle—who in a stovepipe hat loomed tall over the boy—and to turn the man away.

In the late 1960s, Marianne Moore told one of her nieces that she thought half of who she was came from her father. She told another niece that she thought her creativity came from her father. What could she have meant? Surely something beyond her red hair (a Moore trait) and the predilection for circuses, animals, and fine hats she shared with her grandfather. She knew that Captain Moore kept a diary for most of his life and that Louisiana Ricker did as well, besides earning a living as a journalist. But the drive to put pen to paper was just as strong, if not stronger, on her maternal side. Perhaps it was her father's "untiring zeal" she sensed within her, a combination of what she called "perseverance" and "gusto."

Perhaps, too, she identified with his "silence," the silence she associated with her own most profound feelings. "Silence," a 1924 poem, suggests this possibility. The first line, "My father used to say," is followed by a ten-line quotation that ends:

> the deepest feeling always shows itself in silence;
> not in silence, but restraint.

The citations Moore included in *Observations* and subsequent books identify the speaker of the poem's first line as Miss A. M. Homans, thus informing the reader that the father in the poem is not her own. Some critics have seen a feminist irony in the long quotation, the daughter silenced by her father's praise of silence. But Moore perhaps enjoyed another dimension to the irony. The seemingly casual first line, "My father used to say," breaks her family's biggest taboo, their own great silence. Unlike the stereotypical Victorian patriarch, John Milton Moore was not a silencer of women but was himself silenced.

3

Designing Heaven

1887–1896

James Dickey once wrote that if he could choose a poet to design heaven, he would choose Marianne Moore. A utopian impulse does run through her poetry. Not only do poems such as "In the Days of Prismatic Color" directly describe a prelapsarian world but most of her animal and landscape poems create a quirky Eden: "an imaginary garden with real toads in it," as she wrote early in her career, or an "unconquerable country of unpompous gusto," as she wrote later. In an unfinished memoir that Moore began during the 1960s, she makes a utopia of her childhood.

Green shutters adorned the white-frame manse where she was born, and Victorian gingerbread trimmed its porches. On the side of the house opposite the church, a galvanized fence supported jacque-minot roses and a sprawling vine of tiny white clematis. In the back a potted oleander once broke the fall of a three-year-old Marianne from a second-story window. And in front a path led to the picket fence that separated the house from Kirkwood's main thoroughfare. Oaks, acorns, and blue jays impressed themselves upon the memory of the future poet, as did the small persimmons gathered on an upstairs porch to ripen in the frost.

The Kirkwood of Moore's memoir is a place of safety, harmony, and "picturesque estates." On the estate of one church elder a light-house stands next to a small lake. And in the sunroom overlooking the grounds of the estate, a glass case holds two chameleons—probably responsible, she says, for her "extreme interest in lizards." In the vine-yard of another estate, small bags are tied around each bunch of white grapes to protect them from bees and flies.

Kirkwood was utopian by design. As the ills of industrialization reached St. Louis during the 1840s, its residents longed for the fresh air and woodland streams of their agrarian pasts. Yet they were un-willing to forgo urban prosperity. The opening of a fifteen-mile stretch of Pacific Railroad in 1853 made it possible to have both. Kirkwood became St. Louis's first suburb and the first planned community west of the Mississippi. Men could work in the city and yet protect their families from urban dangers such as the cholera epidemic and fire that devastated St. Louis in 1849. The planners of Kirkwood laid out broad streets and in the 1870s planted thousands of elms and maples along-side them to complement the native groves of oaks and cottonwoods. By the end of the century, trees arched nearly every street, and the town boasted a "high location, excellent drainage, freedom from smoke, clear, sparkling water, and high standards of morals."

Social diversity did not appear to threaten those standards. One of the earliest churches in Kirkwood was African Methodist Episcopal, and the suburb attracted Europeans of all social classes. One could wit-ness Kirkwood's diverse population even within Reverend Warner's own household. The family of five employed four servants: an Irish-Catholic nursemaid, a Danish cook, a white country girl, and a black manservant, who had charge of, among other things, the fastidious reverend's clothes.

As a girl, Mary Warner Moore had liked to watch sparrows build nests in the eaves of her father's church. Returning to Kirkwood after her ordeal in Newton, she yearned for a nest of her own. She bore her second child in the upstairs corner bedroom of her girlhood. A large portrait of her father hung over the mantel, and wives of the church elders busied themselves about the room. No one paid attention to Warner, the shy toddler in a white starched dress, or explained to him that he had a sister. Yet he instantly understood, Mary believed, the importance of the new bundle in her bed. When one of the women approached the side of the bed where the bundle lay, he threw back his yellow curls and howled. The women smiled at his innocence, but Mary empathized with his fear, as she imagined it, of the attempted theft against them.

As word of the arrival spread, the parlor downstairs hummed with callers. It was indeed a week for celebration. Two days before the birth of his granddaughter, John Riddle Warner had celebrated his twentieth anniversary at the First Presbyterian Church. Following the anniversary service at the church, one of the church elders invited everyone to a reception at his country estate north of town, and there the elders surprised Reverend Warner with twenty gold pieces and plans for a new church building. One anonymous participant in these festivities described them in detail for the weekly newspaper and included just below the article the news that on Tuesday, November 15, "Mrs. Moore, *nee* Mary Warner" gave birth to a daughter. Mr. Moore was not mentioned.

Following the announcement was an anonymous thirty-two-line poem. "We welcome thee!" it begins, "With loving arms outspreading; / We welcome thee, / To fill our hearts with joy." The child did bring joy to the Warner household. She grew to be, in her mother's eyes, "the most gentle considerate nestling that ever made a bird's nest a thing to be sung about or warm the heart." "And what is the *home*," Mary added, "but a nest, where the young are cherished, and where the old again grow young, beholding childish joy?" The first six years of her daughter's life allowed Mary to indulge such sentiments and brought relief to all three adults—her father, her aunt, and herself—from the years of loss that preceded them.

Even before Warner could talk, he named his sister the "yah-yah" after the sounds that emanated from his mother's room. "The solemnest baby mortal ever looked at" is how her mother remembered the early weeks of her daughter's life. And then, when the baby was first brought downstairs, Warner danced around the baby carriage beating two sticks together. To the astonishment of the adults, the baby burst into laughter, not a child's squeal but according to Mary a genuine laugh.

"Yah-yah" may, in fact, have been Marianne's earliest name, and it remained in the family vocabulary for years to come. Sometime within the first few days or weeks of her life, she was given the name Marian. Her mother always pronounced her name this way, even after changing the spelling a year later to Marianne. The name Marianne honored her great-aunts, Mary Craig Eyster and Annie Warner Armstrong; and her middle name, Craig, honored her maternal grandmother's family.

But the practice of "home names," as Mary called it, started early, if unimaginatively. Warner was called Buddy, and Marianne, Sissy—a name her mother never altogether relinquished in the six decades they lived together. As the children grew into adolescence, they took the practice of "home names" to elaborate heights of fancy and developed a private vocabulary that would preserve their childhood intimacy until the end of their lives. Much of their "home language" drew on the baby talk of their Kirkwood years: *vey* for *very*, *kam* for *calm*, *yah-yah* for *baby*. Mary began early to reinforce the bond between her children, and she, especially, preserved their childish expressions in her conversation and letters. But the children's mutual devotion needed little encouragement.

"One day Warner and [Marianne] were playing they were birds," Mary wrote shortly after Marianne's sixth birthday, "now robins, then thrushes, and again 'chippies': when Warner said, 'When I'm a chippy, *you* have to be a *frush*!' 'O no Buddy,' she replied in a dear little coaxing voice—'*You know we are just almost the same*; and when you are a chippy, I *have* to be a chippy too; and when you are a fwush, *I* have to be a fwush!'"

Warner and Marianne never outgrew this game. Although they assumed many different personae over the years, the one constant past childhood was Marianne's insistence that she be Warner's *brother* and hence *he* in the home language—perhaps so that she and Warner would be "just almost the same." One of Marianne's most vivid memories from these years was a neighborhood birthday party at which boys were divided from girls for a game of London bridge. Even this separation from Warner terrified her. As late as 1945 she wrote, "Every time I go to a party, let alone speak in public, I feel *away* with it. I could just run home the way I did from the children's party in Kirkwood."

The adults in the family enjoyed watching the children's unique personalities emerge. Marianne was the more cheerful of the two children, their great-aunt Annie observed. "Marianne is very well—bright and happy," said her grandfather, "and one of the most charming companions you ever saw. I could not begin to tell you of her sweet winning ways. She has a quick temper, a real little 'spitfire,' but is soon over it and will kiss and caress you two minutes after she has been scolding you severely."

A few years later her mother reported an incident revealing Marianne's "funny mixture of dignity and impatience." The servant girl was filling glasses before dinner and asked each person, "Will you have some water?" According to her custom, she would not pour a drop until receiving an answer. When she reached Marianne and slowly asked her if she would have water, Marianne sat "straight as a ramrod" to conceal her irritation and answered calmly, "I *always* take *water*." People who knew Moore later in life recognized her quick—and quickly suppressed—temper by a flash of red in her cheeks.

Concepts of childhood changed rapidly during the nineteenth century, and Mary reared her children under different assumptions from those under which her grandparents had reared her. Although her grandparents and aunts and uncles doted upon her, they considered whipping and scolding essential to her upbringing. Good was instilled through memorizing the catechism. Mary recalled that her elders "demanded perfect righteousness of *everybody*, of me more than of all the rest," that they "filled my life with *Don't*." There were no birthday presents, no parties, no playmates. Her most vivid memory of childhood was playing with her shadow on the wall while her grandparents read the Bible by candlelight.

By the time her own children came along, Mary subscribed to a Victorian understanding of childhood that was born of the industrial age. Children were seen as emissaries of God, and their innocence required protection against the corrupting influence of industrialization—thus, the appeal of suburbs such as Kirkwood. While Mary's child-rearing methods were gentler than her grandmother's, it never occurred to her that children could get too much parenting or ever outgrow the need for it. Overindulgence, or "spoiling," was considered a real threat, and no imperfection was trivial enough to pass without correction.

As her children entered adulthood, Mary's attachment to the concept of childhood became central to her moral and religious vision. She often advised Marianne in college to "be a little child again" and wrote to Warner as a young man: "Remember how well Peter Pan flew, till he began to consider the manner of his flying. Oh! don't be introspective! We are bidden to be like little children that we may enter the kingdom of heaven." The child as a model for Christian faith is a frequent theme in Mary's letters. The ever youthful Peter Pan captivated the public imagination in the first decade of the twentieth century, and Mary remained a devoted admirer of J. M. Barrie, Peter Pan's creator, long after the public lost interest in him. All three adult Moores read children's books and shared them with one another. Most notably, in 1914 they read Kenneth Grahame's *The Wind in the Willows* and adopted its woodland personae for themselves.

What most distinguished the new view of childhood from that of previous generations was its emphasis on play as a necessary stage in a child's development. Mary encouraged her children to play and fantasize but had lingering doubts that she should have directed their play more than she did toward "ennobling purpose." The validation of play created a new market for toys and child-size furniture among parents and grandparents entranced by the world of childhood. Warner and Marianne were indulged with both. Although Marianne later described dolls as "abhorrent and meaningless" to her, she owned at least two.

Not surprisingly, she preferred toy animals and recalled "a sheep with wool and green glass eyes that could baa, a horse with real skin, [and] a rubber elephant." There were real animals, too: a baby alligator, Tibby, brought by Mary Eyster from Florida, and Toby, the pug dog of a friend in St. Louis. Both would survive as family personae: Toby for Warner and Tibby for Marianne.

Kindergarten, the phenomenon most responsible for widespread changes in the attitude toward play, encouraged children to impersonate birds and animals, as Warner and Marianne did then and later. They started kindergarten in May 1893 just after a long article on the kindergarten movement appeared in *The Century*. In contrast to the prevailing method of teaching through recitation, kindergarten encouraged children to develop their own imaginations and follow their natural curiosity.

A mainstay of kindergarten was the object lesson, during which the children would sit in a circle while the teacher presented for their scrutiny a natural object such as a seashell, quartz crystal, or flower. Following an object lesson about a bird's nest, the children might sing a song about birds, play a game pretending they were birds, or hear a story about birds. Along with gardening and nature walks, such activities directed the child toward close observation of the natural world and toward a sense of connection with its forces.

Kindergarten also included playing with special toys, called "gifts," designed to develop the imagination through manipulation of abstract forms. To give their play an underlying geometric structure, children played with these gifts at long tables etched with a one-inch grid. Marianne specifically recalled weaving mats with strips of colored paper and making three-dimensional shapes out of toothpicks and dried peas.

Marianne entered kindergarten at the age of five and attended less than a year. It is at least minimally significant for being her first educational experience outside her own family. At most, it began to shape her modernist sensibility. One of the hallmarks of this sensibility is close observation of nature and especially of its geometric forms: birds' nests built "in parabolic concentric curves," a crape myrtle blossom's "pyramids of mathematic circularity," a seashell's "close-laid Ionic chiton-folds."

Even the stanza she invented in 1915 and 1916 might be seen as a kind of self-imposed "grid" of syllable count and rhyme. In "The Fish," where the stanza's pattern demands irregular breaks in the flow of the sentence, it is not hard to imagine her "playing" against that grid:

> All
> external
>   marks of abuse are present on this
>   defiant edifice—
>   all the physical features of

ac-
cident—lack
   of cornice, dynamite grooves, burns, and
   hatchet strokes, these things stand
      out on it; . . .

Perhaps the most significant legacy of Marianne's kindergarten
experience is her almost instant affinity, when she encountered it in
the early twentieth century, for the work of other moderns. When she
visited New York in 1915, she learned about the theories of Kandinsky
and soon afterward purchased *Der Blaue Reiter*, a large illustrated volume in which Kandinsky explains his concept of "inner necessity."
Closely resembling the theoretical basis for kindergarten—which
Kandinsky attended at the age of three—"inner necessity" is a spiritual force that drives genuine art and that connects artists across geo-
graphical and historical boundaries. It manifests itself in the abstract
patterns of art and nature.

The luxury of taking comfort and plenty for granted ended abruptly
for the Moores. On February 20, 1894, after a short bout of pneumonia, the Reverend Warner died. In later years, Mary would often recall
her father's dying words—"The children oh! the children!"—to convey the helplessness thrust suddenly upon her. A year earlier they had
traveled to Pennsylvania to bury Mary Eyster, the only Grandma the
children ever knew. And now they traveled to Gettysburg to bury
Grandpa. When the family returned to Kirkwood, first Warner and
then Mary contracted scarlet fever and were quarantined in the back
sitting room. Preparations were made for Marianne to stay elsewhere,
but when the carriage arrived to take her away, she refused to go.
    In the late spring, Mary decided to leave Kirkwood. She hired
seamstresses to make new curtains for the quarantined rooms, stored
their furniture, and rented the manse to the new minister. She feared
that if she stayed in Kirkwood, her in-laws would try to contact her.
And so she went to stay temporarily, she thought, with her first cousins Henry and Annie Armstrong, who lived in Ben Avon, Pennsylvania, just up the Ohio River from Pittsburgh. Their mother, Aunt

Annie, died soon after her brother did, and the surviving brother, Uncle Henry, suggested that the three cousins could mitigate one another's grief. Mary and her children lived with the Armstrongs for more than two years.

They were not happy years. Although Mary had gladly removed herself from the flow of callers in Kirkwood, she was unprepared for the loneliness that awaited her at Ben Avon. Despite the beautiful countryside near the Ohio River, the new house had no garden or even chickens to fill her hours, and trips to Pittsburgh were inconvenient and infrequent. She felt indebted to her older cousins for alleviating the loneliness of her childhood but felt no deep kinship with them. Henry Armstrong worked in real estate and—as would later become painfully evident to the Moores—did so with few scruples. Mary pitied Cousin Annie for the way Henry treated her and for the disruptions that Warner's rowdy antics brought to her formerly quiet life.

Ever resourceful in finding female companionship, Mary chose a Craig cousin, the same age as herself, for her confidante and began a correspondence with her that would last the rest of her life. Mary Watson Craig graduated from Vassar in 1885, taught English and math at Wilson College for two years, and then married Ira Shoemaker. At the time the Moores moved to Ben Avon, the Shoemakers lived in Harrisburg, where Ira worked for the Pennsylvania Railroad. The letters that Mary Craig Shoemaker received—and saved—from Mary and later from Marianne document the Moores' lives for more than six decades.

Mary also turned at this time for both emotional and financial support to Uncle Henry, who lived near Pittsburgh with his wife and children. From her earliest memories, Mary had regarded Uncle Henry as the next best thing to her absent Pa. A former bank president, state legislator, and land developer (he founded Aspinwall, a Pittsburgh suburb), Henry Warner had managed his brother's investments for years. After his brother's death, he managed the combined assets of John Warner and Mary Eyster, which provided Mary with a modest income. The estate consisted of two rental houses in Allegheny (the Warner home and her grandfather's store next to it), the manse in Kirkwood, some utility bonds, some undeveloped land in Kansas, and mortgages in Colorado and Montana.

In August of their first summer together, the Moores and Armstrongs traveled east, where they went sightseeing in Washington and Boston, and then went to Cape Ann in Massachusetts. The next summer Uncle Henry took them via Niagara Falls to Canada, to a businessman's retreat at Muskoka Lake, where Marianne recalled writing letters on birch bark and "the pleasure of catching and liberating frogs from the edge of the lake."

"You would laugh heartily," Mary wrote her cousin after the annual visit to Locust Hill, to hear the children reminisce about the pigs and sheep. "Marianne talks lovingly of the dear sheep with their 'stick legs' and fondly pats her own well-rounded figure when partially undressed declaring: 'Now I am a sheep—with a nice fat little body.'"

The children found pleasures in Ben Avon, too: riding a merry-go-round at church picnics by the Ohio River and skipping stones over the water, chasing the ice truck in summer to get chips of ice, and in winter making snow angels in the churchyard. Among the pleasures was the smell of print in new books at Miss Lizzie Dalzell's school. In the fall of 1894 Marianne and Warner both entered primary school, their first formal education other than kindergarten.

Although a dozen years would pass before Marianne thought of herself as a writer, she already had the hum of poems in her head and was sometimes, according to her mother, "possessed with the writing frenzy." In March 1895, while Mary was writing a letter to her cousin, seven-year-old Marianne composed two poems, which Mary transcribed in her letter: "The shadows now they slowly fall making the earth a great dark ball. Pussy in the cradle lies—and sweetly dreams of gnats and flies." Anticipating a key element of her daughter's modernist aesthetic, Mary sagely remarked, "If 'brevity is the soul of wit,' surely this point is early reached in the aspirations of our young poetess." When Mary returned briefly to Kirkwood, Cousin Annie reported that Marianne would have written letters to her mother all of the time had she been permitted to do so.

Marianne's chief literary education of these years took place not at Miss Lizzie's, but at home. As soon as the family returned from vacation in the summer of 1894, Mary began reading her father's sermons with the idea of publishing a selection of them. She devoted much of their first year in Ben Avon to this project and particularly to the fifteen-page biographical sketch she wrote as a preface. Uncle Henry encouraged the project and bought her a mahogany desk—at which Mary braved the battle of justice to her father's memory.

The florid prose of Mary's preface stands in marked contrast to the unadorned style of the sermons themselves. One sermon celebrates the democratic principles of the Presbyterian Church, which from its earliest presence in America "ever strove to educate the head while she won the heart"—the goal apparently of Reverend Warner's own sermons. Another, a children's sermon, instructs its listeners to "look away from yourselves to the very animals," to "see how the Creator intended each one of them to do something, and something that no other kind of animal could do." The one perhaps extreme position taken among these sermons pertains to observation of the Sabbath: not even the purchasing or reading of a newspaper, not even exposure to advertising, should taint the day reserved for worship and sacred rest. Mary paid J. B. Lippincott of Philadelphia to publish the volume, which she dedicated to the congregation in Kirkwood. "Bound in maroon," the book impressed young Marianne "as verity itself."

Mary's grandmother allowed no fiction in the house while Mary was growing up, and so she relished nineteenth-century children's literature as much for herself as for her children. She read to Warner and Marianne as much as she possibly could. During the Ben Avon years she developed a devotion to Jacob Abbott, a Congregationalist minister, educator, and author of 180 children's books. When asked in 1962 to jot down the books "that most shaped your attitudes in your vocation and philosophy of life," Moore put at the top of her list four Abbott characters who provide practical, historical, scientific, and moral instruction to their young charges. Like these gentle mentors, Moore's poems never doubt the reader's appetite for information.

The second year in Ben Avon brought greater hardship than the first. Uncle Henry died in September 1895, barely a year after their move. Mary was devastated. Within three years she had lost Mary Eyster, Pa, Aunt Annie, and now Uncle Henry, her last bastion against the outside world. Although Uncle Henry's bank in Pittsburgh continued to manage her father's estate, Mary had trouble collecting the rent from

Kirkwood and blamed herself for not having made a lease. In April a mortgage she expected to sell for $3,000 brought only $2,000. And unanticipated expenses depleted the rental income from Allegheny. (Cousin Henry oversaw the two properties, as he would for decades, and it is possible that he was already embezzling her profits.) From the late summer through the spring, Marianne had a continual fever. She was often so frail that Mary feared for her life. Mary herself lost hearing in her left ear after Uncle Henry died. She could hardly afford a doctor. She tried unsuccessfully to get a job in a store and considered returning to Kirkwood to take in boarders.

In the spring Mary allowed herself to fantasize to Mary Shoemaker about a cottage of her own, where she could be far away from any neighbors and where her children could play without disturbing anyone's fragile nerves. She secretly inquired of the Shoemakers about housing in Carlisle, Chambersburg, or Greencastle—all in the Cumberland Valley and convenient by train to the Shoemakers in Harrisburg— and about schools that Warner and Marianne could attend together. Chambersburg seemed the obvious choice because her mother's oldest brother owned a thriving lumber business there. But while she would welcome her uncle's protection, she did not want to be under the scrutiny of certain cousins who also lived in Chambersburg.

In August and September, Mary took her children for several weeks to Cape May, New Jersey. (Sea trips and books were necessities to the Moores, not luxuries.) And she made up her mind then to make the move. On their return from vacation, they stopped in Harrisburg to see the Shoemakers, who helped Mary find a house in Carlisle. Carlisle gave Mary distance from her cousins but was only a short train ride from Harrisburg and Chambersburg. The house she rented at 343 North Hanover Street stood, moreover, directly across the street from a school that accepted into its primary department both boys and girls.

4

A Peculiar People

1896–1904

When Mary moved her children the two hundred miles from Ben Avon to Carlisle, she brought with her not only a vision of the childhood for which she had always yearned but also a vision of family—of "love and intensity of feeling and enjoyment in one another's presence"—that she had witnessed among her elders but never fully shared. Although she and her father had sometimes vacationed alone together, she knew that he preferred to spend vacations visiting his brother and sister. "How they did *talk* when they got together!" she recalled. "And no one could say they made religion dull. The walls rang with laughter—jokes—satires—anecdotes—sermons. Bible passages discussed; and then their prayers together night and morning!"

Her vision of family was both ethnic—"the clannish feeling of the Scotch, their almost idolatrous family love"—and religious. "Don't forget that we three are 'a peculiar people,'" she repeatedly told her children, "that is, according to the Scriptures, a people *set apart*. We have a mission to the world; as the old prophets used to call their message, *'a burden.'*"

One of the main attractions of Carlisle as a setting for this family idyll was the presence there of Metzger College, a girls' school that occupied an imposing brick structure and sprawling green campus across the street from their new home. For the first two months that the Moores lived in Carlisle, November and December 1896, they slept and boarded at Metzger while awaiting improvements to their house and the arrival of their furniture from Kirkwood. Since the primary department admitted boys, Warner and Marianne both started school there.

Metzger was in its heyday. Formerly Metzger Institute, it had recently added a college department to its primary and secondary departments and changed its name to Metzger College. It had moreover doubled its enrollment and faculty in two years. One reason for the sudden growth was a generously illustrated brochure that almost certainly influenced Mary's decision to move to Carlisle. It draws attention to Metzger's elegant and spacious interiors, its parklike grounds—including a croquet lawn and tennis court—and its location in Carlisle.

> Carlisle, the site of Metzger College and capital of Cumberland county, was laid out by the Penns, and derives its name from Carlisle, England. It is well known all over the United States as an educational center, and is noted for its healthfulness, historic association, fine scenery, and the intellectual and social refinement of its inhabitants . . . The town has upwards of 12,000 people, wide, well kept streets, a dozen or more churches, a fine public school system, three daily and three weekly papers, good stores, alert, obliging business men, and its citizens number judges, ex-judges, active and retired clergymen, army officers, professors and others prominent in the various walks of life.

One evening, less than a year after moving to Carlisle, the Moores were walking home, perhaps from their favorite ice cream parlor, when Warner exclaimed, "Mother, don't you think we are the happiest people in the world?" The moment was a revelation to Mary, who still thought herself a "bowed, grief-stricken woman." She realized that her dream of happiness had become a reality, at least for her children. She felt more financially secure than she had during the second year in Ben Avon, Marianne had recovered her health, and the family at last enjoyed her much-desired privacy. Although Mary was never meticulous about housekeeping and it took her months to unpack, she loved having a house of her own and took great care in arranging it.

The redbrick row house that for twenty years the Moores called home—or "343," or later "the Nest"—stood five blocks north of the town square on the east side of a tree-lined street. The external doors and windows displayed the colonial-style moldings popular in Carlisle during the 1830s, the most distinctive features being the arched garden door and the circular window of the upstairs sitting room. Double windows admitted light into the street-level parlor, a wide hearth and bookcases lined the parlor's north wall, and French doors perpendicular to the hearth opened to the narrow courtyard that ran beside the dining room and kitchen. A path at the rear of the house crossed the backyard to a small stable at the back of the property. Though not spacious, the courtyard readily accommodated Mary's green thumb. She planted yellow snapdragons, yellow iris, and yellow violets. Upstairs were two bedrooms, one of which the children shared until Marianne was fourteen, and a front sitting room for sewing, reading, and writing letters. A balcony over the courtyard held a hammock for summer reading.

Much of the Moores' home life revolved around books and reading aloud to one another. Mary instructed the children in French and piano and gave them books as rewards for piano practice. Christmases and birthdays also brought new books into the household. "You would have laughed surely could you have heard my daughter's lament that the *poetry* book was for Warner rather than her," Mary wrote her cousin just after their first Christmas in Carlisle. "She *dotes on poetry* to a perfectly horrible degree. I know we shall yet have a poetess in the family and finish our days languishing in an attic (prior to the ages when posterity and future generations will be singing our praises)." (At least as notable as Mary's prediction of a poetess in the family is her vision of *our* days and *our* praises.)

Marianne later claimed that she never liked poetry as a child, especially the poems that she and Warner had to memorize for school. "Strike the tent, the sun has risen," she remembered Warner reciting from the top of the stairs. As for "The Red Hen," which she had to memorize, she resented even then its lack of verisimilitude.

The Moores' favorite site for reading aloud was a rented rowboat on Conodoguinet Creek. To Mary this creek overhung with weeping willows exemplified Carlisle's "English aspect." Part of the appeal of *The Wind in the Willows* would be the memories it invoked of excursions on Conodoguinet Creek. Always in their lunch basket was something to read: one of their many Jacob Abbott books, a copy of *The Youth's Companion*, or a particular favorite of Marianne's, *Stories Mother Nature Told Her Children* by Jane Andrews.

In the summer of 1898 Mary invited Laura and William Benét, who were visiting Carlisle for the summer, to join them for a boating expedition. The Moores were "storybook people to us," Laura recalled, "and we were thrilled." Mary read aloud Nathaniel Hawthorne's "Three Golden Apples," and Warner's affability made the day "a huge success" for the older children.

Ten-year-old Marianne, however, spoke hardly at all. She was "a quiet child—very much of a 'clam,'" according to Laura. Marianne later admitted that she had little use for childhood playmates, especially girls. She disliked games and dolls. She enjoyed the company of kittens, however, and that of Rex, the Shoemakers' Skye terrier.

Mary moved to Carlisle in part because of the anonymity it provided her, and she intentionally selected a house near the edge of town. Having endured in Kirkwood as many as twenty-five callers a day, she now enjoyed the luxury of not returning calls. She was not shy, however, and always had as many friends as she wanted. Her earliest friends in Carlisle were Miss and Mrs. Rose, the aunt and grandmother of the Benét children. Miss Elizabeth Rose was the children's teacher and lived with her mother in a gabled cottage on Metzger's campus.

Mary also joined the socially progressive Second Presbyterian Church, where the congregation included many community leaders. Dr. George Norcross, its pastor since 1869, had earned a doctorate at Princeton and a reputation for scholarship as well as homiletics. He supported the temperance movement and advocated equality for women and racial minorities. When he addressed the Scotch-Irish Congress in 1896, he began his history of the Cumberland Valley when it was "first invaded by the white man." General Richard Henry Pratt, the founder of America's first school for Native Americans, was a member of his congregation. And when members of the community voiced fears about the presence of Indian students in Carlisle, Norcross argued that the school caused far fewer problems than had the army base that preceded it.

Norcross's brother-in-law, Sheldon Jackson, was a missionary to Indian tribes of the American West and later a powerful lobbyist on behalf of native people in Alaska. Jackson is the subject of Marianne's 1940 poem "Rigorists." His daughters Dais, an attorney, and Lesley, an artist, often visited Carlisle from their home in Washington, D.C.

Mary quickly adopted Dr. Norcross and his wife, Louise Jackson Norcross, as surrogate parents. The Norcrosses had lived in Carlisle twenty-seven years before the Moores arrived and were well established socially. But their eldest daughter, Delia, was soon to marry, and the other three—Elizabeth, Mary, and Louise—were away at Bryn Mawr College. Their only son had died in boyhood. They welcomed Mary and her young children into their own family. Barely a year after their arrival in Carlisle, the Moores had Christmas dinner with the Norcrosses and thus began an annual tradition.

Not only did Dr. Norcross provide all three Moores a certain paternal affection—the children called him "Dockey"—but the Norcrosses also provided Marianne with a learned society such as she later sought at Bryn Mawr and in New York. "Blake, Rembrandt, Giotto, Holbein, D. G. Rossetti and Christina Rossetti, Turner, Browning, Ruskin, Anthony Trollope, George Meredith," Marianne recalled, were "household companions of the family and their friends." The Norcrosses gave her *The Divine Comedy* a volume at a time over three Christmases. "Derogation in the Norcross family was unknown," she wrote, "tolerance, commendation if it was appropriate, high quality, sobriety, kindness, art and constancy characterized the members, all."

The Moores' affection for the Norcrosses extended to their housekeeper, Agnes Butcher, and her family. "Aggie" had come to work for the Norcrosses as a girl so young she had to stand on a stool to wash dishes, and she remained with the family until her death in 1923. The Moores sometimes attended weddings and musical programs at Aggie's church, one of three black churches in Carlisle.

•

For the first twelve years of her life, Marianne shared her mother's attention with no one but Warner. "I was hand reared," she said late in life. "I got almost too much individual attention." Then in September 1899, Mary accepted the position of English teacher at Metzger. Marianne would come to value the knowledge of literature her mother acquired, but at the time she deplored her mother's schoolbooks and papers to be graded.

The previous English teacher had a degree from Vassar, and Mary had no college. But the principal had been urged by his friends Ira and Mary Shoemaker to hire Mary, and John Hays, a trustee, enthusiastically endorsed the appointment. She was offered $150 per year plus board for her family and tuition for Marianne. Knowing that the previous teacher had earned $350, she finally agreed to $200 (about $5,000 today) but wondered whether she had been a fool to accept such an offer.

Marianne had attended Metzger for two years when Mary transferred her to public school for sixth grade. Marianne much preferred her new teacher to Miss Rose, who taught all of Metzger's primary grades. But Mary's accepting the teaching position at Metzger and compensation in tuition (thirty dollars per year) meant that Marianne would return to Metzger for the next six years, until she graduated from high school.

Metzger's growth spurt passed quickly. By the time Mary started teaching there, it was a college in name only. Metzger struggled financially throughout the fourteen years Mary taught there, and she was not the only teacher receiving compensation in board. She observed that most of the teachers (nine including the principal) ate in the dining room but only five students did. Nevertheless, she liked the food and borrowed books from Mary Shoemaker to prepare her classes. Throughout Marianne's childhood and adolescence, the family ate three meals a day at Metzger in the company of women such as Miss and Mrs. Rose. Marianne grew up in a society of single, educated women like her mother.

Metzger struggled to recruit enough students to pay the bills and drew fewer still who shared Marianne's academic aspirations. She later said that she "experienced society vicariously" through her tall, handsome, ebullient brother. Warner attended public school, edited the high school newspaper, and "abounded in invitations." She sometimes accompanied Warner to barn dances and hayrides even though, as she recalled later, they "intimidated" her.

Marianne had a genuine fondness for one of her Metzger teachers, Elizabeth Forster, who taught art and German and had studied at the Art Students' League in New York. Miss Forster "made us think we liked teasels and milkweed pods, jointed grasses and twigs with buds that had died on the stem." She also valued the precision of Cornelia Thompson, from whom she took piano and voice lessons, the latter "not because I could sing, because I could *not*." But she would receive little of the academic preparation that she needed to enter college. She was one of two students in Latin, the only student in French, and she "felt considerable antipathy" toward her French teacher, "who inevitably had a cigarette in his fingers smoked to almost nothing."

Mary was Metzger's only English teacher. Marianne remembered reading Spenser, Shakespeare, Milton, Tennyson, George Eliot, and Dickens for her mother's class but with little enthusiasm, especially for poetry. After school, however, she enjoyed adventure books such as *Robin Hood, Kidnapped, Treasure Island, Lorna Doone, Captains Courageous, Rebecca of Sunnybrook Farm*, and *Pilgrim's Progress*.

Marianne said several times in adulthood that she felt as old at thirteen as she ever would again. She had already lost much of her mother's attention to teaching by the time she turned twelve. But before she turned thirteen, she faced a more formidable rival.

Mary Norcross, the third Norcross daughter, returned to Carlisle in 1900 after graduating from Bryn Mawr. She often called at the Moores' house that summer. And by the fall, thirty-eight-year-old Mary Warner Moore and twenty-five-year-old Mary Jackson Norcross had fallen in love. "Will you laugh and say, 'Second childhood!'" Mary wrote her cousin, "when I tell you I have deliberately turned my footsteps after school to South Hanover St., and have indolently taken to the luxury of a college divan covered with pillows, that is owned by Mary Norcross. We have all spent several Saturday evenings there and have stayed all night." A year later she was begging her cousin to accept her new love: "*indulge* me, and *don't* throw me over, but take *her* into the family also, and then you'll understand all about it."

What was there to understand? Although sexual acts between members of the same sex had been acknowledged for centuries, few people in central Pennsylvania would have heard of homosexuality, much less of lesbianism, as psychological proclivities. The terms would not come into common usage until the 1920s. Because the Victorian era assumed that only men felt sexual desire, women often held hands, kissed, and slept together. When Mary was visiting relatives in Chambersburg, Norcross did omit the usual *darling*s and *sweetheart*s from her letters, but this is the only indication of their hiding anything except their most intimate relations from family and friends.

Although none of Mary's letters to Mary Norcross survive and Mary later destroyed most of those she received from Norcross, those that do survive leave little doubt about the physical nature of their relationship. The earliest one is a note Norcross wrote in March 1901. It laments their just missing each other one Sunday afternoon and says that Norcross cannot leave the house for a week while her cousin is visiting. "I fear I shall devour you on Sunday to repay me for my long long wait," the letter concluded. When the next weekend did arrive, the two women took a spontaneous trip to Atlantic City, leaving Marianne and Warner behind, presumably at Metzger.

In a series of letters written in 1904 while she was visiting her cousins in Washington, Norcross refers often to her physical longing. She indicates that it has been seven months since she and Mary slept together and imagines that once they do, they will not get much sleep. She looks forward to their vacation in Monhegan, Maine, the following summer: "Think of having each other at night and all through the day for a whole month, Darling! I've never been so starved before. How I long to hold you in my arms and feel your precious self against me." And: "To think of having you again night after night! I wish the rooms would be so small that Sissy would have to have a room to herself. You see how greedy doing without makes me." But she promises to "be good when we are up in Monhegan and think of your fears, instead of my own gratification."

Mary Norcross's starry-eyed passions required a certain indulgence from her family, and while she had none of John Milton Moore's hilarity, she courted Mary with a similar zeal. She had started Bryn Mawr in the class of 1899 but graduated in 1900 with her sister Louise, the only family member who disapproved of her relationship with Mary. For years Louise would not speak to Mary if they met in public, and Mary avoided visiting the manse if Louise was at home. For in college Mary Norcross had demanded of Louise much more than sisterly affection, insisting that they dress alike and do everything as a couple. Louise thus felt betrayed and abandoned when she returned from a year abroad to discover her sister in love.

The first year after Mary Norcross graduated, she lived at home, but the following spring she accepted a position as Bryn Mawr's assistant bursar. From 1901 to 1903 she lived in the Low Buildings, campus apartments for women faculty and staff, and Mary came to visit her there, sometimes alone and sometimes with the children.

The children came often enough to develop affection for Norcross's roommate, Fanny Borden, a librarian. She must have entertained them often to give the lovers privacy, for they addressed her as "Aunt Ann" and corresponded with her for years. Fanny Borden eventually became the head librarian at Vassar, her own alma mater. There, in 1934, she would make her mark upon literary history by introducing a student and aspiring poet, Elizabeth Bishop, to an old family friend, a friend whom she first knew as "a strange and appealing little creature with bright red hair."

In January 1903, Mary went to the Low Buildings to nurse Mary Norcross through a bout of neuralgia. Not long afterward Norcross resigned her position in the bursar's office and moved home to Carlisle. The condition of "nervous prostration," as Mary called it, debilitated Norcross for more than a year and always sent her to bed when her menstrual period arrived each month.

With her mother's attentions directed elsewhere, Marianne relied for companionship upon "her pugnacious and vivacious brother." "He has scarcely whistled himself into the house and banged the front door shut," Mary wrote in 1902, "till he has demanded her whereabouts; and immediately they are off together on some jaunt or project." Thus, Marianne's introduction to sports. The first one was bicycling. She found cycling difficult at first but soon learned the pleasure of "sweeping down smooth roads and looking at trees in blossom." She once sprained a finger playing basketball. But "tennis," she told George Plimpton in 1964, "is the game that I liked from the first and always have." She and Warner played almost daily on the dirt court at Metzger, next to a large willow tree.

From the time they were small children, Marianne and Warner played verbal games as well, making up stories about themselves and about various animals they knew. During their first year in Carlisle, Mary transcribed one such story, Marianne's explanation for why Warner liked corn mush: "Once in *ante-luvian* times some great strengthy cornstalk grew big and tall, and by and by got crushed, and upheaved by the earth's convulsions, and when Toby (Warner) was made, *he was made of that dust*, and so he likes cornmeal mush, because it makes him grow more of his own kind."

The cats at Locust Hill were characters in other stories. During the five years that Warner and Marianne shared a bedroom, they would lie awake at night entertaining each other. One would begin the story and then they would take turns adding to it. Their own cats and kittens—Willow, Tommy Purr, and Puck lived the longest—provided a constant source of entertainment. And once, while bicycling through the Pennsylvania countryside, they encountered a cow they named Mousetail Furnoze. The activities of the extended Furnoze family provided stories for a decade.

A critical juncture in the family dynamics occurred in the summer of 1901. Mary needed surgery and took the children to stay with the Armstrongs in Ben Avon. After having a potentially malignant growth removed from her uterus, she spent several weeks in the Pittsburgh hospital recuperating. Meanwhile, Warner worked as an office boy for Cousin Henry, and thirteen-year-old Marianne tended to her mother. "Cousin Annie and I never go to see Mother at the same time," Marianne wrote Mary Shoemaker, "so I am learning to go all around Pittsburgh by myself and to wash dishes, make beds, etc. etc., cook, get up early in the morning, and keep house."

Mary recovered more slowly than expected, and the doctor advised taking a sea trip and staying in a deck chair until September. In August the Moores, along with Mary Norcross, took their first trip to Monhegan Island. As Mary continued to recover over the next year, Warner and Marianne took charge of the house and helped Mary with simple tasks such as dressing. They took over the parental role and played that she was their child. This is likely the occasion for their first naming themselves bachelor "brothers" to each other and "uncles" to their adopted orphan child, whom they called "Fawn" or "Bunny." Although their animal personae changed over the years, Warner and Marianne remained "brothers" to each other and guardian "uncles" to Mary for the rest of their lives.

The Moores did not require a doctor's orders to take vacations. Every summer they went to Gettysburg and picnicked by the graves of Mary's parents. They took frequent trips to Chambersburg and Locust Hill and dutiful ones to Ben Avon. In the summer of 1897 they went to the seashore with the Armstrongs. They went sightseeing in New York City one year and in Washington, D.C., another. Mary enjoyed the Library of Congress and especially the excursion to Mount Vernon. "Your hero-worshipper cousin could have shed tears," Mary wrote her cousin, "at any moment of our two-hour stay at *beautiful beautiful* Mt. Vernon." (A similar Mount Vernon sightseer appears in Marianne's 1932 poem "The Hero.") A trip to Florida with the Shoemakers reinforced the family's preference for the rocky coasts of New England. Marianne refused invitations to Florida until 1966.

It was through Fanny Borden's father that the Moores first learned of Monhegan, a rocky, wooded island and fishing village ten miles off the coast of Maine. For Mary and Mary Norcross, the family's first trip there was a lovers' reunion after Mary's monthlong absence in Pittsburgh and also a celebration of their first year together. But if Marianne had reason to feel "old" already, she certainly had reason now as she watched Mary Norcross usurp her newfound role as Mary's caregiver. Marianne mentions in her memoir that Mary Norcross's reading aloud Trollope's *The Warden* relieved certain tensions that arose during the first trip to Monhegan. Such tensions worried Mary enough at the time that she confided in Mary Shoemaker about them. But by the next summer, when the foursome returned to Monhegan for a week, Mary reported with relief that Marianne and Mary Norcross had developed true affection for each other.

The second vacation on Monhegan in 1902 and especially the

monthlong one in 1904 helped solidify Mary Norcross's role as Mary's partner, as they all regarded her, and a permanent member of the family. So deep did Marianne's affection grow that she adopted Norcross as a mentor and confidante, something between a second parent and an older sister. Never again would a fourth person be granted such a degree of intimacy with the Moores. That Norcross was given nicknames—Rustles, because of her taffeta petticoat, and Beaver, because she wore brown—and allowed to use the family language indicate how thoroughly she was included in their private life.

In August 1904 the family indulged in a month at Monhegan to mark their last moment of unity before Warner left for college. Perched on the precipice of change, the vacation fulfilled everyone's expectations and created fond memories. For Marianne, Warner's departure meant losing her only friend and playmate. And for Mary, Warner's growing independence posed imminent danger to the family that she had so tightly woven. Mary Norcross, however, had already begun to plot a future for Mary and herself in anticipation of Warner's and Marianne's leaving home. She imagined farming in some serene location as a means of restoring Mary and herself to health, and they met with a real estate broker about buying an acre on Burnt Head, one of Monhegan's most dramatic bluffs. Warner also looked forward to leaving home. Though sincerely devoted to his mother and sister, he never feared homesickness and already had a social life quite separate from his family. At Monhegan he spent most of the daytime with Marianne, but in the evenings socialized with the girls whom Marianne dubbed "frogs" because of the sounds that emanated from the ice pond around sunset.

It would be difficult to overstate the importance of Monhegan to Marianne Moore's literary imagination. She would return twice more in her life, in 1917 and 1929, both trips precipitating personal upheavals in her life. She tried repeatedly to capture the experience of Monhegan in words. One of her first attempts to write something for the Bryn Mawr literary magazine was a story about a brother and sister at Monhegan, and her last serious literary effort, her memoir, devoted much description to the island. Monhegan is also the setting for three chapters of her novel and the inspiration for much of the sea imagery in her poems.

Visitors to Monhegan today will discover the same rustic beauty that so enchanted Marianne and that has attracted professional artists and Sunday painters since the early twentieth century. The island is only a mile and a half long and three quarters of a mile wide yet rich in sensual stimuli. On the west side are the harbor and fishing village, which partially inspired the setting of "The Steeple-Jack." From there the island rises east to dramatic bluffs, up to 150 feet high, against the Atlantic. Between the harbor and bluffs, an old-growth forest of evergreens muffles the sound of the surf and permits only a few sunbeams to outline the gnarled roots that sculpt the forest floor.

"Endless delight and surprise attended every step taken on Monhegan," Marianne wrote in her memoir. "The woods were tall on a bed of pine needles, the upper branches clashing faintly. At one point in the woods there was a towering rock face covered with moss and tiny ferns. Farther on we would come on brilliant mushrooms, gamboge, vermilion or an occasional gray one. In a thickly wooded area around a closed-in patch of very green grass, there was a fairy ring of white toadstools or mushrooms, amanitas, if harmless or not we did not know. Pushing through alders and brushed by blueberry bushes we would come out at the coast and find to our delight what we called the hippo's bath, a deep pool with three sheer sides as smooth as if a knife had sawed them vertically."

Monhegan provided the adolescent Marianne with what she later called "the kind of tame excitement on which I thrive." If Warner found independence by courting young women, Marianne found a certain liberty of mind by observing the island's endless wonders. Scrutinizing the submarine worlds of tide pools, such as appear in "The Fish," could provide hours of entertainment. Young fir trees, "each with an emerald turkey-foot at the top," appear everywhere along the eastern bluffs. And the recurrence of waves as an image of power in Moore's poetry ("Sojourn in the Whale," "The Fish," "Novices," "What Are Years") indicates that one of her chief enjoyments was watching the Atlantic surf crash against the igneous boulders and cliffs on the island's wild side, the "incessantly panting lines of green, white with concussion, / in this drama of water against rocks."

•

There was never a question of Marianne's and Warner's attending college. When the family moved to Carlisle, Mary had thought the children could both go to Dickinson College. But through the influence of Mary Shoemaker, the Norcross family, and indirectly the Benéts, Warner and Marianne set their sights beyond those of their high school classmates who, if they attended college, went to Dickinson, to State College, or to Wilson College in Chambersburg. William Benét started at Yale and Laura at Vassar in 1903. That same year Warner transferred from public school to Dickinson Preparatory School in order to prepare himself for Yale, and Marianne began studying for the Bryn Mawr entrance exams. Although the Moores saw little of the Benéts in these years, they heard continual reports in the Metzger dining room of their accomplishments—fueling at least on one side an unspoken rivalry. Education was important enough that Mary was willing to draw on principal, if necessary, in order for her children to have the best education available to them.

As soon as Warner left Monhegan for New Haven, the extraordinary verbal bonds of the three Moores began to manifest themselves for posterity. It was not enough for Warner to write home weekly. He received two or three long letters from his mother and sister every week and was expected to reply in kind. Warner's letters addressed to "Dear Family" included Mary Norcross, and at first she tried to keep pace with the letter exchange herself. But she soon gave up in desperation when she realized it took her as long to write a short note as it took the others to write a long, detailed letter.

"It is sad almost to the degree of unbearable," Mary wrote Warner just after his departure, "to think the old life is all gone and will never come back any more." For much of Mary's own childhood, letters had been her sole conduit of parental love, and when Warner left home, she clung to the written word again to keep her family intact. She feared the secular influences of college life—"O I wish I wish you were not out on the wild wild sea of 'this generation'!"—and tried to impress upon Warner the family's distinctiveness: "It's hard to resist those who are our compeers and friends in everything save this *inner life*. But it has to be done, unless we become one of them; and that, surely, is too dear a price to pay for ease." Her worries did not stop at Warner's peers. She instructed him to tell his professors that he could not study on Sundays, that Sundays were reserved for reflection and rest.

When Mary learned that Warner had exchanged a few letters with a young woman he met at Monhegan, she made him promise to send home any such letters received in the future and not to answer them without her approval. Nothing posed a greater threat to the sanctity of the family than the girls Warner courted. "You have long practiced in your interest at various times with certain girls, an amount of secrecy, that under the circumstances was equivalent to deception," she wrote him. "Perhaps you get the trait from me. I look back and see in myself in long past years, enough to make me think it possible I gave you the costly inheritance. But oh Warner the bitter tears, the wringing heartbreaks—that trait brought in its aftermath, has left me emptied and bare in the places where formerly I would have had *hidden things*." Although Mary Norcross once wrote that she hoped Warner "is seeing girls to his heart's content," neither Mary nor Marianne shared such hopes.

Warner soon learned that the aspects of college life that excited him—the football games, the hazing, the annual snowball fight between the sophomores and freshmen—elicited Mary's disgust. He had to negotiate a man's world and a woman's world differently, and he answered his mother's craving for detail by drawing a floor plan of his room and noting the exact placement of every picture on the wall. When his new desk arrived, he described the contents and arrangement of each drawer. Religion, too, was a safe topic. Some of New England's finest preachers visited the Yale chapel on Sundays, and Warner could fill several pages of his weekly Sabbath letter with a summary of the sermon and a critique of its delivery.

Warner never defied his mother, at least not on paper. He accepted her advice and was usually penitent at her scolding. But he learned to withhold information in order to get what he wanted. While Mary Norcross was writing about plans for him to fish on Monhegan during the summer, he was secretly corresponding about summer employment elsewhere. He entered Yale with the intention of becoming an engineer (knowing perhaps that his father was one) and wrote the Steelton Bridge Company about gaining some experience.

His correspondent, a family acquaintance, told him that he could join a bridge crew for the summer but that the class of men that formed such crews was not suitable company for a Christian gentleman such as Warner. The language and behavior of such men did not scare Warner. Having grown up fatherless, he wanted to learn the ways of men. After he had completed the negotiations, he wrote his mother a long letter making a case for the practicality of his plan—without, however, mentioning the objectionable habits of his future coworkers. Mary approved, so long as he did not have to work or travel on the Sabbath.

Language was never a trivial matter to the Moores, and Mary applied the same zeal to rectifying Warner's occasional usage and spelling errors that she applied to his social behavior. And she insisted upon detail. If Warner and Marianne learned from their mother the power of precise diction and detail to make their letters vivid, she learned equally important lessons from them as they initiated her into their own language. At first she addressed her letters sentimentally "Dear Child," but she soon changed to "Dear Toady" and by the spring "Dear My Uncle Biter."

Warner's letters included for Marianne's benefit much teasing about turtles and 'gators. Turtles were Yale students—hence Yale was Turtletown—and sometimes young men generally. Marianne was, by contrast, a 'gator (like their Kirkwood pet Tibby), and Warner's letters often included drawings of combat between turtles and 'gators. There was verbal combat to match. When Marianne began a letter "My dear Biter" instead of the accustomed "Dear Biter," Warner responded that the change was "highly opprobrious" to him: "For that alone, you deserve a most fearful buffet on the snout. Leer not, isolent *lizzard*, thinking that although you deserve said buffet, you'll escape it, on account of the distance between us. I coming home soon. So, it behooves you to repent in 'burlap and thistles.'"

Mary did not attempt to correct Warner's English here. The special language allowed him to resist and even parody her solicitousness and yet at the same time to convey intimacy and affection. On Marianne's birthday, he recollected how Turtle (himself) and Fawn (Mary) were wandering about the swamp one day, Turtle smashing all the 'gator eggs in sight, until Fawn spied a very tiny one that she wanted to keep. Turtle took it in his beak, brought it home, and gave it a warm place in the sun. It hatched on the fifteenth of November. The letter accompanied a Yale pin, inscribed "Fangs," that delighted its recipient.

The names Mary continued to use most often—Rustles, Toady, and Sissy—were almost never used by Warner and Marianne, and they sometimes teased her for misusing their special words. "I greatly regret having taught the Fawn to say 'Camel Brand of turkey Figs,'" wrote Marianne, "for now when I ask her what she's to call Uncle, or something else, she promptly jabbers out the Fig phrase regardless of the order in which the words come." But Mary learned to tease, too: "When I want to torment Uncle, I call him 'Aunt Fangs.'"

Although all three Moores contributed over the years to the evolution of their private language, Warner seems the chief arbiter of it during the college years. The playful language filled up the many pages that his mother demanded, maintained the bonds of affection that were genuinely dear to him, and kept those bonds at a certain distance from the rest of his life. Also indicative of that distance and the importance he assigned to names, he asked his college friends to call him John, his first name. He would henceforth be John to everyone but family.

For Mary, the language maintained the family's innocence—she was the one most likely to interject childhood expressions—and to reinforce their distinctiveness as "a peculiar people." "If we had not the remarkable family life," Mary later wrote, "even to a vocabulary that amounts to a foreign language, we should not be awkward with our friends, and unnatural; but we are like people interrupted in love-making the minute any outside persons come in."

Warner and Marianne never questioned Mary's authority either on their own behalf or the other's. Marianne once wrote a long letter chiding Warner for his poor table manners, but it is so uncharacteristic of her language and attitudes that it was almost certainly drafted or dictated by Mary. Marianne enjoyed the role reversals that came with being Warner's brother. In the family language Mary was a much adored but helpless infant. "If you had a family," Marianne told her, "you might go home, but as you're an orphan fawn I'm obliged to keep you, and do for you."

The special language allowed Marianne to avert confrontation with her mother and yet maintain dignity. And while she could rise readily to the challenge of verbal sparring with Warner, she did not often initiate such games. She preferred to claim authority through the subtlety of her allusions. Sometimes she used language, such as "Camel Brand of turkey Figs," that only Warner could interpret. And one suspects, as was later the case with her poetry, that even Warner did not always grasp her affectionate but impenetrable allusiveness. Although he later claimed to recognize the family's special language in his sister's poems, their meaning baffled him as much as it did outsiders.

Mary also observed at this time that Marianne often made "valuable and pungent metaphors," most of which Mary could not recall for Warner's benefit. But she did conveniently recall one that Marianne made about the brevity of Warner's recent letters, that they "were to real letters, as the frill on a pancake is to the cake." "Like other men of genius," Mary added, "he drops these pearls so unconsciously, that it is impossible for him to recall or gather them up."

5

The Edge of a Precipice

1904–1906

Under the progressive leadership of M. Carey Thomas, Bryn Mawr was by the turn of the century both the most difficult of the women's colleges academically and the most radical in redefining women's roles. Women's colleges of the nineteenth century catered to middle-class girls who expected to teach rather than marry. One did not do both. Brought up in a prominent Baltimore family, Carey Thomas wanted women to have an education equal to that of the men in her class. She did not oppose marriage but warned students against becoming financial burdens upon their families. Above all, she urged students to make a difference in the world.

Through its rigorous academic standards and controversial physical education requirement, Bryn Mawr challenged assumptions not only about women's physical and intellectual stamina but also about their sexuality. Carey Thomas shared her campus home with two successive "intimate friends." In the summer of 1904, Mamie Gwynn, Thomas's partner of twenty-five years, abruptly moved out to get married, and Mary Garrett, with whom Thomas had been having an affair, moved in. Until Thomas built the Low Buildings, on-campus housing for female employees, women faculty at Bryn Mawr and other women's colleges lived with the students as house mothers. The Low Buildings gave women faculty both the freedom to conduct research and the privacy to form romantic partnerships.

First as a student and then as a resident of the Low Buildings for three semesters, Mary Norcross fully embraced the feminist ideology of Bryn Mawr and brought it to the Moore household during the formative years of Marianne's youth.

Entering the male workplace was rarely an option for college-educated women of Mary Norcross's generation, but she nevertheless wanted to "do something that will count and . . . live long after I am dead." She began contemplating her life's work as soon as she and Mary became romantically involved. Rejecting the missionary work of past generations, she preferred the burgeoning field of social work. An urban settlement house (such as Jane Addams's Hull House) would provide the likeliest opportunity for her to engage in such work. But she did not wish to provoke Mary's jealousy over the romantic liaisons, or "Boston marriages," that often formed among women working in settlement houses. Passion for a cause created powerful bonds among women exploring new roles for themselves.

By the time the Moores went to Monhegan in August 1904, Norcross had decided that before she could begin her life's work she and Mary must recover their health. She thought that a cottage on Monhegan would be the ideal setting for their recovery and imagined them weaving and doing a little farming both as therapy and as a livelihood. Eventually she wanted to establish a learning center for mountain people, the rural equivalent of a settlement house, where she could teach weaving and market the handicrafts of local women. Although she and Mary decided to postpone buying land because of the expense of the children's college, Norcross remained in Boston on her way home from Monhegan in order to learn weaving at the Boston Society of Arts and Crafts.

When Mary Norcross returned to Carlisle in November, she moved a loom into Warner's former bedroom and filled the Moores' unused kitchen with vats of dye. She wove rugs and cushions for Warner's and Marianne's college rooms and gifts for other friends and relatives but apparently never sold any weaving. (Mary once quipped that a thousand dollars of dye and labor went into a six-dollar rug). The two women pored over house plans in the Arts and Crafts magazine *Craftsman*, trying to decide which bungalow they wanted to build at Monhegan, and Mary ordered government pamphlets on raising vegetables, chickens, and bees. Impatient to begin her projects, Mary Norcross planted a vegetable garden behind her parents' house and ordered a beehive. She did eventually sell two heads of lettuce—to her parents, who paid double the market price.

When Marianne was not chasing swarms of bees through the streets of Carlisle with her mother and Mary Norcross, she was preparing for her Bryn Mawr entrance examinations. Modeled after those at Johns Hopkins and Harvard, Bryn Mawr's exams were among the most rigorous in the country. Students had to pass fifteen exams, in algebra, geometry, Latin grammar and composition, Latin prose and poetry, English grammar and composition, history, science, and two languages selected from French, German, and Greek. They took the first set of exams after their third year of high school and the second following their senior year. It is no wonder, then, that Marianne recalled being "over-anxious when sixteen." She kept herself on a diligent study schedule for two years with Mary and Mary Norcross providing most of her tutoring. At Mary's request, Bryn Mawr agreed to let Mary Norcross proctor Marianne's exams, which Norcross administered with lemonade and strawberries in her upstairs bedroom.

Because each college had its own entrance exams, students usually applied to just one. Marianne applied to Bryn Mawr just before her sixteenth birthday. Until then, Mary Shoemaker, who disapproved of Bryn Mawr's physical education requirement, had been allowed to assume that Marianne would go to Vassar, her own alma mater. Marianne later claimed that she chose Bryn Mawr because of her admiration for the "very talented and unusual" Norcross sisters. Mary Norcross viewed it as a personal victory over the pressure brought to bear in Vassar's favor. As a young adolescent Marianne had formed her own impressions of Bryn Mawr while visiting the campus with her mother. Especially memorable to her were the field hockey players returning after a game, their hair falling down and their hockey skirts dragging.

•

Whether college ruined a girl for matrimony and motherhood was still controversial when Marianne entered Bryn Mawr. Metzger represented the status quo. It offered a protective, homelike environment and emphasized art and music over academic subjects. Its catalog promised not to *worry* students with examinations because of the widespread belief that worry could endanger a young woman's reproductive organs.

In Marianne's first month at college, the *Ladies' Home Journal* published an anonymous essay arguing against "the popular belief that college women are deficient in home instincts," but the next month a regular contributor rebutted "that the average college woman is not trained for her life work." She found Bryn Mawr the most negligent of women's colleges because it hired maids to clean the dormitory rooms rather than let the students do their own housekeeping. Bryn Mawr students, who all read *Ladies' Home Journal*, scoffed at such notions, and yet still joked about "the celibate influences" of Bryn Mawr, among them biology class.

No one seemed concerned about Marianne's matrimonial prospects. As a child she showed little interest in dolls and as an adolescent read adventure books rather than love stories. The adults she knew best were single women. Although she went to parties in Carlisle and danced a little with girls as well as boys, none of them could measure up to her brother.

Given the conventional wisdom of the day, what is more remarkable than the family's disregard of the matrimonial risks of higher education is their disregard of its health risks. Mary Shoemaker could not have the children she wanted, Mary Norcross's menstrual pain often sent her to bed, and Mary Warner Moore required gynecological surgery. Yet none of them believed that intellectual activity draws energy from the female reproductive system. Despite Marianne's high level of anxiety and poor overall health, her family supported her academic aspirations.

Mary rarely mentioned Warner's health during the Carlisle years, but Marianne's was an ongoing concern. When Marianne was twelve, her delicate appetite and light sleeping worried her mother. And when she was fourteen, Mary took her to Washington, D.C., to receive treatments from Mary Norcross's chiropractor. Not only did Marianne seem frail, but she had developed, due to scoliosis, a protruding rib. The chiropractor treated both Mary and Marianne with massage machines and static electricity and stretched Marianne's spine every day.

The stretching helped temporarily, but two years later Marianne's back was worse. Neither the chiropractor nor the various conventional doctors Mary consulted prescribed any treatment other than fresh air, exercise, and a nutritious diet. Then an "osteopathic physician," as he called himself, moved to Carlisle, and Marianne began seeing him once a week both for her back and for temporary ailments such as an earache and a scaly skin condition. Dr. Krohn worked up a sweat manipulating her back and limbs and, although the treatments did not hurt her, she sometimes felt sore afterward.

After Marianne went to Bryn Mawr, she began seeing another osteopath, Abby Pennock, whose massages gave her the "most heavenly healthy tingling glow." Marianne liked Dr. Pennock but did not think the treatments worth the expense (two dollars per session). Mary would not hear of giving them up, however, and Marianne saw Dr. Pennock weekly throughout her four years at Bryn Mawr.

Even Dr. Pennock was "very much opposed to college for women," Marianne reported in her first semester, "for she thinks they are not strong enough and that there's too much strain." Since a college degree was not then a prerequisite for medical or osteopathic school, it is likely that Dr. Pennock never herself attended college. Quoting President Thomas, Marianne proudly told Dr. Pennock that the health of every class had improved during its four years at Bryn Mawr. The statistic surprised Dr. Pennock, who said she "was always hearing of girls breaking down."

Underweight and barely pubescent, Marianne was a young seventeen when on Saturday, September 23, 1905, she said goodbye to her mother and Warner at the Carlisle train station. A friend who had last seen her a year earlier marveled at Marianne's wearing long dresses and her hair done up. "Won't they all just *love her*," said another friend, "dear little modest girl!" During the weeks of packing, Mary had been "alternately a mountain of tyranny and a fountain of tears," according to Marianne. But probably no tears were shed at the station. Mother and daughter wrote playfully to each other just after they parted. Mary did not worry about Marianne's independence as she had Warner's. Everyone worried instead about homesickness.

The train ride gave Marianne a few hours to study for her examinations on Monday morning, and at the Philadelphia station she met Mary Norcross, who escorted her to Bryn Mawr. It had been three years since Marianne had last seen the campus, and the next day Norcross gave her a tour of the new buildings. "It would do your heart good to see him," Norcross wrote Mary, "he is so wildly enthusiastic over everything."

On Monday morning Marianne took the three entrance exams she had not yet passed. And afterward Norcross took her to find her dormitory room in Pembroke East. The green walls delighted them. "The paper is dark green," wrote Marianne, "there is a big cupboard, two little windows right together, a nice floor, a nice couch, a modest desk chair and two electric lights. The room is very small but therefore all the cozier." A college room had to serve not only for sleep and study but also for entertaining. Norcross supplied the necessary tea table, tablecloth, and tea set and the handwoven pillows that made the bed into a couch by day. Since Marianne could not move in until the following Saturday, Norcross took her to Atlantic City for the rest of the week.

Marianne's letters repeatedly tried to allay her mother's fears. As the residence halls filled the following weekend, Marianne assured Mary that some of the girls who had brought their own furniture could not fit their bureaus through the door, and so she was "as well fixed as the wealthiest." And on Saturday night the Pembroke East juniors entertained the freshmen with cocoa and songs. Marianne was thrilled to meet several "divine" seniors and some of the contributors to the student literary magazine, *Tipyn o'Bob*, which she had been reading for the past year. Mary Norcross had given her a subscription. "There are more splendid people here," Marianne wrote home, "than I had imagined were in the world."

By the time Mary Norcross departed for Carlisle the following Thursday, college life had absorbed her young charge. Teas filled the afternoons, receptions and meetings filled the evenings, and sometimes the classes assembled on the steps after dinner to sing songs to one another. "I have never been in such a rush in my life," Marianne wrote home on the eve of Norcross's departure. "Scores of people call and I invite scores more, so I won't have time heavy on my hands for a long day."

After Thursday there was no break in the tone of her letters that circulated first to New Haven and then to Carlisle. But the letters that Marianne wrote secretly to Mary Norcross sound a different note. "The work is enormous," she wrote the day after Norcross left, "I shall never be able to do it." A few hours later she began a second letter confessing that she was homesick, that she had not eaten since Norcross left, and that she was "tottery on my legs." "I fear unless I can eat soon I'll have to go to bed. Of course I can't come home. I have done my work all right but fear I shan't be able to."

Sunday morning she received an answer (mail was delivered seven days a week and several times a day), and she answered that she was following Norcross's advice. "Don't imagine that I sit solitary and unoccupied thinking of home and my woes," she wrote. "I do everything in my power to make things go right. It seems unpardonable of me to be homesick when the Fawn and you and Biter are not sick or dying. For a while it made me desperate to see the things you'd done for me and the places where we'd gone about, and my pictures. I loathed my room, my clothes and everything I had. But enough of this. Everything will be all right."

The next week she wrote Norcross daily and sometimes twice daily. She tried to take pleasure in a few bright moments, but her sensations were "occasionally indescribably horrible." It was a "satanic malady," a "sick, vibrating, feeling that makes my hands numb and makes me feel like sliding over asleep on someone." "As in the case of seasickness everything is a burden." She knew other homesick freshmen, but they were "hungry for their meals and never reel wild or anything of that sort."

The term *homesick* does not do justice to the intensity of her anguish, which would not be matched until her mother's death more than forty years later. "I suddenly feel as if I were melting away like a snowdrop," she said. Never having formed an identity separate from her family, she feared losing her very self. Yet she never considered giving up. "I know I am going to stay; I have to work. I am having what

I want. It would spoil my life for me to give up." Within a few days Marianne told Norcross that she was "physically all right" and "making steady progress otherwise . . . I feel anxious and dissatisfied a good deal of the time but I don't care to die or run away or feel an impulse to do anything wild."

She wrote Mary and Warner the next Sunday that she was making good progress socially despite her initial trepidations. "Soon after Rustles left it seemed possible for me to make headway in knowing people or to make no effort and sink absolutely into oblivion. The latter course was fascinating as the edge of a precipice is," she bravely added, "but I seem to have come out alright." Norcross honored Marianne's request for secrecy, and neither Mary nor Warner learned about her distress until Christmas vacation. It never dimmed in Marianne's memory. "If anyone was ever homesick, *I* was in college," she said in 1965. "It was very painful. I was at sea two years."

Marianne had little practice in making friends, but she followed Norcross's advice to let people know when she felt blue. She adapted to college by letting the girls on her floor mother her. "I seemed to need . . . mothering by everyone," she recalled late in life.

"One of my small troubles," she cautiously confessed at the end of her third week, was that Judith Boyer, a classmate, "insists on my wearing my hair in the Grecian style so popular here." She sketched a woman's profile with a braid wrapped around the crown. "I loathe the style but like to have Judith intimate and friendly enough to fix my hair for me. She thinks me stubborn and ungrateful because I won't acquiesce. She came in after I was completely dressed for the Senior [reception] and fixed it, the first time. Strange to say everybody said it was absolutely right and becoming and said I simply must wear it that way all the time etc. Sometimes when Judith sees me she says how naughty she thinks I am to wear that horrid knot when I could make my hair look so pretty. I have been artful enough however saying I could never learn to do my hair that way and that it felt as if it wouldn't stay a minute. Judith gives me occasional lessons and swears the braids will stay in place."

Artfulness worked with her mother, too. When a month passed with no objections from home, Marianne admitted that she had lost the knack of fixing her hair the old way and that she liked the new style as well as the others did. She liked it so well that she wore it the rest of her life.

Among the many social events and campus rituals Marianne describes in her letters is a reception for the freshmen at the Deanery, President Thomas's campus home. (Though Thomas had been president for a decade, she was still called affectionately the Dean.) Marianne described this "most newsworthy event" in detail beginning with what she wore— "white wool dress, white hat, white gloves and no coat"—and the Japanese butler who ushered the guests into the library. "When the whole band of Freshmen in starched frills, silk, or fur as the case might be were assembled, Miss Thomas appeared in a cream lace dress trimmed here and there with pink passementerie . . . We were told the traditions of the college . . . and were told that the honor of Bryn Mawr was in our hands. We were in short flattered and warned within an inch of our lives."

Carey Thomas's dramatic entrance at this and other events hardly does justice to the presence she commanded at Bryn Mawr. Her personality and vision permeated every corner of college life. She hired each faculty member, she oversaw each course, and as for the buildings, it was nearly true, as Mary Norcross said, that "every stone was picked specially."

From the age of twenty, when Carey Thomas's father first told her of plans for a college for well-to-do Quaker girls, she had imagined herself teaching there. After attending several American and German universities that refused to grant a PhD to a woman, she earned her doctorate summa cum laude from the University of Zurich. At the age of twenty-five, she sought the presidency of the new college. The board of trustees, all prominent Orthodox Quakers, did not grant her the presidency but in 1884 named her Dean of Faculty, in charge of hiring faculty and designing the curriculum. She served as president from 1894 to 1922. Envisioning a women's college that would grant graduate degrees, support faculty research, and meet the highest standards of American and European universities, Thomas quickly developed a reputation as America's foremost authority on women's education.

Many of Thomas's curricular innovations have become standard practice in colleges and universities today. Rejecting both a standardized sequence of courses and Harvard's total elective system, Thomas designed a curriculum combining free electives with a required core of courses. Bryn Mawr was among the first colleges to offer a survey of British literature and freshman science courses. She adopted from Johns Hopkins the "group" system, a precursor to the college major, but expanded its options. A student chose as her group two related subjects, such as English and French or biology and chemistry, and took twenty hours of advanced coursework in each area.

Among Thomas's innovations was making chapel attendance voluntary. Marianne nevertheless went regularly so that she could hear Thomas's daily extemporaneous talks on subjects ranging from woman suffrage (she was for it) to the spelling reform movement (she was against it) to Henry James's *The American Scene* as it appeared serialized in *The Atlantic*.

The students were both awed by Thomas's erudition and amused by her eccentricities. "When she isn't trying to say funny things," wrote Marianne, "she is witty by accident." Especially her pronunciations tickled them—"the Dean said to pronounce blouse, blooze and of course, B double E N, Bean, and w-e-r-e ware." Marianne so enjoyed Thomas's manner of expression that she kept a notebook to record remarks such as "The students are requested not to return from the depot without being accompanied by the night watchman. A tramp has been seen infesting a bush."

Moore later praised Thomas as "an impassioned emancipator" of women, but what most impressed her at the time were Thomas's literary and aesthetic judgments. If the Dean mentioned an art exhibition or a play in Philadelphia, Marianne made a point of seeing it. The Dean's chapel talks about George Bernard Shaw, Henrik Ibsen, Henry James, George Meredith, and other contemporary authors not only inspired students to see the plays and read the novels but also provoked lively discussions across the campus.

"I was appalled by my incompetence," Marianne wrote of her first two years at Bryn Mawr, "all my instructors strangers to me requiring three times the work for each day's class that I had been accustomed to

prepare at Metzger." Passing all of her entrance exams placed her aus-
piciously among the third of her class who matriculated without "conditions." But she would struggle academically throughout her four
years of college. She later said she was unprepared for solitary study,
that she liked to be "corrected, phrase by phrase" as she was at home.

In her freshman year Marianne took five hours each of Latin, biology, and English. The English requirement consisted of two and a
half hours of lecture each week, two hours of composition, and a half
hour of elocution. Designed by Thomas herself, the two-year survey of
English literature began with the history of the English language and
ended in the fourth semester with Keats. Complementing the lectures
was a "private reading" list so extensive that it would today intimidate
most English graduate students.

For composition, freshmen had to write five short personal essays
each week, and every two weeks write a long one based on the lectures
in literature. Various "readers"—mostly young, underpaid women with
master's degrees—evaluated the papers and met with the students individually, often over tea at the Low Buildings. "My English Comp. is
neither good nor bad," Marianne reported in her first semester. "My
diction is the best thing about it. Ideas are not startlingly abundant
and original and I have to work like a slave to write anything decent."
Although Marianne refused to send home all of her papers, Mary
took great interest in them and for the most part agreed with the readers' criticisms. When Marianne was chastised for writing "a network
of quotations," however, Mary rose to her defense.

Marianne's letters hardly mention Latin, which consisted of a full
year of Horace and a semester each of Livy and Cicero, but she did
well enough that she was able to earn fifty cents an hour tutoring
other students. Early on, she earned "a vast reputation in biology,"
which would be her strongest subject. She did not, as has been often
reported, major in biology. But she took twenty hours in it both because she found her professors inspiring and because she made higher
grades in laboratory courses than in writing ones. Her laboratory in-
structor, she recalled years later, "made biology and its toil, a pleasure
and like poetry, 'a quest.'"

In the early weeks of her freshman year, Marianne yearned for
nothing so much as a corduroy hockey skirt in red, 1909's class color.

She managed to purchase a stick for seventy-five cents from a fellow student but could not afford the shoes and the fabric for the ankle-length skirt. Warner, who had secretly saved all of the forty dollars he earned in the summer, sent her an early birthday present of the necessary five dollars. On her actual birthday he sent her another fifteen dollars. Marianne qualified to play on 1909's second hockey team and in her senior year she played on the first team.

Sports could count for two of the required four hours of weekly exercise. The other two hours were divided between "light" and "heavy" gym. (Students called Henry James "Heavy Jim.") But so fearful were some parents about the dangers of vigorous exercise for women, even in 1905, that 60 percent of the freshmen were excused from this requirement by their doctors, mostly due to "female complaint."

One of the more colorful campus personalities was Constance M. K. Applebee, the Englishwoman who introduced women's field hockey to the United States in 1901. In 1904 Carey Thomas hired her to be the director of physical culture at Bryn Mawr. Applebee remembered telling Thomas, " 'You want all these students to go out and do something in the world, to get the vote. What's the good of their having the vote if they're too ill to use it?' . . . Miss Thomas roared with laughter. She roared with laughter at anything like that."

Applebee tried to instill in the girls her principles of sportsmanship: "There had to be a physical side, not to injure yourself. There had to be a mental side which controlled your actions; you saw the great power and strategy of games. You had to have the spiritual side which said love your neighbor even if you wouldn't let her have the ball." Such ideals contributed to Moore's lifelong appreciation for athletes and athletics.

In the winter the girls worked out in the gym. Marianne mentioned rope climbing, putting the shot, wrestling, tumbling, and jumping. Her favorite exercise was the "ring high," where she sprang from a diving-board-like plank, grabbed two rings, and swung out over a suspended bamboo pole. "I am puny and scrawny compared with most of the girls who go," she wrote, "but have lots of fun and get a great deal of benefit." Also in the winter she took swimming lessons. At the first one she had a rope around her waist as she walked across the slimy-bottomed pool; after learning a few strokes, she was "suspended from a pulley in the deep water like a water spider."

Constance Applebee gave the students annual physicals and took on the responsibility of monitoring their general health. As a sophomore Marianne was found to have "extra large lung capacity" but was "pretty poor otherwise," weighing only 102 pounds. At the end of her junior year, her height was 5'4" and her weight 98. Applebee told her that it was a disgrace to weigh so little and urged her to eat more.

Every Friday afternoon Marianne took the train into Philadelphia for her osteopathic treatments. Regardless of any medical benefit Marianne may have derived, the weekly trips provided not only a respite from academic and social pressures but an invaluable sense of independence as she learned to negotiate the city on her own. She often ran errands for her mother and for both Carlisle and college friends. On one early trip, she could not locate the store her mother had specified and so decided to make a day of it by visiting the Pennsylvania Academy of Fine Arts. She returned often to the Academy and saw exhibits there of John Singer Sargent, James McNeill Whistler (a favorite), Augustus Saint-Gaudens, and Auguste Rodin.

Not all her urban adventures were pleasant. "Am I myself? Or am I somebody else?" she wrote in February. "I wonder what you will think of me. I guess you will want to shake me and feel sorry for me and laugh at me all at the same time." She had purchased theater tickets for several friends and lost them along with a hundred-trip railroad pass. A kind stranger found them on the street and sent them to Bryn Mawr by special delivery. In her detailed account of the incident, Marianne repeats verbatim her letter of gratitude, in which she offered "to further the interests, in every way possible of the Dreydoppel manufacturing company," for which the honest man worked. On her next trip to Philadelphia she found her way through an unfamiliar commercial district in order to locate the company and thank the man in person. She returned to campus with samples of Dreydoppel soap and lotion to distribute to her friends. "Tear me limb from limb about my carelessness if you want to," she wrote Mary. "I know I deserve it. I don't believe you will have another chance for similar misdemeanors."

•

In the throes of homesickness, Marianne longed for the Sabbath, when she could lie on her couch and read *Pilgrim's Progress*, Milton, or the Bible. While most of Bryn Mawr's students were active in one of the two Christian organizations on campus, Marianne's practice of not studying on Sundays set her apart. Even casual socializing on Sundays was against Mary's principles, as was anything that caused others to work. Marianne feared no reproof for not joining the Presbyterian Church. She visited churches of various denominations and eventually went most often to Quaker meeting. But she always walked to church rather than ride the coach, and she did expect reproof for accepting an invitation for a carriage ride one Sunday afternoon.

"I cannot conceive of your thoughts after reading this letter," she wrote Mary, "but know that the deeper and more disapproving they are the greater is the anxiety for me and desire for my good."

Marianne always associated Sabbaths with family and devoted a good portion of the day to writing home. It was not unusual for her Sabbath letter to run twenty to thirty pages. Mary had devised a twice-a-week, round-robin schedule whereby Marianne would write on Sundays and Wednesdays, and then send her letter and Mary's most recent to Warner, who would then send his own and Marianne's to Carlisle. Mary occasionally forgot to forward Warner's letter, and Warner sometimes lagged behind, but Marianne never broke the cycle. She often sent a postcard directly to Carlisle so that Mary would receive something in advance of the long Sabbath letter.

Both children felt protective toward their mother, but for Marianne nothing took precedence over providing Mary a steady flow of words. It was to her not mere filial obligation but almost literally a means of sustaining life. Both Mary and Marianne urged each other not to write so much, but Marianne repeatedly assured Mary that she "simply can't help writing," that she had nothing else to claim her attention on Sundays, and that she enjoyed venting her opinions. Mary explained her own long letters as driven by "a feeling like that which sends a drunkard to his bottle."

Largely due to Mary Norcross's coaching, Marianne put nearly as much effort into her social standing as she did her academic one. In her first semester she counted twenty-nine people she would invite to tea if Warner came to visit. But the next semester she wrote that she had given up expecting to be a "social shark." She admitted that she would have an easier time getting to know certain people if she had money to eat at the White Rabbit and to go for drives. But her letters name a variety of friends, and her closest friend, Frances Browne, was elected class president. She even learned to enjoy dances—usually hosted by one class for another. Sometimes the hosts would wear men's dress clothes and the guests party dresses, but more often the dances were costume parties. It was customary in either case for members of the hosting class to call for their guests and present them with flowers.

The biggest event of Marianne's freshman year was May Day. Initiated in 1900, it was intended to be a quadrennial affair, but President Thomas had postponed it for two years due to scaffolding on the new library. Two twelve-car trains were chartered to bring visitors from Philadelphia to the festival, where the students all wore costumes for the morris dances, masques, and plays that they performed in various locations across the campus. In the grand procession, white oxen carried the maypole itself, and Marianne, an attendant on the May Queen, rode on a Henry VIII float. Much was made of the green dress that Mary had made her for the occasion. Although Marianne and the day student Hilda Doolittle were in two large lecture classes together, they did not become acquainted until a decade later, when Doolittle wrote Moore to inquire whether she was the same "medieval lady" in green dress from the May Day fete. Doolittle's guest for the day was a medical student from the University of Pennsylvania, William Carlos Williams.

In the summer Marianne went directly from Bryn Mawr to a Christian Union conference at Silver Bay, New York, on Lake George. There Marianne came to know Ellen Thayer, a member of the class of 1907 with whom she would later work at *The Dial*, and she succumbed to her second crush of the year. "I have what sad to say corresponds to a crush," she had written in February about a "very peculiar" sophomore. But she rarely saw the girl after that. At Lake George a freshman, Katherine Ecob, captured her devotion. "I have liked her ever since last November," Marianne wrote, "but never would have said as I can now, 'She can have me any time she wants me.'"

6

Possessed to Write

1906–1908

Returning as a sophomore, Marianne reentered a whirl of teas, receptions, and hockey matches. "Really college is so much what I would like it to be," she wrote after the first month, "that I won't know what to make of it if it gets nicer next year." At least that was her ambition. She wanted to succeed academically and socially and above all to please her mother. That meant contributing something toward her college expenses. She turned out the lights in her dormitory for ten dollars a year, she read to a student with bad eyesight for fifty cents an hour, and she sold copies of the *Tipyn o'Bob* in exchange for a free subscription. She also devoted hours each week to the Christian Union, calling on students and inviting them to Bible study, and drew upon her experiences of the previous year to console homesick freshmen. And while her adherence to Mary's Sabbath principles cut out a whole day in which she might otherwise study, she worked hard to do well in her courses.

She sometimes received praise for her personal essays, but her scores on quizzes and exams exasperated her. "English makes me rant and rant inside," she wrote after her midyear exam, "I had just as good a chance as anybody and almost as many ideas, but I *cannot* remember dates and I never seem to express myself clearly. I don't seem to have the grasp or the knack or the luck or winning feeling or something." Though she passed English, she failed her midyear exams in Italian and law.

She did have an ineptitude with numbers. Filling out a scholarship application, she could not remember the year she was born and calculated it to be 1885 instead of 1887; told that her height was 5'4", she wrote it as 4'5"; and while working as a librarian in her thirties, she had difficulty making change for fines. Today she might be diagnosed with a learning disability, dyscalculia. The disability could explain not only her confusion of dates but also her difficulty putting ideas and events in the proper sequence. She always felt that she knew the material better than her exams indicated.

Mary, meanwhile, felt more threatened than ever by her children's growing autonomy. Metzger was suffering financial hardship and, since Mary Norcross was nursing her sister through a fever, she had little time for Mary. In November Warner invited his mother and sister to New Haven for the Harvard football game. Neither had yet visited him, and he made elaborate plans, nearly all of which met with objections from Mary. In response to his proposal that a certain young lady accompany them to a glee club concert and that his roommate escort Marianne, Mary answered that she was "as willing as can be to have her go, if she is *our kind*," but that there was no use "in extending social favors to people that are different in thought and feeling from us," that "being gracious and generous" to such people "didn't do good to anybody." The trip did not go well. Mary was "white and drawn and exhausted and bewildered," according to Marianne, and on the last night in New Haven, tensions reached a climax when Warner decided to cook steaks in his fireplace.

The next day Warner wrote one of his love letters, as he later called them, to restore harmony with his Bunny Fawn. He presented a future in which he would have his own study (like his grandfather) and hire a servant like the Norcrosses' Aggie so that Mary, Mary Norcross, and Marianne would have little to do other than go for country drives and sit around the fire together in the evenings. "Then, *in truth*, Bunny, you will be the 'queen-mother.' You are a queen mother now; but how hard hard are the duties of the queen of our little state!" Vowing to please his mother in everything he did, he gave up engineering a few months later in order to pursue the ministry.

Mary accompanied Marianne to Bryn Mawr on her way back to Carlisle, and the two fared no better alone than they had with Warner. Soon afterward Mary wrote Marianne a long letter warning her that when one is "always acquiring—book knowledge, friends, position etc.—one is in danger of falling into the snare of *self-seeking*." Although she acknowledged Marianne's work for the Christian Union, she worried that Marianne did not give of herself enough. (It did not concern Mary in this case whether the recipients of Marianne's generosity were "our kind" or not.)

Mary's admonitions about ambitiousness and self-centeredness seem harsh in context of Marianne's academic struggles and probably contributed to Marianne's poor performance on her midyear exams. But Marianne took to heart Mary's accusation that she had lost sight of her "own far-off self" by allowing everyone around her to put her into "a different mold." Mary urged "simplicity" and "native unconsciousness" upon her daughter and advised her to see funny things in life rather than erupting in bursts of nervous laughter. "You'll try to quiet yourself won't you, and let the waves rush by you?"

Again and again Marianne's mature poetry extols the virtues of simplicity over artificiality: of the "genuine" over the "derivative"; of "unconscious fastidiousness" over "conscious fastidiousness"; of "nonchalance" over "hard trying"; of "pleasure in my average moments" over "too stern an intellectual emphasis upon this quality or that." At the antipodes of "sophistication," truth will "be there when the wave has gone by."

It would be another year before Marianne discovered her own far-off self, but she was already developing a nose for intellectual and artistic pretentiousness, particularly as manifest in two of her professors: Lucy Martin Donnelly, her English literature professor, and Katherine Fullerton, her English reader. The two were romantic partners at the time and prime examples of what Marianne and her friends called the "pedants"—women who lived in pairs in the Low Buildings, who admired Henry James and disdained marriage, and who assumed the pose of British aesthetes. Donnelly described herself proudly as "a militant Blue Stocking." Although Marianne had written enthusiastically about Donnelly's lectures as a freshman, as a sophomore she called them "confetti." She later enjoyed the attention Donnelly paid her as a promising student writer and decades later as a celebrated alumna, yet she never overcame her distaste for Donnelly's "artistic fakery," as she called it.

As if to echo Mary's concern about the different molds imposed upon her, Marianne in these same winter months experimented with various styles of handwriting. Mary had advised her to collect an alphabet of letters she admired in order to improve her writing, and Cousin Annie Armstrong sent Marianne a book about handwriting analysis. It revealed that Marianne was "ostentatious and loved cheap jewelry" while her friend Margaret Morison was "artistic and direct about things." By the spring Marianne's handwriting had become remarkably like that of Margaret Morison.

Marianne arrived at Bryn Mawr in awe of the students whose work she had read in the *Tipyn o'Bob* but did not submit anything of her own until her sophomore year. She was thrilled when Margaret Morison, a senior and a member of the editorial board, invited her to contribute something. Marianne was already developing a crush on "Margie" and over the course of the year would earn a reputation as one of Morison's "birds," a reputation she enjoyed. In Bryn Mawr parlance, an upperclassman with multiple admirers had "birds."

Marianne's best friend, Frances Browne, thought crushes were silly and warned Marianne against them. But while Marianne disdained "mooning" over upperclassmen and sometimes dismissed her crush as "mostly a joke," her letters home and those to friends indicate that she took her "Dante-and-Beatrice" affections as seriously as she did her "Jonathan-and-David" ones. When a classmate characterized Marianne in an English assignment, Marianne was flattered by the physical description but could not see herself as "the convent type" depicted. She saw herself, rather, as "Byronesque."

Marianne's infatuation with Margie Morison was largely literary, part of her growing desire for a certain kind of identity and recognition. "I'd give anything but my family's health and happiness to have her 'fond on me,'" she said. When Margie invited her to contribute something to the *Tipyn o'Bob*, Marianne did not let on that she had already given something to another member of the staff but instead began immediately writing a new story, which she called "The Man and the Minstrel," about a brother and sister going to Monhegan. When she took the story and a verse about hockey to Margie's room, Margie asked her to sit down. "I love the name of your story," she said. Marianne appreciated Margie's kindness but did not think Margie would like the rest. And she was right.

Marianne made her literary debut in the January 1907 issue of the *Tipyn o'Bob*, which appeared just after midyear exams. "Yorrocks," a story she wrote over Christmas vacation, opened the issue. Two days later the February issue appeared with, to Marianne's surprise, another of her stories and two short verses. Theresa Helburn, who would later achieve prominence as a Broadway producer, had assumed editorship of the *Tipyn o'Bob* in January. She offered Marianne real encouragement as a writer, and Marianne respected her criticism far more than she did that of Katherine Fullerton. Terry "knows," she said.

"My story has been much appreciated but somehow I don't care a bit," Marianne wrote after "Yorrocks" appeared. But she did care. The compliments she received from her favorite upperclassmen were a powerful antidote to the news that she had failed two of her midyear exams. When Miss Fullerton told her the next week that her writing was "incoherent," Marianne wrote home that despite the frustration of writing itself and her inability to express herself, she inexplicably felt "possessed to write."

"Yorrocks" reveals that even before Marianne appeared in the *Tipyn o'Bob*, she was contemplating the life of an artist and the sacrifices it entailed. Like most of the stories she wrote for the *Tipyn o'Bob*, the protagonist of "Yorrocks," Pennel, is an artist and a vagabond—in this case a painter, a follower of Whistler. "He loved color, he loved weeds, he loved solitude." One evening at his isolated studio outside London, Pennel receives a boy, Yorrocks, who has been sent to him as an assistant and model by another artist. Pennel resents the intrusion and resolves to send the boy away. But upon learning that Yorrocks has already left, Pennel feels suddenly "lonely" and "nauseous"—the same feelings Marianne had as a homesick freshman. The artist looks over the precipice of solitude, as Marianne had done, and then recognizes his need for companionship. The protagonists of her subsequent Bryn Mawr stories face similar conflicts while growing progressively more independent.

Like the title character of her third story, "The Discouraged Poet," Marianne felt shy about her verses because she had little to say. What she liked about poetry was the rhythm. The rhythm of a drinking song she found, "Oh, we'll drink once more / When the wind's off shore," inspired one of her verses in the February *Tipyn o'Bob*. And she was "seized with a great admiration for Browning" after discovering a book of his poetry in the drawing room where she waited for mail. "The metre of some of the long poems sticks in my head so it bothers me." A few months later she borrowed a volume of Yeats and was "perfectly carried away" by his "highly-colored, Celtic, impressionistic rhymes."

The sonnet she wrote for an English assignment in May is undistinguished and was not among those read aloud. But she wrote her best poem of the year the next day while visiting a lecture with a friend, Peggy James. Though never published, this exercise in rhythm, called "Noon," received high praise from both Mary and Warner.

NOON

A single tree
A silent sea
A rocking, painted "bell."
A tacking craft
    with heavy draft
Far out upon the swell.

Just after Marianne returned from Easter vacation she was elected to the editorial staff of the *Tipyn o'Bob* by the other editors—a powerful antidote to her low spirits and the news that she had failed her Italian exam on the second try. Her new position gave her a certain status among the "pedants" and among the "English sharks." Peggy Ayer, a senior with a delicious wit, grew jealous of Marianne's infatuation with Margie Morison and wanted Marianne for her own "bird." Peggy told her that she would train her to become a pedant so that

Marianne would outgrow her taste for Robert Louis Stevenson and "all Margaret Morison's Sunday school literature," that Margie might be more lovable but that she, Peggy, knew more. Marianne admitted this was true (Peggy won the Pulitzer Prize for fiction in 1931) but did not shift her affections. Although Frances Browne told Marianne that Margie did not know the first thing about writing, neither did she want her friend to become like Peggy Ayer and "talk like Henry James."

In early May Marianne had her worst disappointment of the year. Lucy Donnelly advised her not to attempt English for her group because her writing was so uneven that she might not graduate. Marianne passed all of her second-semester exams and improved her grades in everything except history. She feared, however, that she might not get her degree because of the controversial "merit rule," the requirement that she make at least "merit" (equivalent to a C) in half her courses. The next year Marianne would choose history with politics and economics as her group, the latter two in the same department and thus one area. She took laboratory courses in biology to earn sufficient merits. Not until her last semester would Marianne feel confident of earning her degree. Yet her grades were at worst mediocre. More than a third of her freshman class would not graduate.

Marianne first noticed Peggy James at a dance in November, and in March she noticed her again—"very handsome and not at all self conscious"—when Peggy appeared in the freshman play. Peggy was a celebrity from the moment she arrived on campus. Her father, William James, wrote the textbook for Bryn Mawr's required psychology course, and her uncle Henry James had visited Bryn Mawr twice in the year before Marianne matriculated.

The day after the play, Marianne stopped Peggy when they met on campus to congratulate her on her performance. "She is tall and has dark hair and eyes and wears queer shades of blue silk and pongees and Boston shoes and handmade watch-chains and pins etc. She is very 'intellectual' and not a bit aware of it apparently," Marianne wrote afterward.

The admiration was mutual. Peggy asked Marianne to help her with her narrative for English and complimented Marianne's stories and poems in the *Tipyn o'Bob* because they "had a real sound." By the end of the term, Peggy, a freshman, was Marianne's "bird," according to the "Bird News," which "deals with all college crushes and comes out daily on the bulletin board."

Over the summer they exchanged a few letters. When Marianne returned to Bryn Mawr as a junior, she found Peggy more enchanting than ever. Her infatuation with Peggy reached a far greater intensity in her junior year than had her crush on Margie Morison. She did not call her feelings a "crush" or dismiss them as "mostly a joke." Since Marianne no longer read aloud for pay or worked for the Christian Union, she and Peggy spent most of their evenings together.

At no point did Marianne feel more enthralled with Peggy than she did at a lecture about Henry James in October. The lecturer was Morton Fullerton, a handsome young friend of Henry James's and the brother of Katherine Fullerton. (He is now best remembered as Edith Wharton's lover; they met soon after he spoke at Bryn Mawr.) Marianne was "wildly excited" about the lecture beforehand because James was so widely discussed on campus. In chapel the morning before the lecture, President Thomas defended the difficulties of James's late prose.

Marianne found Morton Fullerton as pretentious as his sister and his lecture "so-so." But Peggy James did not disappoint. While Katherine Fullerton was "spoiled completely" by the attention she received, Peggy was "no more affected . . . than a six-year-old king in a cradle." Marianne enjoyed watching faculty and students "rush" Peggy. "I've never seen her look so stunning in a white low-necked short-sleeved net dress with pin roses round the neck and a variegated pink silk ornament in her hair."

Marianne's letters home return again and again to Peggy. "Peggy is the staff of life. She is so funny and so unaffected." And a few days later: "Peggy irritates me beyond words." One lengthy passage about Peggy concludes: "She is no devotee of mine yet but my hand closes upon her beautifully. She is exactly like a wild horse—Too beautiful to leave unbroken, and yet too perverse not to make you want to swear."

Peggy reciprocated Marianne's friendship, but Marianne wanted more. On one occasion Marianne was disappointed by Peggy's putting an arm around her shoulders in a "brotherly" fashion. "She largely overestimates my literary ability," she wrote a few days later, "and I must get her out of it. She sees much more in me intellectually than physically anyhow (which is of course the best thing that could be). I mean she plain, *likes* me—She doesn't feel any terrific excitement over me."

Although part of the attraction was surely physical—Moore repeatedly mentioned how "handsome" Peggy was—it is unlikely that she thought of it as sexual. Years later, when she read about her friend Bryher's coming of age as a lesbian, she identified with some aspects of the story but not the sexual ones. She had thought for some time, she told Bryher, "that it is normal for young people to have a sentimental attitude to love and that it is abnormal for them to be aware of the sexual aspect of their relations."

What did Marianne want from Peggy James? Although crushes seem to have been widespread at Bryn Mawr, her letters give no evidence that students openly formed couples as the women faculty did. Marianne's passion for Peggy James was closely associated in her own mind with her passion for writing, and her letters often veer between the two passions. If having Margie Morison "fond on me" meant recognition by the Bryn Mawr literati, having Peggy James's affection meant recognition of a much higher order. In some sense, Marianne wanted to *be* Peggy. She envied Peggy's unprepossessing self-confidence and the literary environment of the James family.

"Peggy's friendship for you gives me the keenest delight," Mary wrote in a letter devoted to the subject. The childlike simplicity, spontaneity, and apparently effortless self-possession that Marianne admired in Peggy James were qualities that Mary repeatedly urged upon her children. She did not question whether Peggy James was "our kind." "It's the people beautiful in mind and soul, that have too an inheritance of the same thing back of them that I yearn for, as companions for you and Toady." Mary encouraged this pursuit more than anything else Marianne undertook in college.

Although Mary did not want her daughter's "little heart ever to be wrung," she wondered if a heart is "worth anything that goes through life intact." Above all, she urged patience. She used her own experience with Mary Norcross as an example. "The love that Mary gave to me was greater than any I had ever known a woman to give to a woman . . . I thought it couldn't last. In my own mind I gave it five years to die in—or be metamorphosed. But it did last, and has proven itself sane and safe and nourishing to all." Although Mary promised not to manage Marianne's relationship with Peggy, her letters, like Marianne's, return repeatedly to the topic, most often to advise patience with Peggy's "artistic temperament," as Mary saw it. She never questioned the worthiness of the goal.

In November Mary went to Bryn Mawr ostensibly for Marianne's twentieth birthday but actually to court Peggy. Since she expected her family to live together always, it made little difference to her whether Peggy chose Marianne or Warner as a partner. She wrote Warner unabashedly about her "artfulness" on his behalf. To attract President Thomas's notice, she sat with the staff at chapel, and to earn the respect of Marianne's classmates, she charmed some and snubbed others.

"As bad old Cassius said—'Now let it work,'" she told Warner. "I don't think I'll go back soon, but I've got accomplished a thing I've longed to do; and I'm somewhat pleased with the developments in general. I wasn't very spontaneous (though spontaneity was my pose!) but I was on business bent, and people are not insincere just because they have their wits about them in a business deal."

Her artfulness did work. "Peggy likes the Mouse (as everyone does)," Marianne wrote Warner the day after Mary left. "I feel like a lamp in the morning with the feeble moths hanging to it of the night before."

During October and November 1907, the months of Marianne's most intense obsession with Peggy James, she wrote and revised her best work to date, the short story "Pym." Peggy appears in the story, according to Marianne, as a "portrait in green of a lady with dark slippery hair." This portrait, based on John Alexander's *A Quiet Hour* at the Pennsylvania Academy of Fine Arts, is the prized possession of the young protagonist, Alexander, and his stimulus for writing. Marianne described the story as "a series of individual impressions in 'my latest style' . . . It is what James calls the record of 'a generation of nervous moods.'"

Told as a series of journal entries, it shows Alexander's conflict between personal obligations to his guardian uncle, who wants him to practice law, and a solitary but independent life as a writer. Alexander has chosen the latter path when the story opens. But even so he must

endure his employer, who (like the *Tipyn o'Bob* editors) wants to pre-
scribe how he writes, and his servant, who (like Mary) interrupts his
writing to remind him it is late and to offer something to eat. Even
his "big aggressive brute" of a dog (one of Warner's personae) demands
his attention.

As the story progresses, Alexander decides to return to his uncle.
He feels greater attachment to the things he must leave behind than he
does to the people and thus chooses two things to take with him: the
portrait that Marianne associated with Peggy James and a dark blue
rug, a private tribute to Mary Norcross. Ultimately, Alexander decides
to "put off the semblance of dignity" and "go in for some actual experience." Not only does the story experiment with Jamesian technique
but it also chooses messy "experience" and family loyalty over sopho-
moric stubbornness, preferences that Marianne would continue to
associate with James as her admiration for him grew in subsequent
decades.

At the end of January, Marianne fell into her usual funk over midyear exams, and the simultaneous appearance of "Pym" did little to
relieve it. "Marianna, your ears ought to burn," Peggy called out from
her table in the dining room, "we're talking about you. Mr. Pym has
gone through many metamorphoses hasn't he? We all like him very
much." The *Tipyn o'Bob* editors also praised the story, but Mary said it
lacked a satisfactory moral ending. Reading it as a victory of law over
writing, she missed the point about experience.

Marianne meanwhile complained of fatigue, a bad tooth, a cough,
and a "perfectly rotten" attitude—but not to her family. Throughout
the spring of her junior year, her letters show a remarkably self-
conscious quest for identity. The letters she wrote to Marcet Halde-
man, like those she had written to Mary Norcross as a freshman,
reveal a rather different version of that quest than do her letters home.
An aspiring actress, Marcet left college just before midyears to return
to Kansas, where her widowed mother was a bank president. (Marcet's
mother was the sister of Jane Addams, founder of Hull House, and
her late father was the sisters' stepbrother.) Marcet and Marianne were
evidently in the habit of discussing their woes with each other, and the
subject of Peggy James was well-trod ground between them. If ever in

her correspondence Marianne was guilty of dramatizing her emotions, it was in the dozen letters she wrote that spring to Marcet. Not that she was insincere. Rather, these letters provide a rare glimpse of Marianne's "Byronesque" side.

Marianne promised Marcet that she would "love college madly" once midyears were over. But she wrote after midyears that "jollying people up, and reading things I like, and working like a dog" often lead to the "sticking point—what *is* the use?" She assured Marcet that she had no "intention of 'committing suicide'" but did feel "the starch of life getting weak occasionally." "I vow I will come out on top sometime," she continued. "But I cannot pretend every minute of the time that I know how it feels to be doing it."

"Trust yourself," Marcet advised, quoting Emerson. She meant that Marianne should trust her gift for writing. "*Try* poetry," Marcet urged in one letter. "Why is it that your letters are nicer than your stories?" she asked in another. Marianne sent Marcet both poems and stories and welcomed Marcet's critiques. She answered that she did not feel as self-conscious writing letters as she did writing stories. While trying to present "the artistic point of view" in her stories, she worried that her mother would think her morally lax, that Warner would think her sentimental, that Peggy would think her pretentious, and that Martha Plaisted, the *Tipyn o'Bob* editor, would think her undeveloped.

Mary as yet offered little encouragement for Marianne's writing. Although she had liked the little verse "Noon," she feared that Marianne's writing for the *Tipyn o'Bob* created unnecessary anxiety and took time away from her studies. After reading the March *Tipyn o'Bob*, in which Marianne had a story, Mary wrote that the best work in it was by Ruth George—because it revealed the girl's "godly parentage."

"I am sorry, Mouse, you feel as you do about the *Tip*," Marianne answered. "Ruth writes better and thinks better than I but that she '*feels*' better I am not willing to confess . . . She is mature in method and attitude and so on but not 'susceptible' as far as I know to distracting influences, devils, wildness and so on . . . I feel as if it is hopeless for me to *be* as I want. I beat the air like a wild beast at night and can but hope, at best, to change the figure that a little truth and sincerity will *burn its way through* like the moon through the trees."

"The Boy and the Churl," Marianne's own contribution to the

March *Tipyn o'Bob*, contrasts a vivacious twelve-year-old boy with his twenty-year-old churl of an aunt, who both envies the boy's freedom and tries to restrain it. The boy feels affection for his aunt but wants his independence, too. He wants to do things on his own without his aunt's worrying about him. Nearly all of the stories Marianne had written thus far involve a wandering youth and a distant but wise paternal figure—suggesting the Calvinist God of *Pilgrim's Progress* and perhaps a yearning for her own father. For the first time in "The Boy and the Churl" the guardian is neither male nor wise. Mary likely interpreted the aunt as an indictment of her own parenting and expressed her hurt by praising the "godly parentage" evident in Ruth George's stories.

The story reveals with surprising candor how Marianne chafed against Mary's possessiveness. But she also told Marcet that the story "takes off Peggy and me." This has to mean that she identified herself with the aunt and Peggy with the free-spirited boy. The story thus marks an epiphany for the young poet: she recognized the loathsome possessiveness in her own feelings for Peggy. Marianne came to view romantic love with deep skepticism, and she eventually adopted Peggy's uncle as her own model of chastity and literary bachelorhood. "Love is the thing more written about than anything else," she wrote thirty years later, "and in the mistaken sense of greed. Henry James seems to have been haunted by awareness that rapacity destroys what it is successful in acquiring."

Throughout February and March, Marianne's letters show a growing detachment from Peggy. The distance between her idealization of Peggy and Peggy herself grew ever wider as she realized that her desires had little to do with the practicalities of long-term, daily companionship. Although she told Marcet that she still cared about Peggy "like all wild Wales," she also told her about new flirtations with freshmen and sophomores.

In April, the self that had eluded Marianne since the beginning of her freshman year at last began to burn its way through the trees. She had described herself a year earlier as "possessed to write" and in February as "a demon needing wild horses to drag me *from* the diabolical profession."

But on April 5, 1908, she decided at last what she wanted: "Writing is all I care for, or what I care for most."

An important factor in her decision was seeing Ibsen's *A Doll House* the night before. The play demonstrated that you could "sacrifice for the people you love even your honor," Marianne said, and still preserve "individual liberty" for all. Ibsen thus addressed the conflict between love and independence that she had been exploring in her stories for two years. A week later she saw *Hedda Gabler.* "I shall never forget it," she wrote afterward. "Ibsen and she—have these two times taught me more than almost anything I have read or anyone I have seen in the way both of artistics and morals. I dash into the ineffable in trying to speak of it."

Over Easter vacation, Marianne decided to seek what she had desired from Peggy in the writings of Peggy's father and uncle, both of whom she would later name as influences upon her life and work. She read the student section of William James's *Talks to Teachers and to Students* and finished Henry James's *The Portrait of a Lady.* Just after she returned to campus, she heard a lecture on psychology and pragmatism and began reading William James's *The Will to Believe and Other Essays in Popular Philosophy* the next afternoon.

The second essay in particular, "Is Life Worth Living?," spoke directly to her own feelings of despair. Arguing against pessimism and the inclination toward suicide, James makes the case for believing in "an unseen spiritual order" because one has the need for such belief. "Be not afraid of life," the essay concludes. "Believe that life *is* worth living, and your belief will help create the fact." The essay convinced Marianne "that the thing to do, is to go *at* the business and see that life *is* worth living." Strong fibers of William James's philosophy run throughout her mature work.

Not coincidentally, two days after Marianne began reading *The Will to Believe*, she pronounced Peggy "a fair wave in my wake." "I shan't play with her anymore," she told her family, "though she is very pleasant. She is unenthusiastic and a little perverse. I don't want to 'waste myself' on her." This time she meant it. A few weeks later she told Marcet that Peggy and she "were on excellent terms but utterly 'uncongenial.'" Although she still found Peggy attractive, she no longer respected her intellect or her judgments of people.

Peggy and Marianne wrote each other the following summer

(there is no apparent lapse of affection on Peggy's part), but the friend-ship did not survive college. Peggy visited the campus during Mari-anne's senior year but did not return to complete her degree. In 1917 Peggy married Bruce Porter, an acquaintance of Henry James's and a prominent member of the San Francisco arts community. Their two children, extended family, and community were the chief concerns of Peggy's adult life.

Marianne had two poems and a story appear in the April *Tipyn o'Bob*. She was excited especially by the acceptance of the poems, "The Sentimentalist" and "To My Cup-bearer," "about six lines long a piece which I drew from a clear sky as it were, for nothing—I mean the construction was not the puzzle that of prosody is as I merely wrote them and gave them in."

Just after the issue appeared, Marianne was "drifting to biology" when Martha Plaisted caught her sleeve and congratulated her. "Haven't they told you?" asked Martha. "Why the Dean read out one of your poems [in chapel] and said the other was good." Marianne learned that President Thomas had first criticized her story for affec-tations that made the college "ridiculous to outsiders" but then praised the two poems and read aloud "To My Cup-bearer."

While one friend was outraged at the public criticism of the story, Marianne was both interested in the criticisms and flattered by the at-tention. "I admire the Dean a good deal and like her for 'taking me up' so shout and squeal."

7

Appropriating

1908–1909

At the same time Marianne was discovering her identity as a writer, she was developing a remarkable talent for conversation. No longer a "clam," she became "a perfect corker," according to Constance Applebee. During her junior year she developed a following among faculty and students both for the way she dressed (Mary was a superb seamstress) and for her unusual perspective on things. When Marianne and Katherine Fullerton found themselves on the same train returning from town, they discussed suffrage and European politics the whole way. At the end of the year, Lucy Donnelly and Katherine Fullerton invited her to tea alone—a mark of distinction as well as amusement among Marianne's friends, since Donnelly had a reputation for pursuing her favorite student writers. The conversation ranged from Latin and Greek to philosophy, to animals and evolution, and then to flirtations, or "playing," among undergraduates. "I love to 'talk,' as you know," Marianne told Marcet, "and Miss Donnelly is fun in a very peculiar way, to talk to. She listens and comments so engagingly."

"The net result of my experiences at Bryn Mawr was to make me feel that intellectual wealth can't be superimposed, that it is to be appropriated," Marianne wrote in 1921. By her senior year, she had learned to "appropriate" from college what she wanted. Writing research papers taught her a method of appropriation she would later adapt to writing poems. Although she thought the writing itself took much longer than it should, she enjoyed the array of books spread out around her. And she took pride in learning to organize her sources and cite them at the bottom of the page. One paper, "Why Artists Are Socialists," drew on the theories of John Ruskin, Walter Crane, Constantin Meunier, and William Morris to argue against the evils of capitalism. A paper on Babylonian poetry emphasized the "animalizing tendency" of the Babylonians to associate gods with animals. "You have an immense amount of material," her professor told her, "but much of it does not bear closely on your subject."

Having earned enough "merits" in the first semester of her senior year to assure her of graduating, Marianne decided to take her first and only English elective in the second semester. For some time she had wanted to take Georgiana Goddard King's Imitative Writing course. Despite being advised that it would be "awfully precarious" for her to do so, she decided to risk it. There were only four students in the class, and they wrote imitations of seventeenth-century prose writers. Asked about her literary influences, the mature poet expressed indebtedness to prose stylists such as Thomas Browne and Francis Bacon, whose prose she parsed in King's class.

King was herself an early adherent of modernism. She knew Leo and Gertrude Stein and had likely seen their collection of Picassos, Matisses, and Cézannes by the time she began teaching at Bryn Mawr. She subscribed to *Camera Work* and posted photographs from it in her classroom. King taught Marianne to "relinquish [her] own notions of things . . . and immerse [her]self in style pure and simple." Thus did she introduce Marianne to an important modernist principle, the detachment of style from content. In one of her first critical essays, "The Accented Syllable," Marianne points out the rhythm of certain prose sentences as a pleasure distinct from that of the content.

Although Marianne's grades fared no better under King than they had in previous English courses, she welcomed the rigor of the criticism she received and wrote home that Miss King "is the best teacher I have had here (for my hobby). She . . . criticizes with tremendous point and acuteness and gets you in a fever of enthusiasm which is no small achievement in as inert and 'wise' a community as this."

Marianne availed herself of the cultural life on campus throughout her college career but in her senior year aggressively attended lectures both on campus and off. A lecture by C. R. Ashbee, a British architect and leader in the Arts and Crafts movement, created a great stir on campus and so impressed Marianne in both matter and manner that she devoted more than half of a thirty-two-page letter to reiterating it.

As a member of the college division of the National American Woman Suffrage Association, Marianne heard the NAWSA president, Anna Howard Shaw, speak and attended a reception afterward at the Deanery. "No decent, half-kind, creature could possibly think of fighting suffrage if he or it had heard her arguments," she said.

She attended lectures on Italian painting, the Roman forum, the ideals of democracy, India, mysticism in the apostle Paul and Emerson, and "the indecency . . . of publishing the letters of celebrities" (she disagreed). After a lecture on Darwin and modern psychology, she resolved to read Darwin on the emotions as soon as possible.

She sometimes attended lectures for classes other than those in which she was enrolled and got permission to accompany a field trip to the University of Pennsylvania's archaeological museum. "Many of the class strayed away and yawned and whispered 'oh! were you ever so bored,'" but Marianne "lost [her] head completely" over the Assyrian, Babylonian, and Egyptian artifacts and especially the array of colors in the carvings and enamels. She was not too engrossed, however, to notice a bird singing in a nearby office.

She decided to teach herself Greek and asked her philosophy professor to help her. She attended several lectures about Greek mythology and culture. And she sometimes visited Henry Nevill Sanders's Greek class. "He is kind as possible but very cruel in humiliating the presumptuous," she observed. "A worthy trait." Later she called him "the most pursued man at Bryn Mawr." She did not explain why he was pursued. He had a wife and daughter. He was grouchy, "very ugly," and "spoiled" by the attention he received. Yet he had "an invaluable ability," according to one admiring student, "to turn all one's preconceived ideas completely upside down, and to leave one looking at everything from a new, bewildering, but interesting angle"—an ability that must have thrilled Marianne.

The primary reason Marianne attached herself to Henry Sanders at first was the interest he took in her poems. After her poem "Ennui" appeared in the March *Tipyn o'Bob*, she learned that Sanders had praised the glyconic meter of her poem in class.

ENNUI

He often expressed
A curious wish,
To be interchangeably
Man and fish;
To nibble the bait
Off the hook,
Said he,
And then slip away
Like a ghost
In the sea.

She had to assure her mother, therefore, that when she went with a friend to call on him a few days later that she was not seeking flattery. Dr. Sanders went to his desk while they were talking and wrote out a different ending for the poem to make the meter consistent. The next day he lectured half an hour on the poem to his class. Although Marianne preferred her own version of the poem, many years later she used the lines he liked in "The Plumet Basilisk."

Sanders confessed to Marianne that he had asked one of the English faculty about the meaning of the poem and then given it up. "I pretended an explanation," she wrote, "but said I really had no hard and fast idea, that I excused myself for writing things that had no idea, by making use of the privilege of youth . . . that it was simply living, in the pleasure of the moment." She had good reason to conceal the occasion for the poem. She wrote the first draft during philosophy class and called it "The Bored Lady."

Throughout the spring, Marianne's letters are full of "Sandy." And he inspired the one story, "Wisdom and Virtue," that she published in her senior year. Like her previous stories, this one depicts a young artist and her elder. But for the first time her youth is female, and the elder is callow, not wise. Miss Duckworth lives comfortably by herself in the bohemian section of a city. She reads Baudelaire and paints. The story takes place when her uncle, whose world consists of "pious women, clever men, and obedient children," visits her studio for the first time. Though he never means to offend, the uncle shows little understanding of his niece's work. (Marianne worried that the story emphasized only Sanders's negative qualities.) Unlike Marianne's previous protagonists, the unflappable, even impertinent Miss Duckworth takes complete mastery of the situation. The story concludes with her judging the uncle—"Gloomy, Janus-headed man"—rather than the other way around.

The *Tipyn o'Bob* rejected at least two other stories Marianne wrote that year and published only four of her poems. Terry Helburn and Martha Plaisted had both graduated, and Marianne had little respect for the new editor. "Shirley is prejudiced against critical poetry, the informal Browning kind, picture-comment and music analysis etc.," she said, "and it is the very thing I like best. It is the most impersonal and un-forced. Spiritual aspiration, love, and meditation are themes no puppy can do justice to." It would be years yet before T. S. Eliot advocated impersonal poetry and Ezra Pound warned poets against sentimentality and abstraction.

Marianne's friends often went to one another's coming-out parties, they met in Europe, and they spent holidays at one another's homes. Such travel was out of the question for Marianne, yet she was considered "very popular" in her senior year. She often sought out faculty at social events, or they sought her, and her letters mention a wide variety of companions with whom she attended lectures, took walks, and at least once went horseback riding.

Marianne had first mentioned Hilda Sprague-Smith in her freshman year after Marianne attended a party in her room. She admired the decor of the room and especially the original Whistler etchings on the wall. But in their junior year, when Hilda invited Marianne to visit her in New York as the Sprague-Smiths' guest, Marianne refused even though she would have liked to see the opera, a Saint-Gaudens exhibit at the Metropolitan, and the Sprague-Smith house itself, which was "supposed to be a 'mecca,'" she said, Hilda's father being an eminent professor and her mother a prominent member of the arts community. Marianne thought Hilda "a deeply cultured, exquisitely clad but un-divinely 'fired' person," whom she did not like well enough to accept such an invitation.

A year later, when Hilda asked her again, Marianne thought there would be no misunderstanding about the friendship, and she accepted. It would not be the last time she would accept the beneficence of an admiring patron. They left on the Saturday after midyear exams, and on Wednesday and Thursday, after they returned, Marianne wrote more than 150 pages describing the four-day trip. Mary was *"aghast"* upon receiving the letters and worried that Marianne would be *"ill, ill!"* from writing so much. She did not write altogether out of duty, for she had to remind her readers of their duty not to skip anything. Rather, she used the letters to "appropriate" the experience—as much for her mother as for herself—and also to test out her skills as a critic.

Marianne did not altogether approve of Hilda's mother, whom she had met already, nor of the Sprague-Smiths' house, an Upper West Side brownstone with original artwork, much Tiffany glass, and "hideous" fireplaces. But she liked Hilda's father. At dinner the first night, Marianne was "careful not to 'blossom out,'" but when Charles Sprague-Smith asked her on the way to the theater if she was a socialist, she did. She was, she said, but not so radical that she would have voted socialist in the last election if she could have. She supported gradual change and experienced leaders such as Taft and Roosevelt. Having recently completed her paper on socialism, she conversed knowledgeably about the subject, and the two discussed it until the curtain rose. The play was J. M. Barrie's *What Every Woman Knows.* If Marianne had had trouble remembering kings in their proper sequence for her history exam the previous week, she had no trouble recounting almost verbatim each scene of Barrie's comedy, to which she devoted fifty pages of her letter.

Charles Sprague-Smith, an activist in various progressive causes, was founder and director of the People's Institute, which brought together Upper West Side intellectuals and Lower East Side tenement dwellers for their mutual benefit and education. On both Sunday and Monday nights Marianne accompanied him to People's Institute meetings at Cooper Union. The main speaker on Sunday was a Colorado judge, a pioneer of juvenile court reform. And on Monday Sprague-Smith hosted a forum on woman suffrage. Marianne sat on the platform with dignitaries and speakers, who included her former law professor, Clarence Ashley; the philosopher and educator John Dewey; Elizabeth Cady Stanton's daughter, the suffrage leader Harriot Stanton Blatch; and the playwright Louis K. Anspacher, whom Marianne thought "the most interesting man" she had seen in New York. "I think I can put him in a story," she said, "that will net me some cold cash."

Earlier on Monday she had accompanied Hilda and her mother to Tiffany's and to two of New York's most progressive art galleries, the Montross and Macbeth. In the afternoon they heard a tenor recital at Carnegie Hall. Marianne's detailed descriptions show that she paid close attention to the design of Carnegie Hall as well as the performance, and to the layout of Tiffany's as well as the jewelry. As for the speakers at Cooper Union, she noted the mode of delivery as well as the content.

People who knew her later in life said that in a museum she often showed less interest in the main exhibit than in something incidental. Her enthusiasm for the peripheral—or, as she put it, her "fatal way of losing the fringe of the important fact"—probably hindered her from earning the grades for which she strove. It made her academic writing seem, according to one professor, "like unsettled coffee." But it gave her courage to let the rhythm of a poem create the mood even if her readers missed the "meaning."

On her last day in New York, she "shook in every blessed fiber" when she heard the great pianist Paderewski play. A few weeks later she heard him play again in Philadelphia. She put a picture of him on her wall and developed such an infatuation with him that her friends teased her about it. Ignacy Jan Paderewski thus became Marianne's first aesthetic exemplar, anticipating the athletes, performers, and animals of her later poetry. Rarely is there evidence of editing or revision in the letters Marianne wrote to her family, but her descriptions of Paderewski after both performances demonstrate great care. He had "a certain captious, animal, whimsicalness but he never smiled," she wrote. "He is abandoned, selfish and autocratic to the finger tips." Egotism and excess are qualities Marianne typically deplores, and she thus attempts several sentences before she gets the distinctions just right: "It's fun to see excess and egotism so exaggerated sometimes, but it is like Salome, also, decadent." She was developing already what a fellow poet would call her expertise in "the collision of truths."

It would be nearly seven years before Marianne returned to New York. In early April, however, she caught a whiff of New York modernism—"a bird from Heaven," she called it—when she crossed paths with a certain Miss Haviland outside the Bryn Mawr library. She had sometimes noticed this striking young woman at church and had met her the month before at a tea, where she learned that Miss Haviland was visiting her aunt and uncle near the campus.

Marianne gave up her plans to go to the gym that morning and agreed to go for a walk instead. "Miss Haviland got a switch and began tipping the plants and fences as we [went] along. We stopped at the brook and sat on the fence. She is the very embodiment of style and fastidiousness and so naive and genial and really 'childish' in so many respects I was thoroughly delighted." Their conversation turned from arranging pansies to color theory, to Miss Haviland's cousin, Paul Burty Haviland, who shared "a photography studio" with "an Alfred Stieglitz." After their walk Marianne showed Miss Haviland some of her sketches, and then the two went to the aunt and uncle's house, where Miss Haviland showed Marianne a new dress and two recent issues of *Camera Work*.

"I was taken by storm," Marianne wrote, "for I thought they would be common garden photographs on dull paper—they are satisfactory in every particular—way beyond pictures (painted)." She described in detail two photographs by Annie W. Brigman and noted the articles by Haviland and Stieglitz. "They are both," she said, "very spirited and young enthusiasm-ists—in very good taste." She wrote down the address, 291 Fifth Avenue, for future reference.

Marianne kept a sharp eye on what her friends did after college. She might have smiled at Peggy Ayer's account of the debutante's life: "I rush home from the dressmaker's and sprint through *Tintern Abbey* and *The Ode to the West Wind* before the manicure woman comes to do my nails for a bridge luncheon. I recite Wordsworth's most elevating sonnets on my way in the cab and come home at five to lie down and skim over *The Atlantic Monthly* and a short story of James' before dressing for dinner and the theater, and return past eleven to read myself to sleep with Lamb's *Letters* or a little French!" But she would not have envied such a life. And although she did envy Mabel O'Sullivan's prose, she did not envy her post-baccalaureate life of "teaching and living narrowly, spending . . . a small fortune on clean shirtwaists."

Marianne attended a meeting for students interested in settlement work, but her letters give no indication that she seriously considered this an option. Another avenue closed after Ethel Walker, a secretary and placement adviser, told her that she did not have the disposition for teaching. Miss Walker suggested secretarial work or publishing, both of which appealed to Marianne.

"I grieve to think of your being bothered about an occupation," Mary responded. "Don't you think it enough to make 'home happy'? . . . Just remember I have lots of work for you at home . . . And you could write—say Saturdays! . . . Have you any fancy for weaving?"

"Basilisk," wrote Warner, "I would not have you do anything other than cheer the family after you leave college. Tis a hard suggestion to one who has such noble traits and fierce ambition as you, but meditate strongly on our great desire and longing for you in that direction."

Marianne's determination to write met with no objections, but neither did she have any delusions about her financial prospects in that area. Margaret Morison sent her information about the Lyme School of Art, but Marianne did not press to go. "About next year I am certainly up a tree," she said. "I know you feel no unworthy pressure on me but if I paint, or if I write, or if I fool time, all of which I shall probably do, I ought to make some money first, until we get some of the money returned borrowed from the Loan Fund. It's silly for me to paint, when I couldn't make a cent at it and when I'd do it badly if I knew I *had* to make a cent at it." The family owed the loan fund five hundred dollars, the cost of a year at Bryn Mawr, and Warner was teaching at a boys' school in Elizabeth, New Jersey, to save money for the seminary.

"As I've said before, dear Nunkey, dinna fret about next year," Mary answered. "We should be so happy at home together—that

surely when worst comes to worse, we should not be *very* badly off."
She advised Marianne to welcome anything advantageous that happened to come along but not to "pursue a definite end."

Miss Walker arranged for Marianne to meet with William V. Alexander, managing editor of the *Ladies' Home Journal* in Philadelphia.
"I want no work of him understand," Marianne assured her mother,
"but I'm going partly out of respect to Miss Walker and partly to see
what there is in the thing." Mr. Alexander told Marianne that he was
hiring only stenographers at the time and did not think the work suitable for someone such as herself. He told her about his own career beginning as an office boy at the *Boston Evening Transcript* and showed
her a letter from a man who had thirty-one rejections before he sold a
manuscript.

After inquiring whether she had published anything, he delivered
"a long and salutary and galling speech on the fruitlessness of writing
verse." (Would that she could have shown him her future contracts
with the *Ladies' Home Journal*; in the 1950s she earned $362.50 for one
poem and $775 for another.) She did send in the application he gave
her, and he answered that he hoped it might benefit her someday.

"Listen!" Marianne wrote at the end of a long letter in May. "Miss
Walker says she can get me, she thinks, a position in Baltimore as a
doctor's secretary if I learn typewriting and stenography this summer.
It's a dandy position. The man is writing a book moreover, needs accessory assistance. May I do it? Tell me about the business college
[Carlisle Commercial College]. Is it open in summer I wonder? *Please*
let me do it. Miss W. says it's a very responsible position which of
course is enticing, but she is sure I can do it."

"You know it isn't easy for me to say yes," Mary said. She warned
that stenography would be hard to master, but that was not her foremost concern. "*What provision would be made to protect you socially?* I
mean, where would you board, and how much would you see of the
'Doctor'? I have a deep prejudice against the morals of *doctors*; indeed
I think with suspicion of the morals of most men, and should wish you
well fenced, Petty, were you to serve any *man*."

"Please do find out if you can about the stenography and typewriting," answered Marianne. "I don't know anything which has fired me
so with 'proper zeal.' I wouldn't be a continent away from you, and it's

the sort of work I should most like doing . . . Baltimore is a very harmless, sleepy town, too, and you wouldn't feel anxious about me." Margaret Morison, who worked as a substitute teacher in Baltimore, had offered to help her find a safe place to live.

"Baltimore is a sleepy town!" wrote Mary. "All towns are. But they are all peopled with rats and cats, and sometimes snikies [snakes], all of which *wake up* now and again; and *all* are *death on pee-wees*."

"Baltimore may be 'a sleepy town' for some people," Warner added, "but it's not for stenographers. Doctors are 'a free and easy' lot of scoundrels; most of those 'writing books' don't care how they work, when, or how long, just so they get done their purpose. I would urge the Fish to work for anyone rather than a Doctor, or a Lawyer."

All of the family went to Bryn Mawr for Marianne's graduation. When Carey Thomas crossed paths with Marianne and her mother just before the ceremony, she stopped them abruptly. "Mrs. Moore," she said, "your daughter has contributed to *The Lantern* a poem of marked originality." *The Lantern*, an annual alumnae magazine, had just published "Ennui" and "A Jelly-Fish," Marianne's finest poems to date.

The following Monday she started business college.

8

Wild
and Glorious
1909–1910

During the years Marianne was in college, her mother and Mary Norcross never completely set up housekeeping together but moved back and forth between the "Manse," as they called the Norcross house, and the "Nest," as they called the Moore house. They had given up their Monhegan plans and decided instead to build a house on North Mountain, nine miles from Carlisle. Marianne had fond memories of childhood picnics on North Mountain and in the summer before her junior year of college spent a week there with her mother and Mary Norcross at a rustic hotel near Sterrett's Gap. Shortly afterward Mary Norcross tried to buy the hotel but ended up claiming squatters' rights by building a primitive structure nearby. Although the drive to Sterrett's Gap was rocky and slow, it was more accessible than Monhegan, and the Norcrosses offered enthusiastic support and financial assistance. Mary Norcross designed the craftsman-style house and with Mary's assistance built much of it herself. Norcross eventually named her house Deepwood, but Mary always called it the Mountain.

Since the two women would spend the summer at the Mountain laying their road, it was arranged for Marianne to stay with friends while she went to business college. She enjoyed the Hayses' spacious house with its shiny hardwood floors, baby grand piano, and litter of puppies. And she liked Ellinor Hays, whom she soon called Honey, as the family did. Three years older than Marianne, Ellinor was in awe of the talkative, erudite young woman whom she remembered as a timid child. "She is one of the most interesting and finely unusual girls I have ever known," Ellinor wrote Mary. "My attitude towards her is that of the country bumpkin who bows and scrapes and says 'Proud to know ye, Ma'am.'" Ellinor gave Marianne *The Oxford Book of English Verse* as a graduation present, and the two spent hours discussing poetry. After her first week at the Hayses', Marianne had so many social invitations that she decided not to go to the Mountain for the weekend as planned. Later in the month, William and Laura Benét, Ellinor's best friend since childhood, came to Carlisle, and she had further opportunity to discuss the literary questions that burned in her mind.

Marianne enjoyed showing off to an appreciative audience but could be, like Henry Sanders, "very cruel in humiliating the presumptuous." One afternoon she went with Ellinor to call on the new minister, Edwin Kellogg, and his wife. The choice of a new minister after George Norcross's retirement had by no means been unanimous, and the Hayses had sided with Mary and the Norcrosses in supporting Kellogg. When the Cochrans, members of the opposition, arrived at the Kelloggs' shortly after Ellinor and Marianne did, Ellinor secretly reveled in the hypocrisy of the situation. Mrs. Cochran and Mrs. Kellogg were soon engaged in conversation, and the usually gregarious Ellinor could think of nothing to say to the two men. Marianne took charge. She knew that Kellogg was a musician and had lived in India both as the son of a missionary and as a missionary himself. After bringing up Chopin, which pleased Kellogg, she felt encouraged to keep on talking about the Upanishads, Vedic hymns, mysticism, Schopenhauer, and the book of Ecclesiastes. While her performance elicited "amazed and delighted looks" and interjections of approval from Kellogg, Mr. Cochran looked on in baffled awe. Marianne thus "wickedly," as she put it, turned to Mr. Cochran now and then for confirmation of her views while his gaze became "wilder and wilder."

After the business college closed for vacation, Marianne spent most of July and part of August at the Mountain. The day after Marianne came home from Bryn Mawr, she had talked nonstop for the first afternoon and then buried herself in a volume of Sappho. And when she arrived at the Mountain later in the summer, she did the same thing. "The youngster talks all the time; every minute!" Mary wrote Warner, "and of course I like to hear what he says—but it is amazing to observe how much he has to say!" But Marianne soon escaped into the stack of books, most of them graduation presents, that she had brought with her. Refusing to assist with the road or other household chores, she used her books and writing to shield herself against the domesticating influence of her family.

At the end of the summer, Marianne and Warner traveled by steamer to Bay View, Michigan, a chautauqua community on the northeast shore of Lake Michigan. Edith Powell Howard, Mary's ebullient friend from the Mary Institute, invited them to her summer cottage there. In September Mary returned to teaching at Metzger, Warner returned to teaching at the Pingry School, and Marianne returned to business college. "The next time I see you," wrote Mabel O'Sullivan, "I shall expect to see your pink hair in the latest fashion, with many 'rats' and curls; you will have two bracelets; and a watch will be pinned on your open-work shirtwaist; and your hat will be a yard square and you will talk of 'fellers.'" At least in principle Marianne had long been opposed to "class feeling," and she mostly resists denigrating her classmates, but the content of business college was another matter. "I am having quite a high time at school," she told Warner. "I take spelling and sit attentive with a pen behind my ear and manage not to smirk when things wax droll." She remained in business college through June 1910.

Marianne left the house every morning with a piece of bread, an apple, and maybe a slice of bacon and did not return until after six at night. In the evenings she often went out, refusing to miss any entertainment that Carlisle had to offer: performances and lectures at the Opera House, sporting and cultural events at the Indian School, and concerts at local churches. One week she reported seeing two plays, one of them in German, and performing with the Oratorio Society. She also joined the Eurydice Club, a women's music club, and the Christian Endeavor, a Protestant youth group.

When she did not go out in the evenings, she read novels. Just after Christmas vacation, Mary wrote Warner that to ease the pain of his departure, Marianne was reading Henry James's *Roderick Hudson*. "He misses you; he does," Mary said, "and as one bad fellow says of another with a head-shake, 'He's been drinking heavily,' so may I mention that he has been pouring in heavily potations of Henry James . . . The little wretch stood under the light with his book, one night, *motionless*; yet with a Sarah Bernhardt look at me, he said, 'I tremble from head to foot when I read a book like this.' "

Besides Ellinor Hays, Warner's vacations, and Henry James, another thing that made Carlisle bearable for Marianne was Edwin Kellogg. Mary had written before Marianne left Bryn Mawr about Kellogg's beautiful voice, inspiring sermons, solemn demeanor, and sidesplitting stories. Still, when Marianne first heard him preach, she said that she was not prepared, that Kellogg was a "great marvel." Besides singing in the church choir and participating in the Christian Endeavor, she sometimes taught a Sunday-school class for Ellinor Hays, "sling[ing] doctrine" at the boys "of as virulent a nature as they can conveniently handle."

Marianne had sent home poems for Mary Norcross to type and send to *The Atlantic* even before she left Bryn Mawr. And now that she could type them herself, she regularly submitted poems and stories to magazines but received nary a nibble of interest. In January the Bryn Mawr *Lantern* invited her to contribute to its 1910 issue. She worked busily at a story for several weeks thereafter but sent it to *The Atlantic Monthly*, *Harper's*, and *Craftsman* before offering it to *The Lantern*. *The Lantern* also rejected it, as it had her story the previous year, but it did take four poems.

Marianne's last publication in the *Tipyn o'Bob* was a sprightly little verse called "Progress."

Progress

If you will tell me why the fen
Appears impassable, I then
Will tell you why I think that I
Can get across it, if I try.

Little of that optimism survives in the four 1910 poems. In one, she hides her "integument of pride" inside her coat. Another asserts the value of the artist's labor even if it is misunderstood. But in "My Senses Do Not Deceive Me," "the light of a candle / Blown suddenly out" illustrates "illusion, / And subsequent doubt." The direst of the four, "My Lantern," uses similar imagery to implicate Bryn Mawr itself for the illusion and subsequent doubt. It employs the glyconic meter Marianne learned from Henry Sanders.

My Lantern

The banners unfurled by the warden
Float
Up high in the air and sink down; the
Moat
Is black as a plume on a casque; my
Light,
Like a patch of high light on a flask, makes
Night
A gibbering goblin that bars the way—
So noisy, familiar, and safe by day.

Bryn Mawr's most important symbol is the lantern. Every student receives one in her freshman year to symbolize the passing of knowledge from one class to the next. Yet in Marianne's poem the banners sink down, the moat is black, and the lantern itself burns no more brightly than a highlight on a bottle. Not only does her lantern fail to dispel the surrounding darkness, but it makes night into a goblin that blocks the very path that Bryn Mawr had opened up for her.

"Are you very sad and dull in the abyss?" wrote Mabel O'Sullivan, recalling her own wretchedness in the months after graduation. The letters Marianne wrote to Warner that year give little indication of any wretchedness. Yet because Warner never admitted to weakness in his own letters, not even injury or illness, Marianne felt even less inclined to reveal dark moments to him than she did to Mary.

In the early 1930s, Marianne wrote a revealing piece of advice to an aspiring poet. "To counteract melancholy," she said, "the best thing is a hard task that requires your full mentality . . . One feels desperate when unable to compel success in the only way in which one would care to have it, but this feeling is part of the artistic problem, and one must conquer it. I am subject to melancholy myself and can be discouraged by the slightest thing. Henry James, though mature and successful at a very early age, was nearly ill at times, through not being intelligently received and in being published not quite heartily . . . Melancholy is nearly always the twin of enthusiasm, and though indignation can be a help artistically, one must as a rule, get away from any sense of grievance or accusation . . . It is never a help to one's art to brood, and the craving for privacy should not mislead one into thinking one is 'working' if one isn't." It is impossible to know how much of this Marianne had learned by the spring of 1910. But the "gibbering goblin" and her furious schedule suggest depths beyond her droll play with Warner.

Marianne deluded no one into thinking that she intended to make home happy forever. Mary reported in December that Marianne balked at any form of housework "and talks as if he expected shortly to bid adieu to this lowly nest and take up his residence on some high tree that sweeps the sky." In April 1911 Marianne received an offer from Melvil Dewey's Lake Placid Club in the Adirondacks. She had stayed in contact with Bryn Mawr about positions and occasionally sent out letters herself, but this offer probably came, unbeknown to Marianne, through the Shoemakers, who had moved to Albany in 1907. Ira Shoemaker worked for the railroad that served Lake Placid, he knew Melvil Dewey, and he had recommended Warner for a job there two years earlier.

Famous already as the inventor of the Dewey decimal classification system, Melvil Dewey was a zealous reformer, whose favorite causes included the metric system and simplified spelling (hence Melvil instead of Melville). Having resigned as New York State librarian and as director of the library school that he founded, he left Albany to focus his energies on making the Lake Placid Club a model of healthful, efficient living and a retreat for the families of clergymen, professors, librarians, and other professionals. The club's stated objective was to offer the "highest standards of helth, comfort, rest, and attractiv recreations" to the "overworkt and nervously exhausted."

Warner urged Marianne to "snout out a nuzzer job" and "Stay at home!" Mary, however, decided to let her go. "She is so 'young' and irritable, so impatient of people and of the common friction of life," Mary told Warner, "that I would gladly keep her where she can be *considered*; but I'll let her have what she wishes, and hope it won't kill her." "He looks worse than ever I've seen him," she told Warner a week before Marianne's departure, "and I think anything will be a change for the better. He is overwrought all the time. If it were not for the healthfulness and joy of our home life [so Mary believed] he would be a nervous wreck. He rises to every occasion, but rises so high his poor little pinions are flapped to tatters."

Ira Shoemaker accompanied Marianne from Albany to Lake Placid on July 5. She was shown to a small guestroom the first night with the expectation that she would move to a boardinghouse in the village the next day. But when Marianne saw the shabbiness of the boarding-house, she decided to keep her guestroom and to dine at the clubhouse despite the extra expense. She made up the difference by doing her own laundry—to Mary's indignation—and thus spent only thirty-five of her fifty-dollar monthly salary on living expenses.

Had Mary been trying to marry off her daughter, she could hardly have found a better place to send her. Dressing as she did, dining in the clubhouse, and regularly attending the club's concerts and plays, Marianne played at the border between staff and guest. She did not envy the guests' idleness but felt more at home with them than she did with her coworkers. She thus welcomed an invitation to accompany one of the guests to a play. After she realized that her hostess was play-ing matchmaker to a Mr. Walker, however, she felt herself the victim of "vile treachery." Though wealthy and well-dressed, Mr. Walker made her "fidget and gnash with indignation." "Wealth is a disadvan-tage," she told her hostess, "when a man is as melancholy and inactive as Mr. Walker. He owes it to society to be a little more responsive."

Not all of the young men made her fidget and gnash. "The 'help' and college boy assistants take such a fancy to me," she wrote the first week, "it is all I can do to keep from laughing. I don't know what is the matter with my looks that distinguish [the] class I belong to." Marianne worked with three other girls, "all splendid, clever and un-stylish," but in the summer the club employed a hundred golf caddies, mostly college boys, which probably accounts for her entourage. "I have seven suitors," she reported in August. "What do you think of that? They are all dandies." Marianne made several teasing remarks about suitors until Mary responded, "Fangs, what means this 'suitor' business? I thought you eschewed such nonsense." Marianne then admitted that her suitors "are has-beens, wilted. I delight to disregard them. I am a 'business' dog as you say; that is just the beauty of it. They chew their chins and look grumpy."

Some of the young men she took more seriously. She counted herself among the admirers of the Deweys' son, who had just graduated from Harvard and served as chauffeur for the club. And she took an interest in "improving" one of his friends, a shy, first-year medical student from Johns Hopkins. She accepted several invitations to go boating in the evenings. One came from a New York journalist whom she met on a hillside when he walked by with a volume of Santayana. Another came from an unidentified "LN," who promised to meet her at the boathouse wearing his wisteria suit next to the red canoes. Although no one at Lake Placid captured her interest as Peggy James and Henry Sanders had done, she had no shortage of companions and enjoyed the attention she received.

Marianne said at first that she did not like Lake Placid as well as Monhegan or even Michigan. But by sleeping on the roof, she became friendly with other guests in her building; she spent time with a Bryn Mawr friend whose family vacationed nearby; and the Shoemakers occasionally visited her. "I am spending a wild life, wild and glorious," she wrote at the end of July. "I lay on the top of Cobble and sunburned for a while and ate blueberries and disturbed what I could find that was alive in the pools of rainwater. The water is soft, as soft as velvet."

She wrote neither poems nor stories at Lake Placid that summer, but she stored up impressions that would eventually appear in her poems. Her favorite perch on Cobble Hill reminded her of Monhegan and anticipates the perspective of "the college student / named Ambrose [who] sits on the hillside / with his not-native books and hat" in "The Steeple-Jack" (1932). She learned to appreciate the precision of lawn bowls—"with lignum vitae balls and ivory markers, / the pins planted in wild duck formation, / and quickly dispersed"—as she later wrote in "Bowls" (1923). And an exhibition of furs at the clubhouse would find its way into her 1921 poem "New York," as would the teepees and war canoes brought out for the annual Indian council fire.

Hundreds of guests dressed up in blankets and feathers for the ceremony. The ironic distance between this storybook version of Indian life, or "savage's romance," and the actual Indians Marianne knew in Carlisle would also find its way into "New York."

Marianne pronounced Melvil Dewey himself "an HM [Handsome Man] a Dream or anything favorable that you wish to call him." Because of his "wonderful command of English" and "horror of Briticisms," she found that "contact with him is liberalizing." His emphasis on streamlined, efficient prose taught her to recognize the potential for poetry in "business documents and school-books" and to recognize, as she would later write, that "Pressure of business modifies self-consciousness and genuine matter for exposition seems to aid effectiveness." She took dictation about saddle horses and baseball, proofread galleys about golf rules, and learned to type the carbon of a letter on the back of the original to which it replied—a practice she would later adopt for herself. When she did proofreading, she was allowed to sit in a Morris chair on the porch. "They are very liberal," she said of the office, "and have every device imaginable to facilitate work, and yet are economical."

Marianne's Lake Placid experience was understood to be probationary. If her work proved satisfactory, she would receive a raise in September and stay through the winter. If not, she expected Mary to "refund my permit to become wild, and receive me." Her supervisor, the exacting May Seymour, did not always approve of Marianne's work and looked askance at her socializing with the guests. But in an era when nervous exhaustion was a real threat to the "overworkt," what most concerned everyone was Marianne's health. After observing Marianne's crooked spine, May Seymour arranged for Marianne to be examined by an orthopedic surgeon visiting the club. And Mary Norcross wondered (understandably) if Marianne's admiration for Dewey and her professed contentment were just bluff. "For heaven's sake," Norcross warned, "stop before there is any danger of your breaking down. Nothing is worth losing your health over." Mary worried about Marianne's getting enough rest and eating enough. She wanted Marianne to lose the "razor expression" she had developed in Carlisle and again be "round and pink" as she was at Bryn Mawr.

Marianne did eat well at Lake Placid. She liked the food, took satisfaction in her work, and spent many an afternoon contemplating the natural beauty around her. For three blessed months, she satisfied the "craving for privacy" that haunted her most of her life.

She was determined to hold on to her "wild and glorious" life as long as possible. At the end of August she asked Mary to send her winter coat with the expectation that she would stay. A week later, however, she announced that she was coming home because her position had been terminated. Despite Dewey's apparent efficiency and the club's rapid growth, it was facing a financial crisis. May Seymour assured Marianne that her work was not to blame. "For the comparative inexpense of a summer," Marianne wrote home, "I have 'permanently become tame' instead of eventually wild." A week later, as she told Warner, she had lost three pounds and her "fashion plate" looks.

The loss of her job was not the only reason Marianne stopped eating. She learned at the same time that Mary Norcross was leaving her mother for another woman. Mary came home one day in September to find Mary Norcross tidying up the Nest. Norcross had been away for two months, and the two had not written for the past month while Norcross was visiting her new love. They wept when they saw each other, and Mary Norcross convinced Mary that she still loved her. Yet Mary did not ask Norcross to break with her new love, and Norcross did not say she would.

The two women had seen little of each other in the past year. Mary Norcross remained at the Mountain during the fall of 1909 in order to oversee construction of the house. After she returned to Carlisle in December, she left almost immediately to visit friends and family for six weeks. It was then she formed an attachment with her wealthy, sickly cousin Letty. Nervous exhaustion and digestive problems kept Norcross in bed for months after she returned to Carlisle. Mary visited her every day but mourned the loss of their former intimacy.

In addition to losing her partner, Mary also believed during the spring and summer that she would lose her job at Metzger. She assuaged her grief and loneliness by cleaning and rearranging her house. For a few sad weeks after Mary Norcross's return, the two women worked together on the Nest. Norcross was in such obvious agony and poor health over her dilemma that Mary could not harden herself against her. "How do you think I feel," she wrote Marianne, "when I suddenly come upon her and see her knotting her hands together looking into space, her face strained and attenuated, and the tears rolling down her cheeks like rain on a window? Not hard and self righteous—at any rate."

Even before Marianne learned that her position would be terminated, she had written Mary Norcross for advice about coming home for the winter. But Norcross did not answer until Marianne said that she would come. "I couldn't bear to spoil your plans, because of my own mistakes," Norcross wrote her, "and yet it was still more impossible that the Fawn spend the winter alone . . . The Fawn needs you desperately, I do not know whether she realizes the need or not, but of course she would never let you come just because of her need. However you can certainly feel assured that you were never more needed in your life and probably never will be more needed than you are just this winter by the Fawn." Thus, Marianne's mentor and confidante, the one who had first opened the door to Bryn Mawr and a path to independence, all but closed that door. Marianne returned to Carlisle in mid-October and would live with her mother for another thirty-seven years. Only rarely did they spend even a night apart. While Mary Norcross could not have predicted the future, she well knew the irresistible effect that her letter would have on Marianne.

The decision to move home was not, however, forced upon Marianne. Before she left Lake Placid, she received another job offer. Mrs. Bates, a friend of May Seymour's, was the librarian for the Columbia University School of Philanthropy (later, the School of Social Work) and asked Marianne to be her assistant. In retrospect, it would have been an ideal job. Not only is it tempting to speculate how moving to New York in 1910 would have affected Marianne's writing career, but she also felt herself well-suited to library work, as she learned later on. Mrs. Bates "is self-possessed and witty," Marianne said. "She is stout, not 'pretty' or commanding . . . but she has the goods. I have never seen anyone to whom I 'took' more." Marianne said that she was flattered by the offer but resolved to go home—"and I *am*," she wrote Mary, "unless you throw me out bodily."

Just as Mary Norcross predicted, Mary did not insist overtly that Marianne move home. "Don't turn away from you anything that you would find valuable work," Mary answered. "I lived in your experiences when you were at [Bryn Mawr] and have genuine exhilaration in anything that brings life to you. At home here you are in danger of shriveling, and that would blight me too. So I beg that you be not blind or bull-headed in going forward in a course you have decreed. Life at home still brims over for me irrespective of comings, goings, or absences, and I [am] vigorously well, so the only thing to consider in taking a position is whether or not it has a return to give you for your labor."

When Marianne first turned down the offer, Mrs. Bates asked her to think it over before she made a final decision. On her way home, Marianne spent a few days sightseeing in Albany with Mary Shoemaker and then visited Warner in Elizabeth, New Jersey. After she arrived in Carlisle, she made little effort to hide her misery. "Sissy feels her home life to be dull, and the air 'without life,'" Mary told Warner, "but she will become more contented by and by, and in the meantime will absorb a good deal that will do her good. I have given her full freedom to go to New York, but have said at the same time that I wished she could be contented to be at home for this winter." After a week at home, Marianne sent Mrs. Bates her final refusal.

Shortly before Marianne's return, Mary Norcross had told Mary, "The Gator . . . has almost a genius" for "making little poems" and "ought to cultivate his talent." And even Mary Shoemaker realized the terrible sacrifice asked of Marianne. After Marianne left Albany, Shoemaker wrote Warner that she thought Marianne needed "a little rest after her busy summer but after she has had that rest I think she needs some place and work more similar to her training than any thing Carlisle has to give. I am glad you are so happily situated and I hope she may find some place equally agreeable and congenial."

Responding to Cousin Mary's concern, Warner offered to find a house where the three of them could live in Elizabeth, within commuting distance of New York. "I don't know that I should care to live in New York even with you," Marianne answered. "I don't know *where* I should like to live unless in a nautilus shell." The Bryn Mawr loan still weighed on her mind, and she worried about the expense of living in New York. Metzger would survive after all, and so there was also Mary's salary to consider. Mary had no interest then in leaving Carlisle. Seeing Mary Norcross about town was not so painful, she thought at first, that she had to leave Carlisle permanently.

Marianne "seemed to hate everything" when she first came home, according to Mary, but by Thanksgiving had become "genial and gay, and very loving." "Loving" meant deflecting conflict. Rather than bristling at Mary's continual admonishments, as she did at first, Marianne resumed the role of indulgent Uncle to her adorable Bunny.

9

An
Intramural Rat
1911–1914

After Marianne returned from Lake Placid, the Byronesque, wild and glorious self of her Bryn Mawr and Lake Placid letters disappears from view. Except for the notebooks in which she recorded quotations, Marianne never kept a diary. Anything she wrote was subject to her mother's scrutiny. She had no privacy at home, no "room of her own," until she began to make a place for herself in her poetry.

Having longed for intimacy throughout her youth, Mary recognized no need for privacy within the family. She regarded Warner's life apart as nothing short of deception. Mary and Marianne nearly always read each other's letters to Warner and often interjected comments or added postscripts. Not only was Marianne unwilling to confide feelings of self-doubt to her brother, but she also decided soon after returning from Lake Placid that long letters were wasted on him. He needed to know that all was well but little else. She wrote him relatively brief, newsy letters once a week. Mary's longer letters indicate her own deep mourning over Mary Norcross but no exceptional concern over Marianne's health or state of mind.

Marianne adapted to home life more quickly after her Lake Placid experience than she did after college but did so by resuming her childlike, precollege persona. Mary thought her a "pampered pup" but did not resent pampering her. What affected Marianne's moods the most, according to Mary, was the intrusion of outsiders. The presence of a sewing woman in the house precipitated a cold, Mary said, that made Marianne "very sad-eyed—very glum, very vipish."

Although Marianne harbored distant hopes of living on her own one day, she mostly resigned herself to the lack of privacy at home. She felt as determined as ever to write, however, and wrote poems throughout the spring of 1911. Hoping to earn an "honest penny," she sent them to *McClure's*, *The Century*, and *Smart Set*. "Gnashings and knottings of the tail," she said of her rejections. Little as she understood relative amounts of money, she wanted never to become a financial burden upon the family.

Meanwhile, Mary decided after Christmas that she could not bear to remain in Carlisle for Easter and the summer. What she wanted most was to spend a year in Europe with Warner and Marianne and after that to leave Carlisle permanently. Marianne visited Baltimore twice in the spring to check it out as a future home for the family. She even arranged to tour the Johns Hopkins Hospital with a view to future employment there. Mary had sold the Kirkwood house in November and, after considering various ways to invest the proceeds, she decided to buy their house in Carlisle. She put the deed in Marianne's name as a form of life insurance in case Warner and she should die. Her plan was to make improvements to the house, rent it out for the year they were in Europe, and then sell it. She immediately hired carpenters to install electricity and gas, two bathrooms, a new bedroom, and new fireplaces—creating further intrusions upon Marianne's privacy.

Among the first carpentry projects was a trapeze for Marianne. The doctor who had examined her at Lake Placid recommended daily stretching on a trapeze to straighten her spine and strengthen her back. After the family left Carlisle in 1916, she underwent an eighteen-month treatment of plaster casts and braces supposed to correct her scoliosis permanently. There is no indication that she continued the use of a brace after that, but she used a trapeze off and on throughout her life. Even late in life she had a trapeze suspended from a doorframe in her apartment—mystifying visitors.

•

Warner entered Princeton Seminary in the fall of 1910. Since it would be difficult for him to travel to Europe anytime soon, Mary began making secret plans to take Marianne to England, Scotland, and Paris for the summer. Mary Norcross's romance with her cousin had not lasted, making her more distraught and confused than ever. Norcross begged Mary not to leave Carlisle for vacations, and so Mary told Mrs. Norcross to offer her daughter the third berth in their stateroom. Mary did not expect the invitation to be accepted, and it was not. She revealed the Europe plans to Marianne while the two were in Ben Avon for Easter, but she confided to Warner that she already wished the trip were over. Making travel plans without her beloved pained her deeply. "I *must do it*," she told Warner. "It is right and necessary to go. Sissy ought to have the change and newness, and I ought to get myself out of the country. I feel directed to go and I must not fail to obey the impulse."

Setting sail from Philadelphia on May 27, they took with them much advice, two fruit baskets, and eleven issues of "The Daily Egg," a newspaper prepared by Warner, one for each day of the cruise. Planned altogether by Mary, their itinerary began with ten days in England's Lake District and then took them to Glasgow. From Scotland, they took the train to Oxford, Warwick, and London. They spent four weeks in London, visited several cathedral towns, and concluded the trip with ten days in Paris. Relying upon their well-worn Baedekers, they visited as many museums and writers' homes as possible.

The letters that both women wrote Warner suggest that they shared little with each other in the way of feelings. Yet both were grieving. Mary had lost her lover, and Marianne had lost her chance at an independent life. Despite constant homesickness, Mary pressed on because she believed the trip was good for Marianne. Marianne hid her own sorrow by saying and writing as little as possible. She wrote to no one but Warner and wrote to him, at Mary's urging, only once a week. When Mary asked her why she wrote so little, Marianne said that she did it to be "pleasant."

Elliptical and infrequent though they were, Marianne's letters suggest that she felt compelled to enjoy herself for Mary's sake. The letters exude enthusiasm. Every letter is peppered with remarks such as "Life is so exciting, that I don't know whether I'm on my sidewheelers or my tail fins." "I shan't be satisfied now till we have an armoury," she said about Warwick Castle, and the peacocks "make your hair stand on end."

For Mary the high point of the summer was Kensington Palace, where she saw Queen Victoria's childhood things, and Kensington Gardens, where Peter Pan and other of J. M. Barrie's "wee folk" roamed. "Since I am very indulgent to my childhood romances, and keep holiday with them almost religiously," she wrote Warner, "*I just bowed the knee* and worshipped; like the Oriental or the Romanist at the sound of prayer bells."

Marianne shared none of this with Mary but instead stood aside watching the horses and riders along Rotten Row. At the Whitehall Museum, Mary wondered at Marianne's close inspection of a relief map of Waterloo. Imagining that her daughter's thoughts ran like her own, she guessed that Marianne was contemplating a "personal Waterloo" still fresh in her memory from Bryn Mawr. She did not recognize Marianne's more devastating "Waterloo" of the previous summer. But given Marianne's fascination with Napoleon, it was probably the map rather than the metaphor that interested her.

The trip did teach Mary that constant criticism failed to improve her daughter. Imagining the day when her children would be alone together, she told Warner to "be patient with anything [about Marianne] that is hard for you to see or to take, and help her to get the fine things in her developed. I think the way to do it is to see only those and let the rest alone. Some people develop by pruning—others by nourishing—and I think she is of the latter kind."

By their fourth day in London, Marianne reported that her "appreciation bag [was] well nigh exhausted," but her "poison bag [was] still potent." There is little evidence of her "poison bag" in either Mary's or her letters except for her frequent infantilizing of "Bunny." Reporting to "The Daily Egg" on the ship over, she depicted herself as the genial General Fangs who was never "separated an instant from his own Bunny . . . At meals the General holds the Bunny on his knee after moving cruets, salt seller and his grape juice (*unfermented*) out of reach." It was a desperately hot summer, and Mary greatly minded the heat. Marianne carried Bunny, she told Warner, in a lettuce-lined basket with a cloth over it.

The Britain that Mary and Marianne saw in the first month of their travels was the terrain of Sir Walter Scott, the Lake Poets, and the Pre-Raphaelites. They saw fairy-tale-like estates overrun with rabbits and the descendants of the deer that Shakespeare poached. On the turnpike was "a coachdriver . . . the regular old thing in a red suit, with sideburns and a high hat."

In London they entered a new century. "Having once seen London," Marianne wrote, "you will live in a blaze of glory all your life . . . 'Buses thread the streets and wheel round each other and across each other and policemen punctuate the town like may beetles. The 'buses are 2-story affairs and most of them motor 'buses; being operated like motor cars, keeping in a rough line (placarded over with advertisements)."

The heat prevented the sightseers from moving about London and Paris as easily as they had expected. Marianne took over as navigator. She got a schedule of London bus routes and spent "happy hours planning tours of minimum exertion for Bunny." Mary, however, held the purse strings and economized by buying their meals from fruit stands. Lunch might consist of bread, butter, plums, and lettuce, and dinner of a can of sardines. They eliminated a planned trip to Cornwall because of the expense, and never do their letters mention a play or concert.

Before they left Carlisle, Marianne had written in her notebook, "Ezra Pound and Ernest Dowson at all costs," and a few pages later noted Elkin Mathews as the publisher of Pound's *Personae* and *Exultations*. One of the few literary pilgrimages that Marianne initiated took them to Mathews's overstuffed bookstore on Vigo Street. Mathews was the primary publisher and advocate for what was then the literary avant-garde in London: W. B. Yeats, Oscar Wilde, Lionel Johnson, Ernest Dowson, Arthur Symons, and the rising star among them, Ezra Pound. Marianne bought *Personae*, *Exultations*, and the just-off-the-press *Canzoni*. She also asked Mathews about Pound and was shown his photograph. It is telling that she first recorded Pound's name with Dowson's. In July 1911 Pound was still a late Victorian.

The next month he showed *Canzoni* to Ford Madox Ford and watched him literally fall on the floor laughing over the stilted language. By the following spring Pound had pared the language of poetry to its barest elements. With H.D. and Richard Aldington, he invented Imagism and launched modernism in English-language poetry.

Marianne did not describe her experiences in the same detail nor with the same critical nuance that she had written about her New York trip two years previously. Yet the summer did feed her appetite for information and experience. In London she liked much of what she saw in the museums but complained of the "great outbreak of [nymphs] in the galleries." The Tate Gallery was "beautifully placed . . . airy and very modern and not very interesting save for the Rossettis and Wattses." The Rubens panels at the Louvre were "atrocities . . . Marie de Medicis and Henry IV's floating in Elysian *'déshabille'* amidst cherubs and fat Homeric porters." But she admired the jewelry, sculpture, and paintings at the Luxembourg Museum, where she saw sculpture by Rodin and paintings by Impressionists and Post-Impressionists. What most excited her were antiquities such as the Winged Victory of Samothrace and the Assyrian rooms at the British Museum and the Louvre.

When Mary and Marianne departed Le Havre, France, on August 19, they brought home an abiding Anglophilia and an appreciation not just for travel but for maps, museums, and travel guides. "Karl Baedeker's contagious impassivity," as Marianne later put it, provided her an extended lesson in the art of observation. She would develop a keen interest in museums and in the 1920s wrote an unfinished poem about "something more mellow than information" in them. One of her most ambitious poems, "An Octopus" (1924), may be read as an analysis of how travel guides and maps direct experience, and a 1929 editorial she wrote for *The Dial* took as its subject the art of the travel guide.

Immediately after Marianne returned to Carlisle, she was asked to take charge of the Commercial Department at the United States Indian Industrial School. The previous teacher had quit suddenly, and Moses Friedman, the superintendent, applied to the Carlisle Commercial College for a replacement. Pacing the tennis court at Metzger and talking it over with Warner, Marianne thought at first she would refuse. Neither the subject matter nor the prospect of teaching appealed to her. Yet Warner had taught for two years and Mary for twelve. Marianne decided that she owed it to them to contribute to the family income. Friedman hired Marianne reluctantly. Even though women had always taught at the school, he wanted a man to control the unruly Indian boys. What Marianne feared most was not the students but her ineptitude with numbers. She would be teaching commercial arithmetic and bookkeeping along with typing, stenography, and commercial English.

General Richard Henry Pratt, who founded the school in 1879, had great confidence in the ability of native people to learn white ways but had little regard for their tribal traditions. He believed that the best way to "civilize" them was to remove the children from their home environments and immerse them in white culture. During his twenty-five years as superintendent, enrollment grew to more than a thousand, and other boarding schools were built on the Carlisle model. Always a subject of controversy among both whites and Indians, Pratt nevertheless succeeded in creating tolerance for, and even pride in, the students within the Carlisle community. Marianne remembered Pratt and his wife as "very substantial and imposing . . . romantic figures . . . intelligent and cultural." She respected them as friends of the Norcrosses and as community leaders.

The Indian School no longer taught young children by the time Marianne started teaching there but instead (mostly for financial reasons) emphasized athletics and industrial training. The Commercial Department had a "large, airy, and prepossessing" classroom, Marianne recalled, and a separate room for typewriters. Five days a week she began teaching at 8:30 in the morning and monitored study hall until 8:00 at night, riding her bicycle back and forth for meals at Metzger. In the summers she worked in the office. Among her students were "some neurotic Sioux and Ojibway boys who were a long way from home and lonesome and unhappy," she recalled, but most of them "were an ideal group," "open-minded" and "intelligent."

Marianne taught at the Indian School during what *Sports Illustrated* called "its golden age," a three-year period when the football team, coached by Glenn "Pop" Warner, defeated almost all of the major college teams. Several of the star athletes, including Jim Thorpe, were Marianne's students. In their mid-twenties like her, they and their wives helped keep the younger students in line. Asked often in later years about Jim Thorpe—regarded as America's greatest all-round athlete—she remembered "James" as "a little laborious" in the classroom "but dependable," "modest," and "casual about anything in the way of fame or eminence achieved." When the athletes practiced after school, Marianne observed "a kind of ease in his gait that is hard to describe. Equilibrium with no strictures; but crouched in the lineup for football he was the epitome of concentration, wary, with an effect of plenty in reserve."

Marianne treated her students with respect, and they in turn respected her. In her second year she developed a course in commercial law to help students protect their legal interests. And she sometimes typed letters on behalf of disgruntled students and teachers. But she took little pride or pleasure in her work. "I felt myself to be an impostor there," she said years later. "I was soldiering; it really wasn't my work."

Friedman made her situation trying from the beginning. A bureaucrat more concerned with discipline than with education, he could never understand why a Bryn Mawr graduate would want such a job. Mary worried about the strain on Marianne's health and, after the first few months, even Warner urged her to quit. But she continued teaching there for three years. Warner provided much coaching, not only in mathematics but also in handling "the old sourball," as they called Friedman.

Student and faculty morale plummeted under Friedman's administration. According to Mary's letters, students were locked in at night and had to be chaperoned if they left campus. Beatings and confinement in "the hole" were frequent punishments. Complaining of inadequate food and lax morality as well as physical abuse, the students petitioned for an investigation. Because the beating of a teenage girl from the Commercial Department figured prominently among the complaints, Friedman accused Marianne of instigating the petition.

"You mustn't hold me responsible for my pupils' stubbornness," she told him. "I crush out disrespect and rancor whenever I see it, and I give the students as thorough a training in political honor as I can."

All three Moores were experts in deflection and diplomacy, and the Indian School afforded Marianne much practice in these arts.

Congress ordered an investigation in early 1914 and fired Friedman. All of the students testified against him. "Sissy has avoided the inspectors as if they were smallpox," Mary told Warner, but eventually Marianne had to testify about the "honor" of a female student. While Mary felt sorry for Friedman, she was glad that he and certain others had to answer for the school's "cruel neglect and abuse" of the students. "It is a horrid, not even a good, prison," she said. "But we continue, when probed, to say we think Mr. Friedman has made many changes that are good, and that it is hard to do justice to every single case when there are a thousand cases." Marianne probably did not share Mary's sympathy for Friedman, but she refused to denounce him publicly.

Enrollment dropped sharply the following September. With only seven students in the Commercial Department, the new superintendent dissolved it. He offered Marianne the opportunity to teach in the general curriculum—without pay until she passed the appropriate civil service exam—but she refused. "Rat [Marianne] is the cheerfulest discharged beast the sun ever shone on," Mary wrote Warner at the end of September. "He hopes Badger [Warner] will not be displeased. I tell him Badger will demand what I do—some flesh on his bones. He replies that if he may lay on his own rug all winter he will not rustle forth weighing 98 only."

Despite the constant strain of dealing with Friedman, the job did provide Marianne a life apart from Mary, and earning a paycheck did give her leverage within the family. "It would never do," Mary decided, for Marianne to have household duties in addition to her Indian School ones, and so Marianne was allowed to devote her weekends to writing and reading.

Throughout her career she insisted that first reading and then people provided her main incentive to write. She developed a kind of social life with the writers she read, and many of her poems from the 1910s, most of them unpublished in her lifetime, address a writer or other real or imagined character. Some praise and others scorn. She subscribed to *The Atlantic Monthly, International Studio,* and *Life,* and brought home more periodicals from the Indian School library over the weekend. Friends gave or loaned her other magazines, and after she no longer worked at the Indian School, she went to Dickinson College and sometimes Harrisburg in search of periodicals.

She kept a scrapbook, in which she pasted a great many articles clipped from newspapers and magazines as well as a few keepsakes. These clippings reveal that she kept company with literary figures such as Kipling, Trollope, Meredith, James, Conrad, George Moore, and Shaw, and reveal furthermore that she followed closely European innovations in the other arts. She saved clippings about Nijinksy, Edward Gordon Craig, Rodin, and Schoenberg. The scrapbook contains several reviews of the New York Armory Show of 1913 and an announcement of *Des Imagistes: An Anthology* from 1914. When she could not clip the articles, she took notes in tiny, unused diaries that Mary apparently received in her youth. (Blank paper never went to waste in the Moore household.) She stopped keeping scrapbooks after 1914 but kept notebooks of her reading for the rest of her life. These notebooks contain many quotations and ideas she later used in poems.

In addition to pursuing her literary aspirations during these years, Marianne devoted considerable effort to the cause of suffrage. Her taking a civil service examination in Washington coincided with the historical suffrage parade of March 3, 1913. The elaborate twenty-page color program, the allegorical pageant, and reports of drunken hecklers helped launch the suffrage campaign from the local into the national arena. Leading the parade were Inez Milholland on a white horse, Alice Paul, Anna Howard Shaw, Carrie Chapman Catt, Helen Keller, and other pioneers of the movement. At the last minute Warner urged Marianne not to participate so that she would not jeopardize her job at the Indian School. But she marched anyway. Years later she told Elizabeth Bishop that she "paraded with the suffragettes, led by Inez Milholland on her white horse." Her scrapbook includes programs and newspaper clippings about the march.

Both Marianne and Mary served the cause at the local and state levels. Mary Norcross took charge of the county campaign and rented a Carlisle storefront to serve as headquarters. She enlisted Marianne to write weekly press releases. Mary and Marianne hung banners and distributed pamphlets at the 1915 state fair in Harrisburg. Onlookers found it remarkable to see Marianne climbing a tree and Mary standing on a ladder. "I've never seen a lady on a ladder before," remarked one Carlisle gentleman. "Isn't it lovely of Mrs. Moore to be willing to do that for suffrage."

Besides Bernard Shaw, Henry James, Gordon Craig, and others with whom she conversed through print, an important influence upon the poet's developing aesthetic was the Reverend Edwin Kellogg and in particular an evening class he taught on Old Testament poetry. The notes Marianne took for this class, along with the poems she wrote over the next decade, indicate that it impressed her deeply.

Not only did she write several poems about Old Testament figures in 1914 and 1915, but concepts she learned about the Hebrew language appear in memorable passages of other poems. In "The Past Is the Present" she quotes Kellogg directly: "Hebrew poetry is / prose with a sort of heightened consciousness. 'Ecstasy affords / the occasion and expediency determines the form.'" In "Novices" she quotes several passages from two texts used in Kellogg's class, A. R. Gordon's *The Poets of the Old Testament* and G. A. Smith's *The Expositor's Bible*, to demonstrate "the spontaneous unforced passion of the Hebrew language— / an abyss of verbs full of reverberations and tempestuous energy." Although the Hebrews are never mentioned in "An Octopus," Kellogg's preference for Hebrew passion over Greek reason is implicit in the long passage about the Greeks, who "liked smoothness, distrusting what was back / of what could not be clearly seen." They do so at their peril, the poem implies. One of its major themes is the powerful forces hidden in a "deceptively reserved and flat" glacier.

Metzger closed in the spring of 1913, and the Moores began eating at home. Marianne could "'drop into poetry' the minute he is through a meal," Mary told Warner, "and at meals." Even the fifteen minutes between supper and returning to the Indian School could be spent on poetry. But for five years after Marianne graduated from college, her only acceptances came from *The Lantern*. It was not for lack of trying. She entered contests. She sent poems both to the most reputable magazines and to those she had never seen.

In January 1914 she at last received some acknowledgment. Floyd Dell, editor of *The Masses*, sent her a handwritten note rejecting the poem she had sent him but asking to see others. "Instead of shaking him as Longears [Mary] seems inclined to do," she told Warner, "I cling to him as a young kitten to a frail sapling (about ⅔ of the way up)." She carefully selected several poems to send him, but the March issue of *The Masses* appeared with poems by Laura and William Rose Benét and none of her own.

Dell subsequently returned her poems but asked to see a book of them sometime. "Seen altogether, I think I would understand better the personality which they half-reveal, and that would help me to understand these broken-mirror-like reflections of it." Dell thus became the first editor to recognize the modernist appeal of Moore's work, but that made his rejection all the more painful.

"Bah! He makes me think of turnip tops," Marianne told Warner. At least with *The Atlantic*, she could blame its "pigheaded and churlish prejudice . . . against anything that is new."

By this time both Mary and Warner supported Marianne's literary aspirations even though her poems rarely earned their approbation. "Whatever you do," Warner wrote in 1913, "don't 'quit.'"

But when Warner ventured a critique of some poems, Mary wrote him confidentially: "Togo dear, let *me* help Uncle to *brace*. But do *you very shortly*—write him a bit of commiseration, or perhaps I should say *praise*—or something that's 'grateful and comforting.' He knows he is a 'slight man'—and that cheer of spirit would carry him over his bridge, and he beats himself continually for his 'oppressed' spirit . . . You see you are Mr. Fangs's lover (to his mind) and a lover must never tell his sweetheart to be more economical, or more self-forgetful, or more soldierly or any of the things the worthless sweetheart ought to be. See Togo?" (Mary often invoked the metaphor of lovers to describe the family's closeness in these years, but there is no evidence that Marianne shared these fantasies.)

Mary assumed the role of first reader of Marianne's poetry and first critic. While her standards were high and her appreciation for innovation limited, she no longer disparaged the effort or questioned the worthiness of the goal. Marianne felt disappointed, according to Mary, when her poems failed to meet her mother's approval. Yet her dogged pursuit of unconventional meter, unsentimental subject matter, and cryptic language ran counter to all that her English-teacher mother held dear.

In 1915, after Marianne had begun to have work accepted, the editor of *Contemporary Verse* revised three of her poems in proof. Mary opened the envelope in Marianne's absence and wrote her that "Masks," the most altered of the three, was now "a distinguished poem." "I am sore displeased that it is not in *me*," she said, "thus to help you *set your jewels*! To think such help should come from a source despised!" No other record survives of Mary's critiques at this time. And so it is noteworthy that she praised this unrhymed, iambic, sonnetlike revision utterly at odds with anything else Moore was writing at the time. Mary was privy to Marianne's disdain for the conservative bent of the editors (hence "source despised") but apparently oblivious to her formal experimentation.

Early on July 6, 1914, the long-awaited acceptance came. Harriet Monroe, editor of *Poetry* in Chicago, sent a postcard accepting five poems. After Marianne left for Washington later in the day, Mary wrote her about "the shining jewel that came to rejoice me this morning." "You must not forget *July 6, 1914*," she said.

Throughout the years that Marianne taught at the Indian School, Mary continued to think of their situation in Carlisle as temporary. Warner marveled that she could put so much of herself into their house and yet think so little of leaving it behind. During Marianne's first year of teaching, Mary spent money on the house "like a cloudburst" yet planned for the family to live in England for a year after Warner finished seminary. Although Marianne loathed the intrusion of workmen, the prospect of England in 1914 made teaching bearable.

In July 1912 Mary traveled alone to Pittsburgh and then to Colorado and Kansas to inspect investment properties she had inherited from Mary Eyster. The trip went a long way toward healing her emotional wounds, and she took satisfaction in her newfound independence. Not only did she report that she was able to fasten the back of her new dress without assistance, but when the conductor offered her a newspaper, she bought one for the first time in her life.

At one business meeting she refused pity for being a lone woman who had traveled all the way from Pennsylvania and at another feigned helplessness in business matters in order to get an agreement in writing. Performer and manipulator that she was, she always succeeded at getting what she wanted. Despite long days at the Indian School and little news to report, Marianne wrote Mary every day. If she felt that long letters were wasted on Warner, her twenty- to thirty-page letters to Mary indicate that she had no such qualms about her mother.

Mary longed for her father that summer. Although she did not often solicit or heed Warner's financial advice, she conveyed the particulars of her business dealings to him only. "I find myself wishing for you when I ought not to be wishing at all," Mary wrote him. "Sometimes I am, as it were, in a dream of reaching out; the way I used to be for the return of my father . . . and then as I quicken to realization, it is you I am reaching for." Months afterward she wrote Mary Shoemaker of the "mother joy" that Warner gave her, his care for her being "that of lover, father, and son all in one."

In his letters at least, Warner does not resist this conflation. He was "thrilled to the soul" when he received a letter from Mary accidentally addressed to her father. And although he courted a series of young women throughout these years, he let nothing threaten Mary's vision of the family's future together. "Well, there's no girl made that can match my mother and that there Basilisk of ours [Marianne]," he wrote in October 1912, "and *should* I run acrost some '*dream*,' why unless she'd be strong fur a family of four *to start with*, why I'd not 'press the case' no further."

He must have brought up the subject of a fourth member of the family when he came home for Mary's birthday the following April. For immediately Mary began to court a possible candidate. She chose Alice Benjamin Mackenzie, a teacher at Metzger, and within weeks "Benjamin Bunny" was part of the family and using family nicknames. Warner understood Mary's designs and tried to cooperate. He met "Ben" in May and wrote her just afterward. Over the summer he consulted Mary about how and how often to write Ben.

Metzger closed its doors for good that summer, and both Mary and Ben were out of work. Ben found a teaching position in Cleveland but would maintain her intimacy with the Moores for several years. "She sends us wonderful letters every week," Mary told Warner in December. "Nunkey thinks they're the greatest letters that have ever come except yours. But don't pursue anything Togo dear with the idea of 'please my family.' Anybody that is *your mate*, your complement, will 'please your family.'"

Although Warner continued to exchange occasional letters with Ben, he jumped at this opportunity and the next month told Mary that he was thinking of proposing to Hart Irvine, a young woman from Mercersburg whom he had known for some time.

"You know in all the years of your brave battling and waiting—when you told yourself there would be a time of release someday, you never put the day of liberty as early as this," Mary answered. "You have been so strong, patient, courageous, doing all your striving without murmuring—even when the fiends have plagued your sore. Is the last straw laid upon you when 'two years more' is put at you?" (In two years Warner would turn thirty.) "You have already far outdistanced *me*. I gave out long before I was your age; but you have my experience to enrich you, and you have some responsibility in having that bit of protection to use . . . But if you have written and the beginning has already been entered upon, I will stand beside you, and give you ever a word but gentle ones."

Warner answered that he would let his "definite move in regard to the Irvines go, provided you are a well and happy Bunny . . . You come first in my heart and plans. Let there be nothing but joy in your heart for if there is not, I shall feel I've neither had *my* cake nor eated *a* cake."

Marianne rarely interfered with such matters, nor was she consulted. But "out of a clear sky" one day she said to Mary, "I don't fully understand the case in this Irvine matter. But . . . I should say by all means help him, Bunny,—don't hold him back. We have seen enough of the selfishness—the cruelty of sacrificing a man's whole life to a mother and sister." (The words *selfishness, cruelty,* and *whole life* are notable here in the context of Marianne's own sacrifices.)

In principle at least, Mary agreed with this. "You and [Marianne] must each make a place for the love of others," she wrote Warner a few weeks later. "Oh! I long to see you each with a mate of *God's choosing*! And for that shall I pray with all my heart."

In March Warner went to New York to see Ben, who was visiting her sister there. He took her for a boat ride and then accompanied her, her sister, and her father to the circus and to dinner. "*I'm done with all 'grasshoppers' and 'frogs,'*" Warner wrote afterward, "and *if I can't catch Ben, I won't hunt at all.*"

Ben enjoyed her boat ride with Warner but could not understand his interest in such an "antiquated rabbit" as herself. She was four years older than Warner. "He couldn't *possibly* enjoy my letters, Long Ears," she told Mary. "I am no good whatever whatever in writing to men bodies—never have been—not having a brother I cannot imagine what interests them."

By the spring of 1914, Mary and Marianne had not yet given up their plans for Europe—Marianne now wanted particularly to go to Italy—and they sometimes talked of including Ben in these plans. Mary, however, insisted that she could never return to England without Warner. Although Ben did call Mary "my playfellow" and Warner once referred to her as Mary's partner, there is no evidence that Mary harbored romantic feelings for Ben.

The Moores discovered Kenneth Grahame's *The Wind in the Willows* in May 1914. All three felt an immediate kinship with its charming animal characters and the bucolic fields and forests where they roamed. In the first chapter, the home-loving Mole wanders out of his burrow one fine spring day, finds himself at the bank of a river, and sees two eyes sparkling at him from a hole on the other side. These eyes belong to the adventurous and worldly wise Water Rat. After Rat invites Mole for an impromptu boat ride and picnic, the two become constant companions. Rat was an attentive friend and sociable fellow except when his mind drifted off into making rhymes. He could often be found with unfinished verses scattered about. Although Mary first identified with Otter and called Marianne "Little Portly" after Otter's lost child, within a few weeks they were calling each other Rat and Mole.

Knowing smiles must have passed between them when they read about the gregarious and magnanimous but impulsive Mr. Toad. No sooner has the wealthy Toad gone in for one fad than he takes up another, the ultimate being a motorcar. Warner had learned to drive the previous summer and had recently (and impulsively) bought himself a motorcycle. Resemblances between himself and the character that bore his name did not please him. Mary and Marianne suggested that he adopt the name of the distinguished but reclusive Mr. Badger. Badger he became.

By claiming the persona of the self-reliant and savvy Mr. Rat, Marianne defined a new role for herself in the family. But she referred to Rat in the third person for well over a year. Rat was her literary self. "He doesn't know what activity he will take up," she wrote Warner after losing her position at the Indian School. "Rat will devote himself to tennis and housekeeping for a while and bend every energy on the amassing of scraps [for her scrapbook] . . . Mole is scampering and carrying on (is too cute for anything) over Rat's jobless condition (and expects to domineer over him, I guess). Mole says Rat may take the Buldy [*Boston Evening Transcript*]. That entrances him. Think of Rat sitting by a bed of coals with his smoking jacket on and a large tin of marshmallows and a Buldy."

Three days after she first saw *The Wind in the Willows* and well before she began calling herself Rat, Marianne sent Warner "Intra Mural Rat":

Intra Mural Rat

You make one think of many men
Once met to be forgot again;
Or merely resurrected
In a parenthesis of wit,
that found them hastening thru it,
Too brisk to be inspected.

As in other poems she was writing at the time, she speaks to her subject. But the poem is also a self-portrait predicting the kind of poet Moore would be. "Intra Mural" means literally "between walls." She would remain hidden in her poems except for occasional flashes in "a parenthesis of wit." The poem is itself "a parenthesis of wit." A decade later she chose it to open *Observations*.

10

A Fine
Steel Blade

1914–1916

The year and a half after Marianne stopped teaching at the Indian School saw the end of her apprenticeship and her emergence as a major voice in modern poetry. She did not, however, keep her promise to gain weight. She lost ten pounds in her first month of unemployment and developed headaches as well. Two weeks after her layoff, her new bathroom burst into flames. Little damage was done, and Marianne was amused at the firemen's efforts to save her "gorgeous bathrobe . . . as if it had been a priceless statue."

But the fire took its toll on her spirits. "Rat hates his [food]," Mary told Warner three days later. "He has had headaches and is the most-done-up rat in all his host. He doesn't stand strain well, and he surely has had days of that. We don't agree either in the matter of some household changes, and he feels low in mind."

The loss of income meant a loss of independence for Marianne, and the household changes included a tighter budget for food and entertainment. After fourteen years of boarding at Metzger, Mary had begun to cook at home. Priding herself on the thrift of her meals rather than their heartiness, she learned that she could get five meals per week out of one chicken or duck and eat cheese or bacon for the other two. She also

cooked fresh spinach and cauliflower sometimes. But without Marianne's salary, Mary felt they could no longer afford such "luxuries." For
the next two years, they lived mostly on the monthly fifty dollars that
Mary had negotiated during her Colorado trip. After Warner finished
seminary, he worked for two years as an assistant minister in Baltimore.
He sent money when he could but not enough that Mary felt obliged
to tithe it. She sometimes drew on principal to make ends meet.

Marianne decided to enter a war poem contest in hopes of receiving the hundred-dollar prize. And as soon as her job ended, she threw
herself furiously into the task. "Rat has been all but killing himself
over his war poem," Mary said. "The Indian never drove him harder
than he has driven himself over this."

The prize money was a strong incentive, but the poem itself indicates that more was at stake than the money. It was her first poem to
address a contemporary political event (the outbreak of World War I)
and also the first to depart from the accentual meter she had used in
her poems thus far. The poem shows her experimenting with a short
stanza based on syllable count (here a pattern of 3-1-5-5 syllables), the
typewriter's tab feature, and an abrupt rhyme scheme.

ISAIAH, JEREMIAH, EZEKIEL, DANIEL,
Bloodshed and Strife are not of God;

What is war
For;
Is it not a sore
   On this life's body?

Yes? Although
So
Long as men will go
   To battle fighting

With gun-shot
What
Argument will not
   Fail of a hearing!

Moore did not invent syllabic verse but made the first serious use of it in English. Syllabic meter is determined by the number of syllables per line rather than, as in most English poetry, the number of feet. It is more audible and therefore more common in unstressed languages, the Japanese haiku (5-7-5 syllables per line) being a familiar example. Moore always said that she wrote in stanzas rather than lines. To call her stanzas "syllabic" does not do them justice, as she pointed out later in interviews, because it disregards the stanzas' intrinsic rhyme scheme and pattern of indentation.

She had experimented with the glyconic meter she had learned from Henry Sanders and with the symmetrical syntax of Hebrew poetry that she learned from Edwin Kellogg. And she had learned what she could about poetic patterns in other languages. But she always claimed that she had no models for her stanza. "No masters, no mystery . . . It was internal pressure." She liked "symmetry," she said, and "a flowing continuity." Her letters to Warner give no indication that she regarded the stanza of "Isaiah, Jeremiah, Ezekiel, Daniel" as a breakthrough. "My war poem is punk, Mole considers, and that is a gloom," she said. But she did mail it.

Marianne's health did not improve over the winter, yet she had time to "amass scraps" and to write poems more prolifically than she ever had. In February she decided to enter a book contest. Erskine MacDonald, editor of *The Poetry Review* in London, proposed to issue a series of single-author books with sixty to eighty poems each. For nearly a week Mary reported that Rat was "tic-tic-ing on his typewriter" all day and all evening "making a *book*." Marianne sent MacDonald sixty-four poems. (Her first books, *Poems* and *Observations*, would contain twenty-four and fifty-three poems, respectively.) Included were the poems accepted by Harriet Monroe the previous summer but not yet published, and recent poems she would send off in a few days to "eight or nine magazines."

Although the book manuscript does not survive intact, the Moore archives contain quite a few unpublished poems of this period—all of them short and many of them typed on a certain blue paper with the Carlisle address in the upper-left corner. If these are remnants of the book manuscript, they attest neither to MacDonald's inanity nor to Moore's genius. They show a poet testing her powers of critical observation upon children and other innocents, upon passages of literature, and upon biblical, historical, and literary figures. They show her experimenting with meter, rhyme, and typographical indentation. By the following September, Moore had received no response from MacDonald, and she wrote to withdraw from the book contest. She had begun by then to write poems quite different from those in MacDonald's possession.

While teaching at the Indian School, Marianne sometimes went to Washington about various health problems, as she did on July 6, 1914, the day her acceptance from *Poetry* arrived. She visited the Library of Congress the next day to investigate the magazine. "*Poetry* is a respectable magazine," she reported, "small and neatly gotten up."

She had probably first learned about the magazine from the reviews of *Des Imagistes: An Anthology* that appeared in the spring. One review in her scrapbook points to precision as a watchword for Imagism and disparagingly notes that precision makes poetry scientific. Perhaps no twentieth-century poet became as precise and scientific as the mature Marianne Moore, but one could not have guessed this from the poems that she sent to *Poetry*. Their subjects are the Old Testament David, the New Testament Nicodemus, Merlin, the "intra-mural rat," and an Elizabethan trencher motto. And unlike the free verse of Imagism, all employ meter and rhyme.

Poetry had been the first magazine to publish the Imagists in 1913, but it published much conventional poetry as well. By July 1914 Harriet Monroe would have had no reason to identify Marianne Moore with Imagism, nor as it turned out would she share the Imagists' enthusiasm for Moore's subsequent poetry.

When Marianne returned to Washington in March 1915, she saw some of the "eight or nine magazines" to which she had just sent poems. "I had a wonderful time at the Library [of Congress] this afternoon," she wrote Mary. "*Blast* is a wonderful publication—compilation of curses and blessings . . . I also read *Poetry and Drama*, *The Egoist*, *The Little Review* and the *International*, all of whom I expect to buy me."

The next day she returned to find some of the books she had read about, including two volumes of Yeats's essays, *Ideas of Good and Evil* and *The Cutting of an Agate*. "Both are worth their weight in gold," she said. "I never have read more earnest fanciful and ennobling prose."

"I *must* have it," she said about Robert Frost's *North of Boston.* "I don't know when, but I must have it." Amy Lowell's latest book, *Sword Blades and Poppy Seed,* was not on the shelf, but she found Lowell's first book, *A Dome of Many-Coloured Glass,* and felt encouraged because of Lowell's maturation since then. She located Ezra Pound's first prose work, *The Spirit of Romance,* but thought it lacked "the ping and pang of *Blast."* "Richly printed," she said, "and very dusty in the hade [head]."

Three of the poems she sent out in February were accepted by *The Egoist* in London. "No money however," she told Warner. "I am so delighted to have them take me I shouldn't mind if they charged me. I like the paper." Two appeared in the April 1915 issue and the third appeared in May, in a special Imagist number. Floyd Dell was thus the first professional editor to notice Moore's poems and Harriet Monroe the first to accept them, but Richard Aldington, poetry editor for *The Egoist,* became the first actually to publish them. By the spring of 1915, Moore had been writing poems for eight years and sending them to magazines for six.

The Marianne Moore whom Richard Aldington published in April and May of 1915 was already a different poet from the one whom Harriet Monroe at last published in May 1915. The diction of the newer poems was harder and sparer, the meter less conventional. Recognizing the name of her former classmate in *The Egoist,* Hilda Doolittle wrote to Marianne to introduce herself as the poet H.D. and the wife of Richard Aldington. "R. has spoken often of your work," she said. "We both think you have achieved a remarkable technical ability:—R. says it is quite the finest that he has seen from America!"

Although Moore never aligned herself with Imagism, her first poems appeared in magazines associated with the movement. *Poetry* had published H.D.'s Imagist poems and Ezra Pound's explanations of Imagism in 1913, but the Imagists stopped sending their work to *Poetry* after Pound turned his attention elsewhere and after Aldington, one of the original Imagists, became poetry editor for *The Egoist.*

William Rose Benét warned Marianne through his aunt to avoid letting herself be influenced by the Imagists. "I'll have to tell Billy or rather show him," she told Warner, "that it's like getting married; I am sorry to disappoint him, but it is not possible to meet his views on the subject and please myself." When Benét asked Marianne a few months later for information about Imagism to use in a ladies' club lecture, she sent him a three-page, single-spaced letter not only giving a detailed history of the movement but also providing her own assessment of its members. But she made it clear that she considered herself "an outsider so far as Imagism is concerned." She resembled the Imagists in her clear, concise diction but not in her adherence to meter and rhyme.

As soon as Marianne returned from Washington, Mary came down with a serious case of bronchitis. Marianne had to learn how to operate the furnace, cook, and take over other household tasks. They kept the severity of the illness from Warner, and he unwittingly sparked a family crisis when he mentioned plans to sell his motorcycle and buy a car. Mary thought it improper for Warner to have a car when his senior minister, Dr. Barr, did not. (Dr. Barr himself abhorred the motorcycle and backed the plan.) If Christ could conduct his ministry without a car, Mary reasoned, then why should Warner need one?

So great was Mary's distress that Marianne wrote a long, confidential letter to Warner. No other surviving letter reveals with such candor how Marianne viewed her responsibilities toward her mother. "Disappointment makes wreckage of Mole," she wrote, "and she takes things so acutely that she will *never*, not in any case, live a very long time. Mole realizes that she must let go . . . and determines not to be tyrannical and selfish while purporting to care for you; that we know; but I didn't know which way to look when Mole was speaking of the automobile. She seemed to sicken and pale so . . . It would seem morbid to you perhaps to think that Mole could get sick again because you thought of getting a car but . . . it isn't so unreasonable, for Mole would wish to think that without a suggestion from anyone, you ought to know just what is unsuitable . . . I am going to make her as merry as I can and look after her and we are going to get [ourselves] in sound condition. *Then we must 'renew' Mole.* I don't care how much it costs. The best way is for us all three to settle in semi-permanence; and the next best thing to do is to get Mole to Europe. You look on Europe as a luxury and as a thing to be gotten in, if possible and to be missed, if possible . . . yet I think it quite possible that Mole might die of a broken heart *without knowing it*, through not having gone to Europe with you."

Marianne blamed her trip to Washington for bringing on Mary's bronchitis and feared that Mary's loneliness and unhappiness while she was at Lake Placid (five years earlier) had permanently impaired Mary's health. In both cases Mary had said she wanted Marianne to go. And so Marianne now took it upon herself to recognize her mother's needs even if Mary protested. "Mole can't be taken literally and be left to fight her way through briars," she said. She became convinced also that Mary needed protection against the Norcrosses. "The Beaver mourns and clings to Mole and makes her do things that will 'do her good' and sogs the life out of her, and Miss Louise . . . [has] no soul fit to understand Mole, and Mrs. Norcross wants to give and sucks Mole's life." Mary said she could take care of herself, but Marianne thought that leaving Carlisle would mean "life to Mole."

Warner proposed renting a house where they could all live together, but Mary answered that she had no desire to live in Baltimore.

Mary took pride in her Scotch-Irish indirection, in what she called "our circling ways, arriving at the East by going to the West, and saying yes by a thousand no's and no by as many yeses" and also in the Scotch-Irish intuition with which insiders were supposed to grasp the truth behind the circuitous words. Warner and Marianne were expected to know "what is unsuitable" without being told.

Marianne did everything possible that spring to avoid displeasing Mary. She practiced with the Oratorio twice a week, served as treasurer for the Home Missionary Society, and agreed temporarily to teach a Sunday-school class. Mary recognized the toll these activities took on her daughter's strength but thought them all good for her. "He is a *good* rat nowadays and swears at nothing," she told Warner. "He knows that it all is a part of life and must be taken cheerfully, perhaps reverently. To have attained knowledge so high is mighty climbing for a *rat*. Rats, you know, are made of snarls and bites and poison fangs."

Meanwhile, Moore continued to write poems—the only outlet for her individuality and ambition—and at last began to achieve the kind of recognition that she had long sought. In July she had five more poems accepted for *The Egoist*. In August she received a warm letter from H.D. inviting her to come to London the following summer. And in October she received an enthusiastic letter from Alfred Kreymborg, accepting five poems for *Others*.

In high spirits over Kreymborg's letter, Marianne wrote to Warner and conveyed her excitement by describing Mary's reaction to it.

"Now with what poems I have published and my general well being," she said to Mary, "I could publish a book anytime."

"I wouldn't publish," said Mary.

"Never?"

"After you've changed your style."

"Huh!" Marianne said. "Well you would omit all these things I prize so much?"

"Yes, they're ephemeral."

This conversation has horrified readers of Moore's letters, especially since similar conversations often accompany other moments of literary triumph. But it is a prime example of Mary's "saying yes by a thousand no's." While it is true that Mary had little appreciation for her daughter's "style," Warner would have understood the pride and affection implicit in this conversation. Had he sensed any disapproval whatever, he would not have risked taking sides.

"I'm so proud of Rat's success," he answered, "that I'll fail to speak adequately of his work to him, but I 'believe in him' and expect that the time will come when even *he* will be satisfied with himself."

October 1915 brought not only Kreymborg's letter but also literary gossip from London. The purveyor of this gossip was an elegantly dressed gray-haired lady, Amy Rhodes. She was a friend of George Plank's, an illustrator and native of Carlisle who lived in London among other American expatriates. (Marianne had reviewed an exhibition of Plank's work for the local newspaper in 1913.) In response to Marianne's eager questions about her "confederates," Amy Rhodes told her that "Mrs. Aldington [H.D.] kept her house spotless and that Mr. Aldington has dispensed with a hat," also that Yeats "has interested himself in spiritualism and is busying himself about that to the exclusion of everything else." Marianne showed Rhodes her poems and loaned her some books and magazines.

"It will be a pretty intrepid fellow that will buzz around Rat now to annoy him," Marianne told Warner, "freshened up as he is, and full of life."

"Ratty looks almost his old self," Mary said. "Sometimes I feel that he is really *husky!*"

Marianne saw much of Honey Hays that fall. They played golf and tennis and went often to the movies. And she wrote weekly press releases for the suffrage campaign. Both the Suffrage Liberty Bell and Beatrice Forbes-Robertson Hale, an eccentrically dressed actress and suffragist, came to Carlisle in October. When Marianne asked Hale about Edward Gordon Craig, the experimental stage designer in whom she took an avid interest, Hale pronounced him "extreme and fantastic in his theatrical schemes" and "clammy and repulsive as a person." And when Marianne spoke of her own artistic ambitions, Hale advised her "to find something economically sound that 'I thought I could get away with' and attach myself to it, leaving once and for all so dead a suburb as me adopted town."

Just after Thanksgiving, Marianne would go to New York with the Cowdrey sisters and make her modernist debut. But earlier in the month she made a trip of a much different nature. As treasurer for the Home Missionary Society, she went to Mercersburg to attend what she called a "Congress of Gospelated Wigeons." She stayed in the home of one stranger and shared a bed with another, "a wealthy, rotundly proportioned, and exceedingly 'smart' old rhinoceros-bill." Though she got little sleep and merely endured the sessions, she had "a splendid time," she told Warner, and had an even grander time regaling Mary with her adventures after she got home.

Rarely are Marianne's "snarls and bites and poison fangs" as evident as they are in her account of the Mercersburg adventure. The chief victim was the "boa constrictor," the mother of Hart Irvine, from whose coils Warner had narrowly escaped two years before. Marianne appeared on the scene as the venomous "cobra" ready to wage battle on behalf of her Bunny. Clothes were their weapons. Marianne felt well armed in her new hat and rendered Mrs. Irvine defenseless in her poor attire.

Mary made no attempt to hide her glee from Warner but claimed to exercise restraint in telling him particulars. "I do not wish to cast stones at anybody," she wrote, and Marianne inserted, "with paws full of them." Warner did not share their pleasure. When he pointed out that Marianne may have formed a different opinion had she seen Hart Irvine herself, Mary retorted: "*He did see her*, he did; and that was one of the 'stones' Bunny retained in her marsupial. Nunkey thought Hart surprisingly plain and poorly dressed [as she passed by in a carriage]; but I do admit that no fine opinion ought to be formed from a mere glance."

It is clear that Marianne managed to transform the dull occasion into rollicking entertainment for her mother and, moreover, that she was willing to indulge Mary's prejudices at Warner's expense. But the real boa constrictor that Marianne faced in Mercersburg was not the harried Mrs. Irvine but the vision of a future punctuated by such gatherings.

The ten days she spent in New York opened up an entirely differ-ent future. There she resumed the erudite flow of conversation she had developed at Bryn Mawr. And she at last met in person people with whom she could discuss new directions in the arts. She found in Kreymborg a much-needed mentor. She read everything she could find that he had written, but what she found irresistible was his boyish appearance and enthusiasm. They liked each other immediately. Kreymborg recognized right away the unique power and innovation of Moore's poems. Never mind that their meaning eluded him. He seemed to admire them all the more because of it. He introduced her to poets and artists with whom she could discuss the ideas that she had long pondered.

"Ratty has came," Mary wrote the day after Marianne's return from New York. "He knows not what he eats nor what he sees, at Riverbank; can think only of the edge of the great sea, where he has sojourned. I look very gravely, not to say sternly, at some of the experiences unfurled—and think I ought to have taken the scull myself;—but I have offered no threats so far of what I must do in fu-ture . . . His tongue went just like this [she sketched a seesaw] un-til after eleven. Then I stuck him into the tub, and he subsided partially until he was taken out and dried when away it went fast as ever."

While the trip to New York encouraged Marianne in her writing, it also convinced her that she could not earn a living as a poet. The magazines daring enough to publish her were too poor themselves to pay their contributors. "Rats need room to experiment and grow," she told Warner, "that is the main thing and *they need pay.*"

Soon after she returned, she decided she would seek employment as a reviewer. Because Samuel Duff McCoy wrote for the *Philadelphia Public Ledger* and had accepted her poems for *Contemporary Verse*, she thought she stood a good chance of getting hired at the *Ledger*. She heard that the *Ledger* paid its reviewers a thousand dollars annually but realized that she might have to begin as an adjunct. "I am just as sure of getting [a position] as I am of eating," she told Warner. "I should like to do books once a week for the magazine section . . . I could tell them that I have followed the work of Edwin Francis Edgett (in the *Transcript*) and J. B. Kerfoot in *Life* and Francis Hackett and Philip Littell in the *New Republic* recently and what with my poems of a critical trend in *The Egoist* and *Poetry* and *Others* and *Contemporary Verse* and my Indian School experience and AB [degree] I could certainly extort the position. I am prepared to review 'poetry, fiction, art or theology.' Music and sport and dancing are the only things I am afraid to tackle."

She wrote McCoy but received no answer. After Christmas she wrote directly to the *Ledger*'s editor. He replied that book reviews were written by the staff and no changes in staff were anticipated.

In January Marianne and Mary went to Philadelphia so that Marianne could apply in person. They went directly to the *Ledger* offices in Independence Square. The editor was out when they arrived and would not see them after he returned. The book review editor, to whom they were next directed, said she wrote all the reviews herself and was not given enough space for them as it was. She referred Marianne to the literary editor of the *Evening Ledger*. When he at last returned to his office, he told Marianne that he did not need new reviewers but was "always on the watch for something better." Marianne gave him copies of two reviews she brought with her but later in the afternoon began to worry that she could do better.

Mary suggested that she write a review of J. B. Kerfoot's *Broadway*, which Marianne had just read. Midway through the review, Marianne

decided she needed a certain quotation, and the two went to four libraries vainly searching for Kerfoot's book. After dinner she remembered
the quotation. ("Was there ever anything so Rat-like?" Mary said.) Mary
stood at one bureau writing to Warner while Marianne stood at another
finishing her review. If the *Ledger* turned her down, Marianne resolved
to promote herself to another paper, "first the Buldy [*Boston Evening
Transcript*], then the [New York] *Post*, and so on, down." After receiving
no answers from any of them, she sadly gave up her newspaper plans.

In April Moore assembled a second book—this time for H.D., who
had requested the manuscript and offered to look around London for
a publisher. H.D. did not succeed in finding one, but she did use the
collection to write the first critical notice of Moore's work. The review
includes three complete poems, the only known contents of the book
manuscript. Two of the three, "He Made This Screen" and "A Talisman," were slightly revised from their original appearance in the *Tipyn
o'Bob* and *The Lantern*. Moore apparently thought H.D. would appreciate their Imagist-like qualities. T. S. Eliot later called "A Talisman" a rare
example of a discernible influence upon Moore's poetry, that of H.D.

A TALISMAN

I.

Upon a splintered mast
Torn from the ship, and cast
Near her hull,

II.

A stumbling shepherd found,
Embedded in the ground,
A sea gull

III.

Of lapis lazuli;
A scarab of the sea,
With wings spread,

IV.

Curling its coral feet,
Parting its beak to greet,
Men long dead.

But he was wrong. *The Lantern* published "A Talisman" six months before *Poetry* published H.D.'s first poems and launched Imagism.

H.D. calls the poems "curiously wrought patterns . . . quaint turns of thought and concealed, half-playful ironies." She presents Moore as a warrior who might be laughing at readers who look for meaning in the poems, but if so, "it is a laughter that catches us, that holds, fascinates and half-paralyses us, as light flashed from a very fine steel blade." Marianne liked the analogy. She thanked H.D. for recognizing her "fighting spirit," as she called it, her "opposition to mediocrity and the spirit of compromise."

Not everyone liked a fighting spirit, especially in a woman poet. Moore was not represented in a special women's number of *Others* edited by Helen Hoyt, who thought Moore's poems "too compact and keen . . . for comfort." William Carlos Williams, however, welcomed discomfort in the special issue of *Others* that he edited. He wrote to Moore in March, requesting "something you are willing to see stand alone—some one thing—new."

A few days earlier Marianne had jotted down in her notebook something Mary had said about a bird refusing to give up a dead worm.

Ambition without understanding
"It's like a person with a samovar (ant w a stick)
it's an elegant thing but what shall one do with it.
N., S, east west."
The whole thing has been of no avail "except that it has had
    the experience of carrying a stick."

As soon as she received Williams's letter, she started writing a poem about "ambition without understanding," an ant with a stick, and a swan she had seen in Oxford. "Critics and Connoisseurs" would be her first mature poem.

She had begun two years earlier to record bits of conversations in diaries similar to those she used for her reading notes, and she pursued this exercise more diligently after her New York trip. She had long enjoyed colorful speech, including her mother's, and often included examples of it in her letters. Not only was "Critics and Connoisseurs" her first poem inspired by actual (rather than imagined) conversation, but its sentences are longer, more relaxed, and thus more conversational than those of previous poems. Here is the entire poem as it appeared in the August *Others*.

CRITICS AND CONNOISSEURS

There is a great amount of poetry in unconscious
    Fastidiousness. Certain Ming
        Products, imperial floor coverings of coach
    Wheel yellow, are well enough in their way but I have seen
                something
      That I like better—a
        Mere childish attempt to make an imperfectly
              ballasted animal stand up,
      A determination ditto to make a pup
        Eat his meat on the plate.

I remember a black swan on the Cherwell in Oxford
    With flamingo colored, maple-
        Leaflike feet. It stood out to sea like a battle-
    ship. Disbelief and conscious fastidiousness were the staple
      Ingredients in its
        Disinclination to move. Finally its hardihood was
              not proof against its
        Inclination to detain and appraise such bits
        Of food as the stream

Bore counter to it; it made away with what I gave it
    To eat. I have seen this swan and
      I have seen you; I have seen ambition without
    Understanding in a variety of forms. Happening to stand

By an ant hill, I have
　　Seen a fastidious ant carrying a stick, north, south,
　　　　　east, west, till it turned on
　　Itself, struck out from the flower-bed into the lawn,
　　And returned to the point

From which it had started. Then abandoning the stick as
　　Useless and overtaxing his
　　Jaws with a particle of whitewash, pill-like but
Heavy, he again went through the same course of
　　　　　procedure. What is
　　There in being able
　　　　To say that one has dominated the stream in an
　　　　　attitude of self-defense,
　　In proving that one has had the experience
　　Of carrying a stick?

Appreciative readers will notice right away the wit of "Ming Prod-ucts," of a swan's maple-leaf-shaped feet, and of an ant "overtaxing his / Jaws with a particle of whitewash." And they will enjoy the varia-tions in rhythm created by phrases such as "unconscious Fastidious-ness" and "pill-like but / Heavy." But they will have to look at the poem, rather than listen to it, to discover that *Ming* rhymes with *some-thing*, *on* rhymes with *lawn*, and *his* rhymes with *is*. Moore managed to make the pattern of rhyme and syllables all but inaudible by using longer lines than she had used before and by varying the line length from six to twenty syllables.

Later in the summer she wrote an article about the kind of rhythm to which she now aspired in her poems. "The Accented Syllable" quotes a dozen prose sentences in which the intonations "persist, no matter under what circumstances the syllables are read or by whom they are read." Conventional meter and rhyme, she real-ized, are not compatible with the natural, uneven flow of conversa-tion. And so in "Critics and Connoisseurs" Moore creates for the first time a static grid of syllable count, indentation, and rhyme, over which and through which the natural rhythm of her sentences could flow.

What Moore heard and saw in New York inspired, or at least fortified, the evolution of her stanza. She visited the Daniel Gallery twice
and at Kreymborg's suggestion introduced herself to Alanson Hartpence, an *Others* poet who managed the gallery. Hartpence "knows
the ground," she said, and was "exceedingly cordial and thoughtful
about showing me around."

Hartpence played an important role in educating *Others* poets about
innovations in the visual arts. William Carlos Williams tells a story of
Hartpence showing a painting to a prospective customer. "What is all
that down in this left hand lower corner?" the woman asked. Hartpence
went forward and closely inspected the area in question.

"That, Madam," he replied, "is paint."

For centuries European artists were taught to make their brush-
work invisible in order not to interfere with the view of the painting's
subject. But by the early twentieth century, painters had begun to
draw attention to their paints, canvases, and methods as objects in
their own right—thus creating a tension between the subject represented and the medium of representation. Moore created a similar
tension between what she would later call the "architecture" of her
stanza and its "tune."

Another innovation of this time is Moore's ironic use of quotation.
Her notebook entry suggests that Mary said "ambition without understanding" with contempt. An ant carrying a stick back and forth would
represent for Mary the antithesis of usefulness. Readers of the poem
usually assume that Moore uses the phrase contemptuously, too, in
reference to critics and connoisseurs. But those who look past their assumptions will discover her irony: "ambition without understanding"
is the same thing as "fastidiousness." There is poetry in the inexplicable
waste of effort. There is "a great amount of poetry" in the child's un-
comprehending ambition "to make an imperfectly / ballasted [toy]
animal / stand up" and only a lesser degree of poetry in the conscious
attempts of the critic/swan and connoisseur/ant to make sense of what
eludes them.

"Ambition without understanding" accords, furthermore, with the
pragmatic concept of work to which many New York artists, especially those in the Stieglitz circle, subscribed. "I believe in a large
amount of work," a sculptor once told Marianne, and she repeated this

to herself as a kind of mantra. She agreed with Henry James that art requires "the waste of time, of passion, of curiosity, of contact." And she thought poetry and science analogous in their willingness "to waste effort." Her own willingness to waste effort in the service of art had already sustained her for years.

11

Defiant Edifice

1916–1918

Both Marianne and Mary considered themselves pacifists when war broke out in Europe. But not Warner. Excited by the heightened activity in Baltimore's harbor, he joined a naval reserve unit as soon as he could. He did not, however, tell his mother about Dr. Barr's warnings that the Maryland Naval Militia was filled with toughs who would rather punch you than shake hands. Warner enjoyed the company of women in his private life but in his professional life preferred the company of boys and men. He taught at a boys' school for two years before entering seminary and worked at a boys' camp for several summers. In Baltimore, his primary responsibilities at the church were the Boy Scouts and YMCA. The prospect of his first naval mission in the summer of 1915 thrilled him.

Also in the summer of 1915 Warner came home and announced his intention to marry Mary George White, the secretary at his church. Although they loved each other very much, he said, her family objected because of his father's "affliction." The trauma of choosing between her parents and Warner sent her to bed for the summer. "She has a mind like Mole's," Warner explained. "'Thoughts' make her sick and make her well." Mary made it clear that Warner's abrupt news had brought no joy to his family. "Miss White was taken at the greatest disadvantage in not being made acquainted with our life sorrow" at the earliest opportunity, she told him. She suggested that it would not be too late now for Dr. Barr to write a letter warning other church families. At the end of the summer, Mary White made her decision. "Mole wins," Warner wrote, "Mary said: 'No.'" Although Mary had earlier asked him to wait until he turned thirty, now that he was twenty-nine, she prayed "*Times* and *times* a day . . . that your thought may be utterly away from marriage."

By her late twenties, Marianne had more or less come to terms with her own relationship with Mary. While willing to make sacrifices in her personal life, she refused to make compromises in her art. Poetry offered her "a place for the genuine," as she later called it, and she became a student of nonconfrontational combat. "By- / play," she wrote, is "more terrible in its effectiveness / than the fiercest frontal attack." And "in fine / Surrender, may be conquest." She praised the resilience of the Irish who "have been compelled by hags to spin / gold thread from straw." Although she could never risk open disagreement with Mary, she could write poems such as "Critics and Connoisseurs" that mocked Mary's pieties so subtly that Mary herself would never know.

Warner, on the other hand, rarely came home for more than a day or two at a time but had greater difficulty reconciling his personal needs with his filial responsibilities. The conversations while he was home in December 1915 opened, he said, "a new era in our lives." Though still in love with Mary George White, he held only a dim hope of a future with her. He decided to look for a church of his own so that the three could "live together for 'next year,' and the years to follow." His most trusted friend and adviser of these years, the father of a former student, urged him to return to teaching. The navy offered to send him to Rio de Janeiro, the Panama Canal Zone, or Japan. But Warner accepted the call of the Ogden Memorial Presbyterian Church in Chatham, New Jersey. His compensation included a white two-story manse with green shutters, newly laid hardwood floors, and the Moores' first telephone.

Honey Hays shed bitter tears when she learned that the move was definite, and Mary Norcross (who had a new love) urged Mary not to go. But neither Mary nor Marianne expressed any regret about leaving their home of twenty years. "Ratty is full of joy in thought of next fall and winter," wrote Mary, "and works on his magazine sorting diligently. We are doing much toward getting our clothes in order once more. I feel a fortification in this respect that is tremendous." They gave away many things and boxed up 250 books to sell. Mary considered selling their house but would leave it empty for the two years they lived in Chatham.

For Mary the move was the fulfillment of a fantasy, the roots of which extended deep into her childhood. Although much older, the town of Chatham was, like Kirkwood, prosperous and verdant. "When we went to Chatham," Mary recalled later, "I was astonished at the beauty of everyone's lawn, and the social energy of everybody . . . We were happy and full of hope." She strove to maintain the respectability she thought proper for a minister's family. No longer could she afford the luxury of not returning calls. Once a week she cleaned house and opened the manse for prayer meeting.

Marianne dutifully played her part at her mother's side—but took "less and less interest" in babies, she admitted after one early call, and eventually pronounced them "repellent larvae." She played tennis at a local clubhouse and joined the Chatham Women's Club. One acquaintance remembered her as "a slender woman with dark red hair piled in braids around her head" and another as "a rather mousy little person . . . shy and modest, but with a vigorous mind."

The first year in Chatham fulfilled much that Marianne wanted, too. Not only did she enjoy Warner's daily presence, but Chatham's train station also put her within an hour of New York. If it took special effort for the people of Chatham to see beyond Marianne's "mousy" demeanor, such was hardly the case twenty-five miles away, where she metamorphosed into "an astonishing person with Titian hair, a brilliant complexion and a mellifluous flow of polysyllables which held every man in awe."

She resumed her connections with the *Others* group after Mary Carolyn Davies wrote her in November. Davies had been invited to the Kreymborgs' party for Marianne the previous year but had not come, she confessed, because she did not like to go alone. "I'm so glad you're like this," Davies told her when they met in New York, "I was so afraid you wouldn't be. Your things are so—they make you afraid. They're so reserved. They're strong like a man's. I didn't expect you to answer my letter." Davies told her all about personalities in the group. William Carlos Williams, she said, is "so *handsome*" and "*so* nice." "He has black curly hair. Oh you will like him."

In early December Moore and Davies went together to the opening of Kreymborg's play *Lima Beans* at the Provincetown Playhouse and to the tea that preceded it. It was the Provincetown Players' first season in Greenwich Village, and *Lima Beans* appeared on the same bill with two other one-acts. William Carlos Williams and Mina Loy played the leads, and the only other part was played by William Zorach, who designed the set. Moore met Loy and Williams for the first time that afternoon. She was agog, according to Williams, over Mina Loy, who appeared at the tea in "gold slippers, a green taffeta dress, a black Florentine mosaic brooch, long gold earrings and some beautiful English rings." The two women discussed Gordon Craig, whom Loy knew, and "the hollowness of fashionable life."

Williams in turn was agog over Marianne Moore. She wore her red hair "coiled around her rather small cranium," he recalled of their first meeting, and stood "straight up and down like the two-by-fours of a building under construction" (probably due to the back brace she was wearing). "She would laugh with a gesture of withdrawal after making some able assertion as if you yourself had said it and she were agreeing with you." They soon became friends. In February he asked her advice about the title of his next book, and Marianne invited him to bring his wife and children to Chatham. What impressed and mystified him over the years was "how slight a woman can so roar, like a secret Niagara."

After *Lima Beans*, Marianne regularly went to galleries and parties. Her notebook contains several conversations with Hartpence at the Daniel Gallery and with Stieglitz at 291. "You interest me," Hartpence said on one occasion, "the way you seize on the corners and single out things, the collections you make." One of the exhibits she saw at 291, its last, was a one-woman show by Georgia O'Keeffe. O'Keeffe and Moore were both born on November 15, 1887, and they both came to the attention of the New York avant-garde in the winter of 1915–1916. "Finally a woman on paper!" Stieglitz famously exclaimed when he first saw O'Keeffe's abstract drawings. The daringly experimental yet mystifying work of O'Keeffe and Moore inspired awe among men such as Stieglitz and Kreymborg.

Stieglitz had promoted the work of women, including Gertrude Stein and Mina Loy, since the inception of *Camera Work* and 291. Members of his circle shared a pluralist, antihierarchical aesthetic that privileged individual expression, or what Kandinsky called "inner necessity," over the realist conventions that had dominated Western art since the Renaissance. Moore learned about the lavishly illustrated *Der Blaue Reiter*, edited by Kandinsky and Franz Marc, during her first trip to New York and bought her own copy soon after. Its essays explain inner necessity, and its juxtaposition of modern art with folk art, children's art, medieval art, and tribal art illustrates the concept. The artwork is arranged intuitively rather than historically or geographically and thus invites an intuitive or even spiritual response. Moore put inner necessity in her own words when she later praised the "genuine" in poetry and when she wrote that the art she liked "must be 'lit with piercing glances into the life of things'; / it must acknowledge the spiritual forces which have made it."

At least one of Marianne's excursions that spring was, as Alfred Kreymborg called it in his memoir, a "descent into the world of the low-brow." "Never having found her at a loss on any topic whatsoever," he said, "I wanted to give myself the pleasure at least once of hearing her stumped about something." He took her to the Polo Grounds to see the New York Giants play the Chicago Cubs. Unfazed by the lurching el train or the crowds of fans, she spoke in a continuous rhythm, "parad[ing] whole battalions of perfectly marshaled ideas" before him, until he gently interrupted her to point out that the game was about to begin.

"Don't you want to watch the first ball?" he asked.

"Yes indeed." She stopped talking and turned her attention to the game.

"Strike!" called the umpire.

"Excellent," she said.

"Do you happen to know the gentleman who threw that strike?"

"I've never seen him before . . . but I take it it must be Mr. Mathewson."

"Why?" gasped Kreymborg.

"I've read his instructive book on the art of pitching . . . And it's a pleasure," she said, "to note how unerringly his execution supports his theories."

Marianne did go to the Polo Grounds with Kreymborg on April 12, 1917, and she must have astonished him with her knowledge of Christy Mathewson's *Pitching in a Pinch*, a boys' book she admired. Kreymborg, however, takes a few liberties. They saw the Yankees, not the Giants, defeat the Red Sox, not the Cubs. Mathewson, who pitched for the Giants, had retired.

The notebook that Marianne kept during her first year in Chatham indicates that it was a heady time for her—her "Middle Pullman Period," she joked. "I came away so loaded with ideas," she wrote after one New York gathering, "I could hardly keep the sidewalk." "Many of these things which I like I don't thoroughly understand," she wrote on another occasion, "and that brings me to a standstill experimentally."

Others announced at the end of 1916 that it would cease to appear monthly and would instead issue occasional pamphlets, including separate ones devoted to H.D., Mina Loy, and Marianne Moore. Around this time Moore assembled a collection of thirteen poems for the series. The pamphlet did not materialize, but the sequence did appear in *Others: An Anthology of the New Verse (1917)*, edited by Kreymborg. More than half of these poems employ the innovations of "Critics and Connoisseurs" and thus were probably written after the move to Chatham. The poems in sequence are "Critics and Connoisseurs," "The Past Is the Present," "Pedantic Literalist," " 'He Wrote the History Book,' It Said," "Like a Bulrush," "French Peacock," "Sojourn in the Whale," "In This Age of Trying Nonchalance Is Good, And—," "To Be Liked by You Would Be a Calamity," "Roses Only," "To a Steam Roller," "To the Soul of 'Progress,'" and "My Apish Cousins." The sequence captured the attention of Ezra Pound and T. S. Eliot, both of whom reviewed the anthology and singled out Moore and Loy for praise.

Moore's most experimental poem of the Chatham years, "Those Various Scalpels," did not appear in the anthology. Perhaps she felt uneasy about it—her uneasiness is explicit in the poem. It appeared in the May 1917 *Lantern* but would not appear where her literary compeers could see it for another four years. "Those Various Scalpels" takes the experiments of "Critics and Connoisseurs" to nearly ridiculous extremes. In the original version, lines range from one to twenty-six syllables, and they break within "re- / Peating," and "su- / Perior." The *aabbx* rhyme scheme is so subtle that *the* rhymes with *re-* and *to* rhymes with *su-*. The first sentence begins with the title and flows through four of the poem's five stanzas.

THOSE VARIOUS SCALPELS

Those
Various sounds, consistently indistinct like intermingled echoes
    Struck from thin glasses successively at random—the
    Inflection disguised: your hair, the tails of two fighting-cocks
                        head to head in stone—like
                        sculptured scimitars re-
        Peating the curve of your ears in reverse order: your eyes,
                        flowers of ice

And
Snow sown by tearing winds on the cordage of disabled ships:
                        your raised hand
    An ambiguous signature: your cheeks, those rosettes
    Of blood on the stone floors of French chateaux, with regard
                        to which the guides are so
                        affirmative—the regrets
        Of the retoucher being even more obvious: your other
                        hand

A
Bundle of lances all alike, submerged beneath emeralds from
                        Persia
    And the fractional magnificence of Florentine
    Goldwork, a miniature demonstration in opulence—a
                        collection of half a dozen little
                        objects made fine

With enamel—in gray, yellow, and dragonfly blue;
                a lemon, a

Pear
And three bunches of grapes, tied with silver: your dress,
                a magnificent square
   Cathedral tower of unbelievably uniform
   And at the same time diverse, appearance—a species of
                vertical vineyard rustling in the
                transverse storm
   Of conventional opinion—are they weapons or scalpels?
        Whetted

To
Brilliance by the hard majesty of that sophistication which is su-
   Perior to opportunity, these things are rich
   Instruments with which to experiment. We grant you that,
                but why dissect destiny with
                instruments which
      Are more highly specialized than the tissues of destiny
                itself?

It has often been suggested that "Those Various Scalpels" portrays the New Woman and perhaps Mina Loy in particular. Five lines of the poem are devoted to the Florentine enamel brooch that Loy was wearing when she and Moore met. But the distinctive hairstyle of the third and fourth lines belongs not to Loy but to Beatrice Forbes-Robertson Hale, the suffrage speaker whom Marianne had met in Carlisle the previous year. She had hair "like corn silk," Marianne had noted, "and a couple of distaffs of it on either side of her head." Although "your hair," "your eyes," and "your cheeks" suggest the conceits conventionally used to praise a woman's beauty, "fighting-cocks," "scimitars," "rosettes / Of blood," and the "Bundle of lances" indicate the potential violence of that beauty. "Your thorns," she tells the rose in "Roses Only," "are the best part of you."

Moore sometimes thought of her clothing as armor, but she never dressed to dazzle, as Loy and Hale did. There are no physical resemblances between the woman warrior in "Those Various Scalpels" and Moore herself. And yet the poem is essentially a self-portrait—based on H.D.'s review of her work. Not only had H.D. compared Moore's work to "light flashed from a very fine steel blade," but she had employed metaphors of weaponry and warfare throughout her review. She called Moore "the perfect swordsman, the perfect technician," unaware apparently of Moore's lifelong attraction to bladed instruments. In "Those Various Scalpels," Moore transforms H.D.'s flattering but fearsome portrait into an ambivalent self-caricature.

In both form and content, the poem exaggerates Moore's technique in order to ask whether she is really the "perfect swordsman" she aspires to be or whether her "very fine steel blade" is too finely honed for its purpose. Yes, her "curiously wrought patterns" and "concealed, half-playful ironies," as H.D. called them, are "whetted by . . . sophistication" (a pejorative for Moore, the opposite of naturalness), and they are "rich instruments with which to experiment." But what good are they to the poet with real battles to fight?

For the first year in Chatham, Warner tried to become the preacher his mother envisioned. But it gave him little satisfaction. His strength as a minister, as he knew when he took the job, was his affability rather than his preaching—which improved little over the year despite the tutoring of the previous minister and the elocution lessons paid for by a church member. Mary's sudden remark at a prayer meeting, "Oh! I wish my father could be here now," impressed upon Warner the depths of her longing and the futility of his best efforts to satisfy it. As soon as the United States entered the war in April, he wrote to the navy about enlisting.

The Moores celebrated the first year of their new life together by returning to their beloved Monhegan. They had not been back since Warner left for college thirteen years earlier. Monhegan was as beautiful as they remembered. Like the townspeople in "The Steeple-Jack," they did not see the approaching whirlwind.

Also visiting Monhegan that summer was a spirited young woman named Constance Eustis. A 1911 Wellesley graduate and president of student government there, Constance was a social worker and self-proclaimed feminist who shared a cold-water flat in Greenwich Village with other career girls. Her father, reared in poverty, had become a Wall Street attorney and made a fortune in real estate. So highly did John Eustis value education that he put all nine of his children— Constance was the fifth—through college. Warner and Constance were introduced at a dance one evening and met the next morning for a swim. Warner hesitated when he saw the low tide. Then Constance dived off the wharf ahead of him and stole his heart. A week later he asked her to marry him.

Warner told Mary and Marianne that he was leaving them—to marry Constance. He later referred to his announcement as "the hideous attack made upon that precious 'Life' that we three have lived together." He did not try to persuade them that Constance was "our kind," nor did he introduce her to them. The less they knew, the better for everyone, he decided.

When the Moores returned from vacation, Warner ended his relationship with Alice Benjamin Mackenzie, whom he had begun to court again. Ben was often in New York visiting her sister, and the Moores saw much of her during their first year in Chatham. Although marriage had been mentioned, Warner claimed that he never said anything to Ben as binding as his offer to Constance. "When I set upon Ben," he later wrote, "I had the cloak and the means of deceiving myself by thinking: 'Whatever else may or may not be right about this procedure, I shall at least be doing right by Mole and Rat.' Of course, I was even then injuring you beyond words." He was deceiving himself, he was injuring Mary and Marianne, but Ben's feelings, whatever they were, seem to have concerned the Moores very little. Her name disappears from their letters. All three understood that it was Mary, not Ben, who felt jilted and betrayed.

Marianne may well have thought that Warner should not have to sacrifice his life for his mother and sister, but her overriding concern now was Mary. If she believed that Warner's buying a car might literally kill Mary, how much greater her fear now. "I don't think you would actually strike Mole," she said to him at this time, "but you might as well do so, if you keep on as you are doing." He recalled a Sunday afternoon on the Monhegan headlands when Marianne told him: "'Sixty or a hundred years from now it will not matter about anything so far as we are concerned except what we are in character. This that you are doing makes for a rotten, perishable character'—not her _exact_ words perhaps, but what she meant. I was seared but not enough not 'to go on.'" His letters over the next two years are full of remorse for the anguish he caused but never for his decision to marry. "My crime," he said most succinctly, "is that while I would count it nothing to die for you, I have refused to live for you."

Constance did not accept Warner's proposal right away. She told him that she needed to get to know him better. And so he visited her often in the Village and also charmed her family at their large house in the Bronx. By Thanksgiving he had won over both Constance and her father. Upon receiving word of the engagement, Warner's own fatherly confidant expressed sympathy for Mary and Marianne, whom he knew, and yet he warmly congratulated Warner on the "wonderful event." Warner refused to make the engagement public until he received some sign of approval from home. He postponed introducing Constance to Mary and Marianne as long as he could. At last in January he brought her to Chatham for an awkward and painful afternoon.

Constance was led to believe that Warner's alleged engagement to Ben was the only reason his family objected. She had no inkling of the complex drama she had inadvertently stirred up. John Eustis sent his eldest daughter, May, to Athens, Ohio, to investigate John Moore's condition. May was told that John Moore had recovered from his illness but was retained as an employee. The Eustises also consulted an expert at Johns Hopkins about the hereditary nature of mental illness and received further assurances.

Meanwhile, Warner joined the navy. In November he requested temporary leave from the church to begin training in Virginia. And in February, after deciding to become a career chaplain, he turned in his resignation and moved to Boston, where for the next two years his ship would bring troops home from Europe. Mary and Marianne remained in the manse until May. It was a cold, difficult winter. Mary was ill, they had furnace problems, their future was uncertain, and yet they strove to maintain dignity. Marianne did little that winter, Mary told Warner, besides "feverishly" serve the church in every way possible "that honor might be reflected upon your pastorate." A surviving résumé indicates that she also did "prose work" for the Chatham Red Cross from April 1917 to April 1918. But there is no indication that she socialized in New York that year. And she did not write to Warner for weeks on end.

On Sunday, May 19, 1918, the announcement of Warner and Constance's engagement appeared in *The New York Times* and *The Chatham Press*. Mary had not budged in her opposition. But since she once said that she did not want to face people in Chatham about the engagement, Warner asked Constance to postpone the public announcement until Mary and Marianne had left Chatham. The two women were sitting on borrowed chairs in their empty house in Carlisle when Marianne opened the mail and read the announcement in the Chatham paper. "It was an hour of great agitation," Mary reported later. "I scarcely knew my way about in my own mind that day." Mary could hardly prevent the marriage now. Still, she tried.

Two weeks before the wedding, Constance wrote to Mary about arrangements. Mary answered the questions cordially and then added that she thought "the marriage ought not to be." "If Warner has been honest in absolutely un-baring himself before you, you are well aware that I feel that his making you an offer of marriage is unethical in a high degree; and that I have resisted him in his doing so with all the Christian philosophy—no—far better than that—with all the child truth—I could bring to bear upon it. A heaven-made marriage is the most beautiful thing this sin-shadowed world has ever seen and it is the one thing I think that a woman is justified in demanding of heaven; that or no marriage at all. It is because I have felt this to be a marriage unblessed of heaven—that I have been unable to enter into the new love that has arisen, and that I resist it as I do. Should it become a part of my life, I shall accept it, as if I had promoted it . . . I shall not be of much worth in merry-making, yet neither shall I allow the world to know my mind . . . I feel justified in shielding Warner from any questioning that would arise were it known that I have tried to hinder his marriage."

Constance offered to postpone the wedding a few months or even a year if that would make any difference in Mary's feelings. But it took place on July 29, 1918, at the Eustis home overlooking the Harlem

River. The newlyweds then went to the Eustis summer home in Black Lake in upstate New York for a week's honeymoon. Mary was true to her promise as far as the outside world was concerned. Just before the wedding she wrote Mary Shoemaker with the news that Warner was to marry and that she was pleased with the bride.

It hurt Warner that he received no letters from home during his honeymoon, and the letters that he wrote after returning to his ship pled for forgiveness and restored harmony. He called himself "a sick, sick boy, coming to life." "Now I think of myself as not separated from you or 'us,'" he wrote, "but as a part of that mystical body called 'we'— only I have been grievously smitten and like a limb paralyzed must be exercised back to life. Exercises are painful for a paralyzed limb but if maintained and improved mean health."

Marianne had believed since college that writing poetry requires experience, a debt she had now paid. One of the poems published during her second year in Chatham, "Black Earth," is a paean to experience. Black Earth is an elephant whose thick skin—his "patina of circumstance," his "rut / upon rut of unpreventable experience"—protects the integrity of his soul. "Black Earth" is the first of many Moore poems to exalt an animal's "naturalness" and "spiritual poise" over the foibles of human egotism.

Published a year after the Monhegan trip, "The Fish" is one of two poems, along with "A Grave," inspired by that trip. Admired for its imagery and technical proficiency, "The Fish" is one of Moore's best-loved and most mystifying poems. As if slipping off a wet rock, the reader is unsettled by the first sentence, in which (title serving as first line) "The Fish // Wade / through black jade." "Black jade" vividly describes the translucence of the ocean, but it is hard, not fluid, and one needs legs, not fins, to wade. The oppositional forces of rock and sea create constant tension in the poem. The reader is never offered a stable vantage point but instead is moved "in and out" among the liminal spaces— the tide pools and crevices—where sea and rock meet. The constant movement can be as gentle as a mussel shell "opening and shutting itself" or as violent as a "wedge / of iron" driven into "the edge / of the cliff."

The Fish

wade
through black jade.
    Of the crow blue mussel shells, one
        keeps
        adjusting the ash heaps;
    opening and shutting itself like

an
injured fan.
    The barnacles which encrust the
        side
        of the wave, cannot hide
    there; for the submerged shafts of the

sun,
split like spun
    glass, move themselves with spotlight swift-
        ness
        into the crevices—
    in and out, illuminating

the
turquoise sea
    of bodies. The water drives a
        wedge
        of iron into the edge
    of the cliff, whereupon the stars

pink
rice grains, ink
    bespattered jelly-fish, crabs like
        green
        lilies and submarine
    toadstools, slide each on the other.

All
external
marks of abuse are present on
this
defiant edifice—
all the physical features of

ac-
cident—lack
of cornice, dynamite grooves, burns
and
hatchet strokes, these things stand
out on it; the chasm side is

dead.
Repeated
evidence has proved that it can
live
on what cannot revive
its youth. The sea grows old in it.

Rarely do critics look for or find significant autobiographical content in Moore's poetry. But if ever they were to find it, surely in "The Fish," the title of which is one of Warner's family names. The poem's appearance in the August 1918 *Egoist* coincided with Warner's wedding. An early draft of the poem includes the phrase "beauty / intertwined with tragedy," describing how Marianne must have experienced Monhegan in the summer of 1917. In the published poem, submerged shafts of sunlight, a turquoise sea, pink starfish, and spotted jellyfish are intertwined with ash heaps, hatchet strokes, and dynamite grooves.

Despite readers' willingness to accept what Donald Hall calls the "mystery of emotion and sense of hidden content" in the poem, the last three stanzas prove particularly baffling. On a literal level they describe the cliff next to the sea, but the language seems almost allegorical in contrast to the vibrant imagery of the earlier stanzas. Like the rutted skin of the elephant in "Black Earth," the cliff shows "marks of abuse." A "defiant edifice," it reveals both the "dynamite grooves" appropriate to rock and the "lack / of cornice . . . burns / and / hatchet strokes" appropriate to a building—or home. Read in light of the events of the past year, the "defiant edifice" is the family into which "a / wedge / of iron" has been driven. Their "youth" can never be revived, yet the edifice will survive. "The sea grows old in it."

"Life is a good deal like the ocean," Marianne wrote Warner soon after "The Fish" appeared, "self-restorative and continuous in its nature." That is as close to a paraphrase of "The Fish" as one is likely to find. "I have a violent distaste for Monhegan," she added, "and I feel overpowered in a curious way by the atmosphere of Chatham but if I should get over either feeling I will be quick to say so."

12

The Secret of Expansion

1918–1920

Warner assumed that Mary and Marianne would return to Carlisle when they left Chatham and encouraged them to. But the women had their own ideas and did not consult him. They chose an apartment on one of the prettiest streets in Greenwich Village. St. Luke's Place is a tree-lined block connecting Hudson Street and Seventh Avenue. Elegant nineteenth-century row houses along its north side overlook a park that in 1918 reminded Mary of squares in London. Although the Hudson Park Library at the end of the block looked like a police station, Mary said, it provided an unending supply of books from the main library. A few blocks away was the Hudson River, where the two spent Sunday afternoons on the pier reading aloud and watching the boats. At the time the Moores signed their lease, number 14 was, like many houses in the neighborhood, being converted into studio apartments to accommodate the working girls and would-be bohemians eager to enjoy the freedoms of the new century.

"14 St. Luke's Place has some of the poetry that we like in a house," Marianne told Warner soon after they moved in, "but it has colossal disadvantages." Unlike the airier rooms upstairs, their apartment, several steps below street level, had low ceilings and windows that provided little light or privacy from the street. The apartment's most attractive feature was its white marble mantel and hearth, where the Moores displayed a mahogany clock and crystal candelabra from Kirkwood and the brass andirons that had belonged to Mary's mother. Yet the single room could barely contain a bed, a sofa, and a few chairs. There was no kitchen, no telephone, no refrigerator. Mary prepared meals on a hotplate in the bathroom throughout the eleven years they lived there. For the first five, before they rented a second room upstairs, they sat on the edge of the bathtub to eat. Sometimes Marianne was served breakfast in the tub.

Mary seems to have considered the possibility of allowing Marianne to move to New York alone, but she convinced herself that her thirty-year-old daughter needed her protection. In a rare moment that summer, Marianne confided to her notebook: "Well, there are reasons why it is better to live away from home. You want to go somewhere— come in at an unusual hour, or you don't want to eat, you want to be alone—My mother comes in sixteen times a day bringing me apples and things to eat, and you can't eat. She doesn't understand, the whole house is upset. Send for the doctor, insist on an exam. Oh my—Well—I can't have it." For several years afterward, Mary occasionally mentioned letting Marianne live by herself. But she never did because she thought "Ratty . . . *too little* to be chased about by big cats."

"Her deepest feelings never appear," Mary told Warner a year after they moved. "Play is utterly gone out of her; and play was so completely a part of our former life that I am sometimes over-awed by her ascetic graveness—almost grim sternness these past two years . . . Her little narrow white face with a monk-like severity—shows her old merry self-indulgent rollicking days gone, and in their place something I can scarcely get acquainted with." Marianne now bore sole responsibility for humoring Mary—Warner had not endured it a year—but she no longer had to sustain the dignity of Warner's pastorate. She socialized often with the *Others* crowd, "the only thing in life nowadays," according to Mary, "that occasions real spontaneity in her."

At the same time Marianne was developing a reputation as one of the most radical of the new poets, she learned to avoid conflict at home by being the child that Mary wanted her to be. Mary called her by her childhood names Sissy and Nunkey and even turned the resourceful and independent Mr. Rat into the diminutive and defenseless Ratty. Mary wrote friends in Kirkwood that Marianne "is as shy today as she was in the old old days when she drew herself in under Grandpa's long arm and pushed against his leg." When Marianne was forty-two and had edited *The Dial* for four years, Mary claimed her as a dependent on their income tax, "dependent" being clearly defined on the form as a child no older than eighteen or someone "mentally or physically defective." Mary controlled their finances and did all the housekeeping and cooking. Marianne depended upon her for all of her physical needs.

Marianne could not risk the wrath that Warner's sexual maturation had brought on. She had become a "he" in the family from the onset of puberty and thwarted her own sexual development, probably unconsciously, by not eating. Photographs indicate that Marianne had plump cheeks as a child. But by her twelfth birthday she had developed what Mary called a "delicate appetite." In her junior year of college Marianne weighed 98 pounds and was told that she ought to weigh 125. After she lost her job at the Indian School, her weight dropped from 98 to 87 in less than two months. Three years after moving to the Village, her weight dropped to 75 "with hat and coat on and bundles in hand." Even allowing for the potential inaccuracy of the public scale, she was extraordinarily thin—so thin that her friends described her as "wisplike" and "a stick of a woman." To her mother she was "the frailest bit o' bones that could presume to be 'a man.'"

Marianne's anxiety, nervousness, and irritability are documented in letters going back to college and adolescence. These are common symptoms of an abnormally low weight. In her thirties, she developed another symptom, hypothermia. She wore a sweater all summer and slept under a blanket and a down comforter on nights when Mary slept with no cover. It exasperated William Carlos Williams that Marianne took no interest in "literary guys," and when Mary tried to advise Warner about what girls wanted in a romantic relationship, she always made an exception of Marianne, who had "no man-instincts whatever." Marianne showed no more sexual interest in women than she did in men. Her lesbian friend Bryher called her "a case of arrested emotional development," who "haunt[ed] places full of potential victims" (victims, that is, of her inadvertent seductiveness). Marianne repeated the diagnosis late in life to explain why she had never been "matrimonially ambitious." Too little body fat causes both amenorrhea and the loss of libido.

Mary did everything she could to get Marianne to eat—except serve appetizing meals. She was by her own admission a negligent housekeeper and developed a certain pride in their subsistence-level existence. Cousins who visited St. Luke's Place were appalled by the apparent poverty, but the Moores were not embarrassed. Marianne explained proudly that they refused to accept "all day remunerative situations of any kind" and yet felt "happier than most people who had lots of money." "Our wildest extravagance has been a Casaba melon," Mary told Warner, who worried about their eating enough. "Near home on Sixth Ave. crabs and lobsters are boiled fresh nearly every day, and sometimes we come home with two crabs still hot! . . . We buy pumpkin pie too for *Rat*; and I make him cup custards once a week that last him two or three days. Thus do I introduce milk into his small body." This was Mary's best effort. On another occasion, she planned to serve onions and prunes for lunch. Then she decided to invite a guest and scraped together a menu of cooked apples, canned corn, salad dressing, and cocoa. For Thanksgiving one year they ate leftover sardines.

Marianne had no privacy at St. Luke's Place. Her body was under Mary's constant scrutiny at meals, in bed, and in the bathroom. Although she might yell a childish "DOANT" when Mary tried to assist with her toilette, she mostly relinquished her body to her mother's care. Long before they moved to St. Luke's Place, Marianne had associated food with an invasion of her privacy. In her college story "Pym," the protagonist expresses annoyance with a servant who, like Mary, constantly interrupts his writing to bring him things to eat. Whenever Marianne refuses food, "the whole house is upset. Send for the doctor, insist on an exam." She recognized the need to gain weight, but her body rebelled. She said that she wished Mary could eat for her. "My stomach has been about as much use to me as a feather duster," she once told Warner, "or a rim for spectacles without any glass in it."

There is little evidence that Marianne ever thought herself fat or tried to lose weight—symptoms that are now commonly associated with anorexia nervosa. Reducing diets did not become fashionable until later in the century. In college Marianne accurately perceived herself as "scrawny" in comparison with other girls. At Lake Placid she enjoyed her food, as she usually did away from home. But after she received news of Mary and Mary Norcross's breakup, she lost three pounds in a week and told Warner that she was no longer "the high-flying fashion plate of looks either that I was two weeks ago."

And yet she did like the streamlined, androgynous body of the New Woman. Throughout the 1920s she wore a mannish suit that hung loosely on her shoulders and revealed nothing of her shape. There is a snapshot from the summer of 1921 that she clumsily retouched with a pen to streamline the bulging outline of her sweater. One could make the case that the modernist aesthetic itself, with its emphasis on minimalism, was anorexic. In later years, she would quote admiringly Warner's advice about writing: "Starve it down and make it run."

Marianne could never have become the poet she was without the four years away from her mother at Bryn Mawr. Painful as her home-sickness was, it allowed her to define an independent identity as a writer. Writing became her means of survival. While she literally had no room of her own at St. Luke's Place, she managed to construct a little fortress on the sofa in which to write. She sat cross-legged in front of the fire—almost year-round—with books and papers piled around her.

Not only would she achieve in poetry the authority and independence that she could not claim in her family, but among her poetry's most notable features are the uniqueness of her voice and what she calls a "passion for the particular." Never does she long for a lover's embrace or for oneness with nature. She comes to distrust unifying metaphor as much as she does romantic love, preferring instead observation, differentiation, and the precise diction of science. Her poems repeatedly protest tyranny, egotism, and "love in the mistaken sense of greed," all forms of forced unity, whereas they praise the Herculean effort required to see with precision and to recognize individuality. In Moore's oeuvre, "relentless accuracy" is both loving and liberating.

Soon after moving to St. Luke's Place, Moore wrote "Radical," a poem about finding freedom in confinement. Belying Mary's observation that "play is utterly gone out of her," she portrays her redheaded self as a carrot and in a relatively straightforward way shows how this "radical" (literally a "root") presses against the constraints of circumstance.

RADICAL

Tapering
to a point, conserving everything,
    this carrot is predestined to be thick.
        The world is
        but a circumference, a mis-
            erable corn-patch for its feet. With ambition,
                        imagination, outgrowth,

nutriment,
with everything crammed belligerent-
    ly inside itself, its fibres breed mon-
        opoly—
        a tail-like, wedge shaped engine with the
            secret of expansion, fused with intensive heat to the
                        color of the set-

ting sun and
stiff. For the man in the straw hat, stand-
    ing still and turning to look back at it—
        as much as
        to say my happiest moment has
            been funereal in comparison with this,
                        the conditions of life pre-

determined
slavery to be easy—defined
    by contradiction—and freedom hard. For
        it? Dismiss
        agrarian lore; it tells him this:
            that which it is impossible to force, it is impossible
                to hinder.

When the Moores first moved to St. Luke's Place, the constant
callers—friends from Bryn Mawr, the Mary Institute, Monhegan,
Chatham, and *Others*—exhausted them. One visitor, however, was

always welcome. Peter, a mangy black-and-white cat with eyes the color of gunmetal, belonged to neighbors who had rescued him from a burning ash can. He was, Mary told Marianne, "the only person with whom you are always gentle."

In her poem "Peter," Moore describes with characteristic wit the cat's appearance—"the small tuft of fronds or katydid legs above each eye"—and behavior—"Springing about with froglike ac- / curacy." Although the hypocrisy of sitting "caged by the rungs of a domestic chair" is beneath him, even Peter lets his body "be flat- / tened out by gravity" or "dangled like an eel" for the sake of a joke to which he is not a party. "He can / talk, but insolently says nothing." Behind Peter's passivity is "an animal with claws" who "wants to have to use / them."

Marianne feared leaving home even for a few days. When Frances Browne, one of the Bryn Mawr friends with whom she had reconnected, convinced her to go to their ten-year class reunion, she had to overcome Marianne's objections about the expense and about leaving Mary alone. Although Mary approved her going, she and Marianne both worried that she would be overtaxed socially and become ill. But Marianne greatly enjoyed the attention she received both from classmates and professors. As the one classmate present who had earned the literary success to which so many had aspired, she was asked to give a short speech at the class dinner and to read two poems. She ate well, and upon her return Mary found her "astonishingly improved."

After the first year at St. Luke's Place, Marianne accepted a half-day position at the public library branch across the street. The thirty dollars a month she earned the first two years and the fifty dollars she earned thereafter made little difference to the Moores' standard of living. Mary sent it all to her banker in Pittsburgh for Marianne to use to go to Italy someday. But the job did provide respite from Mary's hovering presence. Marianne usually wrote in the mornings and worked afternoons at the library. And while she had no access to her money and little sense of its value, she took pride in accumulating it.

Marianne kept the job almost six years. She liked working half days and liked the work itself. On a typical day, she might help a man research the composition of concrete for a business he was starting, recommend a list of romantic novels to a lonely woman, and help a literary society plan its program for the season. The library patrons came from all social classes and sometimes spoke little English. Marianne was generally good with people as well as books. She received high praise from her superiors and advanced quickly.

While Marianne amazed her literary friends with the range of her interests and the flow of her conversation, there is no record of her sharing confidences with anyone. She wrote Warner infrequently and to Mary presented only a "monk-like severity." The many memoirs of Village life in these years note Marianne's red hair, boyish attire, penetrating eyes, and nervous laughter. Her unflinching devotion to her mother annoyed and mystified her literary friends. And yet the mysteriousness of that devotion, the unpredictability of her views, and her "diamond hard . . . observations" captivated listeners and gave her a kind of power over them. Both in her poetry and in her persona, Marianne recognized and cultivated this power. "Mysteriousness" is "formidable," she observed; "to be understood" is "to be no / Longer privileged." "I think I'd be bored to death with [her]," said Robert McAlmon, "if it weren't that I can't get her angle." Williams remembered her as "a rafter holding up the superstructure of our uncompleted building, a caryatid, her red hair plaited and wound twice about the fine skull . . . [She] was our saint—if we had one—in whom we all instinctively felt our purpose come together to form a stream."

Moore began to wield power across the Atlantic, too. The thirteen poems that she published in the 1917 *Others* anthology drew attention from two influential poets who would become friends and lifelong supporters of her work. Ezra Pound reviewed the anthology for *The Little Review*, and T. S. Eliot reviewed it for *The Egoist*. Although the anthology included such notable poems as Eliot's "Rhapsody on a Windy Night," Williams's "Danse Russe," and Stevens's "Thirteen Ways of Looking at a Blackbird," Pound chose to focus exclusively on what he called "the first adequate presentation of Mina Loy and Marianne Moore." He distinguished their poetry from Imagism, which is primarily visual, and from melopoeia, which is primarily musical. He called it "logopoeia or poetry that is akin to nothing but language, which is a dance of the intelligence among words and ideas and modification of ideas and characters." Following Pound's example, Eliot also wrote exclusively about Moore and Loy, but with a strong preference for Moore. He placed her in the company of Pound, James Joyce, and Wyndham Lewis as one who can be counted on to "write living English." Anticipating the critics who would soon complain of the lack of feeling in Moore's verse, Pound noted "traces of emotion" in it, and Eliot praised in particular her "fusion of thought and feeling."

In the summer of 1918, after his review had appeared in March, Pound wrote Moore requesting poems and prose for *The Little Review*. By the time she sent him two poems and a prose paragraph in late November (Warner's marriage intervened), he had to tell her that he was unable to pay her for them but thought them too good to be published without pay. He asked if he could hold them for a quarterly he hoped to start. More important than his explicit invitation on behalf of *The Little Review* was his implicit one to join the handful of writers—he mentioned Yeats, Joyce, Lewis, and Eliot—who were willing to accept his criticism and to accept his assistance in getting published. "Your stuff holds my eye," he said. "Most verse I merely slide off of." He wanted to know how old she was, what she looked like, when she began publishing, and if she had a book in print. If not, he wanted to help her get one. He asked if she had been influenced by the French Symbolist poets (as he and Eliot had) and if her metric (which confounded him) was indebted to his own innovations.

"The resemblance of my progress to your beginnings," she answered, "is an accident so far as I can see." Deferential she was not. And yet she answered most of his questions with the exaggerated humility that would characterize much of her professional correspondence: "I am glad to give personal data and hope that the bare facts that I have to offer, may not cause work that I may do from time to time, utterly to fail in interest." In response to his question of where her work appeared in America, she said, "I do not appear." She gave the impression of having published very little, whereas she had actually published some fifty poems since college. She told him that she was no longer willing to contribute to *Poetry* and that she was not "heartily in sympathy with *The Little Review*." He could keep her poems for his quarterly, she said, and while she did not explicitly refuse his offer regarding a book, she told him that she was growing "less and less desirous of being published, produce less and have a strong feeling for letting alone what little I do produce." Nevertheless, she showed that she had carefully considered his critiques of her poems, even if she rejected most of his suggestions. She enclosed "Radical" and "Those Various Scalpels" with her reply.

Pound pointed out that neither *Poetry* nor *The Egoist* would have accepted work such as hers without his influence but also offered her honest encouragement: "Definiteness of your delineations is delicious . . . Can't have it lost. Must go on with it. You must."

It was a highly charged exchange. Pound's letter maintains the respectful poet-to-poet cordiality of his previous letter, but he enclosed three pages of free verse, full of mythical and historical allusions, about his "lechery" and his willingness to ascend "your Presbyterian stairturn." Marianne apparently ignored these ramblings. Both in her behavior and in her dress, she did everything possible to discourage sexual attention. But she took Pound's encouragement to heart and wrote two new poems that spring.

"Poetry" and "In the Days of Prismatic Color" show her deeply engaged in the aesthetic questions being debated in Village tearooms, as do most of the poems she wrote over the next few years. The blades and wedges of her Chatham poems have all but disappeared, and so has the ironic self-portraiture of "Radical," "Peter," and "Dock Rats." Both "Poetry" and "In the Days of Prismatic Color" attempt to distinguish between art that is "so derivative as to become unintelligible" and art that puzzles but is nevertheless genuine. While "Poetry" concedes "that we / do not admire what / we cannot understand" (a quotation from Mary), it catalogs examples of inexplicable but genuine behaviors that are worthy of admiration:

> . . . the bat,
>   holding on upside down or in quest of something to
>
> eat, elephants pushing, a wild horse taking a roll, a tireless
>   wolf under

a tree, the immovable critic twinkling his skin
                              like a horse that feels a flea, the
                              base-
        ball fan, the statistician.

Why do bats hold on upside down? Why do people become statisticians? As in "Critics and Connoisseurs," Moore demands respect for difference and finds poetry in genuine idiosyncrasy.

Pound had done more to promote Moore's work in recent months than his letter indicates. Not only had he drawn Eliot's attention to her poems in the *Others* anthology, but he had also urged both Margaret Anderson of *The Little Review* and Harriet Monroe of *Poetry* to publish whatever they could get from her. *The Little Review* published Moore for the first and only time in December 1918, but she was "wholly dissatisfied" with the poem, she told Pound, and surprised to see it in print. At Pound's insistence, Anderson had recovered an old poem, "You Say You Said," from her files and published it without consulting the author.

Poetry had by this time fallen from favor with the *Others* poets. But prodded by Pound, Harriet Monroe wrote Moore in the spring of 1918, requesting poetry and prose. Moore wrote three book reviews for *Poetry* that year—on Eliot, Yeats, and Jean de Bosschère—but refused to send poems because, as she tartly put it, "*Poetry*'s approach to art is different from my own." The two women met a year later when *Others* hosted a party for Monroe.

"Miss Monroe," said Kreymborg when he introduced Marianne, "this is the 'enfant terrible' of all New York."

"Yes, and of all poets," replied Monroe, gazing into the air, "the one whom Ezra Pound is adjuring us all to imitate—a thing utterly impossible to do." It was a sweet victory for Marianne.

For the first two years that Moore lived in the Village, *Others* formed the nucleus of her literary and social life. In addition to receiving callers at home, she frequented the local tearooms and attended parties hosted by the *Others* poet Lola Ridge. "The frailest of humans physically and the poorest financially . . . [Lola] kept the movement going," according to Kreymborg, "by giving a party nearly every time she sold a poem or an article." At her parties one might rub shoulders with writers of various political and aesthetic persuasions. As the evening grew late, the poets would often read their work aloud.

It was a momentous occasion when Scofield Thayer, the new editor and co-owner of *The Dial*, appeared at one of Lola Ridge's parties. By the end of 1919, both *Others* and *The Egoist* had folded. A magazine that Maxwell Bodenheim had hoped to start never materialized. Neither did Pound's quarterly. *Poetry* was no longer an option for most *Others* poets. Then the new decade brought them *The Dial*. Bearing the name of the Transcendentalist quarterly edited by Margaret Fuller and Ralph Waldo Emerson, *The Dial* had been reincarnated in 1916 as a fortnightly for social and political commentary. Thayer and Sibley Watson bought it in late 1919, made it a monthly, and transformed it into the leading literary arts magazine of its day. No longer would experimental writers have to appear without pay, for Thayer had inherited a woolen mills fortune and Watson the Western Union fortune.

Thayer arrived late at Ridge's party, according to Kreymborg, presumably to scout new talent. "Reading aloud was soon in order," and "about two in the morning" Marianne Moore "read something one could barely hear about 'England with its baby rivers and little towns.'" "The mystery man from *The Dial*," however, "heard [it] so well, he stole over to her and, after a whispered consultation, induced her to part with it."

"Send it to *The Dial*," he said.

"I did and it was returned."

"Send it again," he said.

If it is true that Thayer could barely hear the poem and had rejected it already, Pound must have alerted him to Marianne Moore in the meantime. Soon after the whispered consultation, Moore sent Thayer "Picking and Choosing" and "England," which he printed immediately. "By all means get some prose from [her]," Pound told Thayer. And so at Thayer's invitation she proposed to write a review of G. W. Rhead's *The Earthenware Collector*, a book she described as "infinitely poetic," its "zeal . . . contagious." But the book review editor did not think readers of *The Dial* would be interested in a guide to collecting English pottery. Asked for alternatives, Moore sent him a list of seventeen books, the titles of which ranged from *The Mechanism of the Sentence*, to *Early Persian Poetry*, to *Helmets and Body Armor in Modern*

Warfare. They finally agreed upon a biography of the medieval mystic poet Jacopone da Todi.

Ever vigilant for publication opportunities for himself and his protégés, Pound had tried to enlist Thayer's backing for a magazine as early as 1915 after Eliot, a boyhood friend of Thayer's, had introduced them. When Pound saw the first number of the Thayer/Watson *Dial* in January 1920, he wrote to inquire if it were true, as he had heard through Eliot that certain writers including Joyce, Lewis, Eliot, and himself would not be refused there and if he might henceforth consider *The Dial* his "spiritual home." Thayer answered that he and Watson could not promise to accept anything until they had seen it, but that they would expect to publish "most everything" Pound sent them. Watson assured Pound a few months later that *The Dial* was "the type of magazine . . . you have been talking about for a long time." Pound was offered $750 a year to solicit work from Europe and would serve *The Dial* in that unpublicized capacity for three years.

Pound played a far greater role than has generally been recognized in garnering for *The Dial* its impressive, international roster of contributors. He recruited Yeats, Joyce, D. H. Lawrence, Miguel de Unamuno, Benedetto Croce, Remy de Gourmont, Paul Morand, Paul Valéry, and Marcel Proust. And he likely alerted Thayer to Loy and Williams as well as Moore.

It took Warner longer to restore harmony with his sister than with his mother. Marianne wrote him only occasionally. When Mary inquired whether she ever felt the need to write him, Marianne replied, "Yes . . . I do. But there's never anything for *me* to say; so I just don't write. Our letters long ago were all play. There is no play now, and surely no one could want it."

The hyperbole, sexual innuendo, and religious rhetoric with which Mary and Warner carried out their drama of reconciliation was a language alien to Marianne. Warner repeatedly compared himself to the Prodigal Son and envisioned a future when the family could be reunited and harmony restored. After he and Constance moved to an upstairs duplex in Vallejo, California, he invited Mary and Marianne to move into the bottom half. Such an arrangement was inconceivable to Mary, but she tried to restore harmony in her own way by accepting

some of the blame for Warner's transgressions, especially his deceptiveness. She was deceitful herself, she admitted, and had set a bad
example for her children. She also empathized with Warner's sexual
temptation, as she imagined it. She described feeling tempted in her
sleep "to put my hands to a passionate body" and waking in time to
pray, "Save me, my Lord!" She assumed that the men to whom Warner ministered were also consumed by sexual desire and provided
much advice about sermon topics to address their discomfort.

As for Constance: "Doubtless it is here that the Prince of Evil will
set his snare for me. I shall be forgetful sometime. Oh there will be
hundreds of ways of temptation! So far, I have only a feeling of mighty
protection concerning her—of desire to take care of her, to let none of
the fires of our sins kindle against her. But I am no soldier. The least
temptation veers me; and there are many open doors. But Christ is
over every one of them."

The Prince of Evil did indeed set his snare for Mary. Although she
believed that firstborns often arrive early, she was horrified to learn
that Constance expected a child not quite nine months after the wedding. For this meant that Warner had let "passion loose" as soon as he
dared. Warner hoped that a namesake might soften his mother's feelings. The baby was named Mary Markwick Moore, and very soon
after her birth, Warner wrote that if anything should happen to Constance, they wanted Mary and Marianne to assume guardianship of
the child. "It is touching indeed that Constance should be willing to
trust her to us if she should die," Mary answered. "I am glad for you
both that she has such splendid health."

A year later Warner wrote that he wanted Mary to assume particular guardianship over their firstborn, to write to her particularly, and
to make decisions about her education. Mary found it hard to believe
that Constance had agreed to such an arrangement and deferred to her
authority in such matters. Despite Warner's eagerness on her behalf,
Mary sensed that she was likely to have more influence over the neighborhood children, who loved the stories she told them, than she would
ever have over her grandchildren. "I never tell stories to the waifs that
beg 'Teacher—teacher—*please*—a story?' that I do not wonder if ever
I shall tell it to Mary Markwick."

·

Marianne maintained an unembarrassed indifference to the sermon topics that consumed many pages of her mother's and brother's letters. She dutifully refused to go to parties on Sunday and told her friends not to call then. But she did so altogether, it seems, out of devotion to her family. Neither at home nor apparently with her friends did she indicate that she did or did not share Mary's religious faith. While her Village associates regarded her as "a churchgoing, cerebralizing moralist, who observes Sabbath day strictly," her mother was stunned when "Marianne said one day out of a clear sky: 'I think the root of Warner's whole trouble was—*lack of faith*.'"

"Marianne's saying this," Mary said, "was a wave passing over my soul, after it had banged against me. For Marianne herself has never professed to have faith;—has almost *said* her soul was dim with darkness and utter lack of faith. Life has come to her in great surging waves the past year however; I know that; but she has made no motion; no show of that fact; so I have not said I knew."

As Moore said of Jacopone da Todi, readers must look to the poems for the truest expression of her inner life. Her poetry and critical prose reveal that she believed in a spiritual world beyond the empirical one and that her heroes possess "a sense of human dignity / and reverence for mystery." Old Testament allusions far outnumber New Testament ones in her work. And *Pilgrim's Progress* meant more to her, the poems suggest, than the Gospel did. Her 1916 poem "In This Age of Hard Trying Nonchalance Is Good, And" portrays "some poor fool" upon whom is conferred a divine "privilege." He might be a Christ figure, for he is humble like Christ, but he fits more closely the paradigm of the Old Testament poet-prophets whom Marianne studied in Reverend Kellogg's Bible class. In her letter to Pound, she named the "minor prophets" (along with Blake, Hardy, Henry James, and Gordon Craig) as "direct influences bearing upon my work." God conferred upon these prophets the power to see a spiritual reality and to write the poetry that Kellogg described as "prose with a sort of heightened consciousness."

"In the Days of Prismatic Color" presents a vision of spiritual truth that is consistent with the ideas of the painters, sculptors, and photographers Moore knew in New York. They believed that Renaissance conventions (epitomized by the Apollo Belvedere, which appears in the poem) had obscured the spiritual in art and sought to recover that spirituality by breaking with Western conventions. Members of the Stieglitz circle and others influenced by Kandinsky used the terms *inner necessity* and *spiritual necessity* interchangeably.

Moore's friends William and Marguerite Zorach, who had studied under the fauves in Paris, painted brilliant, Edenic landscapes to convey what William Zorach called "the mysterious inner world of the spirit."

"I have never seen such primeval color," Mary remarked when Marianne took her to the Zorachs' studio. "It is color of the sort that existed when Adam was there alone and there was no smoke when there was nothing to modify it but mist that went up."

Marianne recorded the remark in her notebook and appropriated it for her poem. "In the Days of Prismatic Color" distinguishes the "blue red yellow band / of incandescence" that preceded civilization, even a society of two, from the murky sophistication that evolved afterward. Truth will be there, the poem concludes, "when the wave has gone by." Moore is no relativist. Yet her "truth" is brilliantly, prismatically various.

Moore never claimed that Presbyterianism is superior to other faiths, only that it was the most meaningful practice for herself. Religious intolerance was as loathsome to her as other forms of intolerance. She agreed with William James's "democratic respect for the sacredness of individuality . . . the outward tolerance of whatever is not itself intolerant."

Warner tried various means to break through his sister's silence. He tried being playful, he tried writing "love letters," such as had sometimes worked with Mary, and he tried to find her a job. A navy captain he met knew the publisher of *The New York Times* and arranged for Marianne to be interviewed. She was sent home with a book to review, the review was published, but she heard nothing more. She asked Warner not to pursue the matter. The "fine distinctions and meditative comment" that she liked to write were not suitable, she realized, for a large newspaper.

When she sent him a copy of the book review, she also sent him "Picking and Choosing," a poem about making those fine distinctions. The poem thrilled him. "Those 'few strong wrinkles' and 'right good salvo of barks' I rejoice in," he wrote. He was referring to the conclusion of the poem:

> Small dog, going over the lawn, nipping the linen and saying
>
> that you have a badger—remember Xenophon;
>   only the most rudimentary sort of behaviour is necessary
> to put us on the scent; a "right good
>   salvo of barks," a few "strong wrinkles" puckering the
> skin between the ears, are all we ask.

Warner was both a dog and a badger in the family, and "pug wrinkles" had long been a family term for curious attention. But Marianne pointed out, through Mary, that the lines came directly from Xenophon's treatise on hunting dogs. When the poem appeared in *The Dial* six months later, Warner again expressed delight in "our own special 'language' but so marvelously handled that the 'aliens' could and can understand them and enjoy them."

Marianne at last reconciled with Warner in the summer of 1920, three years after he announced his engagement. Warner arranged for Marianne and Mary to take a navy hospital ship through the Caribbean and the Panama Canal to California. In several long letters Marianne wrote Warner from the ship, she develops the highly detailed, descriptive mode that would characterize her letters to him for at least a decade. She describes her fellow passengers, including a pair of pet monkeys and a goat with green collar and knobs on its horns, and expresses genuine pleasure in the tropics, especially the exotic lizards and birds. "The most interesting thing about the island," she wrote of St. Thomas, "is the light green water in the bay and the three pirate castles part way up the hill are very romantic. They are supposed to have belonged to Bluebeard, Redbeard and Blackbeard and look like very squat churns of like cheeses." Marianne seems to have written these long descriptions as much for her own benefit as for Warner's, much as other writers use a journal. Bluebeard's tower, its legendary tyrant, and various tropical flora and fauna from this trip would soon appear in "People's Surroundings."

Constance did what she could to make Mary and Marianne feel

welcome. Sensing that Warner needed time alone with them, she went to Los Angeles for eleven days, leaving the baby in their care. Although the trip convinced both Mary and Marianne that Warner and Constance were happy together, and Warner's happiness, Mary said, was their chief concern, it did not succeed in building affection between Mary and Constance. Mary acknowledged how difficult it must be for Constance to accept "the old family one-ness that was and is" and how "baffling and distressing" it must be "to come continually upon ideals and tastes that she does not know what to make of or what to do with." Although she professed "gentleness of feeling" toward Constance, she used her daughter-in-law's perceived dislike of her as a reason to refuse her request that she return in the spring for the birth of their second child. When Warner told Constance of Mary's decision and the reasons for it, she "cried and couldn't believe all I said."

Marianne and Mary returned to New York by train, stopping to visit cousins in Chicago and Pittsburgh and to see Mary Norcross near Carlisle. (Mary bragged that they spent no money for food on the train from Sacramento to Chicago.) "When we got here," Mary wrote of their arrival at St. Luke's Place, "the brass was shining, and Ratty said—privately—'Isn't our little home a beauty!'"

"Miss Leonard [Marianne's supervisor] was enthusiasm itself over our return when we stepped into the Library," Marianne wrote, "and the youngsters on the street nearly annihilated Mole [for a story]. The Italian woman who keeps the store by the Library made a great fuss over Mole, kissed us both and inquired about our trip . . . Peter, after taking a few minutes to recognize us affectioned with an energy that was most amusing."

Imperfect as it appeared to outsiders, the domestic space that Marianne created for herself allowed her to write. That she wrote many of her finest poems at St. Luke's Place proves that she was not deceiving anyone, including herself, when she told her baffled friends that she and her mother "lived like anchorites, and that she could work as she was situated better than anywhere else."

13

Bluebeard's Tower

1920–1921

On September 12, 1920, Marianne convinced Mary to make an exception to their Sunday rule. They walked uptown to see H.D., who was stopping briefly in New York on her way from London to California. When they emerged out of the sunlight through the heavy doors of the Belmont Hotel, H.D. rushed to greet them and led them to the lobby chairs where she and Annie Winifred Ellerman, who called herself Bryher, had been waiting. The four women spent the afternoon together, the hospitable H.D. and the loquacious Mary doing most of the talking. H.D. apologized for not having made a greater effort to get Marianne's poetry into print. But the war had intervened. Her husband had gone to the front. Her brother was killed. She had become pregnant. And in the winter after the armistice, she had nearly died of pneumonia. The Moores learned little about Bryher that afternoon, so little that Mary did not mention her when she wrote Warner the next day.

Marianne never dreamed, she said later, that underneath Bryher's "composure and look of patient inquiry" lurked "so much anarchy." Bryher's father, Sir John Ellerman, was the richest man in England. He made his fortune as a shipping magnate and invested in exportation industries throughout the world. Bryher traveled widely with him as a child and longed to be a boy so that she could join him in business. Going to an elite girls' school during her adolescence did not assuage that longing. At the age of twenty-four, she discarded her fashionable dresses for suits and adopted the name Bryher after a favorite island in the Scilly Isles, off the Cornwall coast. She decided to become a writer. Enamored with Imagism, she memorized H.D.'s poetry and found out where she lived. As soon as she laid eyes on the willowy beauty, she fell in love. The following winter, when she found H.D. dying of pneumonia, she got her to a hospital and hired a private nurse to oversee her recovery. In return for saving her life and that of her unborn daughter, H.D. rescued Bryher from the colorless existence to which her wealth entitled her.

Like many Europeans of the time, Bryher was enthralled with America's skyscrapers, motorcars, and wide-open spaces. Having come to America to escape her war-ravaged homeland and to find the freedom she associated with the new American poetry, she was disappointed by the Moores' formality and restraint. Mary spent much of the afternoon reminiscing about England and extolling the virtues of a country that for Bryher no longer existed. These women were anachronisms, thought Bryher, characters out of a Victorian novel misplaced in the modern frenzy of New York. Why, Bryher wondered, would they idealize an era in which women had so little freedom?

Marianne gave no hint that she did not completely share her mother's anglophilia. (Her recent poem "England," however, challenges stereotypes about national identity.) Nor did she demonstrate the flow of conversation that amazed her Village friends. With her mother beside her, Marianne "sat back in her chair," Bryher recalled, "a Marco Polo stayed at home, twisted to silence by some strange repression." Her "austere boyish head" and "flushed face . . . vivid with excitement" nevertheless captivated Bryher.

Writing to Warner the next day, Mary expressed no regrets about spending Sunday as they had. It was one thing to have ill-mannered bohemians admire her daughter's poems and quite another for this elegant lady from London to do so. H.D. insisted that Marianne's work was "greatly superior to what people were making a fuss over," and "that the world ought not to permit Rat to be a recluse." Recognizing the many demands on H.D.'s attention, Mary felt honored that H.D. had spent the entire afternoon with them. Even the celebrated Amy Lowell had come from Boston expressly to see H.D., but H.D. told the Moores that she did not like Miss Lowell and felt no obligation to spend time with her.

Before they parted that afternoon, H.D. invited Marianne to return to the hotel the next morning for what she called a business meeting. If H.D. sensed, as Bryher did, that Marianne was cowed by her mother's presence, then she probably called the meeting to talk to Marianne alone. Marianne knew that H.D. still hoped to find a British publisher for Marianne's poems and knew, too, that she would refuse H.D.'s assistance. When H.D. had first extended the offer in 1916, Marianne sent poems without protest. Why she changed her mind in the meantime remains a mystery. Whether she had her own reasons or was altogether under Mary's influence, her resistance took the guise, as it had with Pound, of exaggerated modesty. She told H.D. that she thought her output still too meager for a book. Yet she had published altogether some seventy poems since she first began to appear in the *Tipyn o'Bob*. Half of them she liked well enough to include in *Observations* four years later. Marianne was excited by H.D.'s interest, excited enough that she gathered ten poems to take to the meeting. But she said a firm no to the book.

After H.D. and Bryher arrived in California, Bryher wrote to Marianne and confessed to an imperfect understanding of her poems—the poems that H.D. now had in her possession. She allowed for the possibility that "we are so different in thought it makes for barriers." But she urged Marianne to publish a book because of the difficulty of rousing interest in her work otherwise. Answering that "your interest in my poems does me a great deal of good," Marianne explained, as she had told H.D., that she would "not care to have published by itself, what I have done so far." If she "were to have a book of prose published," the poems could be added "as an appendix." (She had thus far published six reviews and essays, three of them quite short.)

Marianne and Bryher, being the letter writers they were, would become friends by the time they met again in February. Bryher sent her *Development*, the memoir of her girlhood that had been published in London earlier that year, and also the manuscript for an essay about cross-dressing in Elizabethan literature. Marianne's praise for both the essay and the book prompted Bryher to send her part of the new memoir she was writing and to inquire if she might call Marianne by a pet name. "I shall like any name you select for me," Marianne replied.

The new memoir, later published as *West*, described Bryher's trip to America and included Bryher's first impressions of Marianne. "I like what you say of me," Marianne replied, "and marvel that you can say anything at all for it is true that I have not expressed so far, any of the things that I particularly wish to say. I should attempt observations in prose I think—nothing absolute. To put my remarks in verse form, is like trying to dance the minuet in a bathing suit." Bryher chose the name Dactyl for her new friend. *West* compares Marianne to "some heraldic version of a pterodactyl stiffly watching from its Jurassic rock, [as] sea anemones open and close to the rhythm of the tides."

That someone of Marianne's talent should have to work in a public library appalled Bryher. She offered to provide the price of a Burmese elephant, five thousand dollars, "extended on the point of a sword," if Marianne would be a "good pterodactyl that will come out of its rock" and write a novel. Marianne had mentioned to H.D. that she hoped to write a novel someday. Afraid that Marianne would take offense at the presumptuousness of the gift, H.D. wrote to explain that Bryher's father liked to send her "little sums" for such projects. Marianne wrote Warner that she was stupefied by the offer and had no novel "in the process of hatching." She wrote Bryher that the offer had brought her "a great deal of happiness" but that money would not, in any case, "drag me from my slough," that "I could work here better than I could in any other place."

Bryher arrived in America as something of a Henry James character in reverse, bringing a capitalist fortune from the Old World to the New. She hoped to liberate America's latent genius and youthful passion from the older generation who, "eager to repeat the faults of Europe, tried to destroy freedom and development." No one epitomized this situation for Bryher like Marianne and her mother. But Marianne refused to be rescued.

•

When Marianne and Mary returned from their afternoon at the Belmont, they found a card from Scofield Thayer reminding Marianne of his eagerness to "get some of your prose for *The Dial*" and inviting her to dine with him. The invitation caused a flurry of excitement not only because of the status of the visitor but also because the floor of the apartment was being painted, and things had to be brought into rapid order. Three nights later Marianne accompanied him to dinner at the Brevoort Hotel. "Sweet Ratty was pleased to death to have the invitation," Mary told Warner, "but as he said '*scared*.'"

A slight but strikingly handsome man with a shock of black hair and flashing dark eyes, the impeccably dressed Thayer also appeared nervous when he came for Marianne. Mary described him as "a staccato, severe sort of man," who "would be very intimidating were he old and big." He was thirty, two years younger than Marianne. The two soon overcame their apprehensions as they found common ground in their literary passions and mordant wit. "Nunkey says he is extremely circumspect and dry in his humor and conversation," Mary reported the next day. "There is no one I think that they did not vivisect—who ever held a pen."

Marianne found Thayer not "very terrifying at close quarters." But she faced a new terror the next week when she was invited to tea at the *Dial* offices to meet the reputedly brilliant but exceedingly reticent Sibley Watson. Tall, blond, and lanky, he always reminded Marianne of a giraffe. She stayed about half an hour and did most of the talking. Yet she reported particulars of the conversation for hours afterward. She was relieved, she told Mary, that she was not asked to work in the office and that no one offered to walk her home.

The Moores knew that Thayer was married and knew that he and his wife lived apart. "His wife has an apartment and he has one," Mary said. "Neither bothers the other, but they visit, and get on cheerfully." Mary thought it "a miserable way to live" but presumed Thayer's attentions to Marianne were "harmless" because he was married. Marianne had confidence that "Mr. Thayer's sense of the proprieties would not permit a breach of any sort" and feared only her own social ineptitude.

They did not learn the particulars of Thayer's domestic situation for several months. Before he married the nineteen-year-old beauty

Elaine Orr, he had leased a luxury penthouse at the Benedick, a building for bachelors on Washington Square. After a yearlong honeymoon
in California, he decided to keep his apartment and rent another for
his wife around the corner. They remained friendly but drifted apart
emotionally. By the time Thayer met Marianne, Elaine and E. E.
Cummings had had a daughter together. Glad to be relieved of some
of his marital responsibilities, Thayer encouraged the affair and supported the child as his own. He remained a friend and patron to the
impecunious Cummings.

A few weeks after Marianne met Watson, Thayer invited her to tea
at the Benedick. Preparing for the encounter once again "rather
knocked [her] out." She could not eat beforehand and took great pains
to dress appropriately. Apart from Thayer's Japanese butler, the two
were alone in the apartment. "Scofield has a gorgeous library," Marianne told Warner, "about 3 walls full of light calf bindings or blue
bindings, a grate full of ashes a foot deep and a yellow desk like yours,
not quite so large . . . He showed me his art treasures (on request), a
large black marble, nude, some Beardsley pen drawings—a 'cubist
painting' and some drawings of dancers. He has in his art room, a set
of real red lacquer, a red lacquer cabinet, three little benches, and a
smoking stand in front of the fireplace. He doesn't smoke and has no
chairs—one I think at his desk but that is all." She did not mention the
room's green velvet window seat, where they looked at the drawings.

"I'm not snuggling," Thayer said as he sat down beside her.

"Snuggling," she said, "takes *two!*"

Thayer and Marianne saw much of each other throughout the
winter and spring. In November Thayer called and asked her to translate an Italian story. When she said she could not, he asked her what
she could do next, "a poem, a prose article, or a review." Moore said
that she would like to review George Moore's *Heloise and Abelard*, and
Thayer promised it would be reserved for her. At a large party in
January, Thayer asked Moore to review Eliot's new collection of essays, *The Sacred Wood*. She told him she would have to think about it,
but before they left the party she told him she would unless it would
be impossible to speak favorably of it. He gave her a week in which to
write it. "Did you remind him it was George Moore you wished to attack?" Mary asked, but Marianne did not. Pound had made it clear to

Thayer that this was an important review. Though Moore was not among the names Pound suggested, he told Thayer when the review appeared that "M. Moore has managed the Eliot rather well."

Thayer agreed. When he received the review, he wrote Marianne to tell her how happy it made him and to invite her to tea. She went to his apartment, again alone, a week later. "Ratty has been far from well for a week," Mary wrote Warner the day after the tea. "*The Dial* has a heinous way of having its contributors entertained socially one at a time after each contribution, and on Monday Ratty was laid on this altar, when for an hour her precious essence went up in smoke to make fragrant the Benedictine apartment of Mr. Thayer . . . Ratty was so overwrought in resolving to seem low-keyed—elegant and calm— . . . that he came home a wraith, and has not eaten a full meal since. He went, assuring me that this time there would be no palpitations; that he was a mountain of ice for coolness, and that really, knowing exactly what to expect, he could not possibly suffer the anguish of uncertainties that attended the other monkish teas . . . Besides we like Mr. Thayer; his classicism, his erudition, his taste in the literary persons of today, are all in general accord with our own feeling on such matters, and there is almost no one we ever see who can talk to Ratty about the subjects in art and letters that are always in his mind. But it is a killing thing to get this bit of pleasure at the price we pay."

Returning from California sooner than expected, H.D. and Bryher arrived in New York during a February snowstorm. They immediately called on Marianne, who was in the process of reviewing *Development* for *The Dial*, and the three saw one another often during the next twelve days, both at St. Luke's Place and at gatherings with other writers. "We have grown to love H.D. and little Bryher very truly," Mary told Warner, "and to take pleasure in their society. I do so enjoy true ladyhood." Mary approved of her daughter's friends who themselves seemed childlike. Bryher was twenty-six but looked eighteen, Marianne said.

Learning that Bryher and H.D. had taken nude photographs of each other while in California only enhanced Mary's esteem. When Marianne told her about the photographs, Mary said she would love to run naked, alone or with others, through Matthew Arnold's hedges. When Marianne asked if by "others" she meant two-year-old Mary Markwick, Mary said no, that she meant someone her own age. The sexual aspect of H.D.'s and Bryher's relationship was not lost on Mary. Contrary to what any of Marianne's Village acquaintances might have imagined, Mary actually preferred the company of homosexuals to that of heterosexuals. Marriage was a continual subject of scorn for her.

When Marianne, H.D., and Bryher were not talking about literary personalities, the conversation turned to getting Marianne away from home. Bryher "tried most of one evening," Marianne told Warner, "to get me to promise to take a check for a Mediterranean trip. I said I couldn't do it. She said to take it and put it away for some future time as a kind of artist's scholarship, but I refused."

"You shouldn't be so insistent," Marianne told her, "and you don't like what I write anyhow.'"

"I don't like what you write," Bryher said, "but I like you."

If getting Marianne away alone was impossible, Bryher was willing to take Mary, too. When H.D. and Bryher arrived in New York, they expected to stay at least until April, when Bryher's father would come to take them home. Bryher invited Marianne and Mary to return with them to London and spend a month or two. "I don't suppose we can go," Marianne wrote Warner, "but I think there is a possibility we might go." The library might grant her leave, but the trip would be "out of the question" if the thought of going would worry Mary.

"Were Rat staying at home with me just to be faithful," Mary told Warner, "I'd send him packing, in a brief moment of time. They think—I believe, that he is, and wish to give him a breathing space. The young need the young is their idea. But *Rat needs a shawl*; he needs, too, a mole for a shawl." While Mary's letters often portray Marianne as the helpless victim of her literary friends, Marianne's own letters and poems never indicate that she wanted or needed her mother's protection. Protection is a recurrent motif in her writing, but her camouflaged and armored animals are misunderstood, self-reliant, and invariably solitary.

On Valentine's Day the Moores hosted a tea to introduce Bryher and H.D. to Thayer and Watson. Mary hid as many of their belongings as she could under the bed, and Marianne did not sleep for two nights beforehand. H.D. and Bryher arrived first and the men a few minutes later, Watson "very silent and well-appointed" and Thayer "shining." "You could almost see the paths in his hair from a brushing," Marianne said, "his shirt advertised the powers of his laundress, his batwing tie sat neatly across his collar and his feet also gave evidence of friction." Conversation started stiffly—about the blizzard outside and about California—but soon gave way to livelier observations about *The Dial* (which Bryher pronounced too conservative), D. H. Lawrence, and H.D.'s amusing tale of Pound attempting to give Bryher fencing lessons. "Hilda was a remarkable guest," Marianne said, "the most dignified and yet the most informally friendly and entertaining that I guess we have entertained."

Afterward Thayer and Watson walked the ladies back to their hotel. Bryher remarked to Thayer, "Wouldn't you like to see Miss Moore in bronze brown and gold?"

"You wouldn't improve on Miss Moore—would you?" Thayer snorted. "I think she is one of the most distinguished persons I know."

If Marianne refused to be rescued, Robert McAlmon was more than willing. Bryher married him at City Hall just hours before the Valentine's Day tea. The son of a strict, abusive Presbyterian minister, McAlmon had spent many hours at St. Luke's Place, apparently enjoying his bad-boy role there. Mary called him "Piggy." When he married "true ladyhood," he became "O shameless, shameful Piggy!" After less than two weeks in New York, Bryher and H.D. decided to return to London with McAlmon. On the eve of their departure, Marianne and Mary attended a small dinner in honor of the newlyweds. Mary told McAlmon that she was angry with him but would not say why. When he asked Marianne, she explained that her mother thought it "unpoetic," "unchivalrous," and "unpatriotic . . . *for an American to steal the choicest possession of Mayfair.*" McAlmon asked what Mayfair was, and Marianne told him "the most beautiful part of London."

Marianne refused to see the humor others saw in the situation. When Thayer gleefully showed her a London *Times* article about the marriage of the English heiress to a penniless American bohemian, Marianne said she thought it an outrage for anyone to marry Bryher in such a fashion. Although she felt loyal to McAlmon as a friend, she respected neither his writing nor his character. "He can write in an hour what it takes a thoughtful person a half day to criticize," she said. "What I miss in Robert," she later told H.D., "is a lack of reverence toward mystery—a failure to understand human dignity."

Bryher and H.D. gave Marianne a pocket Kodak as a going-away gift. And just after they departed, Bryher sent Mary "a little cheque for Marianne—because I think her one of the very few sincere artists and personalities I have met."

"Your check is here and it is to stay—for a while anyhow," Marianne answered. "How could you send it, when we decided that you were not under any circumstances to 'rescue' me? . . . The pterodactyl is not used to spending; how should it know how to disport itself? You and Hilda must come back and supervise your dactyl; not a penny shall be spent without your approval."

Mary sent the three hundred dollars to Pittsburgh. She wrote Bryher that it would earn 4 percent and stay there at least a year, that if Marianne should decide to go abroad in the meantime, it would be an American check that would "float her across the lake." Marianne had no more access to the gift than she had to her own earnings from the library.

By April Thayer's attentions to Marianne were becoming more frequent and had begun to stir a different kind of excitement at St. Luke's Place. Although Mary still "like[d] to talk to Mr. Thayer better than to any one else who comes to the house," she said they "were very unhappy" over another invitation for Marianne to go to tea at the Benedick. "I wondered why this burden had come to us; Rat so icebound in demeanor always, with no man-instincts whatever;—why should he be set upon? . . . As he—Rat—said, 'There is no such thing as Platonic friendship, and it isn't fair to a wife to see another woman as often as he sees me. If he were not married, though, I should be in a far worse plight, for then I should fear he was getting interested, and would be fooled.'" By this time they knew about the Thayers' relations with Cummings and knew that Thayer planned to go abroad in the summer. They may not have known that part of his purpose was to get a French divorce.

No record survives of what transpired on the afternoon of April 17, 1921, but "as it turned out," Mary wrote Warner the next day, "Mr. Thayer was *not* just pursuing Rat for idle chat."

Moore's unpublished novel contains a scene of what *might* have happened that afternoon: a Thayer-like character presents a Moore-like character with a little round ivory box. "It was of ivory lined with velvet, the fine-fitting edges beveled to sharpness; and it held a pendant of square emeralds set in greenish gold filigree. Her favorite stone." Emeralds were indeed Marianne's favorite stone. It would be like Thayer to declare himself with such a gesture and like Marianne to say, as the character does, "I take and take and take, without sullying friendship by reciprocal givings. But I couldn't take this."

It was rumored that Thayer proposed marriage to Marianne. While he clearly felt great affection for her, it seems unlikely given his marital history that he had in mind their living together. What he probably proposed was to make his fortune available to her, much as Bryher had married McAlmon.

"People's Surroundings," one of the poems Moore was writing at the time, suggests that she might well have associated Thayer's "odd notions of hospitality" and his luxury penthouse with Bluebeard and his tower and that she might well have felt herself caught in a "magic mousetrap closing on all points of the compass." She liked Thayer. And she liked publishing in *The Dial*. But she did not want to be a victim of his egotism—"the acacia-like lady shivering at the touch of a hand." Her health indicates how deeply the events of the spring affected her. Letters to Warner repeatedly mention that invitations to the Benedick stilled her appetite. By early June she was faint with starvation. The scales read 75 pounds.

No further invitations to tea arrived, but Marianne's refusal to whatever Thayer proposed that April afternoon dampened neither his friendliness nor his enthusiasm for her work. In May he and Alfred Kreymborg dropped by to invite her to a party so that she could at last meet Wallace Stevens. Though she was too ill to go, she appreciated their courtesy. In June Thayer sailed for Europe. He wrote to apologize for not saying goodbye but said that he had read and reread "A Graveyard" in *The Dial*'s July issue. "Mr. Cummings," he added, "who met me here on my arrival agrees with me. *The Dial* has published nothing whatever finer than The Grave." The Thayers got their divorce, and in the winter Thayer moved to Vienna to begin psychoanalysis with Freud. He would remain in Europe undergoing analysis, collecting art, and sending long dictated letters to *The Dial*'s managing editors for two years.

Bryher and H.D. not only found a publisher for Moore's poems but also enlisted Eliot in their cause. McAlmon wrote Marianne that "T. S. Eliot has asked many questions about you and thinks you the person who has most definitely established an individual, unique, beautiful and musical rhythm, with intellectual content. He rates you more highly than anybody he has spoken of, and we have talked of about everybody . . . Eliot said he knows of no more beautiful cadenced writing of any time than 'like intermingled echoes struck from thin glass[es] successively at random.'"

Just after this conversation, Eliot wrote to Moore for the first time. He thanked her for the review of *The Sacred Wood* and told her that he admired her verse. "I wish that you would make a book of it, and I should like to try to get it published here. I wish you would let me try." Harriet Weaver of the Egoist Press also wrote and offered to publish a book of three hundred copies.

Eliot's letter meant much to Moore, and she told him she was tempted by his offer. "Were I to publish verse, I should be grateful indeed for the assistance you offer." But to publish a book now, she said, "would merely emphasize the meagerness of my production."

On the morning of July 7, 1921, *Poems* arrived at St. Luke's Place. Thus did Marianne learn of the publication of her first book. Letters from Bryher and Harriet Weaver also arrived claiming responsibility for it.

Marianne was furious. "You say I am stubborn," she wrote Bryher the same day. "I agree and if you knew how much more than stubborn I am you would blame yourself more than you do, on having put a thing through, over my head. I had considered the matter from every point and was sure of my decision—that to publish anything now would not be to my literary advantage." She said that she would have made different choices about which poems to include and which to omit and that, although she liked *Poems* as a title, she would have preferred *Observations.* She approved the "printing details," the paper, type, cover, and absence of misprints. "Nothing could exceed my appreciation for the unstinted care and other outlay bestowed on the book." Nevertheless, she had read in Darwin about a species of pigeon that is born without down. "I feel like that Darwinian gosling," she said. After moving to a lengthy discussion of "more important matters," such as her trips to the zoo and the circus, she signed herself, "Your now naked, Dactyl."

"The poems ought not to have come out," she wrote McAlmon the next day. "As the act of my friends, it is testimony of affection; if it were the act of an enemy, I should realize that it was an attempt to show how little I had accomplished." She spared H.D. her anger. She waited three weeks to write her and was altogether cordial and complimentary of "everything about [the book] that is individually yours and Bryher's."

She told Warner exactly what she had told Bryher. But upon receiving a copy of the book itself, he wrote that it ranked "among the two or three smashing experiences of my life." He was amazed, he said, at the number of poems there. And perhaps Mary was, too, especially when Marianne said there were "a half dozen or a dozen that are not there" that should be. Responding to Warner's letter, Mary wrote that "only this morning did I know how much *I really want his writings collected.*"

No sooner had *Poems* arrived on their doorstep than Marianne revealed what the title should be and the selection of poems that should be there. She had adamantly refused to allow the book to be published yet had already privately assembled the book in her mind. She was not at all pleased that her friends had defied her explicit refusal but, as concerned as she was with her "literary advantage," was even angrier that her first book was not the one she wanted.

It turns out that Moore was right about the timing of her first book. Though amply noticed because of her prominence in poetry magazines, *Poems* received far more scorn than praise. Like the Oxford swan in "Critics and Connoisseurs," critics spurned what the poet proffered. Bryher promised to line up sympathetic reviewers at *Poetry*

and the London *Times*—but failed. *The Times* accused Moore of "eccentricities of spacing," "clumsy prose," "no poetic style," "a lack of inspiration," and "superficial unconventionality."

Harriet Monroe refused to let H.D. review the book for *Poetry*, as
Bryher requested, nor would she let Bryher or Moore's young champion Yvor Winters do so. She wrote the review herself. Careful not to
dismiss a poet whom she could claim as a discovery, she calls the review "A Symposium on Marianne Moore" and acknowledges the enthusiasm of H.D. and Winters for Moore's work. Then she quotes at
length several unsympathetic views (including the negative portions of
Bryher's review) before herself pummeling the poet for her "stiffly
geometrical intellectuality," her "grim and haughty humor," and her
"inscrutable perversities."

No notice of *Poems* appeared in *The Dial* for two and a half years.
Eliot was promptly asked to do it but then suffered a nervous collapse
and wrote *The Waste Land*. In the review that finally appeared (a year
after *The Waste Land* did), he apologized for the delay and said he felt
compelled to write now "because I can only, at the moment, think
of five contemporary poets—English, Irish, American, French, and
German—whose work excites me as much as, or more than, Miss
Moore's." He praised her "quite new rhythm," her distinctive use of
American speech that "inspires both the jargon of the laboratory and
the slang of the comic strip," and her "almost primitive simplicity of
phrase."

Meanwhile, Williams wondered why *The Dial* would ignore
Moore's book and let *Poetry*'s "roast" of her go unchallenged. Eager to
reciprocate Moore's generosity toward *Kora in Hell*, which she had reviewed for *Contact*, he wrote a powerful, unsolicited essay for *The
Dial*, in which he used the example of Marianne Moore to explain
what he valued most in the new poetry. He had not quite finished it
when Eliot's review appeared in the December 1923 issue. *The Dial*
would publish his essay, but not until her next book appeared.

Poems includes the ten poems that Moore gave H.D. at their business meeting, ten taken directly from *The Egoist*, two that Moore had
sent to McAlmon for *Contact*, and two others. The last poem of the
volume, "Is Your Town Nineveh?," was probably among the poems
Moore sent H.D. in 1916. "When I Buy Pictures," she guessed, had

been wheedled out of Thayer, who was holding it for *The Dial* until she approved its publication.

When Pound offered to help Moore get a book published, he warned her of "the very great importance of the actual order of poems in a booklet." *Poems* proves his point and also Moore's point that "by- / play" can be "more terrible in its effectiveness / than the fiercest frontal attack." The thirteen-poem sequence in the 1917 *Others* anthology that drew Pound's and Eliot's attention began with the relaxed, witty "Critics and Connoisseurs" and the celebration of ecstasy and expediency in Hebrew poetry, "The Past Is the Present." *Poems* includes neither poem. Rather, it opens with two of Moore's most indignant verses and thus foregrounds the warrior poet H.D. had described in 1916. With "Pedantic Literalist" and "To a Steam-Roller," she steps forth brandishing swords. Nothing in the early part of the book prepares the reader for the playfulness of "Poetry" and "Radical" near the end. By this point the first-time reader might well mistake Moore's irony for pedantry. Even Richard Aldington, who defended Moore against the harsh treatment she received from other critics, complained of her "air of condescension."

All of the poems rhyme, but more than a third precede the development of Moore's mature stanza in 1916. Neither her sympathizers nor her detractors seemed to appreciate the innovation of her stanza. She had developed it when avant-garde poets were wearying of free verse. But now that readers had become accustomed to letting line breaks determine the rhythm of the poem, they regarded Moore's as mere quirkiness. Edith Sitwell, who ranked Moore "among the most interesting American poets of the day," found the division of words at the ends of lines "irritating." Louis Untermeyer accused Moore of neither caring about nor appreciating the function of rhyme. To Harriet Monroe, the geometrical stanzas were "forms which impose themselves arbitrarily upon word-structure and sentence-structure instead of accepting happily the limitations of the art's materials, as all art must." Although Williams praised Moore for exploring the fundamental tension in modern art between form and substance, it was not until 1935 that Eliot called Moore "the greatest living master of light rhyme" and that Stevens explained how syllable count, rhyme, and typographical spacing work together in her stanzas.

Moore had begun to retreat from her alleged quirkiness even before *Poems* appeared. Her first free-verse poems, "When I Buy Pictures" and "A Graveyard," appeared in the July 1921 *Dial* just before the release of *Poems*. She originally wrote both in stanzas, and *The Dial* accepted them that way months before Moore converted them to free verse and allowed them to be published. From July 1921 until the end of 1924, Moore wrote all of her new poems in free verse—no more line breaks in the middle of words.

The most consistent theme through all of the reviews is that her poems come from the head rather than the heart. At best she was witty and brilliant; at worst, insufferably highbrow. "If an ingeniously constructed, intricate little piece of machinery, a dainty little thing with cogs and wheels and flashes of iron and steel, should suddenly be given a human voice to pour its 'soul' into song," wrote one derisive critic, "it would stand revealed as a bit of writing by Miss Moore." "Emotion in her is calcined to a thin ash," wrote an appreciative one.

So strongly did Moore feel misjudged on this point that she henceforth defended the presence of "gusto" in her own writing and of profound feeling wherever it might pass (as in Henry James) as the opposite. In "Novices," one of the first poems she wrote after reading reviews of *Poems*, the suave young sophisticates dismiss as boring "the detailless perspective of the sea." Little do they suspect what lurks beneath that placid surface, a power that Moore equates with "the spontaneous unforced passion of the Hebrew language— / an abyss of verbs full of reverberation and tempestuous energy." The theme of undetected but stormy passion would inform most of the poems that Moore wrote over the next few years.

14

Liberty and Union

1921–1923

I never knew anyone who had a passion for words who had as much difficulty in saying things as I do," Moore told an interviewer late in life. Yet even in college, when she felt the frustration most sharply, it pleased her that Dr. Sanders did not grasp the meaning of the poem he admired. So highly did she value precision that she appropriated for poetry the language of science. Yet enigma gave her power. "Mysteriousness" is "formidable," she said; "to be understood" is "to be no / Longer privileged." Both her admirers and her detractors agreed that her work would appeal only to the elite. Yet at every opportunity her poems undercut "sophistication" and "too stern an intellectual emphasis upon this quality or that."

There is no indication that Mary understood the poems better than anyone else did. It was not easy for her to watch her daughter "pull and tug—build up, and then destroy what is laboriously put together," but she did not begrudge the many hours it took to get the words just right. Her own offhand remarks, such as "There are things that are important beyond all this fiddle," appear prominently in the poems about modernist aesthetics that Marianne wrote in 1919 and 1920. They give Mary a position of privilege in the poems but not the privilege of understanding them. Marianne repeated to several friends—with delighted amusement—her mother's description of *Poems* as "a veiled Mohammedan woman."

While Moore thought poetry and criticism were closer to each other than most poets do—both, for her, demand keen observation combined with imagination—she did not want her prose to mystify. Expressing her critical judgments with as much honesty and respect for the author as possible demanded considerable effort. *The Dial* provided the ideal audience for her "meditative comment and fine distinctions," as well as giving her the opportunity at last to earn real money as a critic. She was paid fifty dollars for her *Jacopone da Todi* review and agreed to write on the *Memoirs of the Empress Eugénie* next.

For nearly a month, she worked on the review all the time she was not at the library. She asked Mary to read the book and to help with "collateral reading." As the deadline approached, Mary began working on the review herself while Marianne was away. She became so immersed in it that she did not leave the house to buy food, and Marianne had to insist that she go to bed rather than stay up to work on it. Then a letter from *The Dial* arrived, requesting a short review unless a longer one had been written. Marianne cut the 5,000-word essay to 150 words, sent it off (with relief), and accepted the two dollars that was standard for Briefer Mention reviews.

After this Marianne sometimes tried out a phrase or an idea on Mary as she was writing a review but did not show it to her until she had typed a first draft. Mary would then comment on successive drafts until it was finished. Even if outsiders confused Moore's circuitous politeness for praise, Mary always knew when she "privately sniffed and squirreled."

Mary was first reader to everything Marianne wrote but played a different role in the poetry than in the prose. "Last evening my hair turned gray, and I took on ten years," she wrote Warner, "when I had to say that poems he has worked on for months,—for days unremittingly and speechlessly—were not just right yet." It is characteristic of these years that Marianne worked on several poems at once and worked on them "speechlessly," that is, without consulting her mother. "I was determined to finish some poems for *The Dial*," Marianne wrote Warner the next day, "but Mole doesn't commend them for presenting so I have painfully and reluctantly scrapped them."

The poems lacked "stinging greatness of truth and high principle that gripped the soul," Mary said. If she did not understand the poems, she nevertheless convinced herself that Marianne would be "blessed of God" for her efforts. The reason Rat was so pursued by Village literati, she told Warner, is *"his true religion and its visible outcome.* Little do his adherents and suppliants think this preposterous thing . . . but *that is* the attraction. Rat himself admits it."

Just after *Poems* appeared, Sibley Watson called at St. Luke's Place to discuss possible reviewers for the book. With Thayer out of the country, he took a more active role in the daily management of *The Dial.* "He is a . . . quiet, 'modest lad,'" Marianne told Warner, "with common sense and no parlor tricks or aesthetic affectations. I like him greatly. He got up to go about ten o'clock, Mole urged him to stay, and to my great surprise he laid down his hat and sat down again meekly as if he had just arrived."

After they agreed upon Eliot to review *Poems,* she showed Watson the three poems she had "reluctantly scrapped" a month before: "New York," "The Labors of Hercules," and "People's Surroundings." Thayer had told Marianne early in their friendship that he liked her poems but did not understand them, whereas "Mr. Watson liked them." Watson took the poems and mailed her a check for forty dollars. Marianne continued to consult him until the poems satisfied her. Watson thus became the first and, as far as is known, the only reader whose opinion could trump Mary's. When Moore was assembling her *Selected Poems* more than a decade later, she asked Watson's advice about including "An Octopus," a poem Mary disliked. He provided the reassurance that she needed.

Marianne worked from July through September revising the three poems. They show a shift in emphasis from the aesthetic principles of her recent work to social and political ones. "New York" addresses the exploitation of the wilderness—both the fur trade and the romanticization of the "savage" with his "calico horses" and "war canoe." The real savages, the poem implies, are those who "plunder" the wilderness rather than "experience" it. The title of "The Labors of Hercules" refers to the difficulty of overcoming prejudices of various kinds and ultimately of realizing

"that the negro is not brutal,
that the Jew is not greedy,
that the Oriental is not immoral,
that the German is not a Hun."

"People's Surroundings" is about looking beyond surface appearances to discover the Bluebeard-like egos who collect wives and other beautiful things. At the time Moore finished the other two poems, it ended with relatively straightforward remarks about the differences between "sophistication" and "knowledge." But later she changed her mind and concluded the poem with a catalog of twenty-five people and twenty places they inhabit. Adapted from a sixteenth-century astrology book, the list includes both those who hold power—"queens, countesses, ladies, emperors"—and the cooks, carpenters, and chimney sweeps who support the "fundamental structure" of power. The rhythmic crescendo of the thirteen-line catalog suggests finality, but it does not "answer one's questions" in any logical way.

It troubled Moore that her verse was deemed intellectual when the response she most wanted was "a few 'strong wrinkles'" between the ears, a response as visceral and unsophisticated as "hands that can grasp, eyes / that can dilate, and hair that can rise / if it must." She frustrated the intellect by hurling at her readers a barrage of data. Often the data are fragments taken from hidden sources, as in these lines from "New York":

It is a far cry from the "queen full of jewels"
and the beau with the muff,
from the gilt coach shaped like a perfume bottle,
to the conjunction of the Monongahela and the Allegheny.

The reader's desire for coherence confronts the inviolate particularity of the fragments. And yet the accumulation of the queen, beau, and gilt coach does suggest a world that is "a far cry" from the conjunction of two rivers with Indian names. The tension resembles that of modernist collage, in which a fragment of sheet music or newspaper retains its own individuality at the same time it contributes to the overall composition. Knowing the source of a fragment—for instance, that the

Monongahela and Allegheny converge at Pittsburgh, a place of significance for the poet's family—makes the choice of names seem less arbitrary, but it does not unlock the door to a coherent meaning. Moore's
assemblages defy logic yet captivate the imagination by half revealing
and half concealing the mind that put them together. A poet's selectiveness must have "more elasticity than logic," she said in "The Labors of Hercules," and yet it "knows where it is going" as surely as
electricity flies along to "areas that boast of their remoteness." "Mere
mysteriousness is useless," she later wrote, "the enigma must be clear
to the author, not necessarily to us."

It is not known if Scofield Thayer ever recognized himself in "People's
Surroundings." But he would have at least two more opportunities to
feel the barbs of Marianne's wrath. After she saw George Moore's *Heloise and Abelard* reviewed in *The Dial* and realized that Thayer had
forgotten his promise to save it for her, she wrote about it for *Broom*, a
new international magazine of arts and letters. This was her longest,
most ambitious, most personally satisfying essay yet. She worked on it
for two months. "I have finished but not copied my article on George
Moore," she told Warner, "with which I expect to stab Scofield and
'have the pleasure to see him lie struggling for life—but with little
noise' like the lion in *Robinson Crusoe*." Her review actually quotes Defoe's paragraph about shooting the lion. And Thayer got the point.
The Dial asked her to review a biography of George Moore the following summer.

After Marianne finished her review for *Broom*, she and Mary became so ill that Warner sent them a hundred dollars (in addition to the
hundred he sent monthly) to go to a hotel so that they would have
plenty of food and heat and could be waited on by bellboys. Warner's
generosity contrasted sharply, as usual, with Mary's frugality. Mary
put the money into savings and remained ill throughout the spring.
Marianne managed to go to the circus and to a couple of lectures. But
"the terrific experience of this winter," she told Bryher, "has cut me off
completely from writing and writers here."

Meanwhile, Warner began making plans for Marianne and Mary
to join him in Bremerton, Washington, for the six weeks he would be

stationed there during the summer. But he kept these plans from Constance. He felt guilty about "the mean trick he is about to play on his wife whom he loves like his own daughters," but he wanted to be with his mother and sister alone. As it happened, there was no need for deception. Constance decided to take little Mary and Sallie to New York for the summer. There they saw much of their grandmother and aunt.

Marianne and Mary took the train to Seattle, where Warner met them at the station and took them the first night to see a twenty-four-hour sawmill at work. "A jewel of mechanism and a juggernaut of destruction," Marianne called it. As would often be the case in her poems, she found herself caught between aesthetic awe and moral repulsion. They next followed Warner's ship to the industrial port of Everett, where Marianne found the monkey puzzle trees, the subject of a future poem, to be "the only thread of romance."

Warner took off two days to drive them to Mount Rainier National Park. They spent the night at Paradise Inn, which is situated in a meadow of alpine wildflowers with magnificent views of the peak. Warner and Marianne rented hiking gear and went on a guided hike to the ice caves. "We had a glorious time," Marianne wrote Bryher. "We inspected Nisqually Glacier, tried the snow slide, examined the flowers and read with zeal the warnings to inexperienced mountaineers." A deposit for the full value of the equipment was required "in case you don't come back," they were told. Marianne based much of her poem "An Octopus" upon this excursion. It winks at Warner through several references to rats and badgers.

For the month of August, Warner rented his mother and sister a cottage in the Bremerton navy yard. It had a view of Puget Sound and Mount Rainier in the distance. The climax of the summer for Marianne was winning a mixed doubles tennis tournament with Warner. The engraved plate they received as a trophy became a regular part of the tea service at St. Luke's Place.

Marianne began jotting down ideas for what would become the two longest poems of her career: "An Octopus" and "Marriage." The repetition of the lines—"men have power / and sometimes one is made to feel it"—throughout the early pages of her notebook suggests that Thayer's marriage proposal was still much on her mind. A quotation from the book of Amos—"the crumbs from a lion's meal, / a couple of shins and the bit of an ear"—alludes to Thayer. And the notebook includes lines, later rejected, about Bluebeard and acacias.

The following January she promised "Marriage" to Monroe Wheeler for a short-lived magazine, *Manikin,* which he printed himself. His partner, Glenway Wescott, had first called on the Moores in October 1921, when he was passing through New York on his way from Chicago to Europe. He was twenty at the time and the youngest member of the Poetry Club at the University of Chicago. Not even Yvor Winters, the leading member of the club, was as enamored of Moore's work as Wescott was. While working as an office boy for Harriet Monroe, he had looked up all of Moore's poems in magazines in order to type copies for himself. He wrote Moore to ask if he might call on her when he was in New York and was invited to tea.

"He is a lovely fellow," Marianne told Warner afterward, "very young but very elegant and accustomed to studio-lounge life." (He had carefully concealed his Wisconsin pig farm origins.) He told the Moores that his friends in Chicago thought Marianne's work "supremely fine." They liked its "elegant—sustained ecstasy" and the wit of its verbal twists.

He repeated what Harriet Monroe had told him when he asked to review *Poems* for *Poetry.* "Dear boy, I could not trust you to take the right point of view; besides there are two ahead of you."

"She can't stand you," he told Marianne, "and insists the best you have ever done is what she published in *Poetry* ten years ago!"

Neither Glenway Wescott nor Monroe Wheeler was yet twenty when they met through mutual friends in the Poetry Club. Wescott, a student, was engaged to be married. Wheeler was working in advertising and dating several women. Their lifelong partnership began when Wheeler, learning that Wescott was hospitalized with the flu, arrived with a rare copy of John Addington Symonds's homosexual essays and three red roses.

Wheeler published a book of Wescott's poems on the small printing press that his father had given him for his eighteenth birthday and next published a book of Winters's poems. While in Europe in 1922, he launched *Manikin.* The first volume was poems by Janet Lewis, Winters's future wife, and the second was ten poems by William Carlos Williams.

Wescott and Wheeler called on the Moores in early January 1923, brought them strawberries, and invited them to tea. Over the next few weeks they came often to St. Luke's Place and charmed the two women completely with their various enthusiasms and refined tastes. "No one ever has come before," Mary told Warner, "that I like so much to see. The three (Rat and they) had spasms of fun out of my innocently telling him [Rat] that it was the oddest thing he should be so completely modern, and yet seem to need nothing for his art that was outré or risqué, at least not so far." "Glenway's fund of conversation, his phraseology and intensity of feeling are all very impressive," she wrote a few weeks later. "His adoration for Rat and Rat's work is very touching and beautiful. It is impersonal yet it seems almost like family love."

When Wescott asked Wheeler to publish a new edition of *Poems* according to Marianne's specifications, Wheeler said it would be too expensive to publish the whole book. But Marianne promised to give him the long poem that she was writing. (Unbeknown to Marianne, Bryher paid the printing costs.) Marianne worked on "Marriage" relentlessly for the next three months and presented it to him at the end of April.

The Moores had grown quite close to Wheeler by then. Wescott was in Europe for six months with his employer, and Wheeler came to regard St. Luke's Place as a second home. He took Marianne and Mary to an exhibition of Chinese paintings at the Metropolitan and shared with them his passion for books and printing. As a sign of their growing intimacy, Mary began inviting him for meals rather than tea and was surprised at how much she looked forward to his visits. "We all chat enjoyably together," Mary told Warner. "He says when Glenway comes home they are going to pattern their way of living as precisely as they can after life at 14 and utterly give up the chase for literary celebrities."

"Marriage" was published in late September as the third and final issue of *Manikin*. Laid inside each copy was a review Wescott had written of *Poems* before he left. "The impulse of the mind is to avoid paths so stony, steep, and winding," he warns. "The artful reader must decide . . . whether he honestly wishes to pursue a delight so hard to get." He advises readers to seek "the excitation of irrational and dreamlike delight—what is loosely called 'emotion'" in Moore's work rather than "meaning" in any familiar sense. Marianne liked the review. She told Warner it was "the most scholarly so far."

Marianne and Mary vacationed in Bremerton again in the summer of 1923 and were still there when "Marriage" came out. By the time they came home in late October, both Scofield Thayer and Wescott were back in New York.

"Scofield turned white at sight of *Manikin*," Wheeler told Marianne and Mary when he met them at the train station. Wescott, who had dinner waiting, was full of news of Thayer's reaction. Thayer was stunned, Wescott said, that the poem appeared in book form before any magazine had a chance to publish it. It made the insult that much worse when it was pointed out that *Manikin* was a magazine. Thayer had never heard of it. He also would have realized, though he did not say so, that Marianne passed up the considerable sum *The Dial* would have paid her for so long a poem. Thayer soon resumed his composure and told Wescott that he looked forward to seeing much of Mr. Wheeler and Miss Moore during the winter. Wescott liked Thayer, who had agreed to publish his novel serially in *The Dial*, but greatly enjoyed Wheeler's victory over so formidable a rival.

Even Mary gloated. "I am so thankful," she confided to Warner, "that a really strong buffer has interposed itself between Scofield and Rat; I mean Glenway and Monroe . . . When Scofield went away, he felt he could preempt Rat *utterly* . . . He knew Alfred Kreymborg had done all of Rat's publishing, and that Dr. Williams was an adherent, but he waggled by *them*, as a *great* poppa dog. Now he finds a pair that are all in all to each other" and "are accepted by Rat as congenial."

Thayer blanched first over the slight to *The Dial* but would have other reasons to do so as he inspected *Manikin* 3 further. He understood why the celibate poet would choose marriage for her subject as few others did. And the personal message in the cover illustration would not have been lost on him. Instead of a married couple, the cover shows the wily Odysseus strapped to the belly of a ram, his unsheathed sword poised for attack. He lies hidden from the blinded Cyclops just as the poet herself lies hidden from her powerful, unseeing adversary.

Marianne must have worked closely with Wheeler to design the book. She always took great interest in the appearance of the written word. And it was probably Wheeler who arranged for Wescott to deliver it to Thayer in person, so that Marianne could vicariously watch him "struggling for life—but with little noise."

Moore begins the poem by calling marriage "an institution" or "enterprise" and thus deflects attention from any personal interest she might have in the subject. The comic tone of this mock-epithalamium and its assemblage of quotations (approximately two-thirds of the poem) seem so removed from any personal motive that readers are likely to believe her later claim that "Marriage" does not "veil anything personal in the way of triumphs, entrapments, or dangerous collo-quies. It is a little anthology of statements that took my fancy." Though the poem seems disinterested at every turn, it is her most personal poem and perhaps her most formidable. Not only had she felt that Thayer betrayed her trust but she also felt betrayed in different ways by Warner and Constance's marriage and by Bryher and McAlmon's.

The poem's most poignant subject is the multilayered paradoxes of her relationship with her mother—who often in the early 1920s re-ferred to Marianne and herself as a "young couple." "I should like to be alone," Eve says early in the poem. And her visitor replies, "I should like to be alone; / why not be alone together?" This is the central di-lemma of "Marriage" and the central dilemma of Marianne's own living arrangements. It is possible to read the poem as a cry for freedom from Mary's tyrannical love, especially if one considers the significance of the letter M for their tiny household:

> turn to the letter M
> and you will find
> that 'a wife is a coffin,'
> . . .
> revengefully wrought in the attitude
> of an adoring child
> to a distinguished parent.

But it is also possible to read "Marriage" as a love poem to Mary celebrating their unorthodox partnership. In the next decade Moore would come to idealize maternal love as heroic and liberating. "Love is more important than being in love," she wrote in a 1932 book review, "as memories of childhood testify." One of the characteristics of Moore's hero, according to her 1932 poem "The Hero," is to look "upon a fellow creature's error with the / feelings of a mother—a / woman or a cat." And in "The Paper Nautilus" (1940) a mother and her "intensively / watched eggs" ultimately free each other, love being "the only fortress / strong enough to trust to." A journalist who interviewed Moore in 1956 characterized the poet's mother as "the least possessive of beings."

"Marriage" does not celebrate a wedding as conventional epithalamia do but asks "what Adam and Eve / think of it by this time." The poem consists mostly of their dialogue. Eve speaks first. She is "handsome," and Adam "has beauty also." Both are egocentric and comically loquacious. Eve can "write simultaneously / in three languages . . . / and talk in the meantime," while Adam is as "unnerved" by the nightingale's silence as he is "dazzled by the apple." Despite "that invaluable accident / exonerating Adam," both sexes bear responsibility for the "savage" state into which marriage has fallen. Hymen, the god of wedding ceremonies, makes an appearance but is "unhelpful" and ridiculous, "a kind of overgrown cupid." Then Diana, the goddess of single women, enters the scene. With her two panthers and dark, bearlike scowl, she commands awe without speaking a word.

For the first nine-tenths of the poem, individual autonomy and marriage seem utterly at odds with each other. But the ending does present the "rare" possibility of their coexistence, a "triumph of simplicity" for those imaginative enough to see it. The final speech of the poem is given to the "charitive Euroclydon / of frightening disinterestedness / which the world hates." The Euroclydon is a violent wind that in the Bible is closely associated with God's wrath. A native of the Adriatic, it recognizes in Daniel Webster a familiar type: the parading Roman statesman and debater whose gestures—"the book on the writing-table, / the hand in the breast pocket"—wield power.

One no more expects to find the secret to marriage in political oratory than to find poetry in business documents and schoolbooks. Yet the paradox of democracy is the same as for marriage. The "essence of the matter" is

"Liberty and union
now and forever."

It is Moore's principle of composition as well. In no other poem do the
assembled fragments resist unity more than they do in "Marriage." Yet
the force of emotion in the poem provides a centripetal force to coun-
terbalance the centrifugal one.

Despite its detached, satiric voice and its seemingly impersonal
amalgam of quotations, there is much violence in "Marriage." Diana's
"spiked hand / . . . has an affection for one / and proves it to the bone."
Besides her two panthers, the poem mentions leopards, snakes, a hip-
popotamus, a crested screamer, two monsters, the serpent, and the lion
from Amos. Besides the frightening Euroclydon, it includes a violent
waterfall, chasms, and a purifying fire. "The strange experience of
beauty . . . tears one to pieces," and true love can "gaze an eagle blind."
The violence suggests that what angered Moore at least as much as
Thayer's egotistical presumptuousness (as she saw it) was his offer of a
loveless union. Like the critics of her poetry, he underestimated the
depth and power of her emotions.

"The deepest feeling always shows itself in silence; / not in silence, but
restraint." So wrote Moore in "Silence," another poem she began writing as she jotted down notes for "Marriage" and "An Octopus." Restraint was not just a literary strategy for her. Mary's letters indicate
again and again that Marianne never spoke about her deepest feelings.
Only her "little narrow white face with a monk-like severity" indicated to Mary that "life has come to her in great surging waves."

When Peter moved away with his owners, Mary told Warner that
she missed him but did not ache for him as Marianne did. A year and
a half later, while Marianne was deep at work on "Marriage," a neighbor gave them a stray kitten. Both women formed an immediate attachment to him, and his antics appear often in their letters to Warner
and Bryher. After much deliberation they named him Buffalo and
called him Buffy. "Buffalo is developing and is cuter and cuter," Marianne told Warner after they had had him a month. "His flower pin
eyes are a pretty amber—and now he sharpens his claws on the hall
rug each time we let him out the door."

The next afternoon Buffy was dead.

"Mole got chloroform and a little box and prepared everything and did it while I was at the library Monday," Marianne told Warner, "and nothing could have been more exact . . . But it's a knife in my heart, he was so affecting and scrupulous in his little scratchings and his attention to our requirements of him. It would have been cruel to him to let him grow and might have . . . seemed like murder to him if we *had* kept him and turned him over to strangers; and a seemingly comfortable life in a shut up room would not be good for any cat so we were kind, but having had him so long as we had made the deed seem foul . . . You can understand if anyone can, these feelings. We tend to run wild in these matters of personal affection but there may be good in it too." It was Mary's decision to kill Buffy, but Marianne reconciled herself to it. They gave Buffy an honorable burial in the Hudson.

"I never speak of Buffy to Rat," Mary said privately to Warner after another month had passed. "His grief drove me frantic." Even four years later Mary mentioned that they never went to their pier anymore because of Buffy and now rode the bus across town when they needed diversion. "If I had a sorrow," says the Euroclydon in "Marriage," "I should feel it a long time; / I am not one of those / who have a great sorrow / in the morning / and a great joy at noon."

Shortly after Marianne gave "Marriage" to Wheeler, she had an opportunity to display her emotions in a remarkably unrestrained way. Matthew Josephson—the critic who had compared her favorably with other women poets because emotion in her work was "calcined to a thin ash"—came to call. Having formerly been associated with the Dadaist magazine *Secession*, he had recently taken over the editorship of *Broom* and wanted Marianne to join its staff. She had supported *Broom* when Alfred Kreymborg and then Lola Ridge served as its American editors, but her loyalty did not extend to Josephson, whom she disliked.

Mary called their conversation "one of the memorable incidents in our lives." It was "as if a man had come with an offer of marriage," she said, "if guarantee would be given in return, of complete subjugation, that no trouble would be given in any case whatever, and all property made over, before the bans were announced."

The conversation began amicably about armor. Then it turned to young writers, and Josephson inquired what Marianne thought of his friend Slater Brown. Since Brown was "a person of undoubted talent," she said, "it was greatly to be regretted that he lacked a disciplined sense of humor and thus was led into writing the very pitiable story for *Secession* that had appeared in the winter." Josephson rose to Brown's defense.

And thus began what Marianne called "a real carnage of skin and fur for two hours or more." When Josephson inquired what she thought of Dr. Williams's article on the Baroness von Freytag-Loringhoven, she told him that Williams was a devoted friend, yet she "loathed and abhorred his lewdness and had told him so many times." Relieved that Marianne's dislike for a work did not extend to the author, Josephson asked whether she had read the book of his own poems that he had recently sent her. She told him that she disliked all but two poems. Josephson inquired what she disliked.

"*Excrement*," she said, and "armpits." "Sherwood Anderson says he likes the smell of excrement. *I do not*, and I refuse to be made to think of it. Armpits would not interest me if you were the first to mention the subject, but it's done to death."

"What do you think of *Broom*?" Josephson asked at last. "Shouldn't you hate to have it given up?" She told him that she could not live without the *Natural History Magazine* or *The Spectator* but could easily give up *Broom*, *Secession*, and even *The Dial*.

To Mary it was "a purple red fight" that lasted hours, "till that young feller was disintegrated." Others who opposed Rat had backed down, Mary said, and Rat let them off easier. But Josephson crossed a line when he said that if Marianne had only lived abroad, she would have learned to tolerate obscenity. She told him that none of the writers whose work she disapproved ever mentioned lewd subjects to her in person, that they would be embarrassed to. Josephson asked what she thought of Shakespeare. "Shakespeare exhilarates me," she said. "These writers don't. When a piece of work focuses attention so strongly upon his grossness or its funniness that you can think of nothing else then all question of the writer's potential greatness disappears; he's not an artist."

"All my stinging legs stand out like the fretful porpentine," Marianne said afterward, "when I am told that if I were cosmopolitan I'd like lewdness too."

By the 1950s she became admittedly prudish. But what offended her in her youth was a lack of respect for the reader or the characters. She objected to lewdness because it dehumanized women. And she objected just as much to other forms of disrespect. She accused Eliot of "cruelty" toward his subject in "Portrait of a Lady." And she disliked Slater Brown's story because it made fun of a child's wetting his pants. "I could not be amused by a child's misery," she told Josephson.

As much as Wheeler and Thayer would enjoy the story of Rat's triumph, Mary refused to gloat over it to anyone but Warner and Mary Norcross. Since Josephson easily found support for *Broom* elsewhere in New York, that evening's "carnage of skin and fur" had little effect upon literary history. For Mary, however, "one of the memorable incidents in our lives" was watching "Rat [rise] like a bird of Paradise with his definite quotations from Leigh Hunt, Henry James, Browne— Milton, many others; reasons floating like plumes."

Never again do her letters call Rat little or defenseless.

15

The Unbridled Leap

1923–1925

Marianne's abiding loyalty to Thayer soon conquered her anger toward him. Three days after she returned from Bremerton, she accompanied him to dinner at the Plaza Hotel and afterward to the theater. He often took her to dinner in the coming months and called at St. Luke's Place. The private allusions in "Marriage," however barbed, pay tribute to his intelligence as well as to the intimacy of their friendship. Thayer seems to have grasped this. For despite his growing suspicion of almost everyone, he never doubted Marianne. She repaid that trust by writing for *The Dial* exclusively for the next six years.

The Dial occupied a redbrick row house at 152 West Thirteenth Street, "an old-fashioned house," Marianne called it, "with marble mantels and mahogany or walnut stairway." Only THE DIAL printed in gold-leaf block letters on the first-floor window indicated the presence of offices in the otherwise residential neighborhood. "The word *office*," recalled Alyse Gregory, "is hardly . . . a suitable one to describe the spacious, square, homely rooms, with their casual collection of shabby furniture—selected, apparently, as little for display as for efficiency. They had something of old New York still lingering about them, its serenity and its leisured dignity."

Upon his return from Europe, Thayer remodeled the third floor as a dining room and decorated it with paintings by E. E. Cummings and Charles Demuth. Marianne was among the earliest dinner guests in a party that included Alyse Gregory, Thayer's trusted friend who would soon become managing editor of *The Dial*; Llewellyn Powys, Gregory's future husband; and Henry Seidel Canby, book review editor for the *New York Post*, whose favor Thayer wished to curry. Thayer's valet cooked and served soup, steak, and apple pie. After dinner they retired to the wicker chairs in Thayer's large office, where they sat around the fire, heard about Canby's recent trip to Alaska, and admired Thayer's just published "Living Art" portfolio, a set of reproductions of the modern art he had collected in Europe.

For both Thayer and Sibley Watson, *The Dial* had always been as much a social club as it was a literary and philanthropic venture. They followed the example of *The Harvard Monthly*, where they had first met, by naming a president, Watson, and a secretary-treasurer, Lincoln MacVeagh. They asked friends from *The Harvard Monthly*, Stewart Mitchell and Gilbert Seldes, to serve as associate editors. Other Harvard friends—Eliot, Cummings, S. Foster Damon, John Dos Passos, and Conrad Aiken—became frequent contributors. From the time Thayer first invited Marianne to tea in his office and introduced her to Watson, he made it clear that he regarded her as one of *The Dial*'s favored writers and a member of its inner circle.

When Thayer and Watson bought *The Dial* in 1919, Watson was studying medicine at New York University. The reclusive Watson wanted equal say with Thayer about the contents of the magazine but had no desire to interact with staff and contributors on a daily basis. After finishing his residency in 1923, he left the city with his wife and children. The family lived in rural Massachusetts for a couple of years before settling permanently in Rochester, New York. Watson traveled to New York once a month for the makeup meeting, at which final decisions were made about the contents of each issue.

In late 1923 Thayer at last persuaded Alyse Gregory to become *The Dial*'s managing editor. She had resisted his pleas for more than three years. She knew that he trusted her literary tastes—"at once adventurous and old-fashioned," as she put it—but feared that she could never meet his exacting standards. Psychoanalysis with Freud had not forestalled the waning of Thayer's sanity, and he wanted to move permanently to his summer home on Martha's Vineyard. Unless Gregory agreed to take over, Thayer told her, *The Dial* would cease to exist. He gave Gregory more authority over the contents of the magazine than he had given any previous managing editor and paid her more, seventy-five dollars per week instead of fifty.

As soon as Gregory accepted the position, Thayer began to recruit Marianne as a backup. He asked in January if she would be willing to work at *The Dial* for a month or even a year, but she refused, saying that her library work just suited her. Marianne was the only person whom Thayer trusted to serve as Gregory's replacement. Gregory knew this and began to groom Marianne to take over in her absence. Marianne agreed to anything Gregory asked of her.

She began attending the monthly makeup meetings in February so that she could write copy for advertisements. Gregory also taught her to write Briefer Mention reviews quickly enough to make the two-dollar remuneration attractive. "How wonderfully you have mastered in your Briefer Mentions that rare art of delicate veracious evasion which is the soul of goodness," Gregory wrote her in July. "Your words run as softly from your pen as coins dropped into a silken purse and only for those whose ears are initiated is that final clink of candor audible." By the fall Marianne was contributing several Briefer Mention reviews per issue.

When Marianne started reviewing for *The Dial* earlier in the decade, she wanted to choose her own books and mostly turned down the ones she was asked to do. If she felt no enthusiasm for a book, she preferred to say nothing at all—unless the author was a friend. She asked to review *Development* not because she admired the prose but because of Bryher's generosity to her. And because she felt that *The Dial* had slighted Williams's *Kora in Hell*, she reviewed it for *Contact* despite serious reservations about it.

Soon after finishing "Marriage," she reluctantly agreed to review the *Collected Poems* of Vachel Lindsay for *The Dial* even though she had no personal relationship with Lindsay and disliked his poetry. In earlier reviews she had often praised a writer's language while abhorring certain of his attitudes (especially toward women). Lindsay provided an opportunity to do the opposite. "It is impossible not to respect

Mr. Lindsay's preoccupation with humanitarianism," she wrote, "but at the same time to deplore his lack of aesthetic rigor." She remained true to her principles and got the distinctions just right. The review pleased her, and she agreed to review a greater range of books.

Marianne had been closely following developments in modern poetry for a decade by the time she started reviewing for *The Dial*. Her most distinguished reviews show a prescient appreciation for the poets who now form the modernist canon. By 1923, she had already reviewed Eliot (twice), Yeats, H.D., and Williams. As soon as she returned from Bremerton, she began writing about Wallace Stevens's *Harmonium* for *The Dial*'s December issue. No other contemporaneous review gave the book the serious attention and praise that Moore's did. Though she had never met Stevens nor corresponded with him, she felt obliged to educate the reading public about a fellow modernist whose achievement was as misunderstood as her own.

Marianne published no new poems for more than a year after she finished "Marriage" but instead focused her attention upon several long book reviews as well as the Briefer Mention ones. In whatever she reviewed, she always managed to find quotations for which she felt genuine enthusiasm. Comparing her to a crow that "picks over an ash-heap and leaves the ashes behind," Yvor Winters once told her that he liked her reviews but distrusted them. Any dishonesty in her reviews is a matter of emphasis, however, for she never let deficiencies pass unnoticed.

In February 1924 Marianne received a letter inviting her to publish a new book of poems with Contact Press, which Robert McAlmon ran and Bryher financed. "We would want it to include *everything* of yours that you find good from the beginning up to the present," William Carlos Williams said in his letter on behalf of the press. His own as-yet-unpublished review of *Poems* would serve as a preface. Marianne was sorry to disappoint Williams and Bryher, but she did not trust McAlmon to publish the quality of book she wanted. Nor did she care to be in company with certain other authors published by his press. She replied with her old excuse, that she did not have enough new work to justify a book.

Upon receiving a similar invitation from Lincoln MacVeagh in June, she immediately regretted her excuse to Williams. The previous year MacVeagh had resigned his position at Henry Holt in order to start the Dial Press, which he ran out of the basement of the *Dial* offices. Warner urged her to accept, arguing that her close ties to *The Dial* would justify it, but she refused out of loyalty to Bryher and Williams.

Later that summer Marianne changed her mind. Knowing that Watson and Thayer wanted to give Marianne the Dial Award if she had a book out before the January *Dial* went to press, Alyse Gregory gently persuaded her to accept MacVeagh's invitation. This time Thayer wrote to renew the offer. Because the press and magazine were financially separate from each other, Marianne did not realize until later that Thayer had instigated the first invitation as well. She humbly and warmly accepted Thayer's offer on August 26, 1924.

Although she and Mary put writing before anything else, she said, she could not have the manuscript ready until the first of November. Family matters demanded her immediate attention. Warner and Constance were arriving in New York just then with a household of belongings and three small daughters. Mary and Marianne had not seen Constance and the older girls for two years and had not yet met fourteen-month-old Marianne Craig Moore. Since Mary had taken ill for a month after Warner's last visit to New York, Marianne was "under oath to myself," she wrote Thayer, "to compass our small domestic responsibilities and protect my mother from unnecessary social strain."

In 1921 she had thought the body of her work too "slight" for a book. The longer poems she wrote afterward—"People's Surroundings," "Novices," "Sea Unicorns and Land Unicorns," and especially "Marriage" and "An Octopus"—would give her second book greater heft. Eliot's *The Waste Land*, which appeared in the December 1922 *Dial*, had demonstrated just how hefty a modern poem could be. Thayer disliked the poem, and Williams famously called it "the great catastrophe to our letters." Marianne called it "macabre." "It suggests that imagination has been compressed," she said, "whereas experience should be precipitate." Everyone agreed, however, upon the significance of Eliot's achievement.

The poetry notebook that Marianne kept during her first summer in Bremerton indicates that she was contemplating a long poem months before she read *The Waste Land*. She may have had in mind just one long poem at first, but the lines and ideas she recorded that summer eventually appeared in three. She completed "Marriage" the following April but worked on "Sea Unicorns and Land Unicorns" and "An Octopus," as she told Bryher, "off and on for two years." To get *Observations* ready for publication, she first had to finish those poems. She sent "Sea Unicorns" to Thayer first. He promptly sent her a check for sixty dollars and wrote her of the great pleasure he and Watson had in accepting the poem for *The Dial*.

Thayer felt sure he had read "upon her lap / its mild wild head doth lie" before, he said, but neither he nor Watson could place it. "Am I right," he asked, "in understanding that the use of quotation marks in your work always does mean that the phrase is a quotation? That you do not make use of quotation marks merely to set things off, as another might use italics?"

Marianne responded with a three-page single-spaced letter providing sources for all of the poem's quotations. Yes, she said, except in cases where a character in the poem is speaking, as in "Silence," her quotation marks nearly always indicate someone else's words. The lines he asked about came from an anonymous poem in *Punch*, she told him, a poem that she disliked except for the lines she quoted.

"Thank you for your extraordinary kindness in being at such pains to illuminate, in every musty coign, my obscure understanding," Thayer answered. "Sometimes your quotations are not only the best, or not only improvements upon the best, but suggest an opposite, or perhaps I should say converse, meaning to that intended by the author, and these points of yours are the best of all!"

Moore had been using quotations in her poetry since college, and she had been using them in the ironic way Thayer describes since soon after her 1915 trip to New York. By the 1920s, both Eliot and Pound had begun to appropriate quotations into their poems, too. But whereas their quotations invoke the authority of the past and erudite readers may congratulate themselves upon recognizing them, Moore's quotations undercut both authority and erudition. She seizes phrases from the verbal ephemera of modern life—articles from *Vogue* and *Scientific American*, a newspaper advertisement, a remark overheard at the circus, a slogan on a statue in Central Park—much as contemporary artists pasted pieces of newspaper onto their canvases.

She does not expect her readers to recognize the quotations, as Thayer assumed he should do, but to open their minds to unexpected sources of poetry. Anonymous lines from *Punch* thus assume the aura of serious literary allusions. Descriptions of the sea come from a seventeenth-century religious treatise. The source notes enhance the wit and irony of Moore's quotations and also show her imagination at work with the "real toads" of her environment.

Marianne sent Thayer "An Octopus," her poem about Mount Rainier, two weeks after she sent him "Sea Unicorns and Land Unicorns." He sent her $140 and another appreciative letter. She was relieved that he liked it, she said, because she feared that her "laboriousness" had obscured "the resplendence of the material." "I should not have been in the least surprised to have you say it was in no way suited to a magazine and even a little heavy for a book of short poems."

"Marriage" and "An Octopus" are Moore's longest poems: "Marriage" has more lines, "An Octopus" more words. Both resemble *The Waste Land* and subsequent examples of the modernist long poem, such as Pound's *Cantos* and Williams's *Paterson*, in their resistance to narrative, their use of free verse, and their dense assemblage of quotations. "An Octopus" also overtly responds to *The Waste Land* with its use of landscape, its juxtaposition of modernity and antiquity, and the large questions it addresses about culture and knowledge. Not only does Moore's far-from-wasted landscape teem with flora, fauna, and glacier-fed streams, but she also presents American pragmatism—or experience—as an alternative to what she considered the "macabre" failure of imagination in Eliot's poem.

Moore's choice of subject, a mythic mountain, as well as the poem's length suggest the magnitude of her ambitions. Her Mount Takoma, or Big Snow Mountain, joins company with other literary mountains such as Homer's Olympus, Dante's Mount Purgatory, Milton's Eden, Bunyan's Mount Zion, and Shelley's Mont Blanc. But in contrast to these divine peaks, dimly glimpsed or imagined from below, Moore introduces us to her mountain from above: "An Octopus // of ice."

Like experience itself, "An Octopus" continually undercuts the reader's expectations. The title leads the reader to expect a poem about a slippery cephalopod but soon reveals the octopus to be a two-dimensional map of an eight-armed glacier system. The glacier system itself is "deceptively reserved and flat." Contrary to its solid and glassy appearance, the glacier is "creeping slowly as with meditated stealth" "beneath a sea of shifting snow dunes." Its arms "misleadingly like lace" can kill prey "with the concentric crushing rigour of the python." To experience this wilderness is to subject oneself to uncertainty: "Completing a circle, / you have been deceived into thinking you have progressed."

Moore's landscape is unabashedly America itself. The fir trees are "austere specimens of our American royal families." Windswept trees find "strength in union," and regulations of the National Park Service, quoted amply in the poem, protect the diversity and freedom of the park's denizens. "An Octopus" juxtaposes the disorienting experience of the American wilderness with the plethora of maps, regulations, and guidebooks that shape this experience for park visitors. A lake "in the shape of the left human foot, / . . . prejudices you in favour of itself / before you have had time to see the others." Even the octopus comes from a National Park Service publication, which calls the glacier system "an enormous frozen octopus stretching icy tentacles down upon every side."

Whereas mountains often symbolize divine truth in literature and myth, in Moore's poem the all-important central peak is missing: "an explosion blew it off." (Mount Rainier is a volcano.) "An Octopus" does not mourn the loss of unifying truth as *The Waste Land* does but instead celebrates American pluralism, a close cousin of William James's pragmatism. The pluralist understands that truth is various and the pragmatist that it is tentative. The pragmatist gains knowledge not by explaining the universe with a single belief system but by seeking exceptions to one's beliefs and keeping an open mind. As in science, experience expands knowledge without ever revealing truth in its entirety. "An Octopus" presents an American Eden in which "liberty and union" easily coexist: "Maintaining many minds . . . Big Snow Mountain is the home of a diversity of creatures."

About two-thirds of the way through the poem, Moore unsettles her reader yet again by shifting attention away from the landscape to the ancient Greeks, whom she compares to "happy souls in hell."

Unlike Eliot and Pound, who superimpose the myths of antiquity upon the disorder of modern life, Moore presents the rationality of ancient Greece as a foil to American pragmatism. At least since 1914, when Marianne studied Hebrew poetry with Reverend Kellogg, she had viewed the Greeks as overly cerebral in contrast to the more spiritual and passionate Hebrews. She claims in "An Octopus" that the Greeks' "hearts were hard" and "their wisdom was remote." Whereas the Greeks assigned a rational definition to happiness—"an accident or a quality, / a spiritual substance or the soul itself, / an act, a disposition, or a habit"—Americans actually experience "what we clumsily call happiness."

The syntax of lines 208–209 rather than their placement within the poem alerts the reader to the poem's most concise thematic statement:

> Relentless accuracy is the nature of this octopus
> with its capacity for fact.

Opposed to the Greeks' intellectual detachment is Americans' relentless, hands-on accuracy. "Relentless accuracy" demands an open mind, tolerance for individual differences, and the "love of doing hard things." Mount Rainier may be "damned for its sacrosanct remoteness," and Henry James, one of America's least rustic products, may be "damned by the public for decorum." But "relentless accuracy" will discover that James's "decorum" is actually "restraint" and that the word *tree* may include wind-stunted survivors whose "flattened mats of branches" grow "flat on the ground like vines."

The "love of doing hard things" is not simply "enjoying mental difficulties" for their own sake, like the ancient Greeks did. For as much as Americans relentlessly pursue fact, they can also be "happy seeing nothing." Americans respect "what could not be clearly seen" and "complexities which still will be complexities / as long as the world lasts." "Relentless accuracy" is required of the poet, the critic, the scientist, and the citizen. It is Moore's democratic imperative.

R. P. Blackmur underestimated Moore's ambition when he called her "a poet bristling with notable facts" who, "content with smallness," never attempts to write major poems. Despite her fondness for understatement and her attraction to the peripheral, Moore addresses large questions of epistemology and national identity in "An Octopus." The next generation of poets—notably, Elizabeth Bishop and John Ashbery—would more fully appreciate this poem about the national construction of the landscape than did modernists such as Blackmur. Until Ashbery pronounced "An Octopus" the greatest of Moore's poems in 1967, it received little critical attention. Marianne considered eliminating the long passage about the Greeks and Henry James when she assembled her *Selected Poems* in 1935. The young poet T. C. Wilson persuaded her not to; Sibley Watson and T. S. Eliot concurred. Today Moore's most astute readers generally agree with Ashbery about the poem's importance.

After sending off "An Octopus," Marianne spent another month assembling *Observations*, which included fifty-three poems, more than double the number in *Poems*. She made at least minor revisions to nearly all of them and revised some substantially. Generally the revisions make the syntax smoother and more concise. In "Critics and Connoisseurs" she changed "A determination ditto to make a pup / Eat his meat on the plate" to "similar determination to make a pup / eat his meat on the plate." When omissions disrupted the syllabic pattern of the stanza, she did not repair the symmetry. In addition to the three poems—"Silence," "Sea Unicorns and Land Unicorns," and "An Octopus"—that appeared in consecutive issues of *The Dial* just before *Observations* came out, she also included five unpublished poems first drafted between 1915 and 1919: "An Egyptian Pulled Glass Bottle in the Shape of a Fish," "To a Snail," "The Bricks Are Fallen Down . . . ," "Nothing Will Cure the Sick Lion but to Eat an Ape," and "Peter."

After reading Marianne's sources for "Sea Unicorns," Thayer suggested that she include them in *Observations*. She then decided to include citations for all of her poems. Since she had not previously kept records of her sources, locating them required considerable research through her own notebooks and books; she could not find them all. Not only do the citations emphasize the wit and irony of her quotations, but they also engage the reader in her process of composition. The poems thus become a "self-portrait of a mind," as Glenway Wescott observed, "to be appreciated not as . . . beauty, but as an experience."

Marianne had realized as soon as she saw the contents of *Poems* that Harriet Monroe would take offense at the omission of the poems *Poetry* had published in 1915, since Monroe regarded those five poems as Moore's best work. *Observations* opens with two of them: "To an Intra Mural Rat" and "Reticence and Volubility." Monroe acknowledged the gesture by allowing Yvor Winters to review the book for *Poetry*. The remaining poems are arranged in rough chronological order, showing Moore's progression from short, cryptic conversational verses to the more ambitious poems of the late 1910s and early 1920s.

Marianne delivered her book to Lincoln MacVeagh a week earlier than promised, on October 23. Thayer insisted that it come out before Christmas. "It can be done," MacVeagh wrote him, "barring strikes and other acts of God. Under ordinary circumstances of course I would not undertake a new manuscript for this year's publication at so late a date . . . But Miss Moore's book is of course a proposition quite out of the ordinary from several points of view." Marianne had no knowledge at the time of the exceptional treatment her book received nor that MacVeagh had little taste himself for her poetry. *Observations* appeared in bookstores on December 27, 1924. MacVeagh suffered a nervous breakdown early in the new year, and Cummings teased Marianne that her book had caused it.

The Dial Award—Marianne always insisted that it was an "award," not a prize for a competition—was designed to help a writer who would benefit from the financial support: $2,000 out of Watson's and Thayer's own pockets. It was announced each year in the January *Dial*. At a party given for Sherwood Anderson, the recipient of the first award, Anderson told Marianne that he had expected her to win instead of himself. Just after *The Dial* published *The Waste Land*, Eliot was announced as the second recipient. Before the third recipient, Van Wyck Brooks, was announced in January 1924, Glenway Wescott told Marianne that "bets are going all the time at the Algonquin . . . You and Cummings are the favorites."

Thayer and Watson's surviving correspondence gives no evidence that they considered giving Marianne the award earlier, but as soon as she agreed to the publication of *Observations*, it was understood between them that Marianne would receive the fourth Dial Award. She learned of it in November, just after *Observations* had gone to press. Thayer sent her a draft of his Announcement. "Dare I permit you to assume such championship?" she answered.

Thayer wanted a review of *Observations* to appear in the January number along with his Announcement, and he wanted Watson to write it. Thayer would address "the practical and moral aspects of the case," he told Watson, "leaving the aesthetic criticism to you." But Watson, who rarely wrote for *The Dial*, would not commit himself. He suggested that Thayer ask "some reliable person" to write the notice and said that he might write "an accessory review" if he felt so moved. He recommended "with hesitation" Glenway Wescott as a possible reviewer and "with still more hesitation . . . [Malcolm] Cowley—noo no!" Thayer answered that he had already determined that "Mr. Wescott was the only alternative" to Watson himself.

Thayer managed to extract from Marianne a new poem, "The Monkey Puzzler," just as the January *Dial* was going to press. "It *must* go into the January number," he told the staff, "which by the by is going to be more a Moore number than any other January number has been an Anderson or an Eliot or a Brooks number. And this is, at last, as it should be. Do not, however, forget that Miss Moore does not herself know what she is in for." In addition to the new poem, Wescott's review, and Thayer's Announcement proclaiming the recipient to be "so incomparably, since the death of Emily Dickinson, America's most distinguished poetess," the whole section of unsigned Briefer Mention reviews, eleven altogether, consisted of those written by the honoree.

Marianne wrote immediately upon receiving the January number to express her gratitude for "the beauty of Mr. Wescott's article," for "Mr. Thayer's brilliant antitheses and criticism," and for the "entirely personal pleasure [of the Briefer Mention section], known only to yourselves and me."

The advance copy of *Observations* that she saw at the same time disappointed her. She objected to "the Renaissance tombstones and horns of plenty" that adorned the title page and table of contents and was dismayed by the typographical errors. But by the time the book came out, Marianne had little energy to fret over such things. "For a week I have done nothing but try to keep Mother alive," she told

Bryher. "She has been acutely ill and now, though she improves, I am in constant confusion." Marianne stayed home with Mary for the next month.

The announcement of the Dial Award did boost sales of *Observations*, as Thayer had intended. By March Marianne was preparing a second edition. The most notable changes are the removal of the Renaissance flourishes, a radically shortened and revised "Poetry," and the addition of "The Monkey Puzzler."

Reviews of *Observations*, like those of *Poems*, assumed that Moore's poetry would appeal only to the most discriminating readers, to the "Imaginative Individual," as Thayer put it, rather than the "Reading Public." Thayer assured *Dial* readers that Eliot's ranking of Moore "among the half-dozen most 'exciting' contemporary European and American poets" was "the consensus of those qualified to judge." Arguing implicitly with Harriet Monroe's attack on *Poems*, Yvor Winters pointed out Moore's "mastery of phrase and cadence," and Glenway Wescott noted the "passages of pure poetry," in which "each word conveys an emotion as clearly as if it were a colour."

The review that did most to promote the book occupied nearly a full page of *The New York Times Book Review*. Thayer almost certainly pulled strings to secure a sympathetic reviewer, Herbert S. Gorman, and arranged for the newspaper photograph that allowed readers for the first time to put a face with the poems. Although her audience was likely to remain small, wrote Gorman, it had "long since overgrown the limitations of a coterie." He commended *The Dial* for broadening that audience: "Certainly no one who possesses a quick interest in contemporary American poetry can afford to remain in ignorance of her sharp, intellectually compact, aristocratic work."

The photograph had as much impact as the review itself. In the previous century, Napoleon Sarony had more or less invented the art of celebrity photography. He created public personae for writers such as Mark Twain and Oscar Wilde as well as many a Broadway star. Though Sarony was long dead, Sarony Studio was enlisted to take the promotional photograph. The portrait shows the seated poet gazing boldly into the camera, her posture erect. Her dark suit and projected left elbow give her body something of a mountainous solidity, which is offset by the softness of her blouse. Her right hand clutches a pair of white gloves in her lap, and her open but carefully arranged left hand draws the eye from her face to her long, delicately tapered fingers. Unlike contemporary photographs of H.D., Edna St. Vincent Millay, and Mina Loy, there is nothing coy or glamorous about this poet. She is handsomely, confidently feminine rather than demurely so.

A week after the appearance of the photograph, Marianne went to Marguerite Zorach's studio for the first of several sittings. Zorach at first made some pencil sketches—one would appear in *The Dial*—and eventually painted a large double portrait of Marianne and Mary. Marianne's pose and attire in the painting replicate those in the photograph. Zorach often painted family members but rarely made portraits of persons outside her household. Her choice of Marianne as a subject is thus itself remarkable. She felt keenly the difficulties of a woman artist, and the portrait shows admiration for the robust, brightly lit, and boldly red-haired Marianne. The woman artist does not work alone, the double portrait suggests, and yet the shadowy, pensive mother in the background seems almost a doppelgänger. "Only a person of [Marianne's] intellectual robustness could have survived such a mother," Alyse Gregory once privately observed. Zorach's portrait suggests she shared that view.

At Marianne's first sitting, Isabel Lachaise, a friend of the Zorachs and the wife of sculptor Gaston Lachaise, asked Marianne if her husband could make a bust of her. Because of Thayer's Harvard friendship with Edward Nagle, Isabel's son by a previous marriage, the Lachaises had close ties to *The Dial*. Marianne sat for Lachaise several times per week over the next two months.

Lachaise had already made a bust of Thayer and would later do Watson and other *Dial* personalities. Yet Thayer expressed surprise when he learned that Marianne would sit for Lachaise. "I know why he thinks that," Lachaise said, "because you are thin." "In sculpture it does not matter what you weigh. We will show them? What interests me is the spirit." Lachaise's favorite subject throughout his career was Isabel's ample nude body. She was ten years older than he and continued to model for him well into her fifties. Lachaise's nudes did not, in Marianne's view, degrade women. "Very elegant and demure" is how she described the first one she saw.

What chiefly impressed Marianne during her sittings was watching

Lachaise work. His "stubbornness and naturalness were a work of art above even the most important sculpture," she recalled. In 1935 Lachaise's friend and patron, Lincoln Kirstein, had the plaster bust cast in bronze. Isabel Lachaise gave the bust to Marianne in 1947. It stood in a corner of her living room until 1959, when Marianne asked Kirstein to present it to the Metropolitan Museum of Art.

A regular feature of the Thayer/Watson *Dial* was the unsigned editorial Comment that concluded each issue. Topics varied from month to month and often took a position against editors of other magazines. The Comments that Thayer wrote for February, March, and April, following his Announcement of Moore's winning the Dial Award in January, reveal the intensity and near obsession with which he tried to catapult Moore's career. He wished "to keep alight, anyhow through these glum winter months, our beacon for Miss Marianne Moore," he wrote in February. Taking issue with Harriet Monroe's earlier accusations that Moore held too tight a rein on her Pegasus, he defended Moore's intellect as "part and parcel of the body. An intellect which smells the May. An intellect capable of seduction."

Thayer pursued the seduction theme in his March and April Comments, neither of which could have made much sense to anyone but Moore herself. Thayer understood "Sea Unicorns and Land Unicorns" to be a conciliatory coda to the feud Moore had initiated with "Marriage." He had already repaid her for Ulysses' unsheathed sword by placing a sculpture of a swordsman between pages two and three of "Sea Unicorns and Land Unicorns" in *The Dial*. He understood "the lion civilly rampant" in the poem to be himself (like the lions from Defoe and Amos) and the unicorn to be Moore.

Both the March and April Comments address Moore's sources for "Sea Unicorns and Land Unicorns" as cited in the back of *Observations*. The March one questions the poet's reliance upon the unscientific belief that unicorns can be captured only by virgins. While repeatedly reminding the reader of Moore's "youth and sex," Thayer chides her for concealing the true means by which she might be seduced and captured. The April one argues with the logic of a sixteenth-century explorer who deduced the presence of unicorns from the presence of lions in Florida. Marianne took the two Comments to be "friendly raillery."

Like "An Octopus," "Sea Unicorns and Land Unicorns" begins with a map, and like both "Marriage" and "An Octopus," it addresses the dilemma of unity and difference. Alluding to the lion and unicorn in the United Kingdom coat of arms, it takes this dilemma beyond the family and beyond America to the world of nations.

> Thus personalities by nature much opposed,
> can be combined in such a way
> that when they do agree, their unanimity is great,
> "in politics, in trade, law, sport, religion,
> china-collecting, tennis, and church going."

In contrast to "An Octopus," which exists in the realm of sensory facts, "Sea Unicorns" deals with "facts" of the imagination, such as the existence of unicorns: "Upon the printed page, / also by word of mouth, / we have a record of it all." Its personal message to Thayer is that while lions and unicorns may overcome their natural enmity, the unicorn can be "tamed only by a lady inoffensive like itself," that is, only by a woman. The reference to "Virgin-Mary blue" suggests the particular woman who can tame her, her mother.

Any injustice done by the obscurity of Thayer's March and April Comments was rectified by the appearance in the May *Dial* of Williams's revision of his *Poems* review. Rather than setting Moore apart from other poets, as most reviewers did, he presented her as a paradigm for the new in poetry. Even readers who are told that "Everything is worthless but the best and this is the best" are bewildered by her poems, he acknowledged, because their "whole preconceived scheme of values has been ruined." Moore exemplifies the modernist attempt to "separate the poetry from the subject entirely." And while he applauded her failure to make the separation complete, he repeatedly praised the white clarity that results from the endeavor. "With Miss Moore a word is a word most when it is separated out by science, treated with acid to remove the smudges, washed, dried, and placed right side up on a clean surface." "This is new!" he said finally. "The quality is not new, but the freedom is new, the unbridled leap."

•

Just after Marianne agreed to let *Observations* be published, Alyse
Gregory asked Thayer to accept her resignation as managing editor.
Because of Llewellyn Powys's tuberculosis, they planned to remain at
their summer retreat in upstate New York during the fall rather than
return to Manhattan. She asked Thayer to convince Marianne to take
her place and hoped that his doing so would not interfere with his
plans for the Dial Award. Marianne was deeply engaged at the time
preparing *Observations* for publication. And so Thayer persuaded
Gregory to fulfill as many of her duties as she could long-distance and
come to New York one week each month. Gregory agreed to the arrangement and served as managing editor in this capacity for the rest
of 1924 until Powys insisted that she give up *The Dial* completely and
move with him to England.

At *The Dial*'s makeup meeting on February 28, 1925, Thayer dramatically and abruptly named Marianne as Gregory's successor. The
next day Marianne wrote him a letter of refusal. Despite her loyalty to
The Dial, she said, she could not physically assume the duties of the
job. She refused in part because of Thayer's manner but mostly because of her mother. Mary had long believed her daughter too frail for
full-time work. Marianne fell sick for three days after the meeting,
and Mary blamed Thayer for it.

Thayer immediately revised his offer. Marianne could work part-
time, he promised, and not have to meet people. She would work
mornings only, earning fifty dollars per week, and her title would be
acting editor. The conditions mollified her mother, and she accepted.
She began work officially on April 27, 1925. The May *Dial* was out
and the June number largely assembled. Her name would first appear
on the masthead in July.

16

Picking and Choosing

1925–1929

Marianne saw more promise in Hart Crane's poetry than other *Dial* editors did. Though she did not like some of his comrades, Matthew Josephson among them, she liked Crane. He was one of the young writers she tried to encourage. *The Dial* had launched Crane's career in 1920 by publishing "My Grandmother's Love Letters" but over the next five years accepted only two more poems despite his continual submissions. "We could not but be moved, as you must know, by the rich imagination and the sensibility in your poem, 'Passage,'" Marianne wrote him about the first poem he sent her. "Its multiform content accounts I suppose, for what seems to us a lack of simplicity and cumulative force." The careful phrasing typifies her rejection letters. Having received countless impersonal rejections during her own apprenticeship, she wanted to show every writer whose work she rejected that she had considered its merits. She believed that unknown writers deserved the same consideration that famous ones did.

Desperate for money, Crane went to *The Dial* during the first year of Marianne's editorship to meet assistant editor Kenneth Burke for lunch and to ask her for reviewing assignments. She said no and candidly explained why. But she expressed sympathy for his plight and inquired about his poetry. Later that afternoon he sent her "The Wine

Menagerie," which she decided to accept with "certain changes." Those changes included cutting nearly two-thirds of the poem and changing the title to "Again." Regularizing the syntax of the remaining eighteen lines, she brought Crane's Dionysian delirium into the bright light of day. The result was, as Burke quipped, the menagerie without the wine. It is hard to imagine two poets more different than Moore and Crane. Moore valued precision and craft; Crane evoked half-conscious myths and moods. Marianne did not underestimate what she had done. "It is so much our wish not to distort or to interfere with an author's concept," she wrote him, "that we had thought to take no liberty and to relinquish the poem; we feel, however, that you may concur with us in the changes we suggest." Crane answered that he admired "the sensibility and skill of your arrangement" and that he agreed that the revision "contains the essential elements of the original." He immediately and "gratefully" accepted her conditions and the twenty dollars she sent him.

The publication of Crane's letters in 1952 revealed to the world his private anxieties over the situation. Anticipating outright rejection of the poem, he called Moore "the Rt. Rev. Miss Mountjoy" and a "hysterical virgin." The epithets proved memorable. Never mind his genuine pleasure, revealed in a later letter, over the poem's acceptance. He did complain to friends about the liberties Moore took, and Matthew Josephson offered to buy the poem from *The Dial*. But Crane refused to withdraw it despite months of opportunity in which to do so.

The next time he sent a poem to *The Dial*, he made it clear that he was unwilling to accept changes. Marianne respected that wish as he continued to send her new work. Although she rejected much of it (Sibley Watson and Kenneth Burke did, too, in her absence), she accepted altogether six poems, among them "To Brooklyn Bridge," which she quoted years later in her own poem about the bridge, and the four-page "Powhatan's Daughter," which she nevertheless thought "vapid and pretentious." When Crane's *White Buildings* came to *The Dial* for review, Marianne read it carefully and tried to choose a reviewer who would not be "denunciatory."

.

Thayer, like many others, hoped that Marianne's part-time arrangement with *The Dial* would allow her as much time to write as her library job had. Alyse Gregory said it would be an "irreparable loss" if Marianne's new duties interfered with her own writing. But Marianne offered her admirers no reassurances. She never mentioned her own writing when she reluctantly accepted the position nor when she even more reluctantly gave it up four years later. "I am busy to distraction," she told Bryher after the first two months, "but enjoy the work. Every part of it is in accord with my inclination." The work is "enthralling," she said a few months later, but it is also "my entire life, for I have allowed myself to be swallowed up in it."

Marianne worked at the office six days a week, from nine until two, reading manuscripts and meeting with the staff. At lunch she would regale Mary with the events of the morning. Then she—and often Mary—worked until bedtime writing letters. Readers of *The Dial* would have been shocked to learn the extent of Mary's involvement in the daily workings of the magazine. Her primary task was drafting letters. Most were routine, but since it was for Marianne a matter of principle that strangers be treated as courteously as friends, she spent an inordinate amount of time, with Mary's assistance, selecting the precise words and the precise tone to take with each correspondent. In some cases Mary drafted more personal letters, including those to aspiring writers whom Marianne offered to assist. There even survive several drafts in Mary's hand of long, personal letters to George Saintsbury, the octogenarian critic whom Marianne had recruited as a contributor. These drafts show a few changes in Marianne's hand but not many. Mary also edited manuscripts, especially those that required cutting.

For her first few months as acting editor, Marianne worked out of Thayer's office. But after Thayer returned for two weeks in July and dramatically repossessed it, she moved across the hall into the office that was already shared by the assistant editor and a secretary. Thayer's office remained empty until *The Dial* ceased publication in July 1929. At the end of 1926, Marianne moved her small wooden desk to the third floor, the former dining room, which became in family parlance Rat's "Palm Tree."

"The Palm Tree's the thing," Mary wrote Warner in 1927. "I doubt that there's any rat in the world that so affectionates its Tree. It pores over its 'pieces,' it 'wonders?' it *b'lieves* it's got something that with 'fixing' will 'do'! Very jubilant. Then it writes; tick-tacks; sends to 'doctor' [Sibley Watson]; sends to the author;—sends to press; reads and re-reads in proof; alters; sends to author; then when the mag. is out? O me! every ad and paragraph is scrutinized and read. It is held off and held near. It is now an exaltation—now a depth of endless descent into woe and disgrace. Were *The Dial* a human creature it would be honored in having such unending solicitude bestowed upon it."

Marianne's part-time status and pay never changed. She wrote many more Briefer Mentions than previous editors had but received no payment for them nor for the longer reviews she wrote. She worked more than full-time hours throughout her tenure at *The Dial.* "I so firmly believe in my work, that I have not the faintest doubt that in time I shall master entirely the hitches and holdups that so far take up forty-eight hours," she told Bryher after a year and a half. "Former editors had leisure for their friends, for books and galleries, the theatre, and so on, so I know that some day I shall."

For the first two years, Warner commuted from Brooklyn for lunch every day. And Henry McBride, *The Dial*'s art critic, occasionally called at St. Luke's Place. But few others did. Thayer gave up his apartment as soon as Marianne took over as acting editor and moved to his summer home in Edgartown, Massachusetts. Glenway Wescott and Monroe Wheeler lived in Europe throughout Marianne's tenure at *The Dial.* She attended literary parties only occasionally. Unlike Thayer, who enjoyed entertaining members of the literati, Marianne shied away from such encounters.

Since Sunday was the one day Marianne could sleep late, she and Mary did not regularly attend church. Sometimes Marianne went to the office on Sunday afternoons. She never missed the circus, however, and later on went to movies, especially documentaries of natural history and ethnography. Marianne and Mary vacationed in Maine the first two summers of her editorship, first at Biddeford Pool and then at New Harbor. Marianne read manuscripts by the sea and kept up a daily correspondence with the staff about *Dial* matters. In 1928 she and Mary went to Virginia for a week to see Warner.

In the summer of 1927 Marianne and Mary spent two months in Britain, intending to see, as they had in 1911, "ruins and museums, bookstalls, zoos, and authors' birthplaces" rather than living writers. Marianne had made arrangements to call on George Saintsbury in Bath and Alyse Gregory on the Dorset coast but no one else (Bryher was in Switzerland). Marianne did conduct a little business in London by restoring good relations with Raymond Mortimer, a *Dial* contributor whom Thayer had insulted. But she did not call on T. S. Eliot, whose office was only a few blocks from their Bloomsbury hotel. She told Eliot afterward that "many unjustifiable calls are made by visiting Americans" and that she had to resist "the impulse to add to them another."

Warner was just beginning three years of ship duty in Europe, and he took off ten days to tour London, the Lake District, and Scotland with his mother and sister. The final destination of the trip was the former coastguard cottage in Dorset where Alyse Gregory and Llewellyn Powys now lived. Marianne called the house itself "the embodiment of poetic scholarly seclusion" and their visit to the Powyses "a thing we shall never forget; and want not to forget." Upon her return to New York, Marianne received a warm welcome at the office and was "in a caper of satisfaction," according to Mary, "over his food, his *'beautiful home' his Dial oh his Dial!*"

Marianne Moore was at the height of her creative powers when she took over *The Dial*. She had written many of her finest poems during the 1920s, and the Dial Award had brought her international recognition. But for seven years after the publication of "The Monkey Puzzler," she published no new poems. Why, her admirers have wondered ever since, would she give up poetry for the sake of *The Dial*?

It was not for the glory of it. "I know well that no one who has held the position before has enjoyed the plaudits of the many or kept any but his or her closest friends," she wrote soon after she started. Although she did occasionally enjoy the plaudits of Thayer, Watson, and a few others, criticism arrived steadily from both private and public quarters. "God, how I hate you," wrote Maxwell Bodenheim, "and

your mean, unfair, half-blind, apprehensively arbitrary, literary group."
She was willing to be "hated" by certain writers, she said, because she
wanted *The Dial* "respected" above all else.

Moore's modernistic aesthetics, as expressed in her poetry and
prose of the 1920s, suggest that editing *The Dial* was a fulfillment of
her principles rather than an abandonment of them. Nothing she ever
did was more gratifying to her. *The Dial* was for her "an aesthetic Gibraltar" where "the elsewhere defrauded reader finds . . . a fearlessness
which both assails and saves him." She took pride in discovering aesthetic excellence where the reader would least expect it, just as she did
in her poetry. Asked in later years about her editorial policy, she said
that she looked for "individuality" and "intensity."

The editor of the *Tipyn o'Bob* held a position of eminence at Bryn
Mawr, and Marianne had witnessed there how an editor could help or
hinder burgeoning talent. When she met Alfred Stieglitz in 1915, she
encountered an artist who was not only a photographer but also a
magazine editor and a gallery curator. Refusing to privilege any of
these arts over the others, she later described 291 as "a kind of eagle's
perch of selectiveness." All three roles demonstrate Stieglitz's arduous
"advertising." Advertising, according to one of her *Dial* Comments, is
the "art of educating visualization."

Whereas earlier art photographers had tried to make their work
resemble paintings by posing their subjects and manipulating their
negatives, Stieglitz and his followers emphasized the art of selection.
They chose compositions with their viewfinders and chose the precise
moment to snap the shutter. Other European and American modernists simultaneously adopted the selection aesthetic by turning collage
into fine art. Duchamp's readymades took the principle to an extreme: an artist could choose a piece of plumbing from a hardware
store, title it, sign it, and call it art. Modernism as Marianne encountered it in New York galleries was very much an art of selection.
Editing for her was as much an act of "picking and choosing" as writing was.

Marianne often chose exhibitions, anthologies, and published series as subjects for the unsigned Comment that concluded each issue
of *The Dial*. She writes most directly about her aesthetic of selection in
the one that begins:

Academic feeling, or prejudice possibly, in favor of continuity and completeness is opposed to miscellany—to music programs, composite picture exhibitions, newspapers, magazines, and anthologies. Any zoo, aquarium, library, garden, or volume of letters, however, is an anthology and certain of these selected findings are highly satisfactory. The science of assorting and the art of investing an assortment with dignity are obviously not being neglected, as is manifest in "exhibitions and sales of artistic property," and in that sometimes disparaged, most powerful phase of the anthology, the museum.

It concludes: "However expressive the content of an anthology, one notes that a yet more distinct unity is afforded in the unintentional portrait given, of the mind which brought the assembled integers together." Moore thus invites readers to regard *The Dial* itself as an assemblage of "selected findings" and as "an unintentional portrait" of its artist/editor.

If the monthly Comments are not quite prose poems, they are surely "observations." Moore abandons the combative tone taken by previous editors. Besides commenting on current events in the arts and eulogizing the deaths of Amy Lowell, Thomas Hardy, and Ellen Terry, she also points out the potential for art in such unlikely places as advertisements, travel guides, maps, typography, handwriting, and folk dancing. Generally she wrote the Comment two months ahead of time, she spent at least a week rewriting and revising it, and in the final stage she would engage Mary's assistance with the dictionary "to get just the right and ticklish word."

The most trying aspect of Marianne's job was maintaining her loyalty to Thayer while at the same time protecting the magazine and its staff from his delusions. He had once, to fool Alyse Gregory, submitted his own writing under a false name, and as soon as Marianne began her duties, he became convinced that Eleanor Parker, his former personal secretary, and Elise DePollier, *The Dial*'s current secretary, were doing the same thing. When Marianne gently broached the matter with DePollier and offered to help with her writing, to Marianne's intense dismay DePollier resigned.

Shortly thereafter Kenneth Burke became the object of Thayer's fears. A decade younger than Marianne, Burke became assistant editor the same week that she became acting editor. He had been a regular contributor since 1920 and during much of 1923 had served as managing editor while Thayer was abroad. From the beginning, Burke and Marianne enjoyed working together. She appreciated his unassuming manner, his wit, and his resourcefulness. He appreciated what he aptly called her "ingenuity and scrupulosity."

Thayer believed that Burke had dishonorably obtained some letters that he intended to use against Thayer. But no one who had worked with Burke could believe there was any truth to the accusation. When Thayer insisted that Burke be dismissed, Marianne threatened to resign. Watson dissuaded her. "Your resignation from *The Dial* would, I think be exactly as serious to [Thayer] (and to me) as closing up entirely," he wrote. Burke chose to leave rather than continue to work under such conditions.

Thayer hired his cousin to take Burke's place. Marianne had liked Ellen Thayer at Bryn Mawr and never doubted her good intentions, but Ellen's incompetence exasperated her. As Marianne and Mary assumed more and more of Ellen's responsibilities, Ellen was left with little to do except further annoy her boss by seeking her attention.

Just after Burke resigned, Thayer asked Marianne to fire three more employees. She refused. She felt compassion for his illness but would not let innocent people suffer the consequences. "I cannot bear the thought that you should be regarded as a monster," she told him. All three women kept their jobs, and through Marianne's influence the Dial Press employed Burke to do some translating. She always chose him to fill in while she was on vacation and eventually made him *The Dial*'s music critic. As Marianne reached the end of her first year, Thayer no longer insisted upon firing people, but he told Watson that he wished to resign as editor. Although Marianne persuaded him to allow his name to remain on the masthead as adviser, she could not dissuade him from writing in the June 1926 issue that he was "happy" to announce his resignation as he announced the change in Miss Moore's status from acting editor to editor.

Before Thayer turned *The Dial* over to Marianne, it was agreed that at least one of his poems would appear in each issue. She pub-

The poet's mother, Mary Warner, and grandfather, John Riddle Warner, c. 1878 (Rosenbach Museum & Library, Philadelphia)

John Milton Moore, the father whom Marianne Moore never knew, c. 1883 (Moore Family Collection)

Marianne Moore at seventeen months with her brother, John Warner Moore, nearly three, 1889 (Rosenbach Museum & Library, Philadelphia)

Mary Warner Moore and her two children, c. 1891 (Rosenbach Museum & Library, Philadelphia)

Marianne and her brother with Rex, the
Shoemakers' Skye terrier, c. 1898 (Rosenbach Museum & Library, Philadelphia)

343 North Hanover Street, the Moores'
home in Carlisle, Pennsylvania (Rosenbach Museum & Library, Philadelphia)

Marianne, Mary Norcross, and Mary Warner Moore near Monhegan Island,
Maine, c. 1904 (Rosenbach Museum & Library, Philadelphia)

"Don't think I have melancholia, hydrophobia, or distemper when you see the proofs," the Bryn Mawr freshman wrote to her mother, 1905. (Rosenbach Museum & Library, Philadelphia)

Mary Norcross, mentor and confidante to the homesick freshman (Moore Family Collection)

Peggy James, whom Marianne cared about "like all wild Wales" in her junior year, 1906 (Houghton Library, Harvard University)

Marianne as a senior—"a perfect corker," according to one professor, 1909 (Rosenbach Museum & Library, Philadelphia)

Mary Warner Moore at home in Carlisle—drawn to write letters, she said, like a "drunkard to his bottle" (Rosenbach Museum & Library, Philadelphia)

Marianne with Hall and Ruth Cowdrey, embarking on their 1915 trip to New York—the poet's "Sojourn in the Whale" (Rosenbach Museum & Library, Philadelphia)

Marianne with the photographer's pony in Greenwich Village, early 1920s (Rosenbach Museum & Library, Philadelphia)

John Warner Moore and Constance Eustis Moore with Mary Markwick Moore, the first of their four children, 1919 (Rosenbach Museum & Library, Philadelphia)

Bryher, friend and patron who defied Marianne's wishes by publishing her first book of poems, 1920 (Yale Collection of American Literature, Beinecke Rare Book and Manuscript Library)

MANIKIN
NUMBER THREE

MARIANNE MOORE

Scofield Thayer, editor and co-owner of *The Dial*, whose proposal of marriage to Marianne infuriated her, c. 1921 (Yale Collection of American Literature, Beinecke Rare Book and Manuscript Library)

Manikin 3, containing "Marriage," published by Monroe Wheeler and secretly financed by Bryher, 1923 (Yale Collection of American Literature, Beinecke Rare Book and Manuscript Library)

Monroe Wheeler and Glenway
Wescott, lifelong friends of Marianne
and her mother, 1927. (Photograph by
George Platt Lynes, © Estate of George Platt
Lynes. Collection of Anatole Pohorilenko)

Marianne and her mother,
1924 (Rosenbach Museum &
Library, Philadelphia)

Publicity portrait for *Observations* and the Dial Award, 1924 (Photograph by Sarony Studio. Rosenbach Museum & Library, Philadelphia)

Marianne and her mother at home, 1932 (Photograph by Morton D. Zabel. Rosenbach Museum & Library, Philadelphia)

Marianne's protégée Elizabeth Bishop with their mutual friend Louise Crane (Yale Collection of American Literature, Beinecke Rare Book and Manuscript Library)

Hildegarde Watson, Marianne's adoring friend and patron, 1934 (Photograph by J. Sibley Watson. © Dale T. Davis, Literary Executor, Estate of Dr. James Sibley Watson, Jr. Rosenbach Museum & Library, Philadelphia)

Marianne and her mother a year before Mary's death, in *Vogue*, July 1946 (Photograph by Cecil Beaton, © Condé Nast. Rosenbach Museum & Library, Philadelphia)

Kathrine Jones and Marcia Chamberlain, who became family to Marianne after her mother died, c. 1947 (Rosenbach Museum & Library, Philadelphia)

Alexander Calder, Marianne Moore, Marc Chagall, and Martha Graham at the Museum of Modern Art, September 1943 (Photograph by George Platt Lynes, © Estate of George Platt Lynes. Rosenbach Museum & Library, Philadelphia)

Marianne in her Brooklyn apartment with family heirlooms and Gaston Lachaise bust, May 1953 (Photograph by Esther Bubley, © Jean Bubley)

The only picture in *Life*'s 1953 photo essay about Marianne that she liked (Photograph by Esther Bubley, © Jean Bubley)

Marianne's favorite portrait of herself, wearing her cape and tricorne, November 1953 (Photograph by George Platt Lynes, © Estate of George Platt Lynes. Rosenbach Museum & Library, Philadelphia)

Marianne typing in the small bedroom of her Brooklyn apartment, where she slept and wrote from 1947 until 1965 (Photograph by Basil Langton, © Basil Langton 1965. Rosenbach Museum & Library, Philadelphia)

Marianne at 260 Cumberland Street, Brooklyn, where she lived for thirty-six years (Photograph by Basil Langton, © Basil Langton 1965. Rosenbach Museum & Library, Philadelphia)

Marianne with Gladys Berry, her friend and housekeeper for twenty-five years (Photograph by Basil Langton, © Basil Langton 1965. Rosenbach Museum & Library, Philadelphia)

May is Senior Citizen's Month in New York State.

"Marianne Moore, 'Pulitzer Prize Poet, is one of New York State's most creative, productive, and admired citizens."

NELSON A. ROCKEFELLER
GOVERNOR

For information on services available to the aging in New York State, write:
NEW YORK STATE OFFICE FOR THE AGING
11 No. Pearl Street, Albany, N. Y. • 342 Madison Avenue, New York, N. Y.

Senior Citizen's Month poster, May 1967 (Image courtesy of New York State Office for the Aging. Yale Collection of American Literature, Beinecke Rare Book and Manuscript Library)

Marianne throwing out the first pitch at Yankee Stadium, April 10, 1968 (Photograph by Bob Olen. Rosenbach Museum & Library, Philadelphia)

Marianne and Ezra Pound, the last of their generation, at the New York Public Library, June 5, 1969 (Photograph by Sarah E. Moore, © Sarah E. Moore. Moore Family Collection)

"Everyone loved her." October 14, 1957 (Photograph by Imogen Cunningham, © 1957, 2013 The Imogen Cunningham Trust)

lished twenty-three altogether as long as Thayer was well enough to send them. They contain lines such as "The disarticulated limbs of life," and "O wry / The morning, wry the noon, and wry the eve and night!" In contrast to the high standards Marianne upheld for other poets, she never attempted to edit his work because of aesthetic defects. She did sometimes comment on the poems privately and once sent a long critique, which she hoped he would accept as a tribute. She drew the line, however, at a verse diatribe against Leo Stein, "Leo Arrogans," which among other horrors described cockroaches crawling over Stein's legs. She asked Thayer's permission not to publish it at all. When Thayer refused, she asked that he at least omit two stanzas. When Thayer refused again, she cabled: "Cannot publish 7 and 8. Marianne Moore." She ran the poem with a note that two stanzas were omitted.

Thayer resumed his psychoanalysis with Freud from the late summer of 1925 through the fall of 1926, when Freud dismissed his case as a waste of time. All Thayer needed, Freud told him, was "self-command." Thayer suffered a severe breakdown less than a month after his return to America and, refusing food or drink, remained in the hospital for several months. His death seemed imminent. The doctors diagnosed him with schizophrenia—according to Watson, "the new name for everything not manic depressive." By late January Thayer's life was out of danger, but the doctors advised against any form of excitement. "Why not run The Dial as we think best," Watson wrote Marianne, "giving as much consideration as possible to Scofield's wishes when he cares to express any."

Until that time Watson had commuted to New York from Massachusetts for the monthly makeup meetings. He and Marianne exchanged many letters, and even though he sometimes failed to deliver what he promised to write, Marianne regarded him as "my strong dependence." During the winter of Thayer's hospitalization, however, Watson became interested in making avant-garde films and moved more than three hundred miles away, to Rochester. He came to the office less and less and began answering Marianne's letters with only a brief yes or no penciled in her margins. When he did make an appearance, he was, according to Mary, like "a disembodied spirit."

In November 1928 Thayer's family had him committed to a sanitarium. When he was briefly in New York just before that, Marianne invited him to call at *The Dial* or at St. Luke's Place, but he did not answer her note. He never again wrote to anyone. Marianne saw him twice in 1949 while visiting Edgartown with a friend. "The first time I spoke, he smiled and said, 'Sorry I can't stop' and the other time we were careful not to burden him with what seemed to impose a strain," she said. "He looked well and his manner was exactly characteristic. He seemed to puzzle but I don't believe he recognized me." He lived in Edgartown until his death at ninety-three.

In one of her early Comments, Moore compares the artist with the zoo director: both must "master . . . the art of refusing." Except for Thayer, none of her friends or *Dial* associates received preferential treatment. Yet rejecting the work of friends pained her deeply. "*Who Look on Beauty* is so full of beauty," she wrote Laura Benét, "that even if you hadn't written it I should be unhappy in returning it." Perhaps her most difficult rejection was an unsigned foreword to H.D.'s *Palimpsest* submitted by Bryher. "I tend to be a bad editor," Marianne answered, "for I am innately a nepotist and so keenly feel the disappointment of not publishing sometimes, the work of my friends and notices of books written by my friends." Assuming that Bryher was the author (it was actually McAlmon), Marianne sent it to *Saturday Review*, *Literary Review*, and *The Double Dealer*, but no one took it. She tried to make up for the rejection by devoting part of a Comment to *Close-up*, the film magazine that Bryher started with her second husband, Kenneth Macpherson.

Marianne has not been blamed for one of *The Dial*'s most notable rejections, which transpired shortly before she joined the staff. Ernest Hemingway had sent Alyse Gregory a story about a bullfighter, "The Undefeated." Watson, Thayer, and Gregory could not agree about it. Gregory opposed the subject matter and also opposed Hemingway's treatment of women. Since Thayer had rejected Hemingway twice before, Watson was the story's most likely advocate. Thayer sent it to Marianne. "I have read Mr. Hemingway's story with great interest," she replied. "As it stands, I would say no." She offered no explanation, and Gregory rejected the story without inviting further submissions. Marianne did once attend a party in Hemingway's honor but never solicited his work. He received sufficient recognition, she believed, without *The Dial*'s advocacy.

Eliot submitted a short story by his wife just after Marianne became acting editor. "Your opinion, as you know, is held in the most profound esteem by the editors of *The Dial*," she wrote him, "and we could not be insensible to the resilience and grace of this story; yet, it has not for us, that finality which you feel it to have."

Marianne held no other *Dial* contributor in as much awe as she did Yeats, and no single work published during her tenure gave her as much satisfaction as did "Among Schoolchildren." Yet not even Yeats could meet infallibly with her approval. In February 1926 a sequence of his poems came to *The Dial* through an agent. Marianne liked one of the poems but not the crazy, love-starved "old Madge" character in the others. Watson suggested that since the agent's letter did not mention *The Dial* specifically, Marianne might be justified in returning the poems. When Yeats later inquired about the rejected poems, she assured him of "my unwavering assent to your work since I have known poetry at all" and also of *The Dial*'s "eagerness" to accept "anything that you might send us." She explained that she did not know that Yeats himself had had *The Dial* in mind when the agent sent the poems, but in any case that "we did and do, want very much for ourselves the first poem of this particular group." "The other poems of the group," she said, "as content did not give us the same pleasure." Yeats continued to send both poetry and prose. *The Dial* published three excerpts from his autobiography under Marianne's editorship.

Marianne admired James Joyce almost as much as she did Yeats. In July 1926 Sylvia Beach sent *The Dial* 112 typescript pages of his new book—published as *Finnegans Wake* in 1939 but at the time called "Work in Progress." "Your review occupies the highest place among reviews," Beach said, "and is the most appropriate one to bring out Mr. Joyce's work." Recognizing that *The Dial* would not risk legal battles such as *The Little Review* had fought over *Ulysses*, she added: "There is nothing that the censor could object to in Mr. Joyce's piece." Watson read the manuscript first and forwarded it to Marianne while she was in Maine; she then asked the office to inform Beach that *The Dial* would be pleased to publish the work in small sections. When she returned to the office and discussed Joyce's payment with Lincoln

MacVeagh, MacVeagh discovered sexual innuendo that he believed *The Dial* could not risk publishing.

After receiving Marianne's note to that effect, Watson cabled that he would "acquiesce" to cutting some sections and using asterisks for omitted words and phrases. Marianne immediately cabled Beach to say that *The Dial* could not publish the typescript verbatim and followed the cable with a letter asking if the author would object to "reducing it by one third—perhaps a half." To Watson she expressed regret that Thayer could not be consulted about the matter but recalled his "speaking emphatically of his disbelief in the present Joyce" before he went away. "I suppose you know without my saying it," she said, "that I am acutely desirous of our having for *The Dial* what it is your wish to publish and it is sickeningly ironic to me to refuse the work of one in whose technique I have much delight. I also am distressed to involve us in the disgrace of modifying an affirmative letter." Marianne decided at last to publish only the first twelve pages, but by then Joyce had asked that the typescript be returned.

It was understood between Watson and Marianne that they would publish only what both approved, as had been the case with Thayer. Most often, they agreed. When they did not, neither was stubborn, though Watson, as he had with Thayer, did most of the acquiescing. The work of Joyce, however, proved to be a test case of Watson's and Moore's differences. *The Dial* received another short section of "Work in Progress" in February 1927. Marianne thought the work "bad . . . intrinsically" and decided to stand her ground despite Watson's eagerness to publish it. "We have elected to exclude obscenity when it was dull, and even the advance guard couldn't think this piece brilliant," Marianne told Watson in a carefully worded letter. (It was true that a number of Joyce's promoters, including Pound, felt no enthusiasm for "Work in Progress.")

Watson and Marianne's disagreement over this manuscript, their strongest ever, was one of principle on both sides. Watson believed in making *The Dial* a forum for important, innovative writers and thought Joyce should appear there whenever possible. Marianne, on the other hand, judged each submission on its own merits. To the extent that she did consider the author, she would more likely take chances with a promising unknown than with Joyce, whom she thought needed neither the money nor the exposure.

In the office and in public, Marianne always insisted that she considered it a "sacrilege to change or add even a comma" to what an author wrote. But in fact revising—not just editing—consumed a sizable portion of her time. She told Warner that in one issue she revised four stories, cut a review from twelve pages to four, and cut another review to improve it. "One of the stories, called 'Justice' [by Howard T. Dimick] is pro-negro and anti Ku Klux Klan," she explained, "and it seemed to *me* imperative that we offer to take it and now it is a good one, but Mice [Mary] and I both worked hard." Some authors were indignant, some compliant, and others grateful for her efforts on their behalf.

Despite her great admiration for Henry James, Marianne never developed an appreciation for his late fiction. Nor did she ever warm to the work of Hemingway, John Dos Passos, William Faulkner, Virginia Woolf, or Katherine Anne Porter. Given her distrust of psychoanalysis, it would not be surprising if the psychological nuances of such writers were lost on her. Yet it would be wrong to regard her rejection of Joyce as a mark of conservatism.

Despite Marianne's resolve to publish no work of her own in *The Dial* other than Comments, Briefer Mentions, and a couple of book reviews written before she joined the staff, she did make a few exceptions. She wrote Watson that she wished to review Gertrude Stein's *The Making of Americans*. "Please do review Miss Stein," Watson told her, "nothing could be more interesting in the way of a review." After a review essay promised for the February 1926 issue did not arrive, Marianne decided at the last minute to fill its place with the Stein review. She read the nine-hundred-page novel, the prose of which rivals *Finnegans Wake* in its difficulty, and reviewed it within a week.

"It was a most rewarding subject," Mary told Monroe Wheeler, "not a stupid page from first to last." Besides the elegance of Stein's prose, quoted amply in the review, Moore notes in particular the dignity with which Stein treats her characters and the American family.

After Stein thanked her for the review, Marianne answered that reading the book "was one of the most eager and enriching experiences that I have ever had." Although Watson did not share Marianne's regard for Stein, he admired the review, especially because Stein "has previously been slighted in *The Dial*."

The next summer Stein sent *The Dial* "Composition as Explanation," one of her most important aesthetic treatises. It would be Stein's first appearance in *The Dial*. The following spring Marianne requested additional work, and Stein sent the first ten pages of *A Long Gay Book*, a highly experimental novella written more than a decade earlier. "It is a happiness to us indeed," Marianne answered, "that you should grant us these pages of 'A Long Gay Book.' Have you sufficient patience with magazines to know that this delight is genuine and yet that we can wish to omit a portion?"

Stein agreed to the omission of four pages for magazine publication. "I do appreciate your liking my work," she said, "more than I can say."

"Your equipoise in respect to the public creates tranquility which was greatly needed," Watson told Marianne during her tenure as acting editor. Marianne wooed back at least two contributors, Raymond Mortimer and Leo Stein, whom Thayer had offended. But one of her greatest achievements as an editor was her successful courtship of Ezra Pound, who published nothing in *The Dial* between 1922 and 1928. In addition to the Europeans he recruited for *The Dial* in its early years, he had himself contributed "Hugh Selwyn Mauberley," five Cantos, and a regular Paris Letter.

In January 1923 he sent Watson drafts of four Cantos to be published as a group. Watson tentatively accepted them but, since he did so on the basis of an unfinished version, told Thayer that there was still time to refuse them if Thayer would assume the burden of doing so. Watson's position was "that publishing Pound's poetry is one of the things *The Dial* is known for and expected to do." Thayer replied that he abhorred the Cantos and abhorred the Paris Letter. He fired Pound as foreign correspondent and asked Burke to send a formal note of rejection about the Cantos.

With Watson's encouragement, Marianne began requesting reviews from Pound soon after she took over as acting editor. He answered curtly or not at all. But she persisted. When Thayer was briefly in New York between his return from Europe and his hospitalization, Marianne brought up the matter of the Dial Award and mentioned Pound and Stevens as possibilities. Thayer said that the award could go only to someone who had published something in *The Dial* the previous year. She asked whether he would object to her getting work from either poet. He did not.

Pound realized when he learned of Thayer's breakdown that *The Dial*'s mistreatment of him was perhaps not as unanimous as he had supposed. He wrote Marianne to acknowledge the difficulty of her position. "Have you ANY knowledge of my experiences with the editors of the Dial who preceded you?"

Assuring Watson that she was not "independently advocating anything," Marianne sent him Pound's letter and told him what Thayer had said about the Dial Award. "With regard to Ezra Pound," Watson replied, "if we feel prepared to take whatever he sends I think he can be persuaded to send something. I should be willing to 'take whatever he sends' and always have been, although his work is varied in the extent to which it interests me. Scofield was never anxious to do this."

Marianne wrote Pound that both Watson and Thayer supported her soliciting poems from him. But she could not, as Watson advised, offer him carte blanche. "Perhaps I am criminal in liking some things better than others," she told him, "even by an author for whose work I have unqualified enthusiasm; and I feel that individuals may sometimes publish what magazines may not. But I have always read your work with delight. Accordingly to have none of it to publish since I have been associated with *The Dial* has been to me a real hardship."

Still Pound sent no poems. When Marianne had just over a month before the January 1928 issue went to press and no one had been chosen for the Dial Award, she notified Watson. He cabled Pound and offered him the award on the condition that he immediately send prose or verse suitable for publication.

Pound promptly sent Marianne Cantos 22 and 27. She could not resist expressing some reservations about 22 when she mailed them to Watson. "Dear Miss Moore," Watson wrote, "I hope you will not feel that I am acting unconscientiously but when I reread this XXII Canto it seemed as though we really must have it for February or March and in the enthusiasm of the moment I wrote Pound much to that effect without alas implying that there had been any doubt in the matter."

"It is I who am lacking in conscience," she answered, "for disapproving of the Canto, and yet being delighted to have it. And I feel it a great gain that you implied no partial objection."

Pound was won completely. As soon as he learned of the award, he began sending Marianne the work of his protégés: Joseph Bard, John Cheever Dunning, and Louis Zukofsky. She published all three. He also sent his own poems and contributed criticism and translations— despite her often asking for changes. They could not reach an agreement about some poems he sent, but when he made a case for retaining a paragraph that she wanted to delete, she relented.

When Thayer announced that Marianne would assume his former editorial duties, he said that he and Watson would continue to choose recipients of the Dial Award. But Marianne played a more important role in the process than has been recognized. Thayer and Watson had already chosen E. E. Cummings as the 1926 recipient when she arrived. But she agreed to write a review, one of her most lyrical, to accompany Watson's Announcement. Watson chose William Carlos Williams, whose work he had long admired, for the 1927 Dial Award. He consulted Marianne about the matter but not Thayer, who was en route from Europe to New York. Both Williams and his wife expressed deep gratitude to Marianne when she asked for poems. She published his new poem "Paterson" (eighty-five lines thus far) in the February issue. And in March she published three more poems along with her own appreciation of his work.

Marianne wanted Wallace Stevens to win the award, but he remained ineligible according to Thayer's stipulations. When she had asked him to review Williams's *In the American Grain* during the first year of her editorship, he answered that "there is a baby at home. All lights are out at nine. At present there are no poems, no reviews. I am sorry. Perhaps one is better off in bed anyhow on cold nights." Her further requests produced no different response.

In July 1928 Marianne reminded Watson that it was time to think about the next Dial Award recipient. "Have you any suggestions?" he wrote. "Scofield last year wanted [George] Dillon or the author of 'The Emperor of Ice Cream' but they seem unsuitable?"

"You are very good to invite me to have an opinion about the Award," Marianne answered. "Though I feel warmly toward George Dillon and also to Wallace Stevens, it is impossible to get anything from Wallace Stevens, and George Dillon has no command of prose . . . Despite Mr. Burke's being our critic, my thoughts turn toward him, the more that there seem in him just now a faithfulness, discipline, and literary susceptibility that I have not noticed before. I enclose a review in which he shows a great gain, I think, over earlier writing. I surely needn't say that I do not wish to magnify the courtesy of your enquiry, and anyone that you select I shall think the right person."

Watson approved her choice but waited until October to inform Thayer. Not surprisingly, Thayer objected and presented his own candidate, Conrad Aiken. Marianne did not want to thwart Thayer, but Watson insisted upon Burke. Burke wrote poetry and fiction at the time as well as criticism. Yet Marianne presciently recognized his promise as a writer of nonfiction. During the last year of her editorship she published six "Declamations," as Burke called them. Part love story and part philosophy, they would become chapters in his semiautobiographical epistolary novel *Towards a Better Life*. Their themes anticipate those upon which he would build his reputation in coming decades as a philosopher of culture and rhetoric.

The Dial published the greatest density of now famous writers and works during the three years Pound was foreign correspondent. By the time Thayer fired him in 1923, Thayer had grown contemptuous both of Watson and of the experimental work upon which *The Dial*'s reputation rested. The managing editors Seldes, Burke, and Gregory more or less appeased Thayer for the next two years until Marianne took over as acting editor. Partly because of Marianne's own exaggerated humility in her *Dial* correspondence and her 1941 essay "*The Dial*: A Retrospect," histories of *The Dial* have dismissed her as yet another lackey of Thayer and Watson. But especially during the last two and a half years of her tenure, with Thayer incapable of participating and Watson unwilling to, *The Dial* was Marianne Moore's magazine.

Unlike many of the avant-garde magazines that preceded it, *The Dial* was never the organ of a particular group and was criticized accordingly for lacking conviction. If only because *The Dial* paid contributors considerably more than other magazines could (a source of resentment for Harriet Monroe), it remained the premier American arts magazine throughout the decade. Even those who disparaged it sent their work there.

Disgruntlement crystallized in early 1927, when the editors of *The New Republic* launched a months-long feud. Its editors accused *The Dial* of failing to encourage "any interesting new American writer" since its first year. To address that failure, the editorial announced, Van Wyck Brooks, Paul Rosenfeld, Lewis Mumford, and Alfred Kreymborg were assembling a new annual review of poetry and prose. When the first issue of *American Caravan* appeared in September, Marianne was gratified to discover that virtually everything in it had crossed her desk first.

Watson responded to the accusations in a Comment for the September *Dial*. Marianne's defense was implicit in the issue itself, an issue in which she took particular pride. It included four American writers in their early thirties—Mark Van Doren, Malcolm Cowley, Roark Bradford, Genevieve Taggard—plus eighteen-year-old Richard Ely Morse. Its three works of fiction include character sketches of Russian peasants by Maxim Gorky, Bradford's cultural study of a black nightclub in New Orleans, and the excerpt from Gertrude Stein's *A Long Gay Book*. An autobiographical essay by Bertrand Russell, a treatise on aesthetics by Leo Stein, and a reexamination of Walter Pater by Logan Pearsall Smith make up the essays. A fourth of the contributors were women: the painters Marie Laurencin and Vanessa Bell as well as Stein, Taggard, and Alyse Gregory. Collectively the issue represents a wide range of styles. Yet—with the possible exception of some of the book reviews—each work demonstrates the "individuality" and "intensity" that Marianne sought.

Marianne could not have replicated *The Dial* of the early 1920s if she had wanted to. Even Pound admitted that finding work such as he obtained then was a matter of "squeezing the already dry orange." Yet she not only recruited the best work she could get from modernists such as Stein and Pound but also introduced to *Dial* readers a far more diverse selection of writers than one might expect from a Harvard gentleman's club. It is no wonder that *The Dial* was "criticized about town" for "having no virility," as Williams put it, "and having petered out." Marianne included women in virtually every issue she edited.

And much of what she published celebrates the dignity of people marginalized by ethnicity and class.

The longest work Marianne printed was a serialized memoir by the Armenian immigrant Leon Srabian Herald. Another of her favorite protégés was the Bulgarian immigrant Stoyan Christowe. She launched the literary careers of the political leftists Meridel Le Sueur, Albert Halper, and Isidor Schneider, who all became known during the Depression for portraying the poor and oppressed. She published the Harlem Renaissance writer Jean Toomer and discovered the Chinese-American writers Kwei Chen, Fang Ling-Yu, and Chi-Chen Wang. Two articles and a long poem by the noted Japanese poet Yone Noguchi appeared in her *Dial*. She introduced to *The Dial* Rainer Maria Rilke, the Irishman L. A. G. Strong, the Spanish modernist Azorín (José Martínez Ruiz), and two Canadian modernists, A. J. M. Smith and W. W. E. Ross. Along with emerging young poets such as the twenty-four-year-old Louis Zukofsky, the twenty-three-year-old Stanley Kunitz, and the nineteen-year-old George Dillon, she also recruited the eighty-year-old critic George Saintsbury.

Moore brought to *The Dial* the same democratic principles and standards of craftsmanship that she brought to her poems. And the same paradoxical combination of self-assertion and self-effacement that characterizes her poetic persona characterized her editorial one. While she took pride in *The Dial*'s "fearlessness" against its critics, she took equal satisfaction in doing far more work than anyone realized, including operating the switchboard during lunch and helping the janitor reupholster a secretary's chair. *The Dial* was too much an expression of herself—of her modernist aesthetics and moral scrupulousness—for her to treat its contributors as "cavalierly" as Thayer advised her to. Her "interweaving of the aesthetic and the ethical is so intrinsically unusual," Burke recalled, "she could be extraordinary even in the attempt to be average."

On January 25, 1929, Sibley Watson came to New York to deliver the news that Marianne had dreaded for nearly a year. He told her behind closed doors that he expected the May issue to be the last. He had yet to discuss arrangements with Thayer's mother and would come to a definite decision within a week or so. She came home from the office that day "much battered," according to Mary, and said she would resume her job at the library at a reduction in annual salary from $2,600 to $600.

Two weeks later Marianne received a letter from Watson saying that Mrs. Thayer did not think it safe to break the news to Scofield just yet; she requested that *The Dial* continue through July. Marianne had already discerned that it was Watson rather than the Thayers who wanted out. She was ecstatic. For two additional issues meant that no manuscripts had to be returned. The following Saturday she took all the manuscripts she had accepted and distributed them among the April, May, June, and July issues; this left only four pages blank in July.

With two notable exceptions, she thereafter refused new submissions. Perhaps out of deference to Thayer, she persuaded Watson to buy two of Aiken's "Preludes," the first Aiken poems that she liked. The more significant purchase was eleven poems by D. H. Lawrence. Surprised at Marianne's interest in his work, Lawrence sent her the entire book manuscript for *Pansies*. She had published a number of Lawrence's stories but thus far no poems despite her great admiration for "The Snake." She asked Watson to approve the addition of eight new pages for the poems. Lawrence's subject matter—the circus, the sea, lizards—had obvious appeal for Marianne, but she also chose several poems that directly and indirectly protest the recent banning of *Lady Chatterley's Lover*. Lawrence liked her selection. She made room in the May issue for "When I Went to the Circus," a poem about the "bright wild circus flesh" of the acrobats and animals. The poem that opened the July issue, "To Let Go or to Hold On—?," contains the word *sperm* five times. Marianne rejoiced, she told Warner, that *The Dial*'s conclusion was "so full of vinegar."

When she learned in June that the publisher of *Pansies* would delete fourteen poems due to their alleged obscenity, she wrote Lawrence a letter of support and thanked him for what his poems had taught her. "In person you could instruct me in many things," she told him, and "I shall always be . . . a learner at your hand." The most censored of modernists had taught her to find dignity and mystery even in carnality. When Lawrence died the following year, she wrote privately of her "deep, indeed reverent, regard for him." And in her reminiscences about *The Dial* more than a decade later, she quoted at length from his letters to her—implicitly acknowledging her own limitations as an editor.

By late May, the July issue had gone to press, and Thayer had been informed of *The Dial*'s demise. The staff and a few others close to *The Dial* found out just after Thayer did. A note in the June issue announced that the next issue would be the last, and Watson's brief announcement thanking the staff, the readers, and the contributors concluded the July number. "I suppose a magazine never was discontinued," said Marianne, "so unnecessarily, or so unsensationally." The surprise and disappointment, even outrage, among some of the contributors offered her some consolation.

Warner, meanwhile, was full of advice and plans to send money; he regarded the whole affair as a financial crisis despite his mother's and sister's repeated assurances to the contrary. "It is *this I care for*," Mary told him, "*Rat's facility with the work* . . . It is *not* the money." Marianne told him, too, that apart from their other sources of income, "I still have myself. Any powers I have are not lessened by the discontinuing of *The Dial*. In fact I owe a prodigious amount to what its name has transferred to me of public confidence." She began working limited hours at the library and in May was offered her former position there.

But by then Mary's "nervous exhaustion," as the doctor called it, had become so severe that Marianne went neither to *The Dial* nor to the library. (Mary's symptoms of fluctuating fever, extreme fatigue, and a yellow tongue indicate severe hypothyroidism.) After the July *Dial* had gone to press, there was little to do at the office in any case except answer mail. Marianne provided the staff with form letters for that purpose, and she declined the library job. For two months she nursed Mary, who was too ill to dress or come downstairs.

Watson sent Marianne a large check from Thayer and himself. "We have monopolized your time and energy," he wrote, "and fear that *The Dial* has received far more benefit than you have from the exchange." Marianne wrote warm thanks to both Watson and Thayer and also wrote of her sadness at leaving. The gift was "too beautiful a thing to be turned to food and shelter," she said. She had never spent her Dial

Award money nor her 1921 gift from Bryher. The new gift also went into savings.

Just as Mary's health improved and Marianne's *Dial* work ended, Warner arrived at St. Luke's Place with a surprise: two tickets to Monhegan, where he had just spent a month with his family, and the news that Constance had paid their lodging for the month of August.

17

Where One Does Not Wish to Go

1929–1932

As soon as the two arrived at Monhegan, Marianne wrote Warner that Mary was "so evidently better, I wish you could see it with your very eyes." She assured him that she, too, was eating well and felt relieved from the anxiety over *Dial* matters that had accompanied her on recent vacations. Constance had reserved two corner rooms at the island's hotel, one room overlooking the harbor and the other with a view of the lighthouse. They preferred just one room, they said when they checked in, but the innkeeper, echoing Constance, insisted they would be more comfortable in two. Not yet adjusted to the demise of *The Dial* and uncertain about their future, they accepted Warner and Constance's generosity with what Marianne called "joy that is a kind of grief."

Marianne liked watching the fishing boats and an occasional pleasure sloop in the harbor. She befriended a family of kittens. And she often took her reading and correspondence to the wild side of the island, where she sat on a lichen-covered boulder, watching the "drama of water against rocks." Although she apparently wrote only letters while there, she stored impressions of lobster traps, island foliage, and fishing houses that would find their way two and a half years later into "The Steeple-Jack."

•

For the previous year Constance had made a real effort to establish better relations with her in-laws. To the thirty dollars that Warner sent monthly from Europe, she added thirty of her own. Mary had resolved never to bring her private warfare with Constance into the open, she told Warner, for fear it would endanger Marianne's financial security if Marianne outlived them both. "It is not primarily the money that makes the situation seem not real," she wrote, as "it is the *impulse there* that is so wonderful."

"I never felt anything more than Constance's solicitude for Mole and me," wrote Marianne, "for we are (practically if not intellectually) in the way very often; members of a family that are poor and proud are notoriously a care."

Also during Marianne's last year at *The Dial*, while Warner was still in Europe, Constance arranged to bring the four children— now including two-year-old John Warner Moore, Jr.—to visit their grandmother and aunt once a month. Mary said that these visits gave her greater opportunity to talk to Constance than she ever had before.

Warner had been urging his mother and sister to move for years. He and Constance felt embarrassed by the St. Luke's Place apartment, and even the children found it "oppressive." But Mary and Marianne continually resisted. "I really should lose my spirit if I were in the outskirts, or in one of the uptown apartments," Mary had said. "Old time and forgotten aristocracy with 'Italians' just at hand is agreeable enough to me; but the outskirts? O no—no—no."

It was true that St. Luke's Place had lost some of its appeal when the city turned the park across the street into a dusty, noisy ballpark. And Mary's illness during the summer of 1929 gave Warner further impetus to move her to a more salubrious address. Marianne did not believe Warner could find an apartment that would suit both his requirements and their own. They wanted a ground-floor apartment and a fireplace. They wanted to remain in the Village and to pay not much more than the sixty dollars they were already paying for two rooms. But as soon as Mary and Marianne departed for Monhegan, Warner began apartment hunting. His first letter mentioned a Village apartment merely to prove to Marianne "that there are a lot of choices about town."

Despite the attractive location, Warner acknowledged that it was on the fourth floor and too expensive at one hundred dollars per month.

Marianne answered that she would help him look after they returned from vacation, and Mary said that she would like to remain at St. Luke's Place at least through the winter in order to adjust to the idea of moving. Marianne felt far from "indolent," she said, and hoped that another employment situation would come along "that would be appropriate and not a drag upon Mole." "I am resolved to attain to something," she said. "I feel that with relentless perseverance it can be done."

For another week, Warner mentioned various apartments but gave each one up before hearing from the potential occupants. Then he announced that he had begun looking in Brooklyn. Brooklyn had never been mentioned as a possibility despite Warner's having shore duty at the Brooklyn Navy Yard for the next three years. "Brace your paws!" he wrote four days later, "for I've went and got you an apartment, ten minutes walk from the Navy Yard. '260 Cumberland Street.' You'll be comfortable, you have a cross draft, two bedrooms, two other rooms, besides a kitchen and a bathroom, also a Frigidaire Refrigerator, a dumbwaiter, permission to sun on the roof, an elevator, exposure East and South . . . I have many a pang about taking you from N.Y., and there's no fireplace; but *join me in fearing nothing.*" He had already paid the deposit and the first month's rent of a hundred dollars. By the time Marianne and Mary returned from Monhegan, Navy Yard workers had moved their furniture. He made no apologies for the rent but told them that he would be sending them $155 a month and $190 after December.

A Brooklyn apartment had been Warner's plan all along. And he chose one that met his priorities of respectability and convenience rather than his sister's and mother's tastes or explicit preferences. Besides the distance from Manhattan, the high rent, and the lack of fireplace, the apartment was on the third floor of a six-story building. Constance approved the apartment when Warner showed it to her and offered to provide rugs and make curtains.

The letters that Mary and Marianne wrote in response to Warner's news do not survive, but it is easy to imagine their sense of helplessness and, when they saw the building for the first time, their private agony. For the yellow brick Beaux Arts facade of 260 Cumberland Street was as tasteless as St. Luke's Place was charming. Marianne would live there for the next thirty-six years.

When she described the place to George Saintsbury more than a year after the move, she did not overtly complain but merely contrasted it with the poetic appurtenances of St. Luke's Place. The apartment was L-shaped, she said, with a living room and dining room overlooking the street. A kitchen was attached to the dining room, and a long hall led to a small bedroom, a bath, and a larger bedroom. She did note that "every room has sunshine some time in the day."

When Mary and Marianne explained to their friends why they had so suddenly moved, they said Warner had moved them for Mary's health. It is unlikely that they protested this reason even between themselves. They did, however, sigh privately over the neglected state of Fort Greene Park at the end of their block, over the shabby architecture in the neighborhood, and over the poor quality and high cost of food. A new subway was under construction and much of the pavement broken. The air was cleaner in Brooklyn, they acknowledged, the streets quieter, and their apartment brighter. And they relished Warner's proximity. He ate lunch with them every day and spent Saturday nights with them. On Sundays they attended the services he conducted at the Navy Yard. The smaller bedroom was designated Warner's and remained so even when he was at sea. Hiding the fact from Constance, Marianne and Mary continued to share a bed in the larger bedroom.

Reminiscing about the move thirty years later, Marianne wrote that she found Brooklyn "congenial" after her fast-paced life in New York, but nothing survives from the first year to indicate any congeniality whatsoever. In the same essay, "Brooklyn from Clinton Hill," she also placed her apartment in the more prosperous neighborhood up the hill from their own. Fort Greene, their own neighborhood, had long been the home of African-American and immigrant laborers at the Navy Yard, and Clinton Hill the neighborhood of those who profited from those laborers. (The essay even calls Fort Greene Park by its former name, Washington Park, not used since 1897.) By the turn of the twenty-first century Fort Greene would become home to an artistic, multiethnic community. But in 1929 one would have to climb Clinton Hill to glimpse through the windows the "maid with starched cap and apron, adjusting accessories on a silver tray" that Moore recalls so fondly in her essay.

When Marianne moved to the Village in 1918, she resigned herself to the emotional confinement of life with her mother. Over the next decade she not only became accustomed to that life but also managed to gain recognition as one of the foremost poets, critics, and editors of her generation. Then *The Dial* was taken from her. And now Warner had heedlessly taken from her everything else that might have supported her in the next phase of her literary career. Although Warner took pride in his sister's achievements, he could not comprehend how a writer might need a fireplace more than a Frigidaire. He and Constance changed residences even more often than military life required. Moving his mother and sister was for him a simple matter of expediency and propriety.

He took satisfaction in providing for Mary and Marianne. But Marianne also took pride in contributing to the family income and had no opportunity to do so anymore both because of their distance from Manhattan and because of Mary's precarious health. The Depression moreover wiped out all of what she called her "earnings": the three hundred dollars that Bryher had sent her in 1921, the two-thousand-dollar Dial Award, her parting gift from Watson and Thayer, and probably much of her *Dial* salary as well. This money had been invested in bonds recommended by Constance's father, and Warner was "so outraged at the thought of our losses," Marianne told Bryher, "that he is almost unbalanced in his determination to make it up to us." The loss deeply aggrieved Marianne. The principal from Mary's inheritance remained safe in Pittsburgh, however, and Warner and Constance supported Mary and Marianne comfortably through the Depression.

A year after their move, Marianne did find something congenial in the neighborhood: the Brooklyn Academy of Music, a magnificent edifice only a few blocks from 260 Cumberland. Each year it hosted more than two hundred lectures, concerts, travelogues, forums on contemporary events, and documentary films. An annual subscription to the Brooklyn Institute of Arts and Sciences allowed her to attend as many events as she wanted, and she sometimes spent the day there. One Saturday she heard a Burton Holmes Travelogue about Egypt in the morning, a personal account of traveling through the Brazilian wilderness with Theodore Roosevelt in the afternoon, and a lecture called "How the Ant Learns" in the evening. She heard a concert by

Stravinsky, whom she called "the most remarkable performer I ever heard," and recalled with particular fondness a lecture on Brahms by the composer Daniel Henry Mason. Documentary filmmakers often came to the Institute to narrate the films they had made. The science lectures at the Institute were, Marianne told Bryher, "a staff on which I lean heavily." She usually sat in the front row with a tiny notebook and a pen attached to a string around her neck.

A favorite discovery during her first season at the Institute were the inspirational lectures of David Seabury, a New York psychologist. Like Moore, he warned against egotism and tyranny. And using artists for his examples, he argued for enthusiasm, courage, and conviction. Such principles steered Moore through her own despondency at the time and appear repeatedly in her poems of the 1930s and 1940s.

The Institute provided Marianne an opportunity to meet writers—both those she knew and those she did not. Before the decade ended, she would meet W. B. Yeats, Robert Frost, and Gertrude Stein for the first time following their readings or lectures. She paid close attention to how poets read their work and how they performed. She had never approved of Edna St. Vincent Millay or her poetry, but watching Millay play the "extreme damsel in distress" at the Institute, she acknowledged that Millay "sells herself well." Sharing the stage with her old friend William Carlos Williams, Marianne read her own poetry there in 1936.

The Institute provided something of a second home for Marianne, much as *The Dial* had. She ought to have a bed there, Mary once teased, and Marianne liked the joke well enough to repeat it in her 1959 essay. Just as she had while working at *The Dial*, she delivered her Institute experiences virtually intact to Mary—"like a mother animal," Mary said, "with prey in mouth for its young."

If the air was indeed cleaner in Brooklyn, it did not improve anyone's health. And the breeze wafting through the upstairs apartment might well have exposed the occupants to worse toxins than the dust of the ballpark. "A cloud of fiery pale chemicals" hung over Marianne's Brooklyn, according to Elizabeth Bishop. And according to Mary, silt from the coal-burning smokestacks along Brooklyn's waterfront could soon cover a freshly made bed. Even the normally robust Warner suffered from fatigue and a series of boils during the first winter in Brooklyn. In January he developed a carbuncle that nearly killed him. For the first month of his convalescence Mary and Marianne spent fourteen-hour days with him at the hospital and afterward nursed him at their apartment. Mary remained frail enough during that first year that Marianne almost never left her to go into Manhattan. In the summer of 1930, Mary at last saw a thyroid specialist, who gave her medicine and advised her to lie down for twenty minutes after each meal. She found the rest refreshing but did not regain her strength. She told her cousin in the fall that she and Marianne were incapable physically and financially of making the half-hour subway trip to Manhattan.

While editing *The Dial*, Marianne had stayed home because of Mary's illnesses but rarely, if ever, because of her own—thus defying her mother's prediction that she lacked the stamina for full-time work. But after moving to Brooklyn, Marianne began to suffer from frequent upper respiratory infections: "what I am calling tonsillitis, laryngitis, pharyngitis, bronchitis, bulldogitis and every other inequity connected with gruffness," she told Monroe Wheeler. Bronchitis would sometimes keep her in bed for weeks. There were more frightening ailments, too. In the fall of 1931 she had a painful but benign lump removed from her right breast. Two years later she received treatment for typhoid fever after returning from vacation at Black Lake and had surgery to remove an infected cyst near her left breast. In March 1938 she was hospitalized a month with spastic colon and had surgery for it in May.

For nearly two decades the two women were rarely well at the same time. Illness became almost ritualized between them. "[Marianne] and I are a good deal like a wigwam of two sticks," Mary explained to Ezra Pound. "When one stick falls the other follows." Marianne often used military metaphors when describing her illnesses to friends: "I have been demolished by a siege of bronchitis" or "This is about my fifteenth captivity this year." Illness became a despot against which the two had little resistance.

Contrary to Mary's fears that Marianne's constitution could not bear the excitement of leaving home even for a few hours, it was more likely a profound sense of isolation that affected her health. Whereas she had previously been at the center of the New York literary world, during her first two decades in Brooklyn she developed a reputation as a recluse.

"I hope, my dear Marianne," wrote Alyse Gregory a year after the move, "that you are never sad—How can you be with your proud vigorous mind—yet how poor a thing is the mind at times—what a wan wavering light it casts over dungeons where the heart is imprisoned." None of Marianne's friends understood the imprisonment of her heart as well as Gregory did. The first time she met Mary, she sensed that Marianne had developed her remarkable intellect as a kind of armor. "Mon dieu! *What* a mother," she wrote Thayer, "so large, pale, refined, washed over by the years, but *inexorably*, permanently, eternally rooted and *not* to be overlooked, and remorselessly conversational, sentences with no beginning and no end, and no place left to jump in and stop them." Yet having sacrificed her own feminist principles to marry Powys and then exiled herself to England and an emotional imprisonment of her own, Gregory felt keen empathy for her friend. She looked forward, she said, to hearing that Marianne was writing again.

"It is most beautiful of you to wish me deliverance from sadness," Marianne answered, for once acknowledging her feelings, "for its omnipresence is a fact there would be few to deny, and we must allow ourselves to be lifted above it." She thanked Gregory for "your faith in me" but said "it would be a mistake for me to write unless I couldn't be happy without writing. I do make a note, however, of books or items that seem valuable, or suggest something to me; so you may know I am not indifferent to the thought of writing." Virtually all of the magazines to which Marianne had formerly contributed were now defunct. She would have welcomed an invitation from Eliot to write for *The Criterion*, but she told her friends that she did not want to send out work uninvited. Remembering how bold she had been in soliciting work for *The Dial*, she now wished to be asked rather than go begging.

At last an invitation came. It had been two years since Marianne wrote anything at all for publication and more than six years since she wrote poetry. On the evening of May 25, 1931, she took up her pen to rewrite "Poetry." "A great deliverance" came when Harriet Monroe asked to reprint the poem, Mary wrote in her diary, but "harm" lurked about on that evening after it was discovered that "we" (meaning Marianne) "had fallen into the ditch of disuse" and there was "no hope of a new road out." Then "the morning brought both words and form. What thanksgiving!!" Mary did not exaggerate the importance of the occasion. It marked the beginning of a prolific five-year period during which Marianne would publish two new books of poems and some of her finest reviews and essays.

Harriet Monroe was preparing a new edition of her anthology *The New Poetry* and asked to add "Poetry" to the four poems from the previous edition. Moore had told Yvor Winters that she thought "Poetry" should "be omitted or be altered" after the first edition of *Observations* appeared. And for the second edition of *Observations*, she cut it from five six-line stanzas to thirteen lines of free verse. When she returned to the poem in 1931, neither version pleased her. And so she sent Monroe a completely new one consisting of three unrhymed syllabic stanzas of five lines each. This is the only example in Moore's oeuvre of unrhymed stanzas, and she soon abandoned it. *Selected Poems* contains a five-stanza "Poetry," only slightly modified from the original version.

Perhaps the unrhymed stanza was an experimental stage between her free-verse poems of the 1920s and the rhymed stanzas to which she would soon return. Or perhaps she was practicing a bit of mischief against her unsuspecting adversary. In her review of *Poems*, Monroe had accused Moore of "forcing her pattern upon materials which naturally reject it" and being "too sternly controlled by a stiffly geometrical intellectuality." With the new version of "Poetry," Moore presents to Monroe's undiscerning eye the stiffly geometrical stanza Monroe herself had described. And without altering a word, Moore could say with impunity "I, too, dislike it" both of poetry and of *Poetry*, Monroe's magazine.

As expected, Monroe took no offense, for immediately upon receiving the poem she invited Moore to do some reviewing. Moore soon supplied two short reviews, one of W. W. E. Ross, whom she had championed at *The Dial*, and the other of Eliot's one-poem pamphlet *Marina*. Her emphasis in both upon the instructive "method" of these poets suggests that she was contemplating her own methods and, in particular, a return to rhyming stanzas. She praises Ross's "unemphasized rhymes" and "retreating verse patterns," and Eliot's "embedded rhyme" and "emphasis by word pattern rather than by punctuation."

Her next invitation came from Williams, who decided to assemble a volume of essays on Pound's *A Draft of XXX Cantos*. Though he did not yet have a publisher, he invited Moore to write the introduction. She had published two reviews each of Eliot, Williams, and H.D., plus important reviews of Stevens and Cummings, but had not yet written about Pound. And so she threw herself into the project and devoted more than a month to it in the summer of 1931. She resolved not only to reread all of Pound's own prose but also to read everything Pound had *read* before she first opened *A Draft of XXX Cantos*. "I have about two or three thousand pages to read for this little article I'm doing," she told Warner, "but it is of permanent benefit."

Although her review chides Pound for his "unprudery," his antiquated views of women, and his careless dismissal of John Calvin, it shows unabashed admiration for his "ambidextrous precision," his use of color, his "unerring ear," and especially his "musicianship." "This book is concerned with beauty," Moore writes. "You must read it yourself; it has a power that is mind and is music; it comes with the impact of centuries and with the impact of yesterday."

Moore enjoyed preparing the review—both the extensive research and the mental immersion in Pound's literary world—and felt satisfied with the result. It became one of a handful of essays that she reprinted both in *Predilections* and in *A Marianne Moore Reader.* At some point before she began actually writing it, she learned that Williams's proposed volume had fallen through. And so when Morton Dauwen Zabel, associate editor of *Poetry*, called on her in August, she agreed to write the review for *Poetry* instead.

Zabel was a doctoral student at the University of Chicago and would have a distinguished career as a poet, editor, critic, and translator. A great admirer of Moore's *Dial* criticism, Zabel did much to recruit new talent to *Poetry* during the 1930s. It was most likely Zabel who suggested to Harriet Monroe that Moore be asked to write reviews. And Zabel persuaded Monroe to accept the Pound essay despite its length. *Poetry* had never published such a long review, Monroe wrote when she sent Moore the proofs, but she did not insist that it be cut.

Meanwhile, Harriet Monroe had written Ezra Pound that she might soon retire, having just turned seventy, and did not believe that *Poetry* could survive financially if she did. Pound answered that he thought her "good for another ten or fifteen years anyhow" but, if retire she must, "the coincidence etc. incites me to the obvious idea that the only person in amurikuh who cd. continue your periodical is Marianne." He added that Moore's "irreproachable respectability" would be an asset in attracting financial backers. After Harriet Monroe went to New York in October 1931, she wrote Pound that, first, she was sure that Marianne would not leave her mother and proximity to Warner's family in order to move to Chicago and, second, she did not think any editor besides herself could secure financial patronage as she had. There is no evidence that she broached the possibility of Marianne's editing *Poetry* when they talked, but she did ask for poems. Soon thereafter Marianne began writing "Part of a Novel, Part of a Poem, Part of a Play" for *Poetry*.

A year later the Moores invited Harriet Monroe to dinner after she spoke at the Brooklyn Institute. While Monroe was as oblivious as ever to nuance, Marianne told Warner, it no longer mattered. "Her praise and enjoyment of the duck we had, and of our good will, touched me to the heart," Marianne said. "We agree about nothing intellectual, but admire one another's humanity and I have a world of help for which to be grateful to her for [the recent requests for poems and reviews]. She is very small, with gray hair beautifully arranged, and is absolutely without affectation—smiles faintly at this and that and quickly turns off a topic that wearies her." That Monroe took an interest in the family photographs went a long way toward pleasing her hosts.

While Moore was finishing the Pound review, she received a request from Lincoln Kirstein, the twenty-four-year-old editor of *The Hound & Horn*, to review two new books of poetry by Conrad Aiken. Zabel had mentioned Moore's interest in reviewing to Kirstein. In November she wrote a long, respectful review of Aiken praising the superiority of his recent poetry over the earlier. Of greater interest to the attentive reader are the rare glimpses it provides into Moore's personal life. The closest she ever comes to complaining, at least in print, about her lack of a writing space appears in this essay. "One goes into a friend's study," she says. "The books, prints, convenient desk, make one feel that one could work in such a place." She also devotes a paragraph of the essay to reiterating some of the themes she had presented more obliquely in "Marriage." Her remark that "Love is more important than being in love, as memories of childhood testify" may be taken as a defense of her decision to live with her mother, and her catalog of those who "may wish to leave love alone"—"Sir Isaac Newton, Washington Irving, Henry James, and Lord Balfour"—as a defense of her unmarried state. The review delighted Lincoln Kirstein, who told her, "it is by far the finest thing of its kind we have ever had to print, and I am so very proud that you were willing to write it for me."

Marianne mentioned to none of her correspondents that she had a lump removed from her breast in September 1931, but Mary told Mary Shoemaker that Marianne had been "frail for a long time" beforehand due to "things that weighed too heavily." Marianne wrote the Aiken review while recuperating from the surgery. Then in early December Mary became seriously ill and remained so for more than two months. Marianne had a prolonged cold in December. In January Warner had a recurrence of boils, and in February Marianne was bedridden for three weeks with bronchitis.

It was during this winter of illness and convalescence that Marianne actually began writing new poems. For illness gave her more space for contemplation than she had otherwise. The second bedroom, Warner's room, also served as a sickroom, and Marianne lay in the single bed there for weeks, watching a steeplejack named C. J. Poole at work on the Lafayette Avenue Presbyterian Church. Construction of the new subway line had made the steeple unstable and the star on top of it crooked. "My 'writing' has been augmented by my illness," Marianne told Bryher in April, "for while recuperating I finished a group of poems that I have been working at for some time." The group appeared in the June 1932 issue of *Poetry* as "Part of a Novel, Part of a Poem, Part of a Play," a three-part sequence that would eventually be printed as individual poems: "The Steeple-Jack," "The Student," and "The Hero."

The setting of "The Steeple-Jack" is ostensibly a New England seaside town. Like the village of Monhegan, it has a lighthouse, a hill overlooking the town, fish nets, a school, a post office in a store, and a plethora of flowers. But also present here is the neighborhood of Fort Greene. Besides C. J. Poole, the poem contains one of Brooklyn's most famous landmarks, the "town clock" atop the Williamsburg Savings Bank Tower, and Brooklyn's own "stranded whale." If it were not quite visible from the windows of the Moores' apartment, the clock would surely be visible from the roof, where Marianne and Mary often sat in warm weather. And an early but unsuccessful submarine, built in 1864 and nicknamed "The Intelligent Whale," was on view in the Navy Yard. Marianne later said that while writing "The Steeple-Jack" she had in mind "both Brooklyn and various New England seacoast towns I had visited."

The conflation of Monhegan and Brooklyn is not mere whimsy. When Mary and Marianne were sent to Monhegan in the summer of 1929, they trusted the attractive orderliness of their favorite vacation spot. Little did they suspect that the vacation would result in permanent exile from their home. Likewise, someone in the seaside town of "The Steeple-Jack" might think it "a fine day" and enjoy the semblance of order in "water etched / with waves as formal as the scales / on a fish"—little suspecting the approaching storm, a storm powerful enough to disturb "stars in the sky" as well as the "star on the steeple." Even the names of the flowers—"giant snap-dragon . . . spiderwort . . . toad-plant . . . tiger[lilie]s"—contain hidden dangers. And while there are "cats not cobras to keep down the rats," there are rats (one unsuspecting Rat in particular). The town is "a fit haven for / waifs, children, animals, [and] prisoners," the poem tells us. Warner had chosen Brooklyn as "a fit haven" for his mother and sister, but by turning them into helpless waifs, he had inadvertently imprisoned them.

Did Warner recognize the anguish in the poem? Probably not. When he read the sequence in *Poetry*, he called it "Rat's noble work" and fondly recalled Marianne's reading it aloud to Mary and himself in "my room" at the apartment.

The three poems in the sequence are about different kinds of seeing. In "The Steeple-Jack," Ambrose, a college student sitting on the hillside with "his not-native books and hat," sees the ironic but real dangers that the residents below cannot see. "The Student," drawn in part from Brooklyn Institute lectures, is about intellectual seeing, about learning "the difference between cow and zebu; lion, tiger;

barred and brown owls" among other facts and distinctions. "The Hero" is about spiritual seeing. Whereas in "The Student" one forms "opinions that fright could [not] dislocate," in "The Hero" everything is frightful. It describes a place of "deviating head-stones and uncertainty," a place "where one does not wish to go" and where "love won't grow." (All eighteen rhyming lines of this musical poem end with the long *o* of hero.) The setting of "The Hero" is as dark and chaotic as that of "The Steeple-Jack" is light and ordered. And whereas "The Steeple-Jack" has a gilded star that stands for hope, in "The Hero" there is no hope "until all ground for hope has vanished."

"The Hero" refers to two Old Testament patriarchs and two Roman consuls who became heroes in their exile. The spiritual journey of *Pilgrim's Progress* is likewise a model of heroism, as is El Greco, whose self-exile in Spain resulted in spiritual masterpieces "brimming with inner light." The hero to whom Moore devotes the most attention is an African-American security guard at Mount Vernon. To the "fearless sightseeing" tourist asking where George and Martha Washington are buried, this "decorous frock-coated Negro" replies:

> . . . "Gen-ral Washington
> there; his lady, here"; speaking
> as if in a play—not seeing her; with a
> sense of human dignity
> and reverence for mystery, standing like the shadow
> of the willow.

Not only must one look past George Washington, the expected hero, in order to recognize the heroism of someone whose racial history and exile have made him virtually invisible, but Moore also assigns to this hero her most esteemed virtues: "a sense of human dignity and reverence for mystery." The hero's "suffering and not saying so," finding hope after "all ground for hope has vanished," and "looking upon a fellow creature's error with the feelings of a mother—a woman or a cat" anticipate Moore's animal heroes such as the jerboa and pangolin.

18

Debts of Gratitude

1932–1934

During the weeks Marianne waited for "Part of a Novel, Part of a Poem, Part of a Play" to appear in *Poetry*, she "felt down a little about the poem," according to Mary. And so she was heartened to receive praise as soon as the poem appeared: first from Lincoln Kirstein, who requested something for *The Hound & Horn*; and then from William Carlos Williams, who was trying to revive *Contact*. "Why should I not speak in superlatives," he wrote, "there is no work in verse being done in any language which I can read which I find more to my liking and which I believe to be so thoroughly excellent. You have everything that satisfies me."

Marianne received these letters just after returning from her class reunion at Bryn Mawr, where she was invited to speak, her expenses paid by an anonymous classmate. She enjoyed herself so much, she told Warner, that she planned to go every year that she could afford to. Her former teacher Lucy Martin Donnelly, the one who had discouraged her from majoring in English, invited her to speak to the English Club the following winter. Marianne did not get sick—to Mary's amazement—and began work on "The Jerboa" for *The Hound & Horn* as soon as she received Kirstein's letter. Within a few days of receiving

Williams's letter she was contemplating subjects for the poem she would send him and told Warner that the plumet basilisk was a possibility. Warner had just left for American Samoa, where he would remain with his family for nearly two years.

Marianne immersed herself in the world of "The Jerboa," the first of several major poems about exotic animals, much as she had with her Pound review the previous summer. She researched both Egypt and the jerboa at the library, spent a day at the Museum of Natural History investigating this reclusive desert rat, and also drew upon notes she had made about Egyptian artifacts over recent years. For almost two months Mary reported that Marianne and her jerboa were "very very deep in the sand" and that Marianne worked twelve hours a day on the poem, "breathless, barely stopping for food." She spent many of those hours on the roof of the apartment building. For weeks Mary "hated" the jerboa, she said half seriously, for usurping all of Marianne's time and for causing "trouble in the family." Despite a few minor ailments, probably exaggerated by Mary's letters, Marianne would remain in good health for nearly a year. And she was eating. By January she weighed 130 pounds.

"Trouble in the family," as usual, did not mean open confrontation. To Mary's disgust, Marianne began saying "cookie dust" with no explanation and said it with what Mary called "*that smile I don't like.*" With Warner gone and with the encouragement Marianne received from Kirstein, Williams, and her Bryn Mawr classmates, she retreated to her rooftop, to her cryptic phrases, and to the jerboa's desert burrow with a kind of furor, "working like a demon," she said in one letter, "to say what is boiling within me" in another. What was boiling within her was survival, as the poem itself suggests.

After the first three weeks of working on the poem, she told Warner that it was "maybe the one and only thing I have ever written." "The Jerboa" weaves together several themes of "Part of a Novel, Part of a Poem, Part of a Play" but with greater wit and subtlety. Like "The Steeple-Jack," it exposes dangers in a society that the members themselves do not see. It exemplifies the research and precision advocated in "The Student." And the jerboa itself is a variation of her "frock-coated

Negro": it is associated with "the blacks, that choice race with an elegance / ignored by one's ignorance," and its beauty, courage, dignity,
humility, and fortitude go largely unnoticed.

The rhythm of the poem pleased her, especially that of the last two
stanzas, which she wrote first and used as a model for the others:

> By fifths and sevenths,
> in leaps of two lengths,
>   like the uneven notes
>   of the Bedouin flute, it stops its gleaning
>   on little wheel castors, and makes fern-seed
>   foot-prints with kangaroo speed.
>
> Its leaps should be set
> to the flageolet;
>   pillar body erect
>   on a three-cornered smooth-working Chippendale
>   "claw"—propped on hind legs, and tail as third toe,
>   between leaps to its burrow.

"The Jerboa" is divided into two sections: "Too Much" and "Abundance." It speaks more directly about the Depression than anything
else Moore wrote for publication. "Too Much" expresses her outrage
over the irresponsible spending that she believed caused the country's
economic collapse. It describes the affluent court of ancient Egypt,
where luxury is not only taken for granted but also depends upon
exploitation of slaves, dwarfs, "the poor," and of a wide variety of
animals. The intriguing detail with which the poem catalogs the Egyp-
tians' toys and inventions indicates Moore's fascination with their
wealth as well as her moral repulsion. "Abundance" presents the self-
sufficient and graceful jerboa as an alternative to "too much" wealth.

Marianne had supported Herbert Hoover during the 1928 presidential election, when she and her mother were virtually alone among
their Village neighbors in opposing New York's governor, Al Smith.
Mary found it amusing how "chock full of the election" Marianne had
been. "You'd think he owned the country and had himself brought up
Hoover." It was not Smith's populism or social progressivism that

Marianne opposed but his early ties to Tammany Hall. "The possibility of having Tammany politics exhibited like a political transparency all over Europe as a picture of America," she said, was "alarming." What chiefly impressed her about Hoover, on the other hand, were his humanitarian relief efforts in Europe during and after World War I, his Quaker origins, and his statesmanlike dignity. She got up at five o'clock on election day to be first in line to cast her vote.

Marianne admired no living president more. In the 1932 election she vehemently opposed Roosevelt—but not because she was unsympathetic to those harder hit by the Depression than she was. She believed rather that the New Deal would degrade the poor by denying them both dignity and freedom. Reflecting these beliefs, her jerboa embodies an ideal of dignity, freedom, and "abundance" without wealth.

While Moore did care deeply about the national situation, her "working like a demon" on the poem suggests something personal at stake as well. Being a "rat" herself, she felt an obvious affinity with the jerboa. And yet the jerboa is a heroic ideal, not a self-portrait. It exemplifies adaptability and survival in the harshest of circumstances. The encouragement Marianne received from Williams and others gave her new confidence that life in Brooklyn did not preclude a literary career. "The Jerboa" reveals an optimism and playfulness that is missing from "Part of a Novel, Part of a Poem, Part of a Play." The jerboa is a native of the desert rather than a displaced exile. And while the desert provides "no water" and "no palm-trees" (as Moore called her office at *The Dial*), the jerboa has learned not only how to survive there but how to thrive upon "nothing but plenty."

As in Moore's subsequent poems about animals, such as "The Plumet Basilisk," "The Frigate Pelican," "The Buffalo," and "The Pangolin," the jerboa is both a paradigm for the artist and a survivor. It survives depravity not by adopting habits of better-known species but by adapting creatively to the unique rigors of its environment. Although Moore's animals do have innately poetic qualities, such as the jerboa's rhythmic leaps, the poems emphasize what she would later identify as her most valuable assets as an artist: persistence and fortitude. Her animal poems are both instructions in the art of survival and acts of survival themselves.

•

The winter of 1932–33 brought some relief from the cultural deprivation Marianne had felt for the past four years. She accompanied her mother every Wednesday into Manhattan, where Mary received dental treatments and Marianne sometimes visited museums and galleries. In December she went for the first time to the Museum of Modern Art, the Whitney Museum of Art, and the Julien Levy Gallery, all of which had opened since she moved to Brooklyn. Julien Levy, who would soon introduce surrealism to New York, was married to Mina Loy's daughter, Joella. And the founding director of the Museum of Modern Art, Alfred H. Barr, Jr., was a family friend, the son of the pastor for whom Warner worked in Baltimore. "Mr. Kirstein of the *Hound* and Mr. Levy and Mr. Barr," Marianne told Warner, "are I believe leverets who were together at Harvard." Still in their twenties, all three men would have a profound influence on the arts in mid-century New York. Marianne followed the surrealist exhibits at the Julien Levy Gallery with keen interest and throughout her life maintained close ties with the Museum of Modern Art through Monroe Wheeler, who joined the museum staff in 1935.

The Brooklyn Institute offered an especially rich program of literary personalities that winter. Alfred Kreymborg and Harriet Monroe were on the program together in November, Yeats spoke on the "New Ireland" in December, and Robert Frost read his poems in January. "Yeats made a very big hit with me," Marianne told Warner. "He has white hair and instead of being retired and rasped by ague as Padraic Colum had given me the impression he was, he is hearty, smiling, benevolent, and elegant with a springiness and vigor that no invalid could very well counterfeit." She told Pound that Yeats spoke "with daring and ease and two of the most remarkable hands, as mimes, that I have ever seen." She met him briefly after the speech. He bowed, she said, "and made some remark about my writing, in the form of a question, but in my excitement I missed it." Celebrities did not usually unnerve Marianne. Yeats was the notable exception.

The highlight of the season was meeting Robert Frost. Consisting largely of socialites dressed in furs, the crowd, according to Marianne, resembled "the starlings that form a blackened cloud on their way to roost on the Metropolitan Museum, evenings." The Institute lecture room was too small for such a crowd. And so Marianne had to sit in the "undertaker's chair back of the last row." "By sitting down and standing up and making a shell of my ear," she told Warner, "I caught the better part of what was said. It was the best thing we've had in the way of contagious sincerity."

Afterward the young woman in charge made a point of introducing Marianne to Frost. Frost himself was recovering from the flu (or grippe, as it was called then), and his manager was trying to steer him away from the crowd as quickly as possible. But when Frost realized who Marianne was, he broke free, took her arm, and led her to a nearby cloakroom so he could speak to her. She recorded the conversation in a letter to Warner.

"Come out here," Frost said, "I've always wanted to meet you and to *see* you. You know I went to see you at *The Dial* one time but you weren't there; I was seeing Lincoln MacVeagh—he's my publisher you know. I'm a very poor letter-writer but I meant to write to you when your first little book came out. I liked some of the poems and I was going to write to you about it but I never did."

"Well . . . that's a great help to me. I never thought of your having the book."

"I've just had grippe and I'm not very well," said Frost. "I don't take good care of my health, but I want to talk to you. I wish I could do something for you, and help you and I think I could. Is your book being republished?"

"No."

"Well, . . . Lincoln MacVeagh is a friend of mine and I'm going to see him about that."

"No, I wouldn't like you to. In fact, I asked him for the copyright the other day and he returned it to me—very pleasantly too, but I'd rather not suggest that."

"Well, someone else then."

Frost inquired about her current work, and Marianne complimented his reading, noting in particular "how unusual and of interest technically it was to have poems read with continuity as regarded periods and commas."

When Frost returned resolutely to the subject of getting her book published, Marianne told him that she did not wish to republish her book just now. "When I write something," she said, "if you see it, and read it, I'll be glad if you just—"

"Just like it?" he said smiling. "All right." Then he was escorted away.

As soon as Marianne sent off "The Jerboa" to *The Hound & Horn* in July 1932, she began working on "The Plumet Basilisk." Basilisk had long been a family nickname, and the poem resembles the second half of "The Jerboa" in celebrating an underappreciated species, an "amphibious falling dragon" from Costa Rica that can run across water on its hind legs. The poem lacks the emotional and political urgency of the "The Jerboa," however, and Marianne regretted while writing it that it did not achieve the "rush and spontaneity" of the earlier poem. She worked on it for five months—but not breathlessly, for she took breaks to review an edition of Emily Dickinson's letters and to write a short poem, "No Swan So Fine," for the twentieth-anniversary issue of *Poetry*. Since Williams had not succeeded in reviving *Contact*, she decided to send "The Plumet Basilisk" unsolicited to *The Criterion*.

And then she waited. Four months later she had heard nothing from Eliot, who had left for an extended stay in America just when the poem arrived. Marianne told Alyse Gregory that although she had always had confidence in Eliot's honesty and liked the rhythm of his poetry, she was too peeved to attend his lecture at the New School. She did, however, invite Eliot to call on her in Brooklyn. And then when she renewed her acquaintance with Edmund Wilson in May and learned that Wilson would be hosting Eliot in New York, she invited Wilson to bring Eliot to Brooklyn. A few days later Wilson telephoned to explain that Eliot's schedule would not permit a trip to Brooklyn and to invite her to a tea for Eliot. At first she resisted. But Wilson persuaded her to come.

Eliot's review of *Poems* had been delayed two years, and "The Plumet Basilisk" had been neglected upon its arrival at *The Criterion*. But Eliot had greater reason to feel trepidation about the meeting than Marianne did. She had scolded him for cruelty in her review of *Prufrock and Other Observations*, and her rejection of his wife's story at *The*

Dial had miffed him. She did not call on him while she was in London in 1928 despite staying only a few blocks from his office. And she told him so.

Marianne later recalled that she "witnessed" Eliot "rather than met him" at Wilson's tea but found him modest and kind. The conversation among the five guests was so strained and superficial that Marianne found no opportunity to ask Eliot about George Herbert and Bishop Andrewes, as she had intended. Eliot complimented Marianne on her letters and said to the group that her letters to editors were very terse. "So are yours," she retorted. And everyone laughed. But he did not mention her poetry, and she privately resolved to send nothing new to *The Criterion* until asked.

This was June 1933. In September, after Eliot had returned to London, she did receive an invitation from *The Criterion* to review the British edition of Pound's *A Draft of XXX Cantos* and to send a new poem. The invitation pleased her. She promptly wrote the review, taking care not to repeat what she had said in her review for *Poetry*. And, with *The Criterion* in mind, she began writing "The Frigate Pelican."

In January, well before she finished the poem, Marianne received an even more gratifying invitation. In his capacity as editor for Faber and Faber, Eliot wrote her about bringing out a British edition of her poems. She replied with characteristic deference that he might not like her new poems, that there were not yet enough of them for a book, and that she had already promised her next book elsewhere. He immediately wrote back addressing her qualms and also sent Frank Morley, Faber's U.S. representative, to call on her. She liked Morley, and they had a friendly conversation about whales. But she told him that she did not want to publish her previously collected poems in a new book.

Then she received a letter from Pound addressing her as "Deraly Beloved Marianna of the Moated ETC." Pound said that he had received a "plaintive communique from the Rt/ Rev/ bro/ in Xt/ T.S. thePossum of Eliot /codirekr of Faber and Faber London/ who . . . wants to pub/ your poems for reefeened circles in the decaYdent city of Lunnon on Thames . . . I think you better display maidely charity and LET HIM DO IT . . . Besides yr/ mother wd/ like it. I mean yr/ being pubd in Dickens Home Town/."

If Marianne did not yet trust Eliot's sympathy for her work, she trusted Pound's. She and Pound had been in regular correspondence since 1931, when he asked her to contribute to his anthology *Profile*. Then in his 1933 *Active Anthology* he included a liberal selection of her new work; besides "Camellia Sabina," which she wrote specifically for the anthology, he also included "The Steeple-Jack," "No Swan So Fine," "The Jerboa," and "The Plumet Basilisk" (which appeared simultaneously in *The Hound & Horn*). His introduction singled out Moore for praise. Although she herself seems not to have been influenced by her contemporaries, he said, "she preceded the successes of others, and may have contributed to them, though I doubt if they suspected it."

Pound's calling Marianne "Deraly Beloved" and referring to her mother set a new tone to their correspondence, and his subsequent letters grew ever warmer. Even though she withdrew her name from one of his manifestos, he had not forgotten her efforts on his behalf at *The Dial*, and he clearly appreciated the two reviews she wrote of his *Cantos*. Pound was typically so captious, as Marianne put it, that she trusted any kind word from him. And while she did not immediately change her mind upon receiving his "Deraly Beloved" letter, she told Warner that it was a "terrific shove from the rear" and the decisive factor in her accepting Eliot's offer.

She agreed to let Faber and Faber publish, as Eliot put it, "a complete volume of your work up to date, leaving out only such poems as the author wished absolutely to suppress." Eliot told her he had in mind "a kind of companion volume" to the *Selected Poems of Ezra Pound* (1928). He wanted to call it *Selected Poems* rather than a fancier title to show that her work was already known.

In the year between Frost's impromptu offer to get her work back into print and Eliot's formal one, Marianne received two other offers. A young publisher who presented himself to various poets as Martin Jay or as James C. Leippert (and would later form the Alcestis Press under the name Ronald Lane Latimer) nearly persuaded her to reissue *Observations* in a deluxe edition—until she resolved against republishing her older poems and against deluxe editions. Then Macmillan inquired about publishing a book of her poems. She had liked Harold S. Latham of Macmillan since he first expressed interest in her work in

1921 and was elated by his letter. She promised that when she had enough new poems for a book, she would send them to him. When Marianne told him of her negotiations with Faber and Faber, Latham was more than amenable to publishing the American edition of whatever she and Eliot agreed upon.

Observations had been arranged chronologically, as Eliot guessed and Marianne confirmed. He suggested that the new book begin instead with her new poems. "At your simplest," he said, "you baffle those who love 'simple' poetry; and so one might as well put on difficult stuff at once, and only bid for the readers who are willing and accustomed to take a little trouble over poetry. I think this will pay better and excite booksellers more." Marianne liked his arrangement so well that she used it for subsequent collections of her poems. Any lingering doubts she had about Eliot's regard for her work were now assuaged.

By May 1934 Marianne had chosen forty of the fifty-four poems included in the second edition of *Observations* plus all five poems she had published since then (except that she eliminated "The Student" from "Part of a Novel . . ."). She included also "The Frigate Pelican," which she had just sent to *The Criterion*. And before the book went to press, she sent Eliot "The Buffalo" and "Nine Nectarines and Other Porcelain."

After Marianne finished typing the selection, Mary "deplored a great deal of it," Marianne told Warner, "and investigated me till my very fleas blushed and I had to do over a great deal of the work." They consulted "synonym books and small dictionaries" as they had in the days when Mary helped her with her *Dial* prose. Her cover letter to Eliot indicates that in some cases she sent two versions of a poem from which he could choose. In the case of "An Octopus," which Mary thought "a vay [very] bad poem," Marianne bracketed for possible omission the large section about the Greeks and Henry James. Upon further consideration, Marianne decided to consult Sibley Watson. Watson approved the uncut version, but by the time Marianne wrote Eliot to convey her preference, the book was in proofs. Eliot had, however, already chosen to retain the lines in question, as he apparently did whenever she gave him a choice.

Eliot could be almost as self-effacing as Moore, which explains why Pound's "shove from the rear" was so critical to the book's coming into being. While both Frank Morley and Henry Latham assumed that Eliot would write a preface to the book, neither Eliot nor Moore did. Before the preface was agreed upon, Eliot had to be assured that Moore in fact wanted one, and Moore had to be assured of Eliot's willingness to support her work in that way. When Eliot sent her the preface in the fall, he claimed that he felt "diffident and miserable about this puny Introduction" and asked her to tell him if she had any objections. She was ecstatic. The introduction affected her, she told him, like a "tidal wave."

Among the accolades Moore received during the three years between Williams's letter about "Part of a Novel . . ." and the appearance of Stevens's review of *Selected Poems* was the Helen Haire Levinson Prize from *Poetry* magazine. She received word of it in October 1933 while recovering from surgery. That Zabel admired her poems enough to press for this honor and that Harriet Monroe had let herself be thus pressed touched Marianne deeply. The check for one hundred dollars that accompanied the award was also welcome at a time when Marianne felt herself needy.

"We have had a violent winter," Marianne told Williams the following spring, characterized by "anxiety, illness, and ineffectiveness." The illness and anxiety began in the summer, when she had headaches and eye problems related to an infected cyst on her left breast. She had the cyst lacerated and then while vacationing at Black Lake in September contracted typhoid fever. After being treated for that, the doctor said that she must have the cyst surgically removed, which would require a hospital stay. At first she refused. She and Mary had decided not to tell Warner about the cyst and its complications, and perhaps she refused because the payment would alert Warner to the situation. But after the doctor offered to let her edit some speeches in exchange for his services, she agreed to the surgery.

Mary and Marianne were not suffering financial hardship. Warner sent them $125 every month. And having at last wrested Mary's inheritance away from Cousin Henry's control, they received sometimes twice that amount from the Pittsburgh savings account. But they lived so frugally that Mary usually put Warner's check into savings. They had various lesser sources of income, too, including some investments and the small checks Marianne received for her writing. But when Marianne learned that their landlord had lowered the rent for another tenant because of Depression-related hardship, she asked that their own rent be lowered, too. The landlord decreased it from a hundred dollars to eighty-three. A few months later she told him they could not pay more than seventy-seven. He again complied, but Mary felt it unfair to take advantage of the situation and called to say they would pay eighty. During the year before Marianne's surgery, Mary deposited nearly $2,000 into savings, on average more than $150 per month.

Three hundred dollars of that amount was a gift from Sibley Watson and his wife, Hildegarde. Marianne had met Hildegarde a few times during her early association with *The Dial*, before the Watsons left New York, but had never taken to her. When the Watsons were in the city during the spring of 1933 trying to launch Hildegarde's singing career, they invited Marianne to dine with them. Marianne reported afterward that Mrs. Watson was "nicer than ever she has been—less formal, and not assumptive or all-knowing." After a few more dinner invitations, a letter arrived: "Would you accept the enclosed check from Sibley and me?"

Marianne did accept it. And then shortly afterward she allowed Bryher to establish an account whereby Marianne would receive about fifty dollars in quarterly interest. Bryher's father had died, and Bryher led Marianne to believe that the interest from this account would go to taxes if Marianne did not accept it. Whereas Marianne had a decade earlier refused to be "rescued" by her wealthy friends, she now decided to accept their gifts. Hildegarde Watson and Bryher would provide Marianne with substantial monetary gifts and, in Hildegarde's case, other material goods for the next four decades.

From the time Mary and Marianne moved to St. Luke's Place, Mary had taken an almost perverse pride in living below their means. And the suffering they both witnessed during the Depression only reinforced Mary's proclivity to save rather than spend. Marianne had no real understanding of the family finances. What she did understand was the power money conferred. She had been urged at Bryn Mawr never to be a financial burden upon her family, and her financial dependence upon Warner and Constance bothered her. Earning even small amounts for her poems and reviews gave her a sense of independence, as did her negotiations with the landlord. "Rat's chief joy" in the Watsons' check, Mary told Warner, was that "Uncle Badger can take a good long breath, and know we're tended to for a *little wile* apart from *'im*."

The Moores scrimped but did not hoard. Mary sent donations of five dollars to a variety of charitable causes. And Marianne took pleasure in sending Mary Shoemaker, who did feel the effects of the Depression, some of the checks she received for her writing, usually amounts of ten to twenty dollars. Sometimes Cousin Mary accepted these gifts and sometimes returned them. The disappointment Marianne felt when her gift was refused gave her new empathy for those whose gifts she had refused. She told Bryher that, having given up her disdain for money, she had come to regard it as an almost "supernatural . . . agent of solicitude and unselfishness." Neither the amount of money nor the neediness of the recipient mattered as much, she said, as "the sense of support conveyed by the feeling which actuated the giving."

One of Mary and Marianne's acts of charity was spending most of December 1933 and January 1934 with Mary Norcross at her mountain home. Norcross had been injured in a car accident and was in a body cast. Mary and Marianne tended to her physical needs, her various pets and livestock, and her three hundred chickens, from whose eggs Norcross earned her livelihood. Marianne developed a cold soon after their arrival there, and she surely had in mind the lonely poverty in which Norcross lived when calling the winter "violent."

When Marianne was not helping with household chores at the Mountain, she was reading Henry James in preparation for an article she had promised to *The Hound & Horn*. She had long identified with James both as a "literary bachelor" and as someone "so susceptible to emotion as to be obliged to seem unemotional." "Henry James as a Characteristic American" is arguably Moore's finest essay and is, like some of the poems she was writing at the time, an indirect self-portrait. Her purpose is not to defend James the artist but to make a case for the man and the citizen. Despite her own illness and her mother's more serious illness after they returned to Brooklyn, Marianne threw herself into the task of writing the essay with much the same vigor she gave to her first review of *A Draft of XXX Cantos* and to "The Jerboa." "Be thankful," she wrote Warner, "you weren't here to usher in the James article!"

Moore organized the essay according to James's American qualities, including his emphatic individualism, his "respectful humility toward emotion," his good conscience, and his "rapture of observation." If these and the other characteristics she describes are recognizably Jamesian or American or both, they are even more recognizably her own. The last paragraph addresses James's "affection for family and country" and makes the climactic point that "family was the setting for his country." The family Moore discovers in James's memoirs is a utopian vision of shared bounty and equality, a model for democracy. She reiterates here, as she had in "Marriage," how the paradox of "liberty and union" might be realized both domestically and politically. James is her model of love and patriotism.

> Love is the thing more written about than anything else, and in the mistaken sense of greed. Henry James seems to have been haunted by awareness that rapacity destroys what it is successful in acquiring. He feels a need "to see the other side as well as his own, to feel what his adversary feels"; to be an American is not for him "just to glow belligerently with one's country" . . . but . . . the American is, as he thought, "intrinsically and actively ample, . . . reaching westward, southward, anywhere, everywhere," with a mind "incapable of the shut door in any direction."

Nowhere else does she present so succinctly her personal and political convictions. When she later received a query about her "outlook on life," she referred the inquirer to this essay.

"One's debts of gratitude," Marianne told Bryher, "must needs be paid to someone other than the one from whom one receives." Realizing that she could never reciprocate Bryher's generosity, she nevertheless could offer her own small earnings to Mary Shoemaker, for whom the money would make a difference. Marianne began to think of literary support in much the same way. She had always resisted, at least at first, offers to publish her books just as she had resisted financial patronage. But after agreeing to let Eliot publish *Selected Poems*, she at last admitted that her initial resistance was "the old story of refusing what one secretly wants."

Instead of feeling herself hopelessly indebted to Pound, Eliot, and Zabel for promoting her work, Marianne decided to pay her "debts of gratitude" to fledgling writers. Urging her to edit a magazine, Pound told her that she "ought to be guiding and correlating the younger generation. Excuse cliché." She soon thereafter had "three pupils— Mary Jones, Catherine Flagg, and Esther Maddux Tennent." Jones was the daughter of a Bryn Mawr classmate, and Tennent a classmate who had married Marianne's biology professor and was now translating Japanese poetry. When Amy Bonner of the Brooklyn Institute then appealed to Marianne for editorial advice, Marianne confided to Warner that she liked Bonner and wanted to help her but was "full of born and adopted kittens to overflowing already." Her "born" kitten was her eleven-year-old niece, whose play she sent to Macmillan. Macmillan did not publish Sallie's play, but *Poetry* did accept the poems that Marianne sent from her other "kittens."

Marianne met the most promising of her protégées in March 1934, the same month she decided to let Eliot publish her *Selected Poems* and the same month Warner and his family returned to New York from Samoa. Marianne had been ill so often in recent months that she was starting to believe Mary's theory that too much socializing zapped her strength. Mary told Bryher that illness was nature's way of punishing Marianne for "the pride that refuses to admit to a frail constitution." But despite her continual "captivities" that winter, Marianne refused to surrender. Seeing her friends, and especially the literary ones, was not for her a matter of pride but of necessity. Monroe Wheeler returned to New York that winter after almost a decade in Europe, and Bryher visited New York in January. There were other visitors, too, including Mary Norcross's former roommate Fanny Borden, whom they had not seen in years.

Borden, then head librarian at Vassar, asked Marianne if she would be willing to meet a student who was interested in poetry. After she realized how ill Marianne had been, Borden withdrew the request, but Marianne replied that she was "interested in college boys and girls" and would meet the "pilgrim" in Manhattan. She designated a bench outside the main reading room at the New York Public Library and forever remembered her first impression of Elizabeth Bishop dressed in a black, sealskin-trimmed jacket, white gloves, and pearl earrings. Bishop recalled that Marianne wore a flat broad hat and a blue tweed suit with a black bow at the neck—looking "quaint . . . but stylish at the same time."

Marianne did most of the talking. They talked about the questions Bishop had brought with her in a tiny notebook and about books and writers. Miss Moore is "simply amazing," Bishop told a friend afterward. "She is poor, sick, and her work is practically unread, I guess, but she seems completely undisturbed by it and goes right on producing perhaps one poem a year and a couple of reviews that are perfect in their way. I have never seen anyone who takes such *'pains.'*" Thus did Marianne present herself to her young admirer. She had just won the Helen Haire Levinson Prize, she had editors competing over her next book, and in the past three years she had published seven poems, six of them long, and nearly twenty reviews and essays.

Marianne agreed to meet Bishop out of a sense of duty, albeit a sincere one, to the next generation, but she liked her chic jacket and reserved demeanor. The next day she was already referring to "my Vassar friend." Unlike Marianne's other "kittens," Bishop did not ask for help with manuscripts.

Instead, she invited Marianne to the circus. According to Bishop's colorful memoir about her friendship with the older poet, they arrived early at Madison Square Garden so that they could visit the menagerie before the show. Marianne brought with her "two huge brown paper bags" of stale brown bread for the elephants. She gave one bag to Bishop and told her to distract the older elephants while she trimmed a few hairs off the heads of the babies for an elephant-hair bracelet. In Marianne's rendering of the excursion, however, she brought two *small* bags of bread. "Miss Bishop fed her slices timidly with new white chamois gloves and protested vehemently, 'It's *breathing* on me.'" Marianne thought her fortunate not to be slobbered on. Marianne liked Bishop and admired her intellect. "It is almost scary," she told Warner, "to find a college student with so much sense." But she did not "mother" Bishop as some of Bishop's critics have supposed she did.

Rather, Marianne cast Bishop in the role of college-girl sophisticate while she herself played mischief with the baby elephants. And while Bishop portrays herself in her memoir as the callow initiate, she instantly understood how to court the elder poet's friendship. Like a big sister, Bishop invited Marianne to the circus. Later she would invite her to animal films and to Coney Island. Bishop's intellectual and sartorial sophistication evoked some of the awe Marianne had felt for certain upperclassmen at Bryn Mawr. "Miss Bishop is 'older' than I am," Marianne once told Warner, after returning from a movie about baboons. During the year after she graduated, Bishop lived in New York. She and Marianne saw each other often, usually at Bishop's invitation. Marianne needed the friendship as much as Bishop needed a mentor. For the first time in many years, Marianne had the kind of literary companionship she had known during her early years in the Village.

Marianne recognized Bishop's promise as a writer long before she had seen any of Bishop's poems. They discussed Gerard Manley Hopkins at their first meeting, and Bishop sent Marianne a biography of Hopkins the next day. But it would be more than a year before she showed Marianne the essay about Hopkins that she had published in the Vassar literary magazine. And it would be more than two years before Bishop consulted her mentor about poems she was writing. Nevertheless, when T. C. Wilson, editor of *Westminster Magazine*, asked Marianne to recommend a young poet of whom he might not have heard, she mentioned Bishop. At this point Marianne had seen Bishop twice, at the library and at the circus.

Wilson, a young poet himself, was compiling an anthology of young poets and invited Bishop to contribute. Upon receiving Bishop's poems, he wrote Marianne that he thought they were not yet ready for publication. Marianne replied that she had never seen any of Bishop's poetry. A month later he told Marianne that he had received a new poem from Bishop, "The Map," that "is her strongest so far . . . You have probably seen it." Again Marianne replied that she had not seen any of Bishop's poetry but had recommended her because "I felt her ability and technical interest, and felt that in taste she was concentrated and selective."

"The Map" is Bishop's first mature poem. Now widely anthologized, it demonstrates Bishop's characteristic themes and techniques. To see it among the other poems Bishop allowed Wilson to publish is to witness a stunning transformation. The others—a Donne-like sonnet and three Valentines—could have been written by many a precocious undergraduate; they are juvenilia that Bishop never reprinted. Departing completely from the lovelorn themes of the juvenilia, "The Map," like "An Octopus," explores the space between landscape and interpretations of it. Its verbal wit, playful rhetoric, and startling precision are nowhere evident in the other poems—making its indebtedness to *Observations*, and to "An Octopus" in particular, unmistakable. Bishop later said that *Observations* was "an eye-opener in more ways than one." "Why," she asked, "had no one ever written about things in this clear and dazzling way before?" "The Map" is itself clear and dazzling. It leaps right over the usual phases of imitation and apprenticeship.

The anthology that Wilson helped compile, eventually called *Trial Balances*, included thirty-two poets between the ages of twenty and twenty-five, each with a commentary by an established poet. The paragraphs Moore wrote about Bishop are not so much descriptive of Bishop's poetry thus far as they are prophetic of the poetry yet to come. Bishop took her poems to Marianne's apartment to ask for advice about what to send. Marianne suggested a couple of minor changes. But her commentary mentions only two Valentines that had been published in a Vassar magazine, indicating that she did not have "The Map" or the other poems at hand while writing her critique. She praises the rhythm of a couple of lines in the Valentines—indeed, overpraises it—and also acknowledges some imperfections in the poems. But by commending such qualities as "unwordiness," "the flicker of impudence," and "selectiveness" (qualities of her own work that are nowhere evident in the Valentines), she lights the path Bishop would follow.

That Moore recognized in Bishop's conversation and a few short letters the potential for a unique poetic sensibility was her greatest gift to her protégée. She had such confidence in that potential that she recommended her friend's work to other editors besides Wilson: Bryher, Eliot, Pound, Zabel, and James Laughlin. These recommendations resulted in the publication of "The Man-moth" and "The Imaginary

Iceberg," among other poems and stories. Harper & Row even expressed interest in publishing a book of Bishop's work because of Moore's remarks in *Trial Balances.*

After a year in New York, Bishop spent the next year traveling with friends in Europe. She arrived home in the summer of 1936. In a self-described state of melancholy, she wrote Marianne that she was considering giving up poetry for medicine. "I have given myself more than a fair trial [at writing]," she said, "and the accomplishment has been nothing at all."

"Interesting as medicine is," Moore replied, "I feel you would not be able to give up writing with the ability for it that you have . . . To have produced what you have—either verse or prose is enviable." She had invited Bishop to send work in progress before, but she now insisted. And thus did Bishop begin sending her current work to Marianne, as she would for the next four years.

The apprenticeship ended abruptly while Bishop was working on the poems that would make up her first book, *North & South.* Bishop spent the summer of 1940 in Florida and often called Marianne about the poems she was writing. Having received discouraging news from two publishers that had formerly shown interest in her work, Bishop was in a low state of mind and in September apologized profusely to Marianne for her own laziness and for making demands on her mentor while offering nothing in return. She had written, she said, only "a half-dozen *phrases* that I can still bear to reread without too much embarrassment." While on her way to New York in October, Bishop sent Marianne what she considered her most ambitious poem yet. The elder poet called the younger one upon receiving "Roosters" and voiced her objection to the phrase "water-closet," which Bishop defended.

Marianne and Mary stayed up late rewriting the poem. They changed the title to "The Cock," made the strict triplet form irregular, and softened much of the diction. The revision has more of Mary in it than it does Marianne. The subject of the poem, Peter's denial of Christ before the cock crowed, proved irresistible to Mary, the revision indicates, and it shows Marianne as deaf to the crude violence of Bishop's original as she had been to the Dionysian mood of Hart Crane's "Wine Menagerie" years earlier. Marianne did, to her credit, express reservations about mailing the rewritten poem. She folded it into a tiny square, sealed it with a gold star, and warned Bishop in the accompanying letter not to read the poem before bed or at mealtime.

Just weeks earlier, Marianne had described Bishop to Warner as "docile and respectful as regards advice." Since she had honed her own unique voice by subtly resisting her mother's, it is possible to imagine her mailing the revision of "Roosters" to her disciple to provoke her out of docility. Intentionally or not, she succeeded.

Bishop had to muster considerable courage to reply. "What I'm about to say, I'm afraid, will sound like ELIZABETH KNOWS BEST," her letter of October 17 began. She rejected all but a few of the changes and defended her own choices of form and diction. Fearing that the letter sounded "cranky," she waited three days before mailing it. This letter was a defining moment for Bishop: she defended her aesthetic choices and asserted her own voice. Never again would she consult her mentor with the same deference.

No one, however, celebrated the victory. It was a blow to Bishop that the person whose support she most trusted had butchered her new poem. And Marianne quickly regretted having exhausted Bishop's already low supply of resilience. The next week Marianne met Elizabeth and Louise Crane, their mutual friend, for lunch. What chiefly impressed her, she told her mother afterward, was the contrast between Louise's philanthropic activity and Elizabeth's inert neediness. Bishop's despondency worried the Moores (as it did Louise Crane, who took her to a psychiatrist). It was time to exercise patience with their young friend, Mary said, rather than to push. She felt "tender and solicitous toward Elizabeth." For years afterward Marianne's letters to Bishop allude apologetically to the transgression.

By the time *North & South* appeared six years later, Bishop had learned to be solicitous of Marianne, too, and even of Mary, whom she disliked. The discipleship had evolved into a mutually supportive friendship. "You have done so much for me, Elizabeth," Marianne wrote during a summer of illness. "I feel a sense of defeat in your not knowing this better."

19

The Sea in a Chasm

1934–1939

With a new book forthcoming and several magazines eager for her work, Marianne had at last attained that "something" that seemed so elusive when she found herself stranded in Brooklyn five years earlier. "It certainly looks as if the water rat's boat had no leak," she told Warner as soon as plans for *Selected Poems* became definite.

She and Mary had seen Warner only briefly upon his return from Samoa in March. And in anticipation of a long summer with him, she worked "like a demon with canton-flannel horns" to finish "Nine Nectarines and Other Porcelain" by the end of June. She mailed it to Eliot in time for it to be included in *Selected Poems*. Then she and Mary joined Warner, Constance, and the children at Black Lake for ten days. When Warner resumed his duties at the Norfolk Navy Yard, Mary and Marianne accompanied him home to Portsmouth, Virginia, where they stayed until September. Warner came home for a quick lunch every day and again at five for dinner, both meals prepared by Constance's cook. After her "violent winter" of illness and anxiety, Marianne luxuriated in what she called a "nutritious summer."

The stifling heat kept the women indoors. They read Edith Wharton's *A Backward Glance* aloud to each other. And Marianne supplemented her own stack of vacation reading with children's authors from her nieces' shelves. The verdant yard bordered with nine flowering crape myrtle trees provided another source of entertainment. Marianne and her mother watched swallowtail butterflies "the size of bats" and "three grown mockingbird fledglings—mouse gray with dark gray speckles on the breast." The young mockingbirds stand "in a row like penguins," she wrote, "chirping without a pause all day, in the tone of a broken carriage-spring; then at night hop up into a pussy-willow tree, about a cat's height from the ground, still chirping, till one after the other, they fall asleep."

The highlight of the summer was a day trip to Williamsburg, where restorations had advanced considerably since Marianne had first been there in the summer of 1928. "These colonial grandeurs and simplicities would not have excited you so much as they did us," she wrote Bryher, "but it was valuable and romantic in our eyes." Her leisurely observations from this summer and the next, again in Portsmouth, would result in a sequence of four poems that she called "Old Dominion."

When Marianne returned to Brooklyn, she decided to postpone all writing until "we have given away or destroyed or re-examined everything we have." She had pruned her poetic oeuvre for *Selected Poems* the previous spring and now purged her papers. Every evening for nearly two months she sent a sack of letters down the dumbwaiter. At the same time, she instructed Warner to stop saving her letters. "I *can't* write no perfect letter on purpose for every eye of lynx and ear of owl to smell," she told him, "and then have it miss fire for the only reason it is *wrote*." For the past few years she had written him with posterity in mind. She saved carbons of her letters and blue penciled them as if for a future editor. Reviewing Emily Dickinson's letters two years earlier had brought her to the realization that her own letters might one day be published, and she thus began shaping her life and persona for public consumption.

Marianne also began looking for a new apartment. The upstairs neighbors played bridge into the wee hours, and another neighbor was a noisy drunk. She had never liked the landlord. But after inspecting, according to Mary, "hundreds of apartments," Marianne at last decided to remain at 260 Cumberland. The landlord agreed to lower the rent to seventy dollars, the same as another apartment she had found. In April 1935, the same month that *Selected Poems* appeared, she moved her mother and their belongings to the quieter apartment two floors above their own. Also that month they transferred their membership from the church they had attended ten years earlier to the Lafayette Avenue Presbyterian Church around the corner. Brooklyn became home at last. Marianne would remain in the same fifth-floor apartment for the next thirty years.

Unlike *Poems* and the first edition of *Observations*, everything about *Selected Poems* pleased its author. She liked Eliot's placement of her recent work at the beginning. His arrangement obscured the chronological development of her earlier work, but the first nine poems demonstrate her progress from the relatively personal themes of "The Steeple-Jack" and "The Hero" to global ones. Five of the nine juxtapose Egyptian and European aristocracies with obscure yet majestic species of the animal kingdom. Following the example of the Hebrew poets she had studied in Carlisle, Moore assumes the role of social critic and political seer in these poems—but under the guise of animal lover and natural historian.

Her warnings and criticisms are most explicit in "The Jerboa," where she describes Egyptian royalty that "looks on as theirs, impalas and onigers" and that gives evidence "everywhere" of their "power over the poor." In the next two poems, "Camellia Sabina" and "No Swan So Fine," she turns to the French, whom she calls a "cruel race." Her attitude toward French horticulture and a Louis XV candelabrum is one of morally ambivalent fascination. Like the first section of "The Jerboa," both poems show the consciously fastidious art that results from generations of power and possession, and both briefly present a natural and more admirable alternative. In "No Swan So Fine," a living swan "with swart blind look askance / and gondoliering legs" can ironically never be as "fine" as the sculpted one with "toothed gold / collar on to show whose bird it was." And in contrast to the French camellias that can tolerate neither "smoke from the stove, nor dew on the windows" of their greenhouse, the Bolzano vineyards of northern Italy provide shelter and occasional nourishment to the mice that scurry in their shadows. The mice have their own royalty, the Prince of Tails, and a baby mouse carried in its mother's mouth resembles a symbol of European chivalry, the Spanish Fleece.

"The Plumet Basilisk" and "The Frigate Pelican" also describe royalty but follow the example of the second half of "The Jerboa" in their emphasis upon reclusive yet regal creatures. In "The Plumet Basilisk," Moore points out the respect given to dragons in other cultures and claims the Costa Rican basilisk as "ours." It "portrays mythology's wish / to be interchangeably man and fish." It is both "our Tower-of-London / jewel that the Spaniards failed to see" and an "innocent, rare, gold- / defending dragon" that hides underwater among treasures lost from a Spanish ship.

More artist than monarch, her frigate pelican "hides / in the height and in the majestic / display of his art." He is another heroic version of the poet herself, admirable for the way he has adapted to the hardships of his environment. "Unturbulent" themselves, Moore's frigate birds "avail / themselves of turbulence to fly."

Crossing Africa, Europe, and the Americas, these five poems contrast plants and animals exploited for human use with their reclusive but free counterparts. "The Buffalo" and "Nine Nectarines" then take the reader to Asia, where Moore finds societies that live in harmony with their environments. In China the red-cheeked peach, or Yu, symbolizes long life, and features of various animals are combined into the mythic kylin, a gentle beast that becomes fierce against its enemies. The Chinese are "a race that 'understands / the spirit of the wilderness.'"

And in India the water buffalo that humbly serves barefoot farm boys is noble enough to carry the Buddha. European and American bison have been killed to near extinction, and all wildness has been bred out of domestic Western cattle such as the Hereford, Holstein, and Vermont ox. But the serviceable and sacred Indian buffalo retains the ancestral horns with which it can convert a tiger to "harmless rubbish."

"I am now preparing something—in verse—about the buffalo," Marianne told Warner in the summer of 1933. After considering the "zebu and the over-drove ox," the poem would present "the water buffalo, as the most fiery." The finished poem does include the zebu and ox, but the main foil to her buffalo is the aurochs. At the Brooklyn Institute, she had seen a water buffalo and tiger fight on film and had seen images of the Indian buffalo in a travelogue about Bali. But what fired her imagination in the poem was Hitler's rise to power earlier that year. In the course of her research, she learned about the aurochs— the extinct wild ancestor of domestic cattle that was so coveted by the Nazis that they funded a project to re-create it through "back breeding."

Bryher had sent her a pamphlet about the atrocities of racial hygiene in Germany and an open letter from novelist Heinrich Mann (brother of *Dial* contributor Thomas Mann) urging writers to join in protest against the Nazis. Moore was outraged and shared the pamphlet with friends. After Al Smith (Hoover's opponent in the 1928 presidential election) spoke at a large New York rally protesting the Nazis, Moore saw him at the zoo with his children and thanked him for supporting the Jews. "The Buffalo" makes the case that naturally evolved species such as the buffalo serve "human notions" better than breeding cattle selectively and annihilating wild bison. By implication, racial diversity also best serves "human notions."

Moore's references in these poems to "a cruel race," "a race that 'understands / the spirit of the wilderness,'" and "blacks, that choice race with an elegance / ignored by one's ignorance" reveal her ongoing concerns with racial injustice. She does not quite avoid her generation's proclivity either to denigrate or idealize non-European races, but she mostly does by focusing attention upon animals rather than humans. In "The Jerboa" she moves quickly from Africa's "untouched" race to its "untouched" desert rat. The sequence of seven poems that begins with "The Jerboa" and ends with "Nine Nectarines" takes as its theme the power of political ideology to shape both human destiny and the natural environment. Yet by focusing on plants and animals, Moore risks being dismissed as apolitical. Bryher perhaps recognized the political implications of "The Buffalo," a poem she especially liked. But hardly any one else did. When Pound urged Moore to pay attention to the economic situation, she replied that she paid "strict attention" to it but believed that "in art some things which seem inevitable ought to be concealed, like the working of the gastric juice."

•

The publication of *Selected Poems* proved that Moore was not, as some had feared, a one-book poet, but it did not significantly change perceptions of her work. It represents the height of her modernist achievement. By obscuring her early development, the arrangement of the poems had the desired effect of making her seem difficult. And since she reproduced Eliot's arrangement in her *Collected Poems* (1951) and *Complete Poems* (1967), she would appear to decades of readers as a kind of Athena born fully grown from the mind of the Modern.

Eliot's introduction includes two widely quoted remarks, that "Miss Moore is . . . one of those few who have done the language some service in my lifetime" and "that Miss Moore's poems form part of the small body of durable poetry written in our time . . . in which an original sensibility and alert intelligence and deep feeling have been engaged in maintaining the life of the English language." One or the other would henceforth appear virtually any time publishers needed to blurb Moore's poetry.

Eliot makes as strong a case as he can make for a living writer that Moore deserves a place in the tradition—the tradition to which he attached such importance in his landmark essay "Tradition and the Individual Talent." Borrowing the concept from Moore's own poetics, he argues that she merits a place in the literary tradition not necessarily because of her "greatness," a quality that only time can prove, but because of her "genuineness."

Assuming that most readers will find her poetry forbidding, he positions himself as the growling dog at the gate. "The moderately intellectual," he warns, may take the poems for mere "intellectual exercises" whereas it requires intellectual agility to recognize the poems' "emotional value." Thus, the critic F. R. Leavis, who remained baffled by the poems despite his admiration for Eliot, had to concede in print that even a studious reader such as himself might be "very much less than moderately" intellectual.

Pound and Eliot had both gone on record as admirers of Moore's poetry in 1918 and Eliot again in 1923. Williams had done so in 1925. And in 1935, with his review of *Selected Poems*, Wallace Stevens added himself to the roster. Eliot and Williams had no taste for each other's work. Nor did Pound and Stevens. But all four modernists concurred that Moore was, as Stevens put it, "A Poet That Matters." Whereas to Williams she represented all that was "new" in poetry, to Eliot she was an enduring member of the "tradition." And whereas Pound praised her early resistance to romanticism, Stevens paid her his highest compliment by calling her a "romantic." "Unless one is that," he said, "one is not a poet at all." Stevens's review explained more precisely than anyone else had how the elements of her stanza—syllable count, rhyme, and indentation of lines—work together to create a sense of rhythm.

Eliot's praise for Moore's highly complex and innovative technique—along with that of Stevens, R. P. Blackmur, and Morton Zabel—made her seem more than ever a poet's poet. If even F. R. Leavis lacked sufficient intellect to appreciate such technique, was there any hope for the "lovers of poetry," whose aversion to the "new and genuine" Eliot also disparaged?

By the time *Selected Poems* appeared, Marianne had already written most of her next book. When Bryher saw "The Buffalo" in the November 1934 *Poetry*, she asked if she might have it for a series of limited-edition booklets she hoped to publish. "The Buffalo" was already taken, Marianne answered, but she had a new poem about mockingbirds ("Bird-Witted") and another about butterflies ("Half Deity") partly written. Bryher met with Marianne about the book when she came to New York during the winter and arranged a second meeting with their mutual friend George Plank, who would illustrate the volume. Later that spring Marianne sent Bryher four poems: "Bird-Witted," "Half Deity," "The Pangolin," and "Pigeons."

The four poems reflect the buoyant mood of her summer in Portsmouth. She had not written anything as light as "Bird-Witted" for a long time. All four showcase her startling precision and her attention to rhythm—punctuated with dense hyphenated sequences, multisyllabic words, alliteration, and both internal and external rhyme. Often the rhythm illustrates the creatures' movements, as it does when she describes a mother mockingbird feeding her chirping chicks:

> Towards the high-keyed intermittent squeak
> of broken carriage-springs, made by

the three similar, meek-
            coated bird's-eye
freckled forms she comes; and when
       from the beak
            of one, the still living
            beetle has dropped
out, she picks it up and puts
it in again.

Inspired by an article in the *Bulletin of the American Museum of Natural History* and by a small bronze pangolin at the Museum of Modern Art, "The Pangolin" is for many readers Moore's quintessential animal poem—beloved for its wittily precise descriptions of the scaled, nocturnal anteater.

Another armoured animal—scale
            lapping scale with spruce-cone regu-
            larity until they
form the uninterrupted central
            tail-row.

"This near artichoke" is not only "another armored animal" but also another of Moore's obscure survivors, solitary wanderers, and unlikely heroes. Its "exhausting solitary / trips through unfamiliar ground at night" in particular recall the first half of "The Hero." Though the pangolin's movements have an unexpected "grace," it has none of the regality of the plumed basilisk or frigate bird.

And while the poem shows the pangolin hunting ants and protecting itself in its natural habitat, the reader sees little of the cultural and political landscape that had so concerned the poet in recent years. Humans here are relatively harmless and powerless, capable of befuddlement but not much worse. Whereas earlier poems idealized the animal's dignity against human greed and shortsightedness, here the pangolin is shown to resemble humans in its postures and its daily toil. By the end of the poem, pangolin and human become conflated in the pronoun *he*.

The prey of fear: he, always
            curtailed, extinguished,

thwarted by the dusk, work partly done,
    says to the alternating blaze,
"Again the sun!
   anew each
   day; and new and new and new,
   that comes into and steadies my soul."

The unabashedly exultant ending is unprecedented in Moore's oeuvre. It is inspirational if not outright religious. Eliot's synthesis of modernity and Christian faith in *The Rock* had impressed Moore deeply when she read it the previous year. Though her ending seems more pagan than Christian, the poem celebrates religious virtues such as humility, reverence, and grace.

Just as Moore was writing "The Pangolin," she told a reviewer of *Selected Poems* that one of her "idiosyncrasies of technique" was her attraction to "the unaccented rhymed syllable." Following the same principle, she liked a poem merely to come to a close rather than "culminating in a crescendo." *Selected Poems* demonstrates this preference: occasional rhythmic crescendos such as the ending of "People's Surroundings" baffle the intellect, and clarifying statements such as appear within "Marriage" and "An Octopus" are rhythmically understated. This technique contributes to the poems' difficulty. With "The Pangolin," however, she abruptly changes course. Here the rhythmic crescendo at the end contributes to an emotional as well as a thematic clarification.

When Marianne returned to Portsmouth for the summer of 1935, she wrote two new poems for Bryher: first, "Virginia Britannia," a landscape poem about America's cultural origins; and then "Smooth Gnarled Crape Myrtle," a defense of "blameless bachelors" such as herself. Before she returned to Brooklyn in early October, she sent Bryher and George Plank her final selection for *The Pangolin and Other Verse*. "Virginia Britannia," "Bird-Witted," "Half Deity," and "Smooth Gnarled Crape Myrtle" made up the sequence she called "Old Dominion." She dropped "Pigeons" and concluded with "The Pangolin," the only poem outside the sequence.

Not only does Moore turn away from social satire and subtle endings in these poems, but she also changes her mind about romance. In her 1922 poem "New York," romance is a form of "savage" greed opposed to the raw experience of the wilderness. Yet she apparently

intended no irony when she told Bryher how "romantic" Williamsburg was nor when she told Elizabeth Bishop that Jamestown was "a
most romantic place."

"Virginia Britannia" is a celebration of those romantic places. It
does question a romanticized view of colonization. But instead of sati-
rizing the abuses of power as she had earlier in the decade, her descriptions of the flora and fauna show the convergence of English, Indian,
and African cultures. "Indian- / named Virginian / streams" run
through "counties named for English lords." The poem points out the
role of "kind tyranny" in this convergence.

The ending of the poem is as overtly romantic as anything Moore
ever wrote. Rather than emphasizing precision and differentiation, as
she had in "An Octopus" and other poems of the 1920s, she writes that
during the sunset

> . . . The live oak's rounded
> mass of undulating boughs, the white
>   pine, the agèd hackberry—handsomest vis-
> itor of all—the
>   cedar's etched solidity
>   the cypress, lose identity
> and are one tree,

In the final lines, the sunset colors expanding through the clouds "are
to the child an intimation of / what glory is": a direct, unironic allusion
to Wordsworth's famous "Ode: Intimations of Immortality."

Just as Moore began writing "Virginia Britannia," she told Bryher
that all of her attempts at verse and criticism over the years had been
"a chameleon attempt to bring my product into some sort of compati-
bility with Wallace Stevens." "Virginia Britannica" nods to Stevens's
recent characterization of her as "romantic."

The Brendin Publishing Company issued 120 copies of *The Pangolin and Other Verse* in February 1936. Moore sent a few copies of the
illustrated volume to friends; otherwise, very few readers would see its
contents until they reappeared in *What Are Years* a half decade later.

•

Marianne wrote some reviews and a couple of poems in the year after she completed *The Pangolin and Other Verse*. But by early 1937 she was telling people that she was committed to "a task of a non-general kind, from which I am not at liberty to take holidays" and therefore would not be writing poems or reviews in the near future. No one except Mary, Warner, and Harold S. Latham, her editor at Macmillan, were privy to her secret until a year later, when she also confessed to Bryher that she was writing a novel.

Latham had first encouraged her to write one in 1921. She had sent him Bryher's novel, and when she went to Macmillan to pick it up, Latham told her he would like to publish her own novel some day. At that time Marianne had begun recording conversations in her notebooks with the idea of using them in a novel, and she mentioned a novel to H.D. She mentions her "story" off and on in the early 1930s, but it was during her second and third summers in Virginia that she began making real progress.

Warner had taken her to a yacht race during the summer of 1931. The nautical idioms he and the yachtsmen used captivated Marianne, and she recorded long passages about boats and sailing in her notebooks. Parts of these conversations appear in her novel with little or no alteration. When she asked Warner to review the idioms, he offered a suggestion about her "over decorated" prose: "Starve it down and make it run." Over the next few years Marianne sent him all of her chapters in progress and even considered naming him coauthor.

Warner had never grasped his sister's poetry. He told her that "Peace," an eight-line ditty she wrote for a contest and never considered publishing, was possibly the best thing she had ever written. And while he wrote exuberantly about receiving *Selected Poems* and *The Pangolin*, he managed to do so without commenting upon the poems. Yet being an accomplished raconteur himself, he was a reliable critic of her fiction. Warner and Marianne's affectionate exchanges over the novel took both back to the days when they made up stories together.

Marianne sent two chapters to Bryher a year apart. Bryher published the first one, "The Farm Show," in *Life and Letters Today*, a magazine she had founded with her second husband. But the editor rejected the second one. Otherwise, Marianne did not seek advice or recognition outside her family until she sent the complete 385-page typescript to Macmillan in late 1939.

"Once upon a time and now are the same, for there is always the temptation to inhabit a fairy tale," the novel begins. One does not expect a pioneer of hard-edged Modernism to indulge in such a temptation, yet that is indeed what this novel does. The various settings based on Locust Hill, Greenwich Village, Monhegan, London, and Oxford allow Marianne to re-create her favorite memories. Her fairy tale admittedly includes neither a big bad wolf nor cruel stepsisters. Nor does it contain the social satire of Trollope's *The Way We Live Now*, from which she takes her own title. Only the barest of plots—a marriage plot at that—connects the vignettes.

The main character, Alec Van Wart, is a composite of Warner, Marianne, and the all-knowing Uncle George character from Jacob Abbott's Rollo books. He is equally at home on the farm, on a sailboat, and at Greenwich Village parties. He shares his family homestead (based upon Locust Hill) with his older brother Hugh, who resembles Mary in interests and temperament. Their widowed sister, Emily, lives nearby with her two children, Arthur and Angeline, who resemble the childhood Warner and Marianne. These two households allow the author to dramatize family memories from various stages of her life.

During the second chapter Alec develops a romantic interest in Eloise Osgood. (Marianne put much thought into the naming of her characters; like Ambrose in "The Steeple-Jack," her favorite names all start with vowels.) Eloise is the sister of Emily's late husband, Arthur, and is an artist, a "modern Audubon." She dabbles in poetry, is secretly writing a novel, and all the while supports herself by drawing fashion ads. When asked "*What* do you do? *Where* do you live? Are you married?"—questions that Marianne was once asked at a Village party—Eloise replies (as Marianne never could) that she lives alone in "a little attic in New York where I read and do some work and a lot of cogitating." If Alec represents the domestically encompassed Marianne, Eloise personifies the unencumbered artist of Marianne's long-held fantasies. Despite Mary's suggestion that Eloise have a mother and father, Marianne insisted that Eloise be an "orphan."

Several minor characters are easily recognizable as Scofield Thayer, Sibley Watson, Monroe Wheeler, Glenway Westcott, and other Village personalities. Two characters in fact suggest Thayer. Sebastian

Such is small, dark, and formal like Thayer and co-owns a newspaper called *The Equator.* But the tall, blond Nicholas Camelford combines Watson's appearance with Thayer's affluent family and arrogant tastes. He is Alec's rival for Eloise's affection. He takes Eloise to the theater, as Thayer did Marianne, and his opinions resemble Thayer's. When he presents Eloise with an emerald necklace, she suddenly feels like "a minnow trapped in a dipper" and realizes that she does not like him as much as she thought she did. He shows a lack of consideration for his parents, Eloise thinks, and a lack of empathy for some parakeets she is tending. Then he insults Hugh, whom Eloise ardently defends.

In the end Eloise overcomes her objections to Alec's being a virtual relative and chooses him, the brotherly "rustic," over Camelford, the Village sophisticate. The reader learns almost nothing of the appearance of either Alec or Eloise except that each resembles the other's sibling: Alec and Emily mirror Arthur and Eloise. Eloise values her freedom but never considers rejecting romance altogether. Nor does she demand of her beau "love that will gaze an eagle blind." The poet of "Marriage" is nowhere to be found. Eloise's choice of family togetherness, the fairy tale in which Marianne had been captive all her life, is as straightforward as "Marriage" is circuitous.

Once Marianne had a complete typescript, Warner encouraged her to send it to Macmillan. Yet he gently prepared her for its rejection. "Hand it to them, as something that has intensely interested *you*," he advised, "as something that will be perhaps of interest to *them* as an exposition of your character, methods of work, and your critical judgment of literary values and production rather than as a novel the general public might be expected to drop their coffee cups and seize with both hands to read for a thrill or 'a good story.'" How right he was.

"The Way We Live Now" does contain choice passages of description. A sidewalk in the Village is "brisk with people—dogs straining forward on leashes, delivery-boys, neat-footed women; business-men burdened by neither dogs nor packages—all impersonally avoiding one another while hastening as if under threat, in contrary directions." And a sudden storm in Oxford produces "a partial lake . . . ruffling and puckering under the squall,—a tiny popocatapetl [volcano] of water springing up for each drop that came down." But otherwise the novel is bound to disappoint Moore's admirers, as it did Harold Latham.

Without a plausible plot, a consistent narrative voice, and especially character development, the novel lays bare Moore's idiosyncrasies. The reader winces in embarrassment—and yearns for the emotional honesty of her poems.

The second chapter introduces sixteen guests at a tennis party. Far more memorable than any of them is a kitten "dashing toward the house, back arched and tail flowing." This kitten never reappears, yet the reader learns every detail of its appearance down to "the tortoise-shell-spotted ridged roof of its mouth." By contrast, Eloise, who first appears on the same page, is merely "a figure in pink, firmly poised on chiseled white heels." For all Moore's attention to the appearance and behavior of animals, she seems remarkably obtuse about people. She might mention a character's height, hair color, and a distinctive nose— but rarely a revealing gesture or facial expression. Admirable characters express Moore's own views. They share her breadth of interests and sympathies but lack her depth.

The conversation at the party ranges from a long anecdote about sailing to observations about the tennis game, to Puritanism, to a movie about alligators, to the politics of the Depression, to "wild-life conservation, the extinct passenger-pigeon, the mourning dove, and the gracefulness of the swan." Dialogue is to be appreciated for its own sake. Most of it is transcribed directly from Moore's notebooks regardless of the character speaking or the situation. Phrases such as "Our mariner becalmed?" erupt without motivation from characters who never again speak that way. And each new setting produces scenes that set up choice bits of dialogue from the locals, such as this paragraph about Hugh and Alec's arrival in Oxford:

> As their Victoria drawn by a horse trotting so vertically its progress was difficult to account for, stopped at the entrance to "Magpie Lane formerly Grove Street," a back-firing motor-cycle swerved out with a series of deafening explosions, the cabman half-turning and remarking as he got down from the box, "Some of the gentlemen is wicked."

Latham wrote Moore a warm letter assuring her that he and others at Macmillan had gone over and over the novel and that they took pride in being her publisher. "We simply do not feel, however, that your novel is one which we could publish with confidence and enthusiasm in the very difficult conditions surrounding us today. In happier times it would have been a nice book to do—a poet's novel and one which would be treated with respect."

Yes, a poet's novel: it foregrounds Moore's keen powers of observation and her fondness for language against her artlessness as a storyteller. The novel was all but finished when, to Mary's dismay, Marianne spent days rewriting it to remove unintentional rhymes. After Latham returned the typescript in January 1940, she made more revisions and cut thirty-three pages. In March she sent it to Houghton Mifflin. Never again is the novel mentioned in her surviving papers. Most of her friends never knew it existed.

If it is difficult to imagine why Moore the artist would devote more than three years of her career to such a project, it is easy to see why Marianne the daughter turning fifty would do so. Those years were fraught with grief, worry, and illness. In February 1938 Mary Norcross died suddenly—alone and poor. Marianne was "crushed," according to Mary, but they did not go to the funeral because of Marianne's digestive ailments.

Marianne spent two weeks in the hospital during March and did not fully recover for months afterward. After ruling out gallbladder problems, the doctors diagnosed her with spastic colon—what she called her "internal quicksilver orangutan." She was prescribed a liquid diet and certain exercises but was advised above all to stop worrying. "Resistance must give place to acquiescence," the doctor told her. Psychosomatic medicine was then in its infancy. Marianne found her symptoms described in Edmund Jacobson's *You Must Relax* and also found useful David Seabury's *How to Worry Successfully.* Yet she continued to answer scrupulously the letters from aspiring writers that filled her mailbox. "Solicitude for others, and the wish that they may write as they please, are almost a mania with me," she said.

The spastic colon caused Marianne to give up her novel for much of 1938, and she gave it up again for the first half of 1939 while Mary suffered a case of shingles and severe neuralgia. Mary wore a bandage over her face to protect her eyes from the light and was so sensitive to noise that it distressed her to hear Marianne talk on the telephone. Marianne told her close friends that they could call only between 8:30 and 9:00 in the morning. And she never left the apartment for more than an hour at a time.

Ezra Pound came to New York that spring for the first time in twenty-eight years. He wanted to meet her. Marianne sent him her address and phone number but said that she was not using the telephone or accepting visitors. "My mother has been ill since December and is still so ill, I don't know why it is not the dissolution of my mind and my heart," she told him. He nevertheless telephoned to invite himself to supper—eggs or cold cuts, he suggested. Marianne agreed to meet him at a restaurant. He asked what she read for "mental food" and was dismayed by her apparent lack of interest in the topic. I "read nothing," she answered when he asked her later about it. "*British Agriculture* by Viscount Astor and B. Seebohm Rowntree is the only thing I have read thoroughly in a long time." After dinner, she allowed him to accompany her to the apartment. He stayed fifteen minutes—far too long, she thought, considering her mother's discomfort—and then she walked him to the subway. "Yes. Ezra P. is a great scalawag," Warner concluded from reading Marianne's account of the visit.

Their conversation could not have been all solemnity, however, for throughout the next decade their letters to each other grew ever more playful and affectionate. Pound's nearly always included newspaper clippings about elephants. In the winter after they met, Pound asked Marianne to edit a magazine he hoped to start. She told him that he should edit the magazine himself but recommended some writers she knew to be in New York.

For the month of June, Marianne and Mary stayed at Hildegarde Watson's farm near Northbridge, Massachusetts. They had the place to themselves and servants to wait upon them. The quiet calmed them both. Mary felt well enough to sit outside, and Marianne was able to resume work on her novel. They spent the rest of the summer on Cape Ann, first in a friend's cottage and then at a community center, awaiting Warner's return from three years at sea.

At some point during the year, Marianne returned to poetry at least briefly. "What Are Years?" appears about two-thirds of the way through her novel. Eloise is feeling discouraged about writing fiction because of her tendency to digress about "things like the amount of alloy in cymbals and statuary bronze, and the speeds at which birds fly" and decides to try poetry instead. She apologetically shows her first poem, "What Are Years," to Camelford.

What Are Years?

What is our innocence,
what is our guilt? All are
   naked, none is safe. And whence
is courage: the unanswered question,
the resolute doubt,—
dumbly calling, deafly listening—that
in misfortune, even death,
     encourages others
     and in its defeat, stirs

   the soul to be strong? He
sees deep and is glad, who
   accedes to mortality
and despite imprisonment, rises
within himself as
the sea in a chasm, struggling to be
free and unable to be,
     in its surrendering
     finds its continuing.

Without noticing the third stanza on the back, Camelford returns the poem. Eloise, the alleged novice, points out that in line two, "the long foot 'All' should be short; and in line four, the short foot 'the' should be long!" But she accepts the inconsistency. Without prompting, she then adroitly changes "The very bird / grows tall and as he sings, steels / his form straight up" in the third stanza to "The very bird / grown taller as he sings, steels / his form straight up."

Like many of her poems thus far—from "Those Various Scalpels" to "The Jerboa"—"What Are Years" is about survival. But no longer is the poet a warrior thrashing swords or a radical with "everything

crammed belligerently inside itself." No longer is she "struggling to be /
free, and unable to be." She had never been so physically confined as
she was during the nine months of Mary's neuralgia. Yet confronting
her own ailments and her mother's mortality had convinced her to
heed the doctor's advice, "Resistance must give way to acquiescence."
In "Sojourn in the Whale," her 1916 poem about the Easter Rising,
Moore had contrasted the expectation that "water seeks its own level"
with water's ability to "rise automatically" "when obstacles happened to
bar / The path." Twenty years later she uses similar imagery to show
that, rising in a narrow chasm, the sea "in its surrendering, / finds its
continuing."

20

Hindered to Succeed

1940–1944

Marianne returned to poetry as soon as she received Latham's letter rejecting her novel. By the first of May, three and a half months later, she had sent off four new poems and was at work on a fifth. She no longer wished to appear in *Poetry* now that Harriet Monroe had died and Morton Zabel had resigned. And she wanted in any case to see if the larger-circulation magazines might like her new, more accessible work. Yet both *The New Yorker* and *The Atlantic* rejected "What Are Years?" *The New Yorker* returned "Four Quartz Crystal Clocks" and "Rigorists" as well. *The New Yorker* had already adopted Elizabeth Bishop, and Marianne enjoyed the irony of the situation enough to tell her about the rejections. "What I think about the *New Yorker*," Elizabeth Bishop replied, "can only be expressed like this: *!@!!!@!*!!"

Marianne could understand why the poems were rejected, she told Warner. "Technical virtuosity is not the essential nourishment we need at this time." The remark would prove prophetic not only for her own work but also for the generation of more accessible, more personal, and more political poets that would emerge in the decades after World War II.

Marianne's poems twenty years ago lacked "stinging greatness of truth and high principle that gripped the soul," according to Mary. But with the outbreak of World War II, words such as *courage, joy, justice,* and *love* appear prominently in her work. Since most of the new poems came out of her "very abundant head" rather than from research, Mary thought them "freer." The looser syntax does make for smoother reading, and the unlikely comparisons—such as the ostrich's head revolving "with compass- / needle nervousness"—are more charming than jarring. The poems still demand "mental attention," as Pound said long ago, but that attention is now rewarded with a meaning closer to what readers expect from poetry.

Just over a year after Macmillan rejected Moore's novel, Latham asked to publish a new volume of her poems. During the spring of 1941, she assembled fifteen poems: seven from the mid-1930s, including those from *The Pangolin*; a newly revised "The Student"; and seven written in the past year and a half. *What Are Years* appeared in October. Like her animal poems of a decade earlier, the new poems are about survival—but there is now greater acceptance of and less indignation toward life's "hindrances." The moral implications are more explicit, and the animals clearly exemplify human attributes such as ingenuity, courage, and hope. A caged bird finds joy in singing, the Eskimo and the ostrich survive extinction, Montaigne thwarts bandits with his dignity, and the eggs of the paper nautilus free themselves from an obsessive mother.

David Seabury's positive approach to adversity pervades the new poems. His lectures at the Brooklyn Institute had guided Marianne through her own hardships in the late 1930s, and his strategies for "how to worry successfully" helped her manage her anxieties. Writing verse no longer got Marianne as "wrought up or excited" as formerly, Mary assured Warner, and she could write a poem that satisfied her in a week or two. Seabury's name appears frequently in her correspondence of the time. She told Monroe Wheeler to " 'Welcome difficulty' as Mr. Seabury says but remember always that difficulty is relentless and escape is from within." Seabury drew upon American Protestant values of self-discipline, perseverance, and humility as well as the Emersonian principle of self-reliance to make the case that all Americans have the power within themselves to lead healthier, happier lives. His advocacy of "victory by surrender," "refusing compromise," honest prayer, and the healing power of laughter along with his aversion to hypocrisy and egotism had obvious appeal for Marianne.

The new poems have far more to say about the war in Europe than has been recognized. Marianne read *The New York Times* to her mother every morning and supported the Allies in her own small way by refusing royalties from Faber and Faber during the war. She got an eyewitness account of the situation in Europe through Bryher: first from Switzerland, where Bryher aided close to a hundred Jewish refugees at her Bauhaus villa, and then from London, where Bryher spent the duration of the war. Through Louise Norcross Lucas, the youngest of the Norcross sisters, the Moores witnessed the German occupation of France. Louise and her husband sheltered refugees in their Cote d'Azur château until the Germans confiscated it. The fifty soldiers quartered there built fires in every room, including those with no fireplace, and soon burned the place to the ground.

Whereas France had been the perpetrator of power in "No Swan So Fine" and "Camellia Sabina," it becomes the brave guardian of truth in "Four Quartz Crystal Clocks" and "Light Is Speech." Louise sent the Moores a speech by playwright Jean Giraudoux, France's newly appointed minister of information, which partially inspired "Four Quartz Crystal Clocks." The poem celebrates "the world's exactest clocks" and Giraudoux's "instruments of truth" for defying the cannibal Chronos. And in "Light Is Speech," written shortly after news arrived of the Lucases' fire, Marianne compares the frankness of the French, their demand for truth, with light. It first appeared in *Decision*, a short-lived anti-Nazi magazine edited by Klaus Mann, Thomas Mann's son. "Rigorists" is a tribute to Sheldon Jackson, the uncle of Mary and Louise Norcross. The opposite of Hitler, Jackson was "a quiet man" who, according to the poem, saved a race. When the destruction of the whale population threatened the livelihood of the Eskimos in 1891, Jackson persuaded the government to let him introduce Siberian reindeer into Alaska.

> . . . The battle was won
>
>   by a quiet man,

Sheldon Jackson, evangel to that race
whose reprieve he read in the reindeer's face.

"We are out of humor with Ireland just now," Marianne told Mary Shoemaker as she was assembling poems for *What Are Years*. She had one more poem to write, "Spenser's Ireland." While she could appreciate the frankness of the French, the poem indicates that she identified with Irish credulity. The world could do with less "obduracy" and more Irish "enchantment," the poem says. "You're not free until you've been made captive by / supreme belief." This is the most obviously autobiographical poem in Moore's oeuvre: she mentions her great-great-grandmother and proudly claims her Irish heritage. Yet the poem concludes:

. . . The Irish say your trouble is their
trouble and your
        joy their joy? I wish
I could believe it;
I am troubled, I'm dissat-
        isfied, I'm Irish.

Despite the atrocities of the Nazi regime, Ireland remained stubbornly neutral during World War II, a position that "troubled" Moore.

"He 'Digesteth Harde Yron'" hearkens back to "The Jerboa" and the other data-dense animal poems of *Selected Poems*. Unlike the other new poems in *What Are Years*, she worked on it for months. The poem has some of the witty precision of "The Pangolin." But humans in the poem are again greedy, brutal, and obtuse in comparison with the elegant, ingenuous, but (like Marianne) nervous ostrich.

Moore had been contemplating a poem about the paper nautilus ever since Elizabeth Bishop sent her the shell of one in 1937. One of her finest poems of the 1940s, "Paper Nautilus" is as elegantly proportioned and streamlined as its subject. There are no esoteric facts in the poem, and it is also, uncharacteristically, an extended metaphor. A cousin to the octopus, the female nautilus secretes her paperlike shell out of four of her eight arms. Those arms remain wrapped around the shell, the other four tucked inside, until it is time to let both shell and eggs go. While the mother nautilus "scarcely // eats until the eggs are

hatched," her feelings toward her "cradled freight" are no more sentimental than those of the mother cat in "The Hero" or the bayonet-
beaked mockingbird in "Bird-Witted." She constructs her geometric
nest neither for artistic fame nor political power. In a time of war, when
politicians base their hopes on "mercenaries," this cephalopod seems
to know that "love / is the only fortress / strong enough to trust to."

By mentioning writers in the first stanza, Moore invites the reader
to regard the nautilus and her papery creation as a metaphor for the
poetic process. But the intricate simile in the second and third stanzas
offers a more subtle invitation.

> as Hercules, bitten
>
> by a crab loyal to the hydra,
> was hindered to succeed,
>   the intensively
>   watched eggs coming from
> the shell free it when they are freed,—

In this three-point analogy, the nine-headed female hydra corresponds
to the eight-armed mother nautilus, and the crab corresponds to the
nautilus shell. Hercules plays the unlikely role of "the intensively
watched eggs." When he defeats the hydra, he frees himself and inadvertently immortalizes the crab as a constellation. The pairing of the
just-hatched eggs with Hercules reveals a startling self-portrait: the
daughter, at once vulnerable and heroic, frees herself from her mother's
clutches while setting loose her rhythmic, yet flawed art:

> leaving . . . wasp-nest flaws
> of white on white and close-
>
> laid Ionic chiton-folds
> like the lines in the mane of
>   a Parthenon horse.

The poem presents maternal love as a paradox: monstrous on
the one hand and "the only fortress strong enough to trust to" on the

other. No longer does the poet regard herself in exile from the "tea-time fame" and "commuter comforts" of New York's literary world. Rather, the power of her mother's love, she acknowledges, has *hindered* her to *succeed* as a writer.

What Are Years attracted a new generation of critics. Those such as Randall Jarrell and Clement Greenberg, who were already familiar with the modernist achievements of *Observations* and *Selected Poems*, barely noticed the shift in Moore's new work. *Time* magazine, however, acknowledged no difficulty in interpreting the "still-life parables" of "the most accomplished poetess in the English-speaking world today." The brief unsigned review—by Schuyler Jackson, husband of the poet Laura Riding—also exemplified a new trend in journalistic reviews. Jackson interviewed Moore in order to give readers a sense of the poet as well as her work. He presents her as a "a greying, mobile-faced, almost reckless spinster," who "for the last twelve years has lived a sequestered life in her mother's Brooklyn flat" picking up "a microscopic living from her writings."

Time's description of the spinster rather than of the poems caught the attention of a Boston heiress who picked up the magazine on her way to the hairdresser. Marianne soon received through her publisher a long fan letter. "The bits about you and your life in the review have roused the keenest interest in me," it said, "the only real reason I can give you for writing you is that I have to, that is all. I do as I'm led." After considering a variety of gifts ranging from a loaf of bread to a new mattress, Kathrine Jones selected something as remarkable for its intimacy as for its value. She enclosed in the letter a pin, in which were set the "very nice" jewels of a deceased friend. "If this seems strange to you I can assure you it seems just as strange to me . . . I seem absolutely possessed with the desire to do something for you," she explained. "That 'microscopic living' affects me. There could so easily flow at least some time things from my easeful life into yours. And there will! I know there will. It won't be any special doing of mine. They'll go themselves."

Marianne did not refuse the gift as she would have twenty years earlier but instead welcomed it—she did love jewels—and the effusive yet self-effacing language, so like that of her own family. "What elfin, what celestial beams have shone into our little 'flat' as *Time* calls it, through you," Marianne answered the day she received the letter. She sent Kathrine Jones a copy of her book and signed the letter with only her first name. The next day she wrote again, saying that she had at last calmed down enough to read Kathrine's letter word by word. Before she mailed the second letter, a box of cheeses, chutney, gourmet soups, cocoa, and tea arrived from Boston. As had been the case with Bryher—another heiress, prolific letter writer, and aspiring novelist— the two became rapid friends. Kathrine Jones, however, did not question Marianne's filial devotion. Rather, having lived with her own mother for thirty years, she may have imagined that the poet's living arrangements were as "difficult" and "restricted" as her own.

As Mary's health declined, Marianne's entourage of patronesses expanded. Bryher continued to write often and to send occasional checks and gifts in addition to the quarterly payments she had set up. Having given up her own aspirations as a performer, Hildegarde Watson began dressing Marianne for her public appearances. At first the statuesque Hildegarde had her own clothes altered—or claimed to. Later she openly bought her friend clothes. The long-sleeved, light blue wool dress that she sent for Marianne's reading at Vassar was a great hit there and again at Harvard. Mary and Marianne kneeled in grateful prayer, according to Mary, when the dress arrived. And Marianne wrote a playful poem, "The Wood-Weasel," that was a reverse acrostic of Hildegarde's name. Hildegarde continued to send generous checks for Christmas and birthdays.

In Louise Crane, Marianne found a third benefactor. Elizabeth Bishop had introduced them when Louise drove the three to Coney Island in 1935. Louise and Elizabeth soon thereafter bought a house together in Key West. Louise was heir to the Crane Paper fortune, and her late father had served both as governor of and senator from Massachusetts. Her mother, with whom she lived in a seventeen-room Fifth Avenue apartment, devoted herself to the arts. As a board member for the Museum of Modern Art, Josephine Crane knew Monroe Wheeler, who informed the Cranes of Marianne's illness in 1938. Louise sent tulips to the hospital and when Marianne was well again began taking her to galleries and concerts.

She evidently never sent checks but attended readily to Marianne's various needs. During Mary's bout with neuralgia, she bought nightcaps for Mary and the size 42 men's oxford-cloth shirts that Marianne requested for herself. A few years later she would send Marianne a phonograph and in later decades a succession of typewriters. Louise "adores *getting things* for other people," Elizabeth told Marianne. Continuing the Crane tradition of supporting the arts, Louise organized a series of "Coffee Concerts" at the Museum of Modern Art in 1941. Performers included the Jubilee Singers and Billie Holiday, who made a great impression on Marianne. Marianne appreciated Louise's "reverence for people's reserves"—that is, her ability to make herself useful without imposing herself.

Marianne wrote Kathrine Jones thirty-two letters over the first three months of their correspondence, and Mary wrote her nearly as often, flirting on behalf of them both. Kathrine quickly caught on to the Moores' game of elaborately praising the other while even more elaborately demeaning oneself. (Marianne played this sometimes hilarious game with other friends as well. Writing Hildegarde Watson, she compared herself to "the terrible kitten that darts between your feet so you nearly kill it and yourself" and to Monroe Wheeler called herself "an incubus being raised by an eye-dropper.") Kathrine continually protested the Moores' idealization of her and exaggerated her own unworthiness. "Now what do you think of me?" she wrote after admitting that their handwriting sometimes baffled her. "I feel myself going down. down. down. Maybe you will never, either of you, write me another word. But, dearly listening, I love you both with all my heart."

The first person with whom Kathrine shared the delicious secret of her new friendship was her "best friend," Marcia King Chamberlain. Kathrine called Marcia a "business woman" who had had to work all her life while she had herself always been provided for. Kathrine's father had made a fortune in the tropical fruit trade, and Marcia, divorced for many years, worked as a bookkeeper. They lived near each other in Brookline. Possessing every virtue in the extreme, Kathrine said, and deficient in faults, Marcia was the amiable one, Kathrine the recluse. The two were family to each other. Their intimacy did not, however, prevent Kathrine's letters to Marianne from taking an erotic turn. Twice she mentions writhing in bed during the wee hours of the morning. "I want to write you so *much*," she said the first time. "How shall I do it, and how shall I not do it? Either way I am wretched, either way I'm exhausted."

"In addition to all my economic, social, and personal theories," Kathrine wrote on the first of June, "I will state in two words the facts of the case. I love you and want to send you 50.00 a month. If you love me you'll take it. If you don't love me you won't." Marianne returned the first check minus the signature and gave the next one to a *New York Times* reporter who was convalescing in the hospital.

When Marianne mentioned to Kathrine that she expected to be in Northampton, Massachusetts, during the summer, Kathrine jumped at the opportunity to meet in person. But Marianne did not want to wait until August. She invited Kathrine to come to Brooklyn in June. (Kathrine regretted that her bangs were not yet long enough to be "seductive.")

"Oh Marianne you were *entirely different* from what I had imagined," Kathrine said after first hearing her voice on the telephone. "It was a shock. You sounded almost *western*. Could I, as a New Englander, suggest anything worse? And then you talk all the time." It was not just the accent that surprised her. The "microscopic living" in Jackson's portrait had so impressed her that she expected Marianne "to faint every other minute." Recalling that Schuyler Jackson had also compared the poet to a buffalo gun, she now noted the strength in her voice. "Well, I will put myself right in your hands," Kathrine said, "and be as putty for the brief period I am with you."

"No hotels," Marianne insisted when she issued the invitation. No one outside the family had ever stayed overnight at 260 Cumberland Street. Kathrine spent three nights with the Moores, taking all of her meals with them and—like family—sharing in their daily worship and prayers. On the third day Mary announced "gravely" that the chicken they had been eating was gone.

"It seemed like a turning point in one's career," Kathrine said later. It was at least a turning point in her visit; she departed a day early. Afterward she thanked Marianne for teaching her to see things for the first time and blamed her for making the conversation of everyone else dull by comparison. Recalling Mary's "eye-opening" threat that she would *"sulk"* if neglected, Kathrine apologized for not showing Mary sufficient affection. Marianne apparently did not respond to Kathrine's flirtatiousness, for it thereafter disappears from her letters.

After Marianne learned about Kathrine's aspirations as a writer, she sent Kathrine's signature (cut from her check) to the handwriting expert whom she had first consulted at the beginning of her own writing career. "By all means cultivate your artistic sense," DeWitt B. Lucas had written her in 1915. "You are original, critical, observant, have good taste, sense of proportion, and are affectionate, but not one to wear your heart upon your shoulder . . . You can be very decided, direct, and verbally emphatic in stating your opinions, are sarcastic on occasion, cultured and refined, with abundant vitality, keen intelligence, good memory, and judgment that is both logical and intuitive. You have perseverance, curiosity, sense of humor, wit, nervousness, and pay good attention to detail." Marianne had sometimes consulted Lucas again in the meantime. Members of the *Dial* staff knew that she analyzed their handwriting, and she sent Lucas handwriting samples of potential secretaries. Lucas apologized when he wrote about Kathrine's handwriting for fear of losing Marianne's confidence. He advised extreme caution with this "highly intelligent and clever woman" who is also "cold-blooded and hypocritical and mentally dishonest." Since Marianne had already told Kathrine about consulting Lucas, she had to invent a new, flattering analysis to give her friend.

Lucas's analysis did not alter Marianne's feelings toward Kathrine though the friendship would have its ups and downs. Exasperated that Marianne refused her checks, Kathrine started sending clothes instead. But Marianne herself lost patience with Kathrine's extravagance and returned silk blouses, cashmere sweaters, and even a fur coat. "Kathrine has gotta be held down and guided," she told Warner. She even made Mary stop writing Kathrine for a time. Kathrine at last resorted to boxes of canned goods—which the Moores shared with neighbors. Marianne later used her influence to get Kathrine's novel, *Miss Gifford's*, into print.

Simultaneously with seeking a broader audience for her poetry, Moore began to create the public persona that would bring her fame. When she read with William Carlos Williams at the Brooklyn Institute in 1936, Elizabeth Bishop told her afterward that she looked nice in her black velvet dress and reassured her about the appropriateness of her shoes. Williams told her she was "BEAUTIFUL! . . . with her greying red hair all coiled about her brows." Still, the strain of the event was evident to her friends. Bishop was "baffled with admiration" at how Marianne answered unexpected questions, and Williams praised her "unspeakably elevating" presence "through all her frail pretences of being this or that."

Four years later, having learned in the meantime to manage her anxieties better, she performed with greater confidence. "I seemed 'entirely natural' and un-nervous," she told Warner after she spoke at Sarah Lawrence College in May 1940, "and was frequently interrupted, and obliged to wait till the flutter and laughter had subsided, before continuing. I threw in asides and minor speculations that they welcomed." The students especially enjoyed "Rigorists" and "Four Quartz Crystal Clocks," at which they laughed out loud.

The success of her performances generated more invitations. She spoke at Vassar the following May, and in December, after *What Are Years* had appeared, she lectured at Harvard on three of her favorite principles: humility, concentration, and gusto. The examples of poetry she quoted ranged from light verse to Spenser and from the book of Psalms to instructions from the Federal Reserve on identifying counterfeit currency. "Your talk won all our hearts," she was told afterward.

T. S. Eliot's brother, Henry Ware Eliot, whom Marianne had admired for years, attended the lecture with his wife. "I am sure that everyone felt that they were seeing and hearing the real *you*," he wrote. "There was a personal quality free of platform aloofness or affectation or superiority in your talk. It was wonderful how sympathetic the audience was—they were with you at every step, and their pleasure was so evident and genuine."

Accused for decades of emotional aloofness, the poet basked in the laughter and warmth of her student audiences. It was no small feat for her to have fashioned at last the natural, spontaneous persona to which she had aspired since her own student days.

•

But her confidence soon faltered. A few months after the Harvard lecture she was invited to spend two weeks at the Cummington School of the Arts near Northampton, Massachusetts. It was a six-week summer program for young artists, and for the last two weeks of August, Marianne would conduct the writing conferences, which consisted both of classes and individual meetings with students. She agreed to go if her mother could accompany her. Although she promised to send her book list within a few days of accepting the invitation, two months later, when Kathrine visited, she was still undecided. She at last chose poetry by Emily Dickinson, Gerard Manley Hopkins, and W. H. Auden, and the prefaces of Henry James. The list includes three writers who had come to be regarded as precursors to Modernism and one whose recent move to America had caused a great stir.

Although Marianne told Warner she enjoyed preparing for the class, Kathrine Jones was privy to her mounting anxiety. "Are you working hard now for Cummington?" Kathrine inquired after her visit. "I hope not too hard. Those shattered looks you had when I was in Brooklyn. I had never seen just that kind of fatigue. And your whiteness one morning."

Marianne feared disappointing her students, but the experience itself turned out to be rewarding, relaxing even. She enjoyed "the Printing-Shop, the pottery studio, the pianos and fiddles, the skunk in the garbage-can, the ping pong, and drawing classes, and dramatic readings . . . the walks in the woods among white pines, the Indian paintbrushes and johnny-jump-ups, the Lady Oldham apples, the old hound Ned and the Ram, Billy." What impressed her most, she told Bryher, "was that instead of rescuing and teaching [the students] and compensating for anomalies, the ideas and help and sense of indomitableness came from the students to me."

If the two weeks at Cummington felt more like vacation than work, Marianne's genuine concern for her students increased her obligations afterward. She continued for months to advise them both in writing and in person and wrote letters recommending their work to editors. (The poet Jean Garrigue would become the best known of these students.) Perhaps the students did fortify her, for by the end of 1942 she had entered a two-year period during which she would write a half dozen new poems, an important lecture about her poetic principles, and one of her finest essays.

The first poem she wrote after Cummington was a draft of what she called her "kiwi." But before she finished the poem, she was, by her own admission, overcome with emotion, and a surprisingly uncharacteristic poem emerged instead. No kiwi appears in "In Distrust of Merits" and, in fact, no animals at all except the black lion symbolizing Ethiopia's resistance to Mussolini. Apart from the patterned stanzas, it is hardly recognizable as a Marianne Moore poem. It eschews indirection and understatement in favor of overt pleas and exclamations—and not just at the end of the poem. Poetic devices conventionally used to heighten emotion recur throughout.

> Strengthened to live, strengthened to die for
>   medals and positioned victories?
> They're fighting, fighting, fighting the blind
>   man who thinks he sees,—
> who cannot see that the enslaver is
> enslaved; the hater, harmed. O shining O
>   firm star, O tumultuous
>   ocean lashed till small things go
>   as they will, the mountainous
>   wave makes us who look, know

> depth . . .

The poem is also uncharacteristic in bringing together—without irony—Mary's remarks about the war, which Marianne had been recording for several years. Marianne thought that even Mary Shoemaker, who had never quite approved of her modernist work, might like it and sent her a copy. She had been reluctant, she explained, to write about the war and surprised herself by deciding to do so. Although she later dismissed the poem as "just a protest—disjointed, exclamatory," she also said she liked it—because it was "sincere." It appeared in the May 1, 1943, issue of *The Nation*, the magazine she would consider her literary home for the next decade.

"In Distrust of Merits" would remain an anomaly in Moore's oeuvre, adored by readers and anthologists yet disparaged for its excesses by otherwise admiring critics. It is best appreciated as a poem of its moment, for in 1943 it struck a chord.

"Oh Marianne, all my congratulations," Elizabeth Bishop wrote her about the poem. "It seems to me so intricately impressive . . . I admire the repetitions, I admire the 'O's,' I admire [the reference to] Job . . . —and 'The world's an orphan's home.'"

Auden told her similarly that it was "the only war poem so far that made any sense, and it made a great deal."

It is hardly surprising that Auden liked it. For the poem owes as much to his *Double Man*, which Moore had reviewed two years earlier and had taught at Cummington, as it does to Mary. Moore praised Auden's view that "We wage the war we are" and his willingness to address directly "the other kind of war . . . from Spain to Siberia, from Ethiopia to Iceland." War in Moore's poem is waged against "the disease, My / Self" (a phrase of Mary's) and is fought "in deserts and in caves," "on crags," and "in quicksands." "The crowning ornament of [Auden's] work," according to Moore, is "paradox at its compactest."

"In Distrust of Merits" is itself a catalog of paradoxes, which culminates in her own version of the "double man," which Auden had taken in turn from Montaigne: "We are . . . double in ourselves, so that what we believe we disbelieve, and cannot rid ourselves of what we condemn." "There never was a war that was / not inward," writes Moore.

> . . . I must
> fight till I have conquered in myself what
> causes war, but I would not believe it.
> > I inwardly did nothing.
> > O Iscariotlike crime!

As soon as she finished "In Distrust of Merits," Moore turned her attention to a lecture she would deliver at Mount Holyoke in August. Like its predecessor, "Humility, Concentration, and Gusto," "Feeling and Precision" uses examples from unlikely sources such as Ogden Nash and the children's book *Madeleine*, a gift from Elizabeth Bishop. It makes as clear a statement as Moore ever makes about her poetic principles and in particular about how seemingly indifferent precision results from powerful emotion. "Precision is both impact and exactitude, as with surgery," she explains. And like an orchestra conductor's downbeat, "To have started such a long distance ahead makes it possible to be exact." The lecture begins with a defense of Moore's own reticence: "Feeling at its deepest—as we all have reason to know—tends to be inarticulate. If it does manage to be articulate, it is likely to seem overcondensed, so that the author is resisted as being enigmatic or disobliging or arrogant."

Critics of *Poems* had accused Moore long ago of being enigmatic and arrogant. And her defense against these charges had been implicit in the poems she wrote in the early 1920s. Other preferences she mentions in the lecture—such as "concealed rhyme and the interiorized climax"—likewise characterize her earlier more than her recent work. Why did she articulate her modernist standards at the same point in her career when her poetry had veered furthest from them? Did she need distance from those principles in order to analyze them? Or did she willingly abandon her standards to please her aging mother and a war-weary public? "It seems so idle," she told Mary Shoemaker, "just to be writing jingles and descriptions, when others are working and talking of their 'overtime.'" It was her patriotic duty not to even *seem* trifling in "these days of homelessness and death."

Marianne and Mary traveled by train to South Hadley, Massachusetts, on a Tuesday, "attended lectures assiduously," and returned home Thursday after Marianne had given her "Feeling and Precision" lecture. The occasion was a monthlong symposium, Les Entretiens de Potigny, bringing together American intellectuals and French ones exiled during the German occupation. The philosopher Jean Wahl and the medievalist Gustave Cohen, Jewish professors from the Sorbonne, had joined the faculty at Mount Holyoke and presided over the proceedings. The participants gathered informally on the lawn under the large shade trees. "The fleeting glimpse we had," Marianne wrote afterward, "of fervent spirits in action, there at Holyoke, dissecting false tendencies of government and analyzing subtleties of the inward ear and outer ear as regards music and poetry will stay with us as a blessing."

The Moores went early to hear Wallace Stevens, whom Marianne had never met. "Wallace Stevens is beyond fathoming, he is so strange," she later told William Carlos Williams, "it is as if he had a morbid secret he would rather perish than disclose and just as he tells it out in his sleep, he changes into an uncontradictable judiciary with a gown and a gavel and you are embarrassed to have heard anything." He spoke so softly that she missed most of his lecture, but she repeated to friends several phrases that impressed her. She sat with Henry and Barbara Church, Stevens's friends who had escorted him there, and discussed French fashion with Barbara. It is hard to imagine the two *Others* poets not looking each other in the eye that sunny morning at Mount Holyoke and exchanging a few words, but Moore's letters about the day do not say that they did. Stevens seemed "friendly and ready to talk to people," she said, but he was surrounded by admirers for the short time between his talk and his departure. There was no time for conversation, and Stevens did not return to hear her speak the next day.

Seven years later Barbara Church invited Marianne to a party for Stevens. The women thereafter became friends and frequent correspondents. At one point early in their friendship Barbara reassured Marianne that she need not avoid Stevens, who had once called her "a moral force in light blue."

When Marianne delivered "Feeling and Precision" again the following April, this time at Bryn Mawr, she had a more satisfactory encounter with a fellow poet. W. H. Auden, who was teaching at nearby Swarthmore, invited her to dinner. But she had already accepted an invitation to dine with Lucy Martin Donnelly and her partner, Edith Finch. Marianne asked that Auden be included, and he was.

She knew Auden already. Monroe Wheeler had tried to get them together soon after Auden arrived in America in April 1939. But because of Mary's neuralgia, their meeting had to be postponed until November, when he called on the Moores one evening. He immediately impressed the older poet as a "genius," and she followed his career as closely as she could. She heard him read from his new work at the public library and lecture several times at the New School. Despite her disappointment in the reading, she told Elizabeth Bishop that she felt "bound to Mr. Auden by 'hoops of steel' and can 'understand' any misfortune,—in fact, like him the better for his adversities and for his indomitableness." She served as a Guggenheim reference for him in 1941 and welcomed the opportunity to praise his poetry and politics when she reviewed *The Double Man* the same year. The friendship was at least as important to both poets at midcentury as Moore's more celebrated friendships with her fellow modernists had been.

In anticipation of a private dinner with Marianne, Auden sent her the manuscript of his new book, which included two long poems, "For the Time Being: A Christmas Oratorio" and "The Sea and the Mirror," so that they could discuss it when they saw each other. Characteristically, Marianne spent many hours reviewing the manuscript and, since she knew their dinner would not be private, composed a long letter of detailed commentary.

Marianne had read her work to select gatherings at Bryn Mawr before but had never been feted as she was the evening of April 19. A tea in the Deanery preceded her lecture. Students in silk dresses crowded the large drawing room, and the cookies, she noted, were homemade. The setting evoked memories of Carey Thomas sitting in a blue chair in that very room. Holding *The Lantern* in her hand, Thomas had pronounced Marianne the best of Bryn Mawr's student writers. Lucy Martin Donnelly, now in her seventies, gave her former student a grand introduction, and after the lecture "hordes & hordes" of students came up to meet the illustrious alumna. The dinner party for six, also served at the Deanery, included Donnelly and Finch, two young English professors, and the two poets. Having given much thought to her own attire, Marianne noted that Auden wore a "brand new tweed coat and *very* old trousers and shoes."

After dinner Auden accompanied Marianne to New York. Their commuter train arrived at Philadelphia's Thirtieth Street Station at exactly the time the New York train was supposed to depart. Carrying Marianne's briefcase for her, Auden sprang off the train, dashed through a tunnel, and climbed an escalator three steps at a time in order to hold the train until Marianne caught up with him. She arrived home at 10:30, full of details about the day and "glowing with freedom," as Mary put it.

Both Marianne and Mary were ill during much of the fall and winter of 1943–1944. But Marianne nevertheless managed to socialize with artists whose company, like Auden's, fortified her. In September she attended the opening for an Alexander Calder exhibit at the Museum of Modern Art. "I don't see how so many surprisingly individual charmers could be magnetized into a co-operating throng, without short circuiting some currents, somewhere," she wrote afterward. Monroe Wheeler's friend, the photographer George Platt Lynes, guided her about the exhibit and photographed her throwing her head back in laughter with Marc Chagall, Martha Graham, and Calder himself, of whom she considered herself a "strong adherent."

In February she returned to the museum to meet Lincoln Kirstein, who had invited her to look at some photographs of Anna Pavlova in the museum's archives, in hopes that she would write an essay about them for his new magazine, *Dance Index*. Kirstein wanted to enlist Moore, one of his favorite writers, in his project to transform ballet, one of the nineteenth century's most romantic art forms, into a modernist one. Ballet had first captivated Kirstein at the age of twelve when he saw Pavlova perform in Boston. Though reluctant at first to take on the assignment, Marianne soon became "bewitched" with Pavlova and produced one of her most lyrical essays. Her "impeccable prose," wrote the dance critic Edwin Denby, "has the floating balance, the light pauses and the recurrent soaring instants of classic dancing." The essay delighted Kirstein, as it did the author herself.

At a *Partisan Review* tea in May, Marianne met Margaret Marshall, poetry editor of *The Nation*, for the first time. She had already developed great respect for Marshall both from her reviews in *The Nation* and from her editorial suggestions about Marianne's own work. "Never hold back," Marshall told her. "Send me a lot of things. You couldn't send me too much." Alan Tate and Louise Bogan were there as well and took her aside to tell her that they had served with Morton Zabel as judges for the Harriet Monroe Memorial Prize. "We are going to give it to you and you must be *glad*," they told her. She was touched by this and also by Tate's saying that he wanted to meet her mother. Edmund Wilson had told him that Mrs. Moore was "one of the most intellectual women he ever met."

The assemblage artist Joseph Cornell had first written Marianne in the spring of 1943, thanking her for liking a series he had published in *View* magazine. His letter, like his subsequent letters to her, was itself a work of collage that included engravings of a pangolin and an armadillo cut out and pasted among other engraved figures. Moore responded appreciatively. And after finding him to be "generous, quiet, considerate, discerning," invited him to tea during the summer of 1944. They then went to dinner nearby. Moore and Cornell were "kindred artists," as Monroe Wheeler said, both making poetry from found objects. Cornell lived with his mother and with his disabled brother, to whom he was devoted. When he telephoned the next day, he praised Mary's "almost silent way of saying important things." "Thought after thought came back to me," he said about her conversation, "as having lasting significance for me, that at the time was expressed so quietly I almost failed to grasp the depth of it."

Observing her student Harry Duncan print Stevens's *Notes Toward a Supreme Fiction* on a handpress was one of the highlights of her Cummington summer. Duncan, who ran the Cummington Press, liked to publish works by the visiting writers and asked Marianne if he might have something of hers. In the fall of 1943 she offered him six poems, but because of her contract with Macmillan told him she must first ask permission. Latham asked to see the poems—she had completed four at that time—and replied that although it was unusual to issue such a small book, Macmillan wanted it. A shrewd decision, as it turns out.

After "In Distrust of Merits," Moore returned to her more characteristic subject matter and witty indirection. In the next two poems she wrote, "a strawberry / that's had a struggle" exemplifies fortitude, and the elephant, one of her favorite animals, exemplifies wisdom. When Mary Shoemaker saw "Elephants" in *The Nation*, she wrote to inquire if the last two lines were political. Marianne was thrilled, she said, and told her she was the first person to notice what was for her an important element of the poem. But when Shoemaker then said she was thinking of the Republican Party, Marianne bristled in defense of her noble elephant. "I *refuse* to lend an elephant to the Grand Old Party," she said, " 'Political,' . . . I thought of as 'international.' "

"Elephants" proves the superiority of "equanimity" over ferocity: "Who rides on a tiger can never dismount; / asleep on an elephant, that is repose." In "Nevertheless," the title poem of the new book, "The weak overcomes its / menace, the strong over- / comes itself." Whereas Moore chastised Ireland for its neutrality in "Spenser's Ireland," in "A Carriage from Sweden" she praises another neutral country for being "responsive and / responsible" and for providing sanctuary to Denmark's eight thousand Jews. In these and in "The Mind Is an Enchanting Thing," generally regarded as the best of the poems in

Nevertheless, she advocates nonviolence as the best strategy against injustice.

"The Mind Is an Enchanting Thing," the poem she referred to as her "kiwi," appeared in *The Nation* almost a year after "In Distrust of Merits" had. Its obvious subject is the mind's iridescent adaptability. But it may also be read as exploring further the problem of the "inward" war described in "In Distrust of Merits." The mind can be both "enchanting" and "enchanted." Besides the enchantments of art and nature, one thinks, in the context of war, of Hitler's power over his followers. The mind can avoid violence: it "tears off" the veil of "temptation," analyzes "dejection," and conquers "confusion." Though easily enchanted, it can, like a gyroscope, be "trued by regnant certainty." Finally, "it's / not a Herod's oath that cannot change." One of Moore's best critics, Cristanne Miller, has pointed out the suggestion of Hitler in "Herod's oath." This is a connection Moore acknowledged. "One doesn't get through with the fact that Herod beheaded John the Baptist, 'for his oath's sake,'" she told an inquirer, "as one doesn't, I feel, get through with the injustice of the deaths died in the war, and in the first world war."

Nevertheless appeared in bookstores at the end of September 1944. The little fourteen-page book cost just $1.25. Although Marianne usually disliked small books of poems and would not have chosen red for the cover, she told Warner that she liked *Nevertheless* more than any of her books. It felt "neat and businesslike." Bookstores could not keep it on their shelves, and by Christmas it had gone into a third printing.

This was largely the doing of W. H. Auden, whose review in *The New York Times Book Review* brought the book as much attention as the *Times*'s notice of *Observations* had twenty years ago. Auden took an entirely different tactic than Eliot had in promoting *Selected Poems*. Instead of taunting the reader to join the elite group that could appreciate Moore's greatness, Auden placed himself among those readers who had—he blushingly confessed—been unable to join that group. He encouraged similarly intimidated readers to try her again. "There is certainly no poet of comparable rank so unknown, even to habitual readers of poetry," he said, "as Miss Moore." He praised her "musical and structural" innovations and candidly admitted that he had "stolen a great deal" from her.

Marianne's old friend, Henry McBride, wrote her after Christmas to complain that he had been unable to find as many copies of the little book as he had wanted to give as Christmas presents. "Congratulations on being a best-seller," he told her. "After all, it's one of the goals."

21

Perseverance

1945–1953

The breeze from the East River drew Mary and Marianne to the roof on warm summer evenings. During the war they watched rooftop Victory Gardens proliferate in the neighborhood. They could see the tops of the elms and pines in Fort Greene Park and beyond those the heightened activities at the Navy Yard, the "twinkling lights and plumes of steam and planes flying toward the intersecting search-lights." The two had begun roof sitting at St. Luke's Place after Mary's osteopath prescribed a daily dose of sunshine.

By the end of the war, Mary rarely climbed the stairs to the roof anymore. But a neighborhood gardener might well look up from her vegetable patch and see an amazing sight: a fifty-seven-year-old poet skipping rope against the skyline.

Marianne resorted to rooftop rope skipping only when she could not find a tennis partner. She once improvised a net in her building's courtyard and paid the caretaker's son to play with her. She sometimes played in the church gymnasium during winter months. And one summer, when she was having trouble sleeping, Mary encouraged her to recruit a neighborhood boy to play tennis with her in Prospect Park. Word spread, and she soon had six whom she taught to play: "Scotty and Tommy and Buddy and Earnie and two Jimmys."

She had first met these boys when she asked them to stop playing ball in the middle of her street. It was not just the boys' shouts and the occasional crash of glass that wafted through the open windows at 260 Cumberland but also the honking of cars trying to get through. When the boys lost interest in tennis and returned to playing ball in the street, Marianne approached them again. Tommy, their leader, fired back "with all his pugnacious little rhinoceros strength." Boys from the Brooklyn Technical High School would not allow the younger boys to play in Fort Greene Park. But Marianne reasoned with him and a few weeks later accompanied him, his father, and another boy to the park administration building in Prospect Park. They succeeded in getting permission for the boys to play in a nearby field until a junior ball field could be built after the war.

The socialist ideals of Marianne's college years were partly realized in her multiracial, multiethnic Brooklyn neighborhood. Mary and Marianne treated all of their neighbors, even the homeless ones, with equal solicitude, and they impressed the local merchants by bringing their own shopping bags. (So radical was Mary's commitment to what was then called conservation that she once traveled by bus to the bottling plant in Manhattan to deliver an unclaimed milk bottle.) In turn the shopkeepers often held back for them the items they liked and added goods to their shopping bags at no charge. When Warner returned from the South Pacific after the war, he brought cigars for these merchants and regaled them with stories.

Fellow tenants of 260, the Scovells, brought Christmas dinner to the Moores during a winter of illness. And Marianne attributed Mary's recovery the following spring to the meat Mr. Scovell brought home from Armour, his employer. Mrs. Scovell once altered a dress for Marianne on short notice. In turn, Marianne tutored the Scovells' son daily for most of a year to help him make up school work he had missed.

Although the Moores attended church regularly by the early 1940s, Marianne's comments about it indicate that she did so skeptically and reluctantly. She complained repeatedly of the pastor's "insulting didacticism." Even Mary said of one prayer meeting that the chief interest was watching Dr. Magary take his glasses off and put them back on. By 1944, however, Marianne often wrote approvingly of Dr. Magary's sermons and attended his weekly Bible study classes. To Warner she called herself a "religious alligator."

Why the change? The war was surely a factor. It united the nation around a shared sense of tragedy and injustice. Even the intelligentsia no longer disdained religion as it had after World War I. Auden wrote openly about his religious faith. Eliot published his overtly Christian *Four Quartets*. And the most celebrated up-and-coming poet of the time, Robert Lowell, became a self-described "fire-breathing Catholic C.O."

The theologian Reinhold Niebuhr first came to Marianne's attention through Elizabeth Bishop, who heard him speak at Vassar and recommended him as "the only 'minister' I have ever liked." Shortly thereafter Marianne heard Niebuhr lecture at her own church on "Unsuccessful Substitutes for Christianity." "Twenty-seven people were there," she wrote Bishop, "of whom there were only two we had seen before, and seven were Negroes . . . To my satisfaction he said Christianity in comparison with the simplicity of its substitutes, is complex and mysterious; . . . that evil is . . . the exaggerating of what is in itself good, and harmless; that I am not myself evil but if I expand myself into a persecuting autocrat which I present as an object for general idolatry, then I sin, exaggerating reasonableness into an evil."

As suggested by these remarks, Niebuhr, born in Missouri to German immigrants, fiercely opposed the Nazis. His political activism combined with his "reverence for mystery," as Moore would call it, both strengthened her personal faith and her willingness to identify her beliefs as Christian. During the 1950s, when she attended Auden's annual birthday parties, she became personally acquainted with Niebuhr and his wife.

Marianne and Mary read aloud from the Old Testament in the morning and from the New Testament at bedtime. And during the war they timed their daily prayers to coincide with Warner's, first when he served as chaplain for the Coast Guard Academy in Connecticut and later while he was stationed in the South Pacific under Chester Nimitz, admiral of the Pacific Fleet. Nimitz had known Warner since they worked at Bremerton together, and in July 1943 Nimitz asked Warner to serve as chaplain of his flagship and as chaplain of the Pacific Fleet. It was by far the most prestigious commission of Warner's naval career, and the most dangerous. He left not knowing if he would ever see his mother again. And since he often toured ships under enemy fire, Marianne and Mary worried the same about him. Because of military censors, Marianne praised him effusively in her letters and suppressed her usual irony.

Even more than the exchange of letters, the prayers kept the three-some close. When asked about her religious beliefs in later decades, Marianne always defended the efficacy of prayer. "I believe in prayer," she said, "as a mystery which can endow one with more power per-haps, than any other spiritual mystery."

In the months after *Nevertheless* had gone to press, Moore wrote a few more poems indirectly addressing the war, but by the end of 1944 she told Warner that she had "plenty of 'rhymes' [in her head] but no very pressing theme!" Perhaps she told Auden the same thing. For in Janu-ary she received an invitation from Walter H. Pistole, Jr., of Reynal & Hitchcock to translate the *Fables* of La Fontaine. Auden, he said, had suggested the project.

The idea thrilled her. "What enticed me to translate the *Fables* was their verbal harmonies and pattern of rhymes," she later said. She be-lieved at first that she would be the first to translate all 241 fables into English verse. In fact, there had been several translations but none by such an accomplished poet. With Mary's help, she quickly prepared a sample fable. They liked the result, and so did Pistole.

Marianne demonstrated proficiency in French and German while at Bryn Mawr but had never attempted translating for publication un-til Gustav Cohen, whom she met at Mount Holyoke, persuaded her to translate his book on medieval history. She told him from the first that she was not the one to do it, but she did work at the project for a short time. Then in early 1945 Auden asked her to contribute to an anthol-ogy of translated poems. She was still pondering the idea when two weeks later she received Pistole's letter.

Pistole at first envisioned an illustrated volume and showed Moore's sample fable to Robert Motherwell, who was starting to gain recogni-tion in New York as an abstract expressionist. Motherwell prepared some sketches, which Marianne approved, and was ready to sign a contract when Pistole had to inform him of Marianne's objections. "I have respected and admired your work all my adult life," Motherwell then wrote her. He asked whether it was illustrations generally or his work specifically to which she objected. She answered generously that "your violets and crimsons and orange-yellows are what I have—in a clumsy way—been pursuing all my life." She praised his "poetry of the brush" but told him pictures did not suit her plans for a compact, inexpensive volume. "I wish I had a long arm," Motherwell replied, "that could reach out and protect you and your mother; but this is silly. You need no protection with a spirit so strong."

Although Pistole had assured Marianne that a book of translations would not interfere with her contract to publish the next book of "her poems" with Macmillan, James Putnam of Macmillan was stunned when she told him of her plans over the phone. He accused Reynal & Hitchcock of selfishly taking her away from the "creative work" for which Macmillan had contracted. Later he insisted that her translations were "her poems" but reluctantly agreed to grant her a release for the project.

It was June before she actually signed a contract. She agreed to complete the translation within a year. Since the *Fables* consisted of twelve books, this meant one book, about twenty fables each, per month. In the meantime, she prepared three sample fables for Pistole to show Harry Levin, a professor of comparative literature at Harvard. Levin pronounced one "a masterpiece" but recommended changes in the others. "Most translators," he wrote, "since they cannot reproduce the effect of the original, are doubtless wise to be literal and pedestrian. But here, I agree, you have a striking exception: if anyone in English can manage La Fontaine's intermixture of the casual and the artful, innocence and urbanity, it must be Miss Moore; and she has demonstrated it here." Marianne valued Levin's praise and welcomed his corrections.

In April, Henry Allen Moe of the Guggenheim Foundation called at 260 Cumberland to offer her a fellowship. Having written many letters recommending others for Guggenheims, she had never presumed to apply for one of her own. Moe told her that he had asked Alan Tate and Louise Bogan what to do with leftover money he had that year, and they recommended it go to Miss Moore. She agreed to write a proposal to translate La Fontaine, and Moe told her she would receive her $2,500 fellowship in monthly installments over the next year. Marianne conscientiously informed Hildegarde Watson and Bryher of her new source of financial support—they continued to send money anyway. And she felt justified in refusing an advance from Reynal & Hitchcock. She believed on principle that she should receive royalties only after the publisher had the money from sales in hand.

Also before she signed the contract, she completed another translation. Auden's friend Elizabeth Mayer engaged Marianne to help her translate *Bergkrystal*, a Christmas story by Adalbert Stifter. Theirs was the first English translation of anything by Stifter, a follower of Goethe and an esteemed prose stylist. Mayer, a native speaker of German and experienced translator, wrote a literal first draft, and Marianne gave Mayer's English the sparkle of poetry. *Rock Crystal* appeared in stores in late October. Reviewing it in *The New York Times*, Auden praised the translators' patience as well as their skill at capturing the artful simplicity of the original.

Marianne faced a much greater challenge with La Fontaine, for she wanted to preserve not only the nuances of his meaning but also his French rhythms and intonations. She kept at hand a Canadian paperback of the original, Nicolas Boileau's treatise on French poetics, and a 1933 English translation by Edward Marsh, a British scholar with close ties to the Georgian poets. Marianne used the Marsh to check the literal meaning of words but felt no temptation to adopt either his verse forms or his much "heartier" reading of La Fontaine. She finished Books I and II by the end of the summer. Pistole responded enthusiastically, praising Book II especially as "quite easy and true."

A few weeks later Pistole announced his resignation from Reynal & Hitchcock to take a position elsewhere. Marianne received assurances from Curtice Hitchcock that everyone at the press shared Pistole's enthusiasm for the project, and Marianne was assigned a new editor, Elizabeth Ford. (In 1997 her husband, Harry Ford, as senior poetry editor with Knopf, would publish Moore's *Selected Letters*.) Marianne worked doggedly through the fall on Books III and IV until she and Mary fell prey to their usual winter illnesses.

They regained enough stamina in February and March for Marianne to complete Book V. And then they both fell ill again for the rest of the summer. Marianne was so sick with bronchitis that she had to cancel her appearance before the American Academy of Arts and Letters to accept a thousand-dollar grant. But their greatest concern over the summer was Mary's difficulty swallowing. Unable to get the nourishment she needed, she lost weight rapidly. She was diagnosed with damage to the nerve that controlled her palate but, in fact, as would become evident after her death, had a severe case of goiter, her thyroid extending deep into her chest.

Marianne first relied upon the advice of their osteopath and later read books about vitamins and nutrition as she took over food preparation for the household. Vegetable juice was her passion. Monroe Wheeler gave her a large juicer in 1944, and at Marianne's request Louise Crane exchanged it for a small cast-iron grinder called the Health Mine. "I am belly deep in vegetable juice," Marianne wrote Warner. "I have the craze *very bad* . . . The Health Mine . . . makes splendid carrot and beet juice. It tastes like a fruit juice, not like vegetables at all . . . I have a notion that regular juice will prolong Bear's [Mary's] life; and maybe cure us both of aches, itches, fatigue and all manner of things." She urged Warner to try a mixture of half carrot and half beet juice. The following year, she added brewer's yeast, vitamins, and cod liver oil to their daily regimen. And she fed Mary okra juice as a digestive aid. During the final months of Mary's life their meals consisted almost exclusively of milk and vegetable juice.

The Moores had first hired a nurse to take care of them in March 1945, when they became so ill with bursitis, bronchitis, laryngitis, and fever that they were unable to care for themselves for five weeks. Then, from January through the summer of 1946, they hired a succession of variously qualified and variously reliable women to clean house, wash clothes, and sometimes prepare meals for them.

On an errand to the bank in October, Marianne met Gladys Berry, who was mopping floors there. They had an instant rapport, and Marianne hired her on the spot for five afternoons per week. Gladys arrived at two and stayed as long as she was needed. At long last Marianne had found someone whose daily presence was a joy rather than an annoyance. "It will take me months (serially) to tell you of Gladys's courage, initiative, delicacy, trustworthiness, thrift, gratitude, punctuality, affectionate interest in us, and her goodness of attitude in right ideas for us all," Marianne wrote Mary Shoemaker a few weeks after Gladys's arrival. "She is so civic-minded and honorable—very young, she seems, but has a little girl of 12 and little boy of 10 'and a husband.'" Gladys Berry would work for Marianne for the next twenty-five years.

With Mary's and Gladys's encouragement, Marianne was able to work on Book VI "after supper" during the fall. When Elizabeth Ford received it in January, she told Marianne that it was her favorite book so far and asked to call at the apartment to discuss it. Marianne welcomed Ford's assistance with "inaccuracies," as she called them, and decided to revise Books I through VI before continuing with Book VII.

Mary's condition seemed to improve in May—enough that, at Mary's insistence, Marianne went into Manhattan occasionally. Her first outing in a year was to hear Eliot lecture on Milton at the Frick Collection. A few weeks later she was inducted into the National Institute of Arts and Letters. And in June, at Warner's urging, she visited Eliot at the home of graphic artist E. McKnight Kauffer and textile designer Marion Dorn. Marianne already knew Kauffer and had long admired his work. But this gathering initiated a deep friendship with the couple and brought her friendship with Eliot, whose brother, Henry, had just died, to a more intimate level.

Marianne looked forward by late June to an easier summer for Mary and herself. But it was not to be. On July 2, a Wednesday, Mary fell twice, was severely nauseated, and could barely speak. At a loss for what to do, Marianne called Warner, who called an ambulance. It arrived at the apartment and took both women to the Brooklyn Hospital a few blocks away. Mary recovered enough the first night that she felt ready to go home.

"You must not be scared," Marianne told her. "We've never been safe a day at 260, and here, we're safe, for we have so much help."

For the next week Marianne slept on a cot in the room, which had large windows overlooking Fort Greene Park. During the day the two took pleasure in watching the wind toss the upper branches of the elms and whip a flag straight out from its pole. Mary slowly declined, and by the following Tuesday, she and both children had come to accept the inevitable. The three were alone together when she departed on the morning of July 9, 1947.

Marianne spent the afternoon at home writing letters. "We were helped beyond belief," she told Mary Shoemaker, "by the Hospital, by circumstances, by the Unseen, and even we ourselves got past our refusal to part with her for she could not eat or drink yesterday and fought very hard . . . It was a few minutes before half past nine this morning, and we were both with her holding her hands and everything made us grateful."

In the evening Marianne returned to the hospital to arrange Mary's hair and to dress her in the clothes she had saved over the years for the occasion. Gladys Berry and three neighbors stood with Warner and Marianne as they bade farewell to their mother's body before it went to the crematorium.

The next day Warner drove Marianne and the urn of ashes to his home in Bethesda, Maryland. The funeral took place Saturday morning in Gettysburg at the Marsh Creek Church, where Mary's father had been pastor when she was born. Monroe Wheeler came from New York, and several Craig cousins came from nearby. Warner assisted with the service, and then the small party delivered Mary's ashes to Evergreen Cemetery to be buried next to the graves of her parents.

After the funeral Marianne spent a few days with Warner and Constance in Bethesda. Her letters to friends repeatedly express gratitude for Warner's consoling strength and also praise Constance's protectiveness toward her. But in fact tensions escalated until all three realized she had to leave. "I kept her just as long as Constance could act sanely under the strain it was to her to have Marianne," as Warner put it. At first he wanted his sister to live permanently with him. But Constance saw the matter differently: the death of her mother-in-law provided the opportunity for Warner and Marianne to develop at last a "real" brother-sister relationship—that is, one in which the sister is the outsider rather than the wife.

Jealousy was Constance's weakness. It was understood in the family that Constance could never have tolerated Warner's having a church where he would work as closely with women as he did with men. His stories and boyish exuberance had always attracted women, and he never stopped enjoying their attention. He also learned long before he met Constance to tell the women in his life what he thought they wanted to hear. His deceptiveness only exacerbated her suspicions.

Constance's jealousies intensified during the years following Mary's death. Warner described her as "*ill* in certain mental responses and reactions." He wrote of trying to "cure" her "just as if she were an *alcoholic*." But Constance was no fool when it came to her in-laws. She knew to distrust their private language and especially their letters. As soon as she and her children started using the nicknames Mole and Rat, her husband and in-laws started using different names among themselves. Since early in his marriage, Warner had asked his mother and sister to send mail to his work address so that Constance would never know the extent of their correspondence. And he occasionally wrote two versions of a letter: one playful and effusive; the other, for Constance's benefit, sober and short. After Warner retired, he kept a secret post office box for Marianne's letters. Constance forbade him from writing letters while he vacationed with the family at Black Lake, but he usually managed to send off a note or two. After Mary died, she also forbade him from seeing Marianne or even Mary Shoemaker except in her presence.

Marianne hoped that Mary's death might improve relations with her sister-in-law. But Constance's behavior in Bethesda so alarmed her that she immediately transferred her concern for her mother to Warner. Constance, she observed, regarded her husband as "Ulysses among the sirens."

Marianne participated in her brother's deceptions insofar as she refused to give up private communication with him. She did, however, try to appease Constance when she could. Her letters to friends show her training herself to say Constance's name first instead of Warner's when referring to them as a couple. At one point she complied with Warner's scheme to "cure" his wife. She wrote Constance an otherwise frank letter thanking her for her kindness, apologizing for having "been the cause of strain for you, many times," and expressing her strong desire "to cement the family, and ensure certain peace of mind." Then she added (as a ploy) that she might see a psychiatrist about her tendency to put off tasks and to mislay things. She asked Constance to accompany her.

A year after Mary died, Warner turned sixty-two, the navy's mandatory retirement age. He apparently expected the deferment often granted to chaplains but was denied because of the surplus of young officers after World War II. The news in any case came as a blow. "I lost my grip a little," Marianne said, "in seeing him flinch and then rally." She could not eat afterward and came down with a cold. For nearly a year Warner's desperation for something to do exacerbated Marianne's sense of helplessness.

In late September he called to say that he would be moving in with her the next day. Following months of tears and angry threats, he and Constance had agreed to separate. Later the same evening they decided to make a final effort to save their marriage. "Terrible as it is to say so," he wrote Marianne the next day, "I burned to be off to you." Marianne opposed the separation not only on moral grounds but also because of the pain it would cause him and his family. Yet for three years after Mary's death, she worried that Warner would suddenly need her, and she wanted to be available to him if he did.

Then, in the summer of 1950, while attending a Moral Rearmament conference in Michigan, Constance decided to let go of her jealousy. Tensions with Marianne began to ease. Though Constance still insisted on no secrets and thus no private communications between Warner and his sister, the marriage began to heal as well. By this time Warner had found satisfying employment at a boys' liberal arts school, the Gunnery, in Washington, Connecticut. The marriage survived those difficult years, and the couple remained together—happily so, according to their children—until the end of their lives.

Warner and Marianne continued to correspond privately and to meet on the sly—often during Constance's beauty parlor appointment. At least once they met in Elizabeth, New Jersey, at the home of Warner's former girlfriend. And in the early 1960s they met regularly in New Haven, where a Yale art professor was painting Warner's portrait.

•

Besides Warner, the person Marianne most wanted to see right after Mary's death was Mary Shoemaker. Being with Cousin Mary was as close as Marianne could get to feeling her mother's presence again, and her filial devotion would grow ever deeper until Cousin Mary's own death eight years later. Her letters to her cousin during these years reveal a level of intimacy deeper than that with Warner, whom she tried to shield from worry. A few days after her mother's funeral, Marianne went directly from Bethesda to Hagerstown, Maryland, where she spent a week with Cousin Mary before returning to Brooklyn.

Gladys had done much cleaning and laundry in Marianne's absence. Marianne began to give away, throw away, and burn Mary's possessions during the few days she was home. She accepted her friends' offers to provide for her. The Watsons, who had family concerns of their own at the time, sent her money to help with medical expenses. In appreciation for their ongoing generosity, she sent Mary's diamond wedding brooch to Hildegarde.

Louise Crane invited Marianne to join a small party of family and friends at a rustic lodge in the Berkshires that Louise's father had built for his guests. Marianne spent a week there. "The household is indeed innocent and delightful," she wrote, "and the air reviving." In nearby Dalton she toured the house where Louise had grown up. With its Constables and Peales on the walls, it reminded her of the governor's palace in Williamsburg. And the little museum that occupied the original paper mill charmed her. A notoriously fast driver, Louise got Marianne to Boston just in time to meet her train to Bangor.

Kathrine and Marcia brought Marianne from Bangor to Marcia's childhood home in Lamoine, near Ellsworth, Maine. Marianne found in their company exactly the balance of companionship, easy laughter, and solitude that she craved. "I am much improved since being here with Marcia and Kathrine," she wrote Mary Shoemaker. "Life is quiet and encouraging; driving to Ellsworth or to the rocks, is great recreation to me." She had planned to stay a week but ended up staying a month. In the mornings she resumed work on the fables. Her hostesses had rented her a typewriter, and with Kathrine's help, she translated La Fontaine's two prose prefaces and one fable. In the evenings they might go to a church supper or a picnic by the sea. "Marcia lets me dry dishes sometimes," she said, "and water the flowers but keeps me working at my fables and is *so solicitous and kind*."

By the end of the month, they were calling one another "Baby Moore," "Baby Jones," and "Mama Marcia." Marianne was even persuaded to accept money from Kathrine.

Marianne returned to Brooklyn in early September. The Navy Yard had employed more than seventy thousand workers during the war, and their departure brought unwelcome changes to the neighborhood. Marianne had already stopped going to the Brooklyn Institute because of muggers, and several people urged her to move to a safer place. She had become attached to 260, however, and prided herself on her sixty-dollar rent. Warner, who paid the rent, told her new landlord that he would pay seventy-five in exchange for improvements. But Marianne liked to do her own haggling. "We do live in a second class building," she told the landlord, "with people strewn over the front door steps in soiled muslin dresses . . . babies in mere harnesses crying at their mothers' skirts—rusty water, crass paint and elevator—robberies and noisy floors." Since tenants as dependable as Miss Moore were hard to come by, he agreed to paint the building for no increase in rent and to install a new stove in her apartment for a mere six-dollar monthly increase.

Although unwilling to change addresses, Marianne did change bedrooms. She moved from the larger room she had shared with Mary into the smaller one with a single iron bed. She kept her typewriter there, too. For the next eighteen years, she slept in that room every night and wrote there every morning.

Years of grief before and after Mary's death took a toll on Marianne's own fragile health. She dropped things, lost things, and broke things. Her hair whitened. Her skin sagged. Crying made her eyes puffy. She looked exhausted and old beyond her sixty years. In the company of others she ate well but at home ate little because she so hated dining alone.

Soon after Mary died, Warner began urging her to do something about her appearance. The family had been shocked by the way she looked in *Vogue* the previous year, in photographs taken by Cecil Beaton, known for his glamour photography. Warner suggested that she get facials and massages, as Constance did, and make regular trips to the beauty parlor. "Now, my boy, you and I now *can* do something about 'that face,'" he wrote her. Warner had probably forgotten this face when he wrote the next day, with typical grandiosity, about their mother's: "So must we now go about the business of God, and qualify ourselves to see her face once more, as it is raised in glory." Marianne underlined the sentence and wrote a short poem called "A Face."

A FACE

"I am not treacherous, callous, jealous, superstitious,
supercilious, venomous, or absolutely hideous":
    studying and studying its expression,
    exasperated desperation
        though at no real impasse,
        would gladly break the glass;

when love of order, ardour, uncircuitous simplicity,
with an expression of inquiry, are all one needs to be!
    Certain faces, a few, one or two—or one
    face photographed by recollection—
        to my mind, to my sight,
        must remain a delight.

It is the first unequivocal love poem in Moore's oeuvre.

The poet had spent the first half of her career negotiating the confines of her filial devotion. She learned to survive and even thrive artistically in that narrow chasm. By midcareer her confinement had metamorphosed into "the only fortress strong enough to trust to." The love that appears in her late poems is neither the rare but passionate "love that will / gaze an eagle blind" nor love "in the mistaken sense of greed." It is love as other poets mean it, the antidote to loneliness. "I don't seem to grow up," she told Mary Shoemaker months after Mary died. "The greatest support to morale is being loved and I feel surrounded and upheld by affection."

Though loved by many, she felt lonelier than she had since her freshman year in college. She tried to focus upon the affection of her friends. For Louise Crane, who had had a hospital bed installed in the

Moores' living room during Mary's final illness, she wrote "Voracities and Verities Sometimes Are Interacting." The poem makes several private allusions to Louise and subtly praises her dazzling "unobtrusiveness." "Love can make one / bestial or make a beast a man," declares "Efforts of Affection," a poem written soon after Mary's death. When it came out in *The Nation*, the poet's name appeared, at her request, as Marianne Craig Moore. The "Craig" itself was a nod of affection. Cousin Mary, a Craig genealogist and devoted reader of *The Nation*, had wondered for years why Marianne did not use her middle name.

"Can you conceive of such irresponsibleness?" Marianne wrote soon after taking on the La Fontaine project. "It is, moreover, like asking a katydid to construct a B-29." From the beginning, the very enormity of the task, even its laboriousness, gave her a certain satisfaction. She wondered at times whether it was mere stubbornness that kept her going, but the repeated assurances she received from Reynal & Hitchcock right up until Mary's death gave her confidence "that they really want the thing."

Then, just after Mary died, she received a letter from Chester Kerr, vice president of Reynal & Hitchcock, asking to see Books I through VI before she proceeded. Curtice Hitchcock had died, and changes in the firm were under way. Marianne proceeded with her revisions through the fall and sent them to Elizabeth Ford. The task anchored her against the tides of grief that threatened to overwhelm her. Kerr told her in November that Ford no longer worked for the firm and that sending work to her was not the same as sending it to Reynal & Hitchcock. Then he telephoned three days before Christmas to advise her to find another publisher, the firm having decided that the project was a "doubtful sales risk."

Marianne was not allowed to visit Warner over the holiday because of surgery in his family. Kathrine and Marcia again provided the family support she needed. They spent Christmas in Brooklyn, and with Gladys's help, Marianne cooked Christmas dinner for them: steak, potatoes, tomatoes, celery, and salted almonds. Her letters to Warner express optimism that Macmillan would take the fables. Yet to Cousin Mary, Kathrine, and Marcia, she confided how small she felt and how helpless. She did not feel grown up enough to take care of herself, and she spent most of January in bed.

Before approaching Macmillan, she sent a few revised fables to Harry Levin. He told her that he liked them as well as the originals. "I marvel," he said, "at how you manage to catch and sustain, not only the original verse form, but the whimsical tone of La Fontaine, while continuing—not least of the attractions of your version—to sound like yourself."

Marianne had by now a long relationship with Macmillan. Not only had the company published her last three books but it had since 1943 employed her to review manuscripts. Harold Latham sometimes enclosed a personal note with her annual royalty check and in 1945 told her it was a "deep satisfaction" to publish her work and receive her literary advice. The note meant a great deal to the poet. She did not like to admit that her fables had been rejected, and she wrote multiple drafts of her letter to Latham before she got the wording just right. The editors at Reynal & Hitchcock who supported her project, she said, had taken positions elsewhere.

It was James Putnam who answered, Latham having gone abroad. At Putnam's request, she sent him Books I and VI in early February. She then heard nothing until May, when they ran into each other at a tea. Putnam asked her to lunch. When Marianne requested that he dispense with formalities, he hesitated. She asked if Macmillan had found that it could not use the translation. With none of Latham's delicacy, he admitted that was true. Ten days later she received a letter in which his "condemnation was so thorough-going" that she felt "suspicious of every comma." She acknowledged the errors he pointed out but thought she could correct them. Putnam later told people, so she heard, that if the fables could be translated, Miss Moore was not the one to do it.

To be thus treated by her own publisher was a greater blow than the broken contract with Reynal & Hitchcock. And a year had not passed since her mother died.

She regarded the fables as a "godsend" at this point in her life and could not bear losing them. Not wanting to proceed if she had no ear, as Putnam implied, she sent Ezra Pound some sample fables. Pound's own translations and the technical expertise he attained from doing them had influenced her to undertake the La Fontaine project from the start. There was no one whose expertise in meter and diction she trusted more. The "encouraging energetic enthusiasm" with which Pound responded to her letter provided the "tonic" and "reprieve" she so badly needed. He offered to find her a publisher in England.

But Marianne already had, since March, another publisher in mind. Monroe Engel, who had worked at Reynal & Hitchcock when it contracted for Moore's fables, now worked for Viking Press. He was appalled at her treatment by his former employer and said that he would like to see her translation if she had not yet found another publisher. After receiving Pound's reassurances, she sent sample fables to Engel, who quickly responded with an offer.

This time she consulted Monroe Wheeler and Glenway Wescott before signing the contract. She asked that Harry Levin be given 10 percent of the royalties for serving as her consultant, but Levin refused payment for work he considered a pleasure. (Later on, after the fables were published, she had Viking put the first thousand dollars of her royalties into a college fund for Levin's daughter.) On July 20, 1948, she signed a contract with Viking to complete the translation by 1951.

She would encounter still more setbacks before the fables saw publication in 1954, but her most formidable were self-imposed. While translating Book VII, she decided that it was worth the effort to match the vowel and consonant sounds of La Fontaine's rhymes as well as his rhyme scheme. Thus, if La Fontaine's rhyming syllable was *oeur*, she would use an English equivalent such as *fur, air,* or *ear.* The challenge of finding English rhymes to match La Fontaine's was one thing. But to position those words within natural English syntax was quite another.

One wonders, if Mary had been living, whether she could have persuaded her daughter not to make things so difficult for herself. Pound tried to. Williams and Stevens both suggested to her privately that she gave too much of herself to the fables.

But her grief demanded of her a project of Herculean proportions. "My fables are a kind of penance at times and then again a pleasure," she told Mary Shoemaker. She needed the arduous discipline of the task to survive, and working on the fables provided a good excuse for her to stay home when she needed to. Self-discipline in both art and society is a "confirmation of one's freedom," she told an inquirer at this time. "Perseverance," she told another, "is my one qualification as a translator."

Neither Levin nor Engel expressed the same enthusiasm over Books VII and VIII as they had over the first six books. Marianne began to doubt her own ear. In the spring of 1949, on her way home from receiving her first honorary degree, she visited Ezra Pound at St. Elizabeths Hospital in Washington. He was "very severe" but nevertheless "encouraging" about the new work she showed him. He offered much advice but told her above all "to avoid the reversed order of words."

It took Marianne a year and a half to translate Books VII through XII and then almost another year to redo the first six books according to her self-imposed rigors. Meanwhile she worked sporadically with Engel on revisions. He took a five-month leave during 1949 and thereafter worked only on Tuesdays. At the end of 1951, after approving revisions only to Books VI through X, he resigned to go to graduate school.

Senior editor Pascal Covici took over the project. Since he had little background in poetry, Viking hired Malcolm Cowley as a consultant and sent him two books of fables that Engel had already approved. Cowley returned twenty-five foolscap pages of corrections, which Engel forwarded to Marianne. While Engel recommended she consider the remarks, he thought many of them "arbitrary." Marianne agreed that some corrections were "essential" but the bulk of them mere strutting—"justifying his job as language authority."

"There is no one writing whom I value less than Malcolm Cowley," Marianne had confided to a friend shortly before she began editing *The Dial.* Cowley at the time was associated with Matthew Josephson and other young *Secession* writers for whom she had little sympathy. She did publish his book reviews and poems in *The Dial.* But one can imagine how little she would have trusted advice from the champion of Hemingway, Faulkner, and Hart Crane. Cowley himself had translated several books from French into English, but no poetry. His fluency in French far exceeded Marianne's, and his comments at first focused on the literal meaning of the French. Unlike Levin, he was often condescending, and he lacked Levin's appreciation for Moore's poetic voice and sense of rhythm. She took Cowley's advice not to follow her rhyming principles too slavishly but told him she refused to violate, even for meaning's sake, the natural order of words.

Marianne met her 1951 deadline. She had completed all twelve books to her own satisfaction when Cowley took over and was eager to move on to other things. It took Cowley all of 1952 and half of 1953 to get through the twelve books. Marianne complained that she felt like a citizen of Pompeii, forced into paralysis before finishing her work. Her resentment toward Cowley grew and grew. She made no attempt to disguise it in her letters to him or to her friends. Yet she resolved to meet his demands whenever possible for the sake of her publisher.

Having devoted the past eight years to La Fontaine, Marianne delivered her final revisions to Viking at the end of June 1953. To finish was undeniably a relief. Yet she felt that her last " 'absolutely faithful' undigressing version" had lost much of its earlier "dash and color." The banality of some rhymes disappointed her, and she thought the verse too often sounded "labored and uneuphonious." "Anything done with stubborn theoretic determination is hazardous," she admitted after the fables were in print. She thought it "fanatical" to have translated all 241 of them.

Marianne sent a few of her best fables to *The New Yorker* at an editor's request. But *The New Yorker*, which did not at the time publish translations, deemed her work too close to the original and returned it. The editors had expected her fables to be variations on La Fontaine.

22

A Luminescent Paul Revere

1950–1956

Marianne was just up from three weeks in bed when, at nine o'clock on the evening of February 28, 1950, she addressed a large, formally attired audience at the Museum of Modern Art. Despite the snowstorm outside, many of her friends and two of her nieces turned out for the double-bill reading with Auden. The occasion marked her unofficial emergence from mourning and her transformation, at age sixty-two, from Brooklyn recluse to beloved performer.

Her appearance was a collaborative effort. Constance had provided the black velvet dress with rhinestone buckle. The pearl earrings and gardenia corsage came from Hildegarde. Her next-door neighbors, Eleanor and Sadie Padley, and their friend Jimmy Reilly called a taxi and escorted her through the storm to Manhattan. Underneath her elegant exterior was her own concoction: she had salvaged a pink-and-black diagonally striped petticoat from the basement and lengthened it with scraps of an umbrella she found on the street.

She began by thanking Monroe Wheeler and members of the museum's poetry committee for creating "an uncommon *sweetness* in the air as Blake said of fairies he'd seen." She would fulfill her promise, she said, to read some "verse"—though would "scruple to call it poetry."

The audience erupted in laughter.

Her unique blend of easy erudition and disarming humility combined with a comedienne's sense of timing won their hearts. She began with two poems just written, "Armor's Undermining Modesty" and "The Icosasphere," and concluded with a fable, "Rabbits." The crowd was electric, said one observer, and rewarded her with five minutes of applause and whoops of approval. When Auden took the platform for the second half of the program, he said that he felt like "*a great flat foot*" in comparison.

Marianne had long been a student of performance. She was first attracted to Peggy James while watching her perform in the freshman play. Paderewski made a great impression upon her in college, too, as much for his manner as for his music. Circus animals and acrobats captivated her. And she had carefully observed how Yeats, Frost, and Edna St. Vincent Millay performed at the Brooklyn Institute. A month before the Museum of Modern Art event, she attended the dress rehearsal for Eliot's Broadway play *The Cocktail Party*. She would see the performance at least seven times. And because she had heard that Dylan Thomas was the best reader since Yeats, she made a point of hearing him read that spring. Thomas's "wry gusto and, as it were, incompatible daintiness evade characterization," she said afterward.

Despite its apparent effortlessness, Moore's success as a performer did not come naturally. She disliked crowds and never, according to her private letters, outgrew her childhood shyness. Because a public performance or party was often followed by two to three weeks of illness, she learned to pace herself to allow recovery time. When possible, she refused social invitations that immediately preceded or followed her performance. Using her Bible class as an excuse, she often arrived at parties late in order to conserve strength. Even so, her doctors and friends warned her repeatedly not to overtax herself.

Journalists and memoirists struggled to find words for the unique effect Miss Moore had on people. Donald Hall, who observed her meandering among the "Mount Rushmores of the literary moment" at Harvard's 1956 Summer School, realized: "They are all afraid of her. She is five foot three and a half inches tall, weighs less than a hundred pounds, talks in a low mumble while looking at the floor, continually disparages herself while praising others—and they are all terrified of her." Marianne refused to acknowledge anything unusual about her presence. Henrietta Fort Holland called it Marianne's "evanescent firefly quality" and quoted William Carlos Williams that "she walks on roses."

When Marianne once entered a city bus and realized she had forgotten her purse, "the fiercest of bus-drivers," according to Holland, "insisted that she accept the fare from him and on no account leave the bus." One of the doctors who attended Mary in her final illness refused to bill Marianne for his services. Elizabeth Bishop imagined her friend flying over New York, "above the accidents, above the malignant movies, / the taxicabs and injustices at large,"

> with a black capeful of butterfly wings and bon-mots,
> with heaven knows how many angels all riding
> on the broad black brim of your hat.

The magnetism was not new. In 1915 Marianne had emerged upon the New York art scene as "an astonishing person" whose conversation "held every man in awe." Despite her nervous laughter, androgynous figure, and reputation for prudishness, her power seemed almost sexual to sexually alert admirers such as Bryher and Williams. "I never saw a more sexual woman," said Kenneth Burke, "who was more remote from all those things." "Everyone loved her," recalled Williams in his 1951 *Autobiography*.

Now that she looked at least a decade older than her sixty-something years, everyone still loved her. She might pass for someone's grandma, said *Time*, yet was a spinster who walked around arranging words in her head like a Japanese garden. Magazines such as *Time* and *Life* that advertised to young suburban families routinely identified her as a spinster.

Marianne had long studied the seemingly effortless behaviors of animals. Her poems praise the grace of the awkwardly built pangolin, the measured leaps of the jerboa, and the "wisteria-like" effect of an elephant's uplifted trunk. As an artist, she understood that the effect of effortlessness requires hard work and perseverance as well as gusto. She preferred her late poems over her earlier ones because of their greater ease. And she attained the effect of effortlessness even more fully as a performer.

Through observation, imitation, and practice she cultivated the elusive personality trait now called charisma. One scholar of performance has described charisma as the "apparently effortless embodiment of contradictory qualities simultaneously: strength *and* vulnerability, innocence *and* experience, and singularity *and* typicality among them." Marilyn Monroe had it. James Dean and Elvis Presley had it. Cultural icons were as readily consumed by postwar society as were no-iron fabrics and panty girdles. For the reading public, literary distinction could be as enticing as sex appeal, especially in an award-winning poet who claimed to "dislike" poetry. The sexual ambiguity of a Truman Capote or Marianne Moore was itself alluring to literate consumers.

Marianne did include some early poems in her public readings, but when she assembled the volume of poems that would make her famous, she no longer took satisfaction in the modernist experiments and obscure political commentaries of *Selected Poems*. She had undergone a sea change since *What Are Years* appeared, and the only group of poems that she still liked, she told Mary Shoemaker, were the six poems in *Nevertheless*. The rest she dismissed as "my 'cats and dogs' of former days" and as "hard reading."

When T. S. Eliot turned down the opportunity to publish *What Are Years* in 1941 and *Nevertheless* in 1944, he said that he wanted Faber to publish her *Collected Poems* after the war. In June 1946, he called on Marianne and her very ill mother to discuss the project. She gave him copies of *Selected Poems*, *What Are Years*, and *Nevertheless* marked with changes along with typescripts of newer poems. He mentioned the book again in 1948 after she had written to request that he receive all the royalties from *Collected Poems* in memory of his brother. (Eliot did not accept this extraordinary offer.) And in June 1950 he requested at last a table of contents.

Marianne responded promptly. Except for the omission of four very early poems from *Selected Poems* and four from *What Are Years*, her table of contents follows the order of her previous three books. Under the heading "Hitherto Uncollected" are nine poems published since *Nevertheless*: two war poems, four written in the wake of Mary's death, and three light verses written for public performance.

Collected Poems appeared in Britain on September 14, 1951. It was a modest volume of seventy-one poems. Although it included more poems and more pages than *Selected Poems*, its outer dimensions, including its thickness, were smaller. The paper was thinner, the margins were narrower and, because the poems appeared continuously on the page rather than each poem appearing on its own page or pages, the book had far less white space than its predecessor. Was the greater condensation of type the publisher's decision? Or had the poet, who had always exercised as much authority as she could in designing her books, learned from the popularity of *Nevertheless* that smaller books sell better? In any case, sell it did. The American edition, issued by Macmillan on December 17, 1951, remained in print for more than twenty-five years.

Her omission of eight poems was less remarkable than the radical excisions she made to her longer poems, especially those of the 1930s. Most shocking is the reduction of "The Steeple-Jack" from twelve stanzas to eight. Among the other affected poems, "Nine Nectarines" and "The Frigate Pelican" are each reduced by half. "The Jerboa" loses a stanza and "Elephants" two. Three and a half lines vanish from "The Buffalo" and thirty-two lines from "An Octopus." Ellipses appear in "The Buffalo" and "Nine Nectarines" where cuts were made but not in other poems. By dividing the last two lines of each stanza in "Camellia Sabina" into three, Moore revealed a rhyme pattern that the former arrangement had obscured. There were numerous other changes as well. She deleted passages that seemed tangential to her themes but rarely repaired the pattern of the affected stanzas.

Readers had had a hard enough time distinguishing her stanzas from free verse when the stanza patterns were typographically consistent. But their fragmented appearance in *Collected Poems* and the resemblance between overrun lines and indented lines all but prevent detection of her stanzas' patterns. (Later she moved overruns to the right of the page.) Moore was working on Book VIII of La Fontaine at the time *Collected Poems* went to press and becoming ever more meticulous about reproducing La Fontaine's poetic form. Yet the revisions to her own poems make the emphatic point that she cared more for verbal concision than formal consistency.

Moore did have misgivings about the book, she told Bryher. She appreciated the honesty of a reviewer who said that "the war poems are embarrassing and he shudders to think what I may be in old age if my present sentimentality grows on me."

Reviews of *Collected Poems* were nevertheless overwhelmingly positive. They took Moore's status among four or five major living poets for granted. This stature was due in part to the growing accessibility of her poems over the past decade and also to a major shift in thinking among literary critics. New Criticism, which valued literature that demands close analysis over that which does not, was in its heyday, and Modernism was no longer a fringe movement. The subtleties, ironies, and paradoxes of Moore's poems that had so irritated early critics became marks of her greatness. John Crowe Ransom and Cleanth Brooks, two leaders of the New Criticism, had contributed to the special issue of *The Quarterly Review* that was devoted to Moore in 1948. R. P. Blackmur and Randall Jarrell, two other critics associated with the movement, had already gone on record as her champions. And Alan Tate had helped choose her for the Harriet Monroe award.

Reviewing Moore's *Collected Poems* at length for one of the chief organs of New Criticism, *The Sewanee Review*, Wallace Fowlie said that Marianne Moore's "warmly human" poetry established a "dyke" between readers and the more difficult modern poets: "What might appear in other poets as capricious and confused, is here lucid and organized." Self-respecting critics might now complain of her sentimentality but no longer of her inscrutability.

Barely a month after the American edition of *Collected Poems* appeared in bookstores, it received two major prizes: the Bollingen Prize for Poetry, then in its fourth year; and the National Book Award, then in its third. Six hundred people attended the National Book Awards banquet at the Commodore Hotel in New York. During the press conference that preceded the ceremony, someone pointed out that James Jones's *From Here to Eternity*, winner of the fiction award, had sold 250,000 copies and Rachel Carson's *The Sea Around Us*, winner of the nonfiction award, had sold 180,000 whereas Moore's *Collected Poems* had sold about 5,000. Marianne retorted that she was surprised it had sold one.

"I think you have to work to read poetry," interjected thirty-year-old James Jones, "and most people don't like to work while they read."

"It ought to be work to read something that it was work to write," said Moore.

In her formal acceptance speech, she said that she could "see no reason for calling my work poetry except that there is no other category in which to put it." She then proceeded to quote R. P. Blackmur, Wallace Stevens, Chaucer, Confucius, La Fontaine, and contemporary art critic Harold Rosenberg about the impetus for poetry. Stevens "puts his finger on this thing poetry," she said, when "he refers to 'a violence within that protects us from a violence without.'"

"I could live to ninety," Warner wrote Marianne after the ceremony, "and not find life boring merely to relive those moments at the Commodore." It was the first time he had seen his sister perform. He observed how people admired the other two winners but *loved* her. He told her that her clothing was a "triumph," that her face looked "composed," and that she had "a fine light" in her eyes. He was relieved that she did not look "worn and wrinkled" but still urged her to see a hairdresser and get a massage.

Marianne answered that a great deal of care had gone into her clothes and that she was sure Mary would approve of her new dressmaker, Gilda Serla. She had not taken time away from her speechwriting and busy schedule to get a facial or a massage but had drunk lots of orange juice and vegetable juice and eaten steak almost every day. To please him, she would see the Swedish woman in her bank building about a massage.

At the time of the National Book Awards ceremony, there were rumors already that *Collected Poems* would win the Pulitzer, too. And it did. The two-person jury consisted of Moore's early champion Alfred Kreymborg and one of her most disparaging critics from those years, Louis Untermeyer. Moore had won Untermeyer over, he had told her already, with *What Are Years* and *Nevertheless*.

The following year she won two more awards. On May 19, 1953, Moore became the first artist and first Bryn Mawr graduate to receive the M. Carey Thomas Award of five thousand dollars. It was given every five years to an eminent American woman. Jane Addams and Eleanor Roosevelt were previous recipients. At another ceremony on

May 27, Glenway Wescott presented her with the Gold Medal for Poetry from the National Institute of Arts and Letters. And on June 11 she received her fifth honorary degree, from Long Island University. She had previously accepted degrees from Wilson College in Chambersburg, Pennsylvania; Mount Holyoke; the University of Rochester; and Dickinson College in Carlisle.

This was also the year that Moore adopted as her signature the black cape and tricorne hat. She had never, even when younger, thought herself photogenic and always said that she hated close-ups. But she learned to be a media darling through the assistance of the freelance photojournalist Esther Bubley and the fashion photographer George Platt Lynes.

Working on assignment for *Life* magazine, Bubley first photographed Marianne at the M. Carey Thomas Award ceremony and then, after taking more shots of her at Bryn Mawr the next morning, brought her back to Brooklyn, stopping at an antique store on the way. The following week Bubley spent another day with Marianne, this time shooting her in her Brooklyn neighborhood and at the Bronx Zoo. Marianne had brought a cape to wear as a wrap, and Bubley convinced her to wear it in the photos.

"I like you in the *cape*," Bubley told her. "If you are too warm, could you put it on for the picture? It is just right and identifies you." All of the outdoor shots that day show Marianne in her cape and a black straw cartwheel hat.

Marianne described Esther Bubley as "heroically diligent, gentle, expert, and considerate." Two of Bubley's photographs delighted her: a full-length shot of herself posing next to an antique boar from a carousel and another of children and balloons at the zoo, where she appears as little more than a silhouette in the background. After the fiasco, as she considered it, with Cecil Beaton and *Vogue*, she always asked to censor any pictures of herself that she disliked. She was told that *Life*, as an exception, would allow her to do so. But the promise was forgotten or ignored. When the photo essay appeared in the September 21, 1953, issue, she was disappointed that both of her favorite shots were "suppressed" in favor of others that made her "look like a gorilla."

The poet was not famous enough to be identified by name in the *Life* headline. But she was famous enough to be called "famous": "Life Goes on a Zoo Tour with a Famous Poet." "Marianne Moore is a 65-year-old spinster," begins the text, "who lives in Brooklyn, wears wide straw hats, is interested in everything from snails to steamrollers and is, in the opinion of many literary critics, the finest living American poet." A two-page photo spread shows Miss Moore with elephants, swans, a baby chimp, and zebras next to lines from her poems that describe these animals. The two columns that follow on successive pages show the poet's domestic life: wearing an apron in her kitchen, shopping in a local store, and holding a baseball bat among neighborhood boys. *Life* makes the "famous poet" an adorable eccentric, a kind of Brooklyn Mary Poppins. Moore thought all the photos "hideous" except the one with the baseball bat and thought the text condensed her into something unreal.

George Platt Lynes, a close friend of Monroe Wheeler and Glenway Wescott, had been photographing Moore since 1935. One portrait of her had appeared in a 1949 issue of *Life* as part of an article about Lynes's literary portraiture. When she sat for him in November 1953, he took what would become her favorite portrait of herself wearing a black cape and tricorne hat. It made her look, according to Elizabeth Bishop, "like a feminine, luminescent, delicate re-incarnation of Paul Revere."

Neither the cape nor the tricorne was new to the poet. Marianne had requested her first black cape while a sophomore at Bryn Mawr. Mary made her one. This was not long after she had observed President Thomas wearing a long sealskin cape over her nightclothes while rushing to a (false) fire alarm. Nearly two decades later, when Mary and Marianne were flush with Marianne's *Dial* salary, they purchased a Knox cape for seventy-five dollars (nearly nine hundred dollars today). Marianne enjoyed the attention it drew from passersby as she walked to work, and she wore it occasionally after moving to Brooklyn. After Hildegarde Watson's mother died in 1950, Hildegarde gave Marianne a similar cape that had belonged to her mother. Marianne told Hildegarde that it was Mrs. Lassell's cape she wore in the Bubley photographs.

The tricorne also dates from Marianne's sophomore year. "I am wild for a hat some time in colonial shape," she wrote just before her nineteenth birthday, "of heavy black felt with nothing on it." At some point thereafter she acquired a green straw tricorne that she wore for nearly a decade until the dye started flaking off.

While preparing her clothes for the National Book Award ceremony in 1952, she decided she needed a new hat and spied a tricorne in a Fifth Avenue window as she rode by on a bus. When she later returned to the store, it had been sold. She next went to a Brooklyn milliner.

"Could you get me a black velvet tricorne?" she asked.

"No, it's out of season, but I'll make you one."

"No," Marianne replied, "I have to try it on. If it's too small it will sit on my head like a napkin ring and I'll look like an organ grinder's monkey. I want a sort of George Washington Federal Troops hat, with tails in back."

"Well . . . I have a felt one in the window that could be adapted. We could curve it upward with velvet." After receiving assurances that the woman had once made hats for Mrs. Astor, Marianne agreed to the purchase.

"The hat did it!" said Warner after the National Book Awards ceremony. He especially admired the impact of the tricorne in a newspaper photograph of the three winners. In 1957, when Marianne briefly lost the hat, Hildegarde had Henri Bendel's make an all-velvet replacement and ordered one for herself as well. It thrilled Hildegarde, as Marianne well knew, to dress her famous friend and to wear clothes identical to those she gave Marianne. Hildegarde sent Marianne a gardenia corsage, and later an orchid, before every performance.

Some of Marianne's friends found it endearing that she cared for clothes as much as she did—especially after buying almost nothing new for herself during the decade surrounding Mary's death. She spoke and wrote at length to friends about planning her outfits for public appearances. While she continued to live frugally, she was now willing to pay for designer dresses and accessories. Her public persona demanded a sense of style, and she received such a steady supply of grants and prizes in addition to monetary gifts from her friends that she could well afford to dress the part. A favorite designer in 1950 was Hattie Carnegie, whose opening Marianne attended the day after her

Museum of Modern Art event. Her friends also continued to supply her with clothes. Louise Crane procured a nutria coat from Buenos Aires to ward off Marianne's winter colds.

While traveling to Vassar by train in the spring of 1954, Marianne was recognized for the first time because of her tricorne. A Princeton student who had seen the Lynes photograph approached her, and the two "discussed the ethics of individual responsibility quite hard for a few minutes" as they reached Poughkeepsie. She liked being recognized and until the end of her life often wore the tricorne on her day-to-day excursions about town.

The Lynes photograph and Moore's celebrity status created a market for her *Fables* that no publisher could have imagined when she began the project a decade earlier. In addition to the trade hardback, Viking released a signed collectors' edition bound in coral buckram with a black slipcase. Moore gave up her royalties for the first thousand books in exchange for a hundred copies of the collectors' edition to be sent to friends. Viking gave a tea in her honor on the release date, May 17, 1954, and the next day she took her lunch to the office "like a construction worker" and signed more than four hundred copies of the special edition. The hardback, bound in indigo linen with the Lynes photograph on the dust jacket, went into a second printing within the first month and into a third printing six months later. Faber and Faber brought out a small edition of *Selected Fables* in Britain. And a decade later, in 1964, demand for the *Fables* was still so great that Viking issued a paperback edition, for which Moore was allowed to make corrections. It went into a second printing within the year.

Reviewers with expertise in La Fontaine's poetry lauded Moore's work. In *The New York Times Book Review*, Wallace Fowlie, a scholar of French poetry, praised Moore's fidelity to La Fontaine's verse forms and meters and especially the way she captured the complexity of La Fontaine's rhymes. Howard Nemerov, however, wrote in *The Sewanee Review* that "as poems to be read in English," the translations "are irritatingly awkward, elliptical, complicated, and very jittery as to meter." Moore liked the more balanced review that a young Hugh Kenner wrote for *Poetry*. At worst, Moore gets "preoccupied (understandably) with tucking all the words into the given rhythms and rhyme schemes," says Kenner. But while the resulting English can be tortuous, the "normal excellence" of her translation "is surprisingly sustained." She creates a "climate of mind, not heretofore available in English, in which the wit of the Fables can thrive."

Viking rolled out new books for Moore's readership as fast as she could assemble them. In May 1955 it brought out the first volume of her prose, *Predilections*. The two most explicit statements of her poetic principles, "Feeling and Precision" and "Humility, Concentration, and Gusto," appear first in the book. These are followed by "Henry James as Characteristic American" and nineteen other essays, including reviews and recent lectures about Stevens, Pound, Eliot, Auden, Williams, Cummings, and Louise Bogan.

Like a Bulwark, a volume of eleven new poems, came out in 1956, and *O to Be a Dragon*, with fifteen poems, came out three years later. Moore's poems of the 1950s no longer show "a violence from within that protects us from a violence without." Rather, they show the poet as performer—appearing in person or in print to fulfill her campy, colonial-patriot role as unofficial poet laureate. A Christmas poem, "Rosemary," appeared in *Vogue*. A poem written for a Phi Beta Kappa event appeared in *Ladies' Home Journal*. A pharmaceutical company paid her five hundred dollars to write a poem about medicine for its in-house periodical. The copyright page of *Like a Bulwark* shows not just the periodicals where the poems first appeared but the names of the editors who requested and bought the poems.

Moore no longer wrote poetry "to say what is boiling within me," nor did she spend days researching her subjects in museums and libraries. Rather, she wrote primarily to please her recipient. This is not to say that she wrote thoughtlessly. The poems of these years show off her wit, her mastery of cadence, and her facility with rhyme.

"Ah Marianne! How *do* you do it," Elizabeth Bishop wrote about "Sycamore." "I like that one as much as Hopkins's 'dappled things'— and it is so much better without that emotional *rushing* effect he produces. Perhaps it is the uncanny meter."

Still, not all of her poems rose to the standard of the lovely "Sycamore," and most everything, she told a friend, came back from the editor for "repairs."

Like her public performances, these poems delight without challenging the reader. Even their subjects show her attention to performance. In "Tom Fool at Jamaica" she wrote about a racehorse, his jockey, and other "champions of harmonious speed": Fats Waller, Ozzie Smith, and Eubie Blake. Others describe a tennis player, a flamenco dancer, the Lipizzaner stallions, the Brooklyn Dodgers, a performance of *The Magic Flute*, and a company of Russian folk dancers. The poems extol heroic virtues such as courage, equanimity, nonviolent resistance, humility, individual freedom, and ardor in one's work—but gently so. No fine steel blades flash. No avalanches are launched. Overcoming racial prejudice was among Hercules' labors in a 1921 poem. In 1955, a sycamore and "a little dry / thing in the grass" illustrate

A commonplace:
there's more than just one kind of grace.

If the poems Moore wrote in her sixties and seventies no longer express the depth of feeling that her earlier work had, it was not because her feelings had grown slack. Her loyalties to friends and family remained as fierce as ever, as did her outrage over injustice.

Surviving correspondence suggests that the person in whom Marianne most honestly confided her feelings after her mother's death was Mary Shoemaker. Marianne withheld from Warner, as she often had in the past, her disappointments, her illnesses, and her deep loneliness. She loved him more than anyone, even adored him, but did not want to worry him. Her letters to Cousin Mary during those years are as sincere as any she ever wrote and as colorful. Much as she had entertained her mother while at Bryn Mawr, Marianne amused her elderly cousin with the comings-and-goings of her literary life. "What would trust and people's chivalry mean to me," she wrote just before the National Book Awards ceremony, "without a meaning in it for you? and those I love (who are to me as it were synonymous with Mother)?"

Marianne adopted Kathrine Jones and Marcia Chamberlain as family, too. For five of the six years after Mary died, Marianne spent August in Maine with them. She visited them in Brookline every spring, and they came to New York every December. Although Marcia and Kathrine supported Marianne's work, their affection for her had little to do with her public personality. It is possible that they never saw her perform before an audience. Although Marianne exchanged many letters with them over the years, very little of the correspondence from either side survives. It was destroyed apparently out of respect for the intimacy of the friendship. Kathrine and Marcia had no desire to share the limelight of their friend's fame.

Kathrine died of cancer in July 1952, five years after Mary's death. Marianne said her goodbyes in May, returned to Brookline for the funeral, and then spent August and September with Marcia in Maine. When Marcia came to New York for ten days in December, Marianne so wanted her friends to meet Marcia that she accepted invitations for every evening. Louise Crane drove them to Connecticut one day to see Warner and Constance. Monroe Wheeler and Glenway Wescott gave them a dinner party, to which they also invited Tennessee Williams and the Sitwells, Edith and Osbert.

Marcia developed stomach pains before she left New York, and a week later severe indigestion turned into a paralyzing stroke. Marianne was "in misery about her" until she could get to Boston in January. She gave a series of lectures at Yale just after Marcia left New York and had already agreed to teach a six-week poetry seminar at Bryn Mawr during February and March. But as soon as her course was over, she returned to Marcia's bedside. For three years Marianne spent as much time as she could with Marcia, who recovered her speech and movement on her right side but remained bedridden. At Marcia's insistence, Marianne took driving lessons while in Brookline and earned a license. Marianne also enjoyed there the company of Cousin Mary's great-nephew, John Stauffer, a medical student at Harvard. Marianne read to Marcia from Mary Baker Eddy's *Science and Health* (Marcia was a Christian Scientist, as was Hildegarde Watson) and helped her work crossword puzzles.

"How magnificently you are her friend," Hildegarde wrote Marianne after visiting them. "Your care of her, how adorable. I understand how you help her stand it." Hildegarde was reminded of Marianne's "electric touch" when Marianne had once massaged Hildegarde's head and neck following an illness. The doctors were amazed at how Marcia rallied in Marianne's presence. Marcia lived until the end of May 1955.

Marianne attended her funeral and went from there to accept honorary degrees at Smith and Rutgers. In early August Wallace Stevens died. And later the same month Cousin Mary died at the age of ninety-four. Marianne was vacationing in Maine with Malvina Hoffman, the sculptor, and did not attend the funeral. There were other invalid friends whom Marianne visited regularly, and she tried to get to Washington once a year to see Ezra Pound at St. Elizabeths.

In the years following Mary's death, Marianne maintained what she called "a subterranean career" of encouraging the forlorn. Her letters generously offer affection, comfort, and encouragement to anyone in need of them. But E. McKnight Kauffer was a special case. In 1937, when the Museum of Modern Art gave the American-born artist a one-man show, Kauffer was enjoying great success in Britain for his poster art. Then, with the outbreak of war in 1940, he and Marion Dorn moved to New York. He despaired over his poor reception there until his death from alcoholism in 1954.

Marianne had been pushing Monroe Wheeler to give Kauffer another show when she visited the Kauffers and Eliot just before her mother died. A year later she wrote an impassioned two-page letter (in contrast to her usual paragraph) recommending Kauffer for a Guggenheim. He greatly appreciated Marianne's interest in his work and they began corresponding. Kauffer told Marianne that he kept one of her letters in his Bible, and she often alludes to biblical figures in her letters to him. Several times she quotes Daniel 8:27: "And I Daniel fainted and was sick certain days. Then I arose and went about the king's business." She urged humility and gratitude upon him. "Courage," she said, "is not courage, Edward, merely the force lent us by humility." Marianne got through to him as no one else could. He thanked her profusely for her friendship and faith in him, as did Marion Dorn.

T. S. Eliot visited New York regularly during the 1950s. Marianne already regarded him as "my chief aid professionally," and in their mutual concern for the Kauffers their friendship grew deeper. A framed George Platt Lynes photograph of Eliot hung in Marianne's apartment, and the two engaged in a brief flirtation. In the spring of 1956 Eliot invited "My dear Marianne" to dinner with Marion Dorn and Robert Giroux, his publisher. He signed the note, "With much love Tom." The day after the dinner he sent her a heart pierced with an arrow sketched in pencil on yellow paper. All it said: "To Miss Marianne Moore from a grateful anonymous admirer."

It is no wonder Eliot was in a flirtatious mood. The sixty-seven-year-old poet was secretly in love with his twenty-nine-year-old secretary, Valerie Fletcher. No one except Fletcher's parents knew of the romance until after the marriage was made public in January 1957. In an interview thirty years later, Gladys Berry said that Marianne was heartbroken over the news. Marianne did care for Eliot. It is possible that she even had a little crush on him. But it was Eliot's failure to confide in her that caused her grief. She believed that their friendship merited such trust, and it made little difference to her that he had confided in no one. She waited six months before congratulating the newlyweds.

Marianne's professional loyalties ran deep as well. In early 1953 she learned that Margaret Marshall, her much-admired editor at *The Nation*, had been fired—ostensibly because the magazine was cutting costs but actually, as Marshall and others believed, because of her political differences with the editor, Freda Kirchwey. Other staff of the book review section were fired, too. Marianne wrote Kirchwey a letter of protest, and when *The Nation* next asked for a review (of a book that interested her), Marianne refused out of loyalty to Marshall and said so.

Marianne had another beef with *The Nation* when Marshall was fired: she objected to its vilification of Eisenhower's "honest, auspicious, genuinely devoted speeches." These were words she regularly used in defending Eisenhower to her literary friends, nearly all of whom supported Adlai Stevenson in the 1952 election. "Well, I'm sure Eisenhower is a good man—but Marianne—he reads Westerns," wrote Elizabeth Bishop. "Detective stories are all right—but not Westerns, never."

Just after Marianne severed ties to *The Nation*, she received her first acceptance from *The New Yorker*. Despite a warm invitation to contribute to *The New Yorker* in 1945 and despite Louise Bogan's glowing reviews of *Nevertheless* and *Collected Poems*, Marianne had never succeeded in placing a poem there.

Marianne Moore is "our most distinguished contemporary American poet," Bogan wrote in 1944. And Miss Moore's receiving the Pulitzer Prize, the Bollingen Prize, and the National Book Award, said Bogan in 1952, "should be a source of pride and pleasure to all members of the population who read American poetry with any attention." Marianne wrote Bogan immediately upon reading these remarks and said that they had brought her to the verge of tears.

The same day, Marianne also wrote Louise Crane that if her new poem, "Tom Fool at Jamaica," came back from the editor to whom it was promised, as she half expected, she would send it next to *The New Yorker*. Elizabeth Bishop meanwhile encouraged Marianne to give *The New Yorker* another chance. Bishop was by then in regular communication with Katharine White, *The New Yorker*'s fiction editor, and William Shawn, its editor. They "feel very badly about some old mistake or other," Bishop said, "and would give their eye-teeth to print a poem of yours."

"Tom Fool at Jamaica" marked Moore's *New Yorker* debut in June 1953. But for the next five years the magazine returned everything she sent.

23

Coney Island
Fun Fair Victim

1957–1968

By the time Marianne turned seventy, she had proved wrong all those early critics who said her audience would never be large. She had throngs of admirers who loved her quaint courtliness and sparkling, inoffensive wit. But her celebrity persona was losing its novelty and her oft-repeated accolades wearing thin.

Five years after the debut of her tricorne at the National Book Awards ceremony, Marianne appeared as the subject of a *New Yorker* profile. Its inaccuracies and condescending tone took her by surprise. While some admirers enjoy the discontinuous, poetic flow of her conversation, according to the profile, other habitués of New York teas and salons regard her as "a quite outrageous chatterbox." And her apartment—cluttered with ivory elephants, porcelain tigers, and other less identifiable "bric-a-brac"—is like her poetry, "the apotheosis of snugness."

Winthrop Sargeant, the magazine's music critic who had thus far published one other profile, does attempt to describe the appeal of Moore's poetry. But her awards and critical acclaim are the only evidence he gives of its importance. He diminishes the poet along with her subject matter: "The connoisseurs who regard Miss Moore's poems almost literally as self-portraits are convinced that all those tiny beleaguered organisms surviving in adversity by means of fortitude, intelligence, and patience represent Miss Moore herself."

"I take it very hard, Chester," she told a friend.

The one part of the article that Marianne liked was the portrayal of Warner as a "tall, spare, white-haired gentleman" who gives "an impression of dignity, dependability, and kindliness." But Warner's dignity comes at his sister's expense: "his thoughts tend to run on a logical track rather than by free and headlong association."

Two months after the appearance of the profile, *The New Yorker* published in its back pages an exchange of letters between Marianne Moore and the Ford Motor Company that upstaged whatever harm or good Winthrop Sargeant had done to the poet's reputation. David Wallace, Ford's marketing director, first wrote Marianne in October 1955, inviting her to participate in the naming of a new automobile. He had already market-tested some three hundred names, but no favorite had emerged. The name should convey "some visceral feeling of elegance, fleetness, and other advanced features and design," he told her. "And, of course, our relations will be on a fee basis of an impeccably dignified kind."

He succeeded in piquing Marianne's interest. She had been entering advertising contests since adolescence. Bon Ami "removes the blur along with the dirt," she once wrote its manufacturer. And she had long regarded her own poetry as a form of advertising, of "educating visualization." "If you fear that you are / reading an advertisement, / you are," she wrote in "The Arctic Ox (or Goat)."

Marianne put serious thought into the first name she proposed. She even did a little market research of her own by consulting Warner. The name she came up with—Ford Silver Sword—fulfilled David Wallace's stipulations and moreover echoed the rhythm of what he considered a successful Ford name, Thunderbird. Marianne had no intention of signing the contract that Wallace drolly insisted was required in business arrangements. Had the correspondence ended there, it would never have garnered public interest.

But Wallace, no mean letter writer himself, urged the poet to set her imagination free from practical considerations such as those suggested by her brother. And she did. Among the more fanciful of some forty names she suggested are Bullet Cloisonné, Mongoose Civique, Pastelogram, Plima Piluma, Turcotinga, and ultimately in a letter of its own: Utopian Turtletop. Wallace responded to that one with a Christmas bouquet of two dozen white roses sent "To our favorite Turtletopper." A year later he informed her that a name had been chosen: Edsel.

These letters lodged themselves more firmly in the imagination of the general public than anything else Moore wrote. Is the poet as hilariously remote from the modern world as the letters indicate? Or is she the savvy performer of a Chaplinesque dance through the cogwheels of mid-century consumerism? She did think Charlie Chaplin "a genius." "So simple and unprotective," she called him.

David Wallace's gift of flowers rather than a check indicates that he, at least, understood the spirit of play in which Moore proffered her lists of names. But to certain of Moore's posthumous defenders, notably Helen Vendler, the Ford letters constitute the nadir of Moore's career—the point where she crossed the line between pop culture diva and court jester. Four decades after the poet's death, Moore scholars rarely mention her Ford names although reporters and bloggers still rediscover them from time to time.

Marianne did not regard the letters as an embarrassment. She allowed them to be published in *The New Yorker* and gave the Pierpont Morgan Library permission to print them in a hardbound limited edition. She so enjoyed the attention they received that she included them in *A Marianne Moore Reader.*

Moore's letters to the Ford Motor Company do merit attention within the trajectory of her career, not for their foolhardiness but for how unguarded, how "unprotective," they are. Not only are they her first published letters, but their appearance marks an about-face change from her younger, armored self—the poet who refused to appear in *Poetry* because it did not meet her aesthetic standards, the poet who cared so much about her literary reputation that the publication of her first book infuriated her. She no longer cared about exclusivity as a measure of her artistic worth but instead gave her public whatever it wanted—even to the point of exhausting herself and jeopardizing her health.

•

During the fall of 1957, Elizabeth Bishop and her partner, Lota de Macedo Soares, gave a party to introduce Lota to Bishop's New York friends. The piano duo Arthur Gold and Robert Fizdale provided their apartment. Marianne arrived late and was "encouraging James Merrill," as she put it, when an unassuming young man in a bat-wing tie "crouched down" beside her "like a catcher on the diamond."

"May I talk to you?" he said. "I am on *The New Yorker.*"

"Indeed you may," said Marianne. "I read *The New Yorker* and like a great deal of it but somehow I can't get on with Howard Moss." Moss was the poetry editor.

"*I* am Howard Moss," he said, "and I'm afraid you don't understand. You see, we don't act individually but as a *board* . . ." and so forth.

"You have done us all a service, Mr. Moss, by your compliments to Juliette Marglen," Marianne soon told him, in reference to his recent satiric poem about a cosmetics advertisement.

"Do you know she replied in verse?" he said, obviously pleased, "very *bad* verse; took me literally, as if what I said really was a compliment."

The following summer Marianne was elated to receive Howard Moss's letter accepting "The Arctic Ox (or Goat)," a poem she had written "with much zeal." Moss requested a few changes. He asked her to turn the footnote about the source of the poem into a headnote and asked her to clarify a word and change a punctuation mark. Marianne proposed other changes, to which he replied that he preferred the original. After three weeks of negotiations they agreed on a final version. Marianne respected Moss. She had always liked a good editor.

"We are overjoyed with the poem," Moss wrote when he accepted "Saint Nicholas," the next poem Marianne sent him. "We are so happy to have this poem and so eager to have others that I wonder if you would consider signing a first-reading agreement with us." The agreement provided considerable financial incentive for favored authors to submit their work to *The New Yorker* before sending it elsewhere.

"Whether you can use my work or not," she replied, "you, Mr. Shawn, and *The New Yorker* have my everlasting gratitude." After asking for a few clarifications, she did sign. Moss did not accept everything Marianne sent him over the next decade and often asked for minor changes in what he did accept. But from 1953 through 1970, *The New Yorker* published twenty-three Moore poems. She thought Moss and *The New Yorker* "phenomenally liberal" with her, both "editorially and fiscally." She took pride in her association with *The New Yorker*. It made her feel, she said, "literarily affiliated with the writing-world."

"It has taken *The New Yorker* sadly long, I think, to discover that there is a *real* New Yorker, *New Yorker* poet," wrote Elizabeth Bishop in 1961, "just the kind of thing they must have dreamed of when they were younger and better—sophistication, wit, up-to-date,—and informed." If it is true that *The New Yorker* at last recognized "a *real* New Yorker, *New Yorker* poet," it is just as true that after signing her first-reading agreement in 1958 Moore wrote nearly all her poems specifically for *The New Yorker*. Readers of the magazine expected writing of a high caliber and did not mind reading a poem several times to grasp its meaning. But they sought amusement primarily, not aesthetic risks such as *The Dial* had taken. Like *New Yorker* cartoons, Moore's 1960s poems are more topical than political. And like her family letters of long ago, their wit and wordplay reward the astute reader with an in-the-know sense of intimacy.

As she had while editing *The Dial*, Marianne devoted more hours of the day to answering mail than to any other activity. Each publication and performance generated more and more letters, often up to fifty a day. When she left home for a week or more, she faced towers of books and mail upon her return. She answered every query, sometimes at length, whether from journalists, graduate students, or seventh-graders. She told them what she ate for breakfast: "half a grapefruit or orange juice, honey, an egg, hard-boiled or scrambled"; how she composed poems: "I do for the most part hear the number of syllables, not count them"; and what she thought of the Vietnam War: "desperate."

She did not copy answers verbatim from previous letters but did hone her replies to complex questions into ever more concise reiterations. To questions about politics and the state of the country, she stressed "FREEDOM for press, churches, and in private life." She valued "self-sacrifice," "tolerance," "family solidarity, and religious faith." "We should be embarrassed," she said, "that other nations should be able to see self-interest supplant love of freedom."

"My anonymous mail does sap my strength and insult my intelligence," she complained to friends. But she continued to answer it and tried to encourage aspiring writers. She often commented on the presentation of the work. "Careful typing, reasonably good paper, and *numbered pages* are tremendous factors in sharpening the reader's sense of obligation to the writer," she wrote regarding some contest entries. The more generous her responses, the more poems arrived for commentary. But she could not stop herself.

"I think you write so many letters because you *like* to write letters," observed Malvina Hoffman during one of the summers she and Marianne vacationed in Maine. She did enjoy it—though called herself "a kind of Coney Island fun fair victim."

Her telephone rang constantly. And strangers, sometimes drunk, arrived at her door at all hours of the night and day. Yet her willingness to help aspiring writers became legendary; she even allowed them to call upon her in her sickbed. The *New Yorker* profile indicated that she liked to receive visitors so much that she insisted upon paying their return subway fare to Manhattan. And then *Time* magazine's 1959 review of *O to Be a Dragon*, in an attempt at cleverness, published explicit directions to her apartment. "I am being obliterated by trespassers," she said. "I might say thugs! Letters upon letters also."

"I beg to be neglected," Marianne said in a 1965 *McCall's* interview. In the early 1960s she had postcards printed, modeled after Edmund Wilson's, listing all the requests with which she would not comply. But she sent relatively few, and when she did send them could not resist adding a handwritten note. If the recipient of such a card took offense and wrote back, she might well answer at length.

By the mid-1960s, Marianne's nieces helped her with mail, and concerned friends hired her a succession of secretaries. Yet when a teacher offered a spin in her yellow Corvette in exchange for advice about teaching poetry to college freshmen, the bedridden eighty-one-year-old scrawled: "Dear Miss Elizabeth I cannot go. (am convalescent) Tell the students they must first of all [be] natural; then strive for lucidity, force, and ease."

•

In the last two decades of her life, Marianne's devotion to her fans confounded her literary friends as much as her devotion to Mary had early in her career. Theodore and Beatrice Roethke were shocked to receive a full letter in answer to a mere Christmas card. This had long been Marianne's practice though she sent no Christmas cards or gifts herself. "Dear Marianne," Beatrice Roethke wrote her, "you mustn't be so conscientious! Of course, we love your letters, but I don't think we merit them." Dorothy Pound screened all of Ezra's mail. He read none of it except for very special letters, such as Marianne's, that she selected for him. Donald Hall was horrified to receive not one letter but two in appreciation for a potted plant he sent her. He resolved never to give her another thing. "Try to be a little ruthless with your admirers," advised Valerie Eliot. "I am afraid the instinct of self-preservation was left out of your make-up!"

Feeling needed meant more to Marianne at this time than did proving herself as an artist. The void Mary's death had left in her life could never be filled, and she wrote to strangers with the same compulsiveness with which she had long ago written her mother. She even wrote letters to friends whom she saw regularly. Writing tired her less than phone calls. After telling her caller she could talk for only a few minutes, she would herself keep talking a half hour or more while giving her listener no chance to interrupt and end the call.

"They say time heals grief," Marianne wrote fourteen years after Mary died. "It doesn't; it emphasizes it." Marianne bristled at the implication that her mother had ever stifled her art. "My writing suffers constantly for the lack of incentive she afforded me," she told an interviewer, "and for lack of her literary finesse . . . She did not interfere with what I initiated—did all kinds of incidental work for me because I was 'doing something important' as she would say."

Mary's absence did free Marianne to travel as she never had before. Morton Zabel had been trying to get her to Chicago for years when she at last agreed to go in October 1953. She read her poems at the University of Chicago and lectured on her *Fables* at the Arts Club. The response to both performances pleased and energized her.

In the late 1950s she made three trips to the West Coast. She took her first flight in 1956 to give a pair of lectures, "Idiosyncrasy and Technique," at UCLA and stopped again in Chicago on her return trip by train. A year later she read before a large audience at the San Francisco Museum of Art. "My reading was 'kind of a hit,'" she told Warner, "roars of laughter, applause; laughter more applause." She gave other readings in the area. And in the fall of 1959 she went on a three-week tour that included the University of Washington, the University of British Columbia, the University of Wisconsin, and Scripps College in California. She meanwhile maintained a busy schedule visiting campuses closer to New York. "Every college is Thermopylae," she told Hildegarde after speaking at Wellesley. "It's be natural, overcome self-destruction, or the hemlock."

By the mid-1950s she no longer had to plan for illness following each event, thanks to Dr. Nagla Laf Loofy, a Syrian woman and specialist in respiratory diseases at the Brooklyn Hospital. Marianne received inoculations once a month and took various antibiotics and vitamins to defeat her infections. One night in San Francisco, a month before she turned seventy, she felt herself getting hoarse. She took a niacin capsule, put on her "emergency underwear" for warmth, wrapped her neck in a towel rubbed with omega oil, and went to bed. The next morning she felt restored. She managed to stay healthy for the rest of the trip despite socializing past midnight and getting up at six every day.

Mary's death also meant that Marianne could take vacations again. After Marcia Chamberlain's stroke, Marianne sometimes traveled with Malvina Hoffman. Both members of the American Academy of Arts and Letters and both single and close in age, the two became friends in 1950 while Hoffman was caring for her dying sister. Hoffman escorted Marianne to Chicago in 1953, and they got along so well that Marianne joined Hoffman at her rented cottage in Kittery, Maine, during the summers of 1954 and 1955. Marianne helped Hoffman revise her memoirs and took up watercolors under her tutelage. "Malvina is a rare companion," Marianne said of her friend, "learned, kind and wise—so affectionate and patient with me." In 1957 they spent ten days together at Rye Beach, New Hampshire, and they returned to Maine, first Spruce Head and then Prouts Neck, in the summers of 1959 and 1963. "We grew up together," Marianne told a reporter at Hoffman's funeral.

Also in the late 1950s Marianne revived her college friendship with Frances Browne. The spacious house that Frances shared with her sister Norvelle in New Canaan, Connecticut, provided Marianne with a convenient and relaxing retreat. The three traveled to Bermuda together in 1957 and to Florida in 1966. In an effort to put an ocean between Marianne and the incessant demands upon her in New York, the Brownes escorted her to Greece and Italy in 1962 and to England and Ireland in 1964. Frances and Norvelle looked after her "as if I were a tot of 4," she said, helping her safeguard her money and reminding her to rest.

Marianne fulfilled her Macmillan contract with the 1951 publication of *Collected Poems*. Even though James Putnam had been fired in the meantime, she still smarted over Macmillan's treatment of her fables and switched to Viking as soon as she legally could. Like Macmillan, Viking wanted to issue as many books by the best-selling poet as possible. It published four new books by her within five years. But it had nothing to compete with Macmillan's *Collected Poems* until it brought out *A Marianne Moore Reader* in 1961, the day after the author's seventy-fourth birthday. Its bright orange dustcover displayed the Lynes photograph of Marianne in cape and tricorne, and its three hundred pages of verse and prose captured as much of her public persona as a print volume could.

The fifty-four poems and twenty-four fables in *A Marianne Moore Reader* essentially made up her performance repertoire. Only twenty-three of the poems came from *Collected Poems*, and only six of those had survived from *Observations*. Everything else had first appeared since 1951. Notable among the omissions is Moore's best-known poem, "Poetry." Notable among the revisions is the restoration of previously omitted stanzas from "The Steeple-Jack." And notable among the inclusions is "Marriage," which Marianne occasionally performed, despite its length, for laughs.

She did not revise "Marriage" but attached to it a disclaimer that distanced herself from the emotional entanglements with Scofield Thayer that gave rise to the poem: it does not "veil anything personal in the way of triumphs, entrapments, or dangerous colloquies. It is a little anthology of statements that took my fancy—phrasings that I liked." She said so in public readings and in her foreword to the *Reader*. The disclaimer is reduced to "Statements that took my fancy which I tried to arrange plausibly" in the notes to her *Complete Poems*.

Most of the twenty prose selections in the *Reader* postdate 1951 as well. They include her Ford Motor Company correspondence, reviews of her friends' books, and two essays of reminiscence: one about being sixteen and the other about Brooklyn. What best conveyed the poet's history and public persona, however, was her *Paris Review* interview with Donald Hall. Although Marianne had the opportunity both to prepare answers in advance of the interview and to emend her answers afterward, the interview captures the wit and spontaneity of her most successful performances. It includes remarks that Marianne made at readings and humanizes her as nothing else in writing yet had.

A Marianne Moore Reader did not generate the critical attention that *Collected Poems* had but sold well, first in hardback and then in a Viking Compass paperback edition. Marianne felt little enthusiasm for it. She disliked the title, chosen by Viking because of the success of *A Hemingway Reader*, *A Faulkner Reader*, and *A Henry Miller Reader*. She had suggested instead "The Arctic Ox and Other Pieces: A Viking Reader." Also, since Viking had asked her to cut sixty to eighty pages of poems from her original selections, it miffed her to see the complete contents of *Like a Bulwark* and *O to Be a Dragon* in the galleys. She had not been consulted.

By the time *A Marianne Moore Reader* appeared, Moore was already known as a Brooklyn Dodgers fan. She wrote a poem about them, "Hometown Piece for Messrs. Alton and Reese," at the request of *The Hudson Review* and, in tribute to the amateur band that serenaded the fans at Ebbets Field, set it to the tune of "Hush, Little Baby." After it was returned by *The Hudson Review*, *The New Yorker*, *Life*, and *Sports Illustrated*, Moore sent it at last to the *New York Herald-Tribune*. To her surprise and to Warner's enormous delight, the newspaper printed it on the front page to mark the opening day of the 1956 World Series, when the Dodgers again faced their Goliath, the New York Yankees.

When Robert Cantwell, a writer for *Sports Illustrated*, saw Marianne read "Hometown Piece" on *The Jack Paar Show* in 1959, he was as stunned as Alfred Kreymborg had been forty years earlier to hear the lady poet speak knowingly about baseball. He requested an interview and discovered at her apartment that she had taught at the Carlisle Indian School during its "golden years" and knew Jim Thorpe and other famous Native American athletes. Readers had become accustomed to seeing Marianne Moore's name in women's magazines such as *Ladies' Home Journal* and *Vogue*, but little did they expect to find a five-page spread about her in *Sports Illustrated*.

Although she rarely attended live sports events, her enthusiasm for sports added a fresh dimension to her public persona. She saw the Dodgers play at Ebbets Field only once and had never been to a racetrack when she wrote "Tom Fool at Jamaica." But she read the sports pages every day, watched sports on television, and savored the gusto in athletes' speech. It was not the racehorse Tom Fool that inspired her poem but the jockey's remarks about the horse as quoted in *The New York Times*.

The literary journalist and sports enthusiast George Plimpton took Marianne to Madison Square Garden to see the Floyd Patterson–George Chuvalo fight in 1965 and afterward to a party he arranged at Toots Shor's restaurant. She met Norman Mailer, whom she liked immensely, and was photographed there with Muhammad Ali, whom she already knew through Plimpton.

Marianne had already written a poem about the New York Yankees, "Baseball and Writing," when Plimpton introduced her to the Yankees president, Michael Burke. Burke invited her to Yankee Stadium for the opening game of the 1967 season, and she threw out the ball to open the 1968 season. The rookie player who caught the ball, Frank Fernandez, planted a spontaneous kiss on the eighty-year-old poet's cheek and ultimately hit the home run that won the game.

Marianne had never seen a professional fight when she wrote the liner notes for Cassius Clay's record album, *I Am the Greatest!* This was before he defeated Sonny Liston to become heavyweight champion and before he became Muhammad Ali. The queen of understatement and self-abnegation praised the poetry of Clay's braggadocio decades before rap musicians and Henry Louis Gates, Jr., taught white listeners about the oral black folk tradition of "playing the dozens."

She invoked Shakespeare and Sidney to describe Clay's rhymed taunts. Clay is "a master of hyperbole" and "a master of concision." When asked, "Have you ever been in love?" he said, "Not with anyone else." Noting also his "fondness for antithesis," she called him "a smiling pugilist."

Marianne liked athletes who persevered against their rivals and admired especially those who prevailed against personal and racial obstacles. She had been a Jackie Robinson fan from the time he joined the Dodgers in 1947 but became a Dodgers fan, she later claimed, while watching Roy Campanella, who joined the team the following year. She liked the swagger of his gestures and idiom as well as his skill as a catcher. An automobile accident paralyzed Campanella from the neck down in 1958, and his autobiography, *It's Good to Be Alive*, came out the next year. "This book is more persuasive—inherently— as emphasizing the injustice, indeed hatefulness, of race prejudice, than any book I know," she wrote the publisher. "What an incentive to accept grief and disability, not just stoically but with joy."

A few years later she developed similar enthusiasm for *Victory over Myself*, the autobiography of the boxer Floyd Patterson. She urged it upon Elizabeth Bishop as well as upon readers of *Seventeen* magazine.

Unlike most whites of the time, Moore did not identify African Americans by their race when she wrote about them. Those who first read her 1961 poem "Arthur Mitchell" in an anniversary program for the New York City Ballet would have seen the accompanying photograph of Mitchell, the first black principal dancer in a major ballet company. But the poem itself gave subsequent readers no indication of his race.

Moore's concern for the racially oppressed did not go unnoticed by African Americans. James Baldwin, whom she called "a fine youth," called on her in 1954 and stayed for supper. She and fellow Missourian Langston Hughes had developed a friendly admiration for each other by the early 1950s and saw each other at various literary events in the 1960s. She introduced Hughes at an Academy of American Poets event in April 1966, and a year later he spoke at a Poetry Society of America dinner, where she was honored with an early birthday cake and the society's Gold Medal for Distinguished Achievement. Four hundred people, including many dignitaries, attended the event at the

Plaza Hotel. After Robert Lowell called Miss Moore "the best woman poet in English," Hughes called her "the most famous Negro woman poet in America." Marianne loved the uneasy joke.

In February 1968 the singer, actor, and civil rights activist Harry Belafonte hosted *The Tonight Show* for a week in Johnny Carson's absence. Among those he invited to the show were Bobby Kennedy and Martin Luther King, Jr., as well as friends in the entertainment world, most of them black. After Marianne accepted his invitation to appear on the show, he and his agent visited her at home for two and a half hours. Marianne's niece Sallie was there and recorded the conversation in shorthand.

Belafonte told the octogenarian poet that he did not want the broadcast to be superficial, that he wanted to give the kids of this country a figure they could identify with, to give them a way of expressing themselves besides protesting in the streets. He asked about her political views and tried to get her to talk about hardships in her own life. When he asked her to describe the most terrible thing that had ever happened to her, she told him of a dream she had while Warner was stationed in the Pacific. He was trapped under a huge pile of logs, and she could do nothing to help him. The dream still haunted her.

Her answers for the most part did not give Belafonte the kind of political fodder he sought. She recognized and abhorred social injustice and was stirred by stories of it. But she had never thought herself a victim of it. Asked about the most significant event of her own lifetime, she paused for a long time before she answered: "Lincoln's assassination." She told Belafonte that the war in Vietnam was "an agony to me" but that she favored finishing the war, even if it meant military escalation, rather than abandoning the South Vietnamese. And when he asked what she thought of the late President Kennedy, she told him she "did not like that young man" and did not have time to give him "the thousand reasons." Belafonte had thought of putting her on the same show with the late president's brother; he agreed not to.

Marianne appeared on Wednesday night, February 7, 1968, along with the actor Sidney Poitier and the singers Dionne Warwick, Petula Clark, and George London. When Belafonte introduced her, he said that three years earlier he was feeling depressed about the civil rights movement and the Vietnam War when someone recommended Miss

Moore's poetry to him. Rather than answer his first question, whether she enjoyed life, Marianne asked to interpolate a commercial and then made a pitch for the Harlem School of the Arts to receive a $5,000 grant for which it had applied or else to receive the same amount from private donors. During her portion of the show, Sidney Poitier read lines from "In Distrust of Merits":

> . . . The world's an orphan's home. Shall
>   we never have peace without sorrow?
> without pleas of the dying for
>   help that won't come? O
> quiet form upon the dust, I cannot
> look and yet I must. If these great patient
>   dyings—all these agonies
>   and wound bearings and bloodshed—
>   can teach us how to live, these
>   dyings were not wasted.

She was told later that Belafonte was brought to tears by the lines and for a moment could not speak.

24

Senior Citizen
of the Year

1961–1972

During the 1960s a new kind of woman poet began to captivate the American public, one who would eclipse Marianne Moore for decades. Readers need not be connoisseurs of poetry to be roused by *Ariel*, the collection of poems that thirty-year-old Sylvia Plath wrote furiously in the five months between her separation from Ted Hughes and her suicide in 1963. That was the year Betty Friedan's *The Feminine Mystique* became a bestseller and the year that Adrienne Rich published her third book of poems, *Snapshots of a Daughter-in-Law*, in which she began to politicize the repressed anger of women forced by social norms into domesticity. Anne Sexton, another poet with young children, meanwhile wrote about her uterus, her battles with depression, and other formerly taboo subjects. The American publication of *Ariel* in 1966 made Plath an inadvertent martyr for the cause of women's liberation, and the 1971 appearance of her autobiographical novel, *The Bell Jar*, catapulted her to the realm of myth. All three poets touched a nerve in the openly rebellious 1960s.

By the time Moore died in 1972, the same year that *Ms.* magazine was launched, the new generation of white, middle-class feminists had come to regard the Plath/Sexton/Rich paradigm as a nearly universal female experience: an imaginative girl who idolizes her father gets duped into marriage, motherhood, and powerlessness by a patriarchal society. To deny the resulting anger was both cowardly and dishonest. Rich's influential feminist manifesto, "When We Dead Awaken: Writing as Re-Vision," delivered to the Modern Language Association just weeks before Moore's death, calls upon women to embrace their female anger and sexuality—unlike Marianne Moore and Elizabeth Bishop who, according to Rich, keep theirs "at a measured and chiseled distance."

In the new era of identity politics, Moore became the wrong kind of woman with whom to identify. Little did Rich and her adherents imagine in the 1970s and '80s that the fatherless Moore had been reared by lesbians and educated by feminists. Although Moore became an attractive subject for feminist academics during the 1990s, her rightful position as the major woman poet of her generation—between Dickinson in the nineteenth century and Bishop in the late twentieth—is still far from secure.

Readers familiar with Moore's early work have never doubted her prominence among America's major modernists. But her reputation reverted abruptly after her death to what it had been before World War II: she was a poet's poet, unread by all but the elite.

It is hardly surprising that the wizened, androgynous, admittedly prudish little lady in the tricorne would come to seem irrelevant, even embarrassing, within the youth culture of the late 1960s and '70s. After all, she lauded Lyndon B. Johnson's stance on Vietnam as strongly as she did his stance on civil rights. Unlike her friend Robert Lowell, who publicly refused an invitation to Johnson's inauguration as a way of protesting the war, Marianne called herself "one of Mr. Johnson's most fervent admirers—both of his objectives and of his words in defining them." Only her frail health prevented her from accepting her own invitation to the inauguration. The following summer she did attend a luncheon at the White House and spoke to Lady Bird Johnson, whom she called "a stately and grave, ardent hostess."

She included among her admirers other members of the establishment. The mayor of New York, John V. Lindsay, attended the Poetry Society dinner in her honor and read aloud "Granite and Steel," her poem about the Brooklyn Bridge. He called her "truly the poet laureate of New York City." The following year he and Marianne were paired together to read poetry in Bryant Park. Adrienne Rich and John Ashbery were among the other pairs invited to participate.

Marianne also included among her friends Governor Nelson A. Rockefeller, who had become an advocate for America's elderly population while serving in the Eisenhower administration. As governor he designated May the state's Senior Citizen Month. In May 1967 Marianne Moore's picture appeared on subway posters throughout New York along with Rockefeller's statement:

Marianne Moore, Pulitzer Prize Poet,
is one of New York State's
most creative, productive, and admired citizens.

Two years later he presented her with the Governor's Award to the Senior Citizen of the Year in New York State. Marianne thanked him for giving "an award to tenacity."

If Adrienne Rich failed to recognize the feminist politics in Moore's early work—"men have power / and sometimes one is made to feel it"—Moore succeeded even less in understanding identity politics and the new generation of feminists. While she tried to be open-minded about contemporary verse, the kind "that whines and wanders and merely ceases, instead of concluding" vexed her. She did support Planned Parenthood—but as a solution to the population explosion rather than as a means of reproductive freedom. Not only did she distance herself from the "female anger" in "Marriage" with her disclaimer about the "little anthology of statements that took my fancy," but she also refused the role of fairy godmother to Sylvia Plath.

Moore and Plath first met at Mount Holyoke, where Moore was one of three judges and Plath one of six contestants for the 1955 Glascock Poetry Prize. Plath, then a senior at Smith, studied Moore's poetry in preparation for their meeting and liked her immediately. "She must be in her late seventies and is as vital and humorous as someone's fairy godmother incognito." Moore, actually sixty-seven, commended Plath as more technically proficient and "more patient with life" than her closest competitor. She and John Ciardi chose Plath for the prize.

In June 1958 Plath and Ted Hughes added themselves to the throngs of young writers who climbed their way up the narrow stairs at 260 Cumberland. (The elevator was often broken.) By this time Plath was writing in syllabic verse. She thought of Moore and Edith Sitwell as "ageing giantesses and poetic godmothers" and aspired to join them one day in the first ranks of women poets. Marianne served her guests strawberries, sesame crackers, and milk while, according to Plath, talking "a blue streak."

Encouraged by Moore's friendliness, Plath sent her eight poems just afterward and asked for a letter of recommendation. Moore responded "warmly" to Plath but coldly to the poems, calling them "grisly" and "unrelenting." The letter devastated Plath. That Moore praised the "largess of a first copy" that Hughes sent in contrast to the carbon copies that Plath sent added salt to the wound.

Three years later, while pregnant with her second child, Plath nevertheless listed Moore as a reference on her Guggenheim application. Moore had known Henry Allen Moe, who ran the Guggenheim Foundation, since the 1940s. Every year she sent him a letter evaluating several applications, with a paragraph for each one. She wrote with candor, as to a trusted friend, and often compared applicants with others for whom she had written. She had endorsed Ted Hughes's successful application some years earlier.

"I thought and think her very gifted but feel cold toward this 'project,'" she wrote about Sylvia Plath. "You are not subsidized for having a baby especially in view of a world population explosion. You should look before you leap and examine your world-potentialities of responsibility as a contributory parent. Sylvia Plath has been specializing lately in gruesome detail, worms and germs and spiritual flatness. Her husband Ted Hughes has moral force and twice the talent that she has, won the YMHA verse-book contest with W. H. Auden, Stephen Spender, and me as judges and I'd rather give the money to him to continue his work than give it to Sylvia."

First because of her mother's illness and then because of translating La Fontaine, Moore had twice refused an appointment as poetry consultant to the Library of Congress, the position that later evolved into

U.S. poet laureate. But during the last two decades of her life she did use her fame and talents in the service of her country. Her patriotism was the cape-and-tricorne variety rather than the flag-waving kind. And her mode was that of the witty, urbane fabulist, like La Fontaine, rather than the Hebrew poet-prophet of her early work. Yet in both word and deed, she repeatedly urged her fellow citizens toward greater responsibility. "Talent, knowledge, humility, reverence, magnanimity involve the inconvenience of responsibility," she wrote, "or they die."

In December 1960 Marianne watched a CBS News documentary called *Rescue, with Yul Brynner* and, while hospitalized for a month that winter, wrote a poem called "Rescue with Yul Brynner." The program showed the movie star visiting refugee camps around the globe in his capacity as special consultant to the United Nations High Commission for Refugees. What chiefly impressed Marianne was how Brynner used his fame for humanitarian ends. Her poem presents him as a consummate citizen and artist. Multilingual and multitalented, Brynner visits the camps not "to dazzle" (in contrast to his role as the king of Siam) but to bring hope to the children growing up in them. The poet calls herself a "pygmy citizen" by comparison.

The power of the arts to counter enmity is a frequent theme in Moore's late poems. Russian folk dancers in "Combat Cultural" create harmony between nations engaged in a Cold War. "Carnegie Hall: Rescued" praises Isaac Stern's campaign to save the historic arts venue from encroaching real estate developers. "Dream" and "In the Public Garden" also extol public support of the arts. In "Granite and Steel" a German engineer envisions the "catenary curve" and then actualizes it in the Brooklyn Bridge: "implacable enemy of the mind's deformity."

A poem she wrote about another New York landmark, "The Camperdown Elm," helped save an ailing tree in Brooklyn's Prospect Park. So successful was the poem in raising money for the Greensward Foundation that Marianne was named its honorary president. In lieu of flowers at her funeral, Marianne requested that donations be made to the Greensward Foundation, which created the Marianne Moore Remembrance Fund to care for trees in Prospect and Central parks.

•

Between her seventieth and eightieth birthdays, Moore published thirty-three new poems and ten books, eleven if one counts the much emended paperback edition of her *Fables*. She also wrote sixty-five pages of an unfinished memoir, called "Coming About." The first of her books was *Idiosyncrasy & Technique*, from the pair of lectures that she delivered at UCLA; the University of California Press issued 1,000 copies in 1958. In the same year the Pierpont Morgan Library published *Letters from and to the Ford Motor Company*. *O to Be a Dragon* came out from Viking in 1959 and *A Marianne Moore Reader* in 1961.

Moore published her first and only play in 1962. She had based *The Absentee: A Comedy in Four Acts* upon Maria Edgeworth's novel after seeing T. S. Eliot's plays performed on Broadway. She told Martin Browne, Eliot's producer, that she wanted the stage actress Gertrude Flynn, a friend of Louise Crane's, to play the leading role. Browne read the typescript in 1954 but advised Moore that there were too many scene changes to make it practical to produce. Viking rejected it two years later. "Now that you are formally recognized as an immortal," Pascal Covici told her, "I don't think this ancient script deserves your time and talent. You have more important things to do. There's your poetry, your literary essays and, what I believe supremely important, your memoirs." When House of Books, a dealer in rare books, asked her for something to publish in its Crown Octavo series, she provided *The Absentee*.

In 1963 Macmillan brought out Moore's translation of three Charles Perrault fairy tales: *Puss in Boots, The Sleeping Beauty, and Cinderella*. Ezra Pound had encouraged her to translate Perrault's fairy tales when she first mentioned the La Fontaine translation. And so when Macmillan's new children's book editor, Michael di Capua, invited her to translate a few Perrault fairy tales, she readily accepted. The same year she allowed the Museum of Modern Art to publish her *Eight Poems*, illustrated and hand-colored by Robert Andrew Parker, in a limited edition of 195 copies.

Faber and Faber did not publish either *O to Be a Dragon* (because it was too short) or *A Marianne Moore Reader* (because that kind of "omnibus" did not sell in Britain). But as soon as Moore had enough new poems to make forty-eight pages of text, Eliot published *The Arctic*

Ox, which combined the poems from those two books that had not yet appeared in Faber volumes with four new poems that had not yet been collected in book form.

Moore's last book of new work, *Tell Me, Tell Me: Granite, Steel, and Other Topics,* appeared just days before she turned seventy-nine. With eighteen poems and four prose pieces, it was considerably longer than either *Like a Bulwark* or *O to Be a Dragon* and, according to a handful of reviewers, more successful. Writing in *The New York Times Book Review,* James Dickey called it "the finest" of all her books. And although John Ashbery said it contained "her least good published poem," "Carnegie Hall: Rescued," he pronounced *Tell Me, Tell Me* "her longest and best collection since the 1935 *Selected Poems.*"

No subsequent critic has written as persuasively as Ashbery did in this review about the achievement of Moore's late work, which he attributes to the discipline of translating La Fontaine. "Forced to avoid digressions and to keep syntax and verbal texture uncluttered, Miss Moore created a style whose tense, electric clarity is unlike anything in poetry except perhaps La Fontaine." She thus replaces the "dazzling obscurity" of her early work with a "new, tough simplicity." As for the La Fontaine translations themselves, they "ought to be required reading for every beginning poet."

Tell Me, Tell Me includes Moore's most ambitious self-portrait since "The Paper Nautilus." "Blue Bug" is a poem about seeing and being seen, about the "reversible" and "revolving" eye of an observer. It was inspired, the headnote says, by a photograph in *Sports Illustrated,* the magazine where the poet's own photograph had appeared some months earlier. Eight polo ponies are looking over a fence. The caption names none of them, but Moore assigns Blue Bug, a name briefly mentioned in the accompanying article, to the horse on the far left, the one whose head appears in profile. Only as astute an observer as Marianne Moore would recognize in this horse's eye a half-reluctant celebrity like herself. Its face, "triangle-cornered" like her own in a tricorne, is "a mere container for the eye." The poem begins:

> In this camera shot,
> from that fine print in which you hide
> (eight-pony portrait from the side),

you seem to recognize
a recognizing eye,
    limber Bug.

Since the poet knows from experience that there is "Nothing more punitive than the pest / who says, 'I'm trespassing,' and / does it just the same," she refuses to ask the origin of the horse's name. Blue Bug is an eye, she guesses, blue like her own. The rest of the poem demonstrates how the observing eye—or mind—may be trained to reverse itself as agilely as a ballet dancer, polo pony, or Chinese acrobat may.

On the morning of her eightieth birthday, November 15, 1967, Marianne appeared on *Today* to promote *The Complete Poems of Marianne Moore*, issued the same day. It was the only public appearance her doctor would allow. Major newspapers, including *The Wall Street Journal*, observed the occasion. Her apartment overflowed with flowers and gifts of food. She received twenty-four telegrams, including one from President Johnson and the First Lady. In the evening she enjoyed a quiet dinner with Monroe Wheeler, Glenway Wescott, Warner, and Constance, Wheeler having a unique ability among Marianne's friends to put Constance at ease.

The one thing that nearly all reviewers noted about *The Complete Poems* was its incompleteness. Although the book included 120 poems and nine fables, representing all phases of Moore's career, a separate page just before the table of contents announced:

Omissions are not accidents. M.M.

The poet, in short, still asserted authority over her ever-shifting oeuvre and let her silences speak for themselves. The most flagrant omission was the reduction of "Poetry" from twenty-nine lines to three; she included the longer version among her endnotes. As she had with *Collected Poems*, she arranged the contents according to the books where the poems had first appeared, beginning with *Selected Poems*. She added "To a Prize Bird" to her *Selected Poems* section even though the poem had not appeared in book form since *Observations*, and she eliminated the longer, more interesting "Melancthon," which had appeared in both *Selected Poems* (with the title "Black Earth") and *Collected Poems*. She made countless major and minor revisions but often with no apparent rationale other than the assertion of her prerogative to do so.

In his review of *Tell Me, Tell Me,* John Ashbery had claimed that Miss Moore was possibly, with the exception of Pound and Auden, "the greatest living poet in English." "After rereading her in this magnificent volume," he wrote of *Complete Poems,* "I am tempted simply to call her our greatest modern poet." Other reviewers praised Moore's accomplishments, but the omissions and revisions baffled them. The major awards that year went to younger poets: the Pulitzer to Anne Sexton, the National Book Award to Robert Bly. *Complete Poems* was not even a finalist for the National Book Award as *Like a Bulwark* and *Tell Me, Tell Me* had been.

Thirteen years later, in 1981, Macmillan and Viking issued a revised, "definitive" edition of *Complete Poems*. It includes minor corrections Moore made to the 1967 edition before her death and a few late poems. Reviewing it for *The New York Times Book Review,* the art critic Hilton Kramer took Moore to task for her "farcical" exchange with the Ford Motor Company and for allowing the media to turn her into "the very archetype of the quaint literary spinster." "What remains imperative for us to understand just now," he continued, "is that this fabricated image had nothing whatever to do with the poet's real achievement." Virtually all of Moore's critics since then have agreed with this assessment. Not only do they mostly ignore her late work but they also shun the photographs that once made her famous.

The omissions and inexplicable revisions in Moore's *Complete Poems,* her advocates claim, account for her relative obscurity among the major modernists. The book omits nearly half the poems she published before 1951 and includes virtually all those she published afterward. Until 2002 the only way to recover Moore's early work was to search through archives and rare book rooms. In that year the University of California Press published *Becoming Marianne Moore: The Early Poems, 1907–1924,* in which Robin Schulze makes available not only a facsimile reproduction of *Observations* but also facsimile reproductions of Moore's magazine publications from the *Tipyn o'Bob* through *The Dial.*

The much anticipated *Poems of Marianne Moore*, published by Viking in 2003 and edited by Moore's friend and protégée Grace Schulman, was expected to restore the "omissions" of *Complete Poems* for the general reader. Unfortunately, it errs in the opposite direction. It includes 230 poems, nearly double the number in *Complete Poems*. Of the 110 added poems only a third were published during Moore's lifetime. The remaining two-thirds are unfinished and unpublished verses gathered from Moore's archive by its first curator, Patricia C. Willis. Since Schulman arranged *Poems of Marianne Moore* in loose chronological order and made no distinction between published poems and unpublished fragments except in the endnotes, the reader encounters nearly a hundred pages of juvenilia before reaching the poems that Moore was willing to collect in book form.

Moore continued to receive awards and honorary degrees in the last decade of her life. In 1965 the Academy of American Poets awarded her a $5,000 fellowship. The Ingram Merrill Foundation, established by James Merrill, awarded her another $5,000 the following year. In August 1967 she became the first woman to receive the Edward MacDowell Medal, and the same month the French ambassador named her Chevalier in the Ordre des Arts et des Lettres. Members of the National Book Committee and all former judges of the National Book Awards chose her for the 1968 National Medal for Literature, which included a gift of $5,000. "This medal and gift to me have done a great deal to make a dent in my diffidence," she said in her acceptance speech. "My writing is the result of books I have read and of persons I have known and I don't see why gratitude should be given a medal."

After Marianne's nephew, John, shocked a taxi driver by saying that his elderly aunt lived alone at 260 Cumberland Street, Warner and his family insisted that Marianne move to a safer neighborhood. She had already had a cylinder lock installed on her door and had for some years been using a car service provided by Louise Crane. Though she felt reluctant to leave her home of thirty-six years, she admitted that the neighborhood had become "lawless," and she let Louise find her an apartment in the Village. Her nieces Sallie and Bee (Sarah and

Marianne) helped her pack and organized her papers into files and file cabinets. She moved in November 1965 to the seventh floor of 35 West Ninth Street, a redbrick apartment building with a doorman. Reporters from *The New York Times* and *The New Yorker* visited her in January and published stories about her move.

Marianne had suffered her first stroke in late 1958. She lost her ability to speak clearly but mostly recovered it within a few months. She experienced a number of "backsets," as she called them, over the next decade and came to depend increasingly on friends and family members. Sallie took an apartment in the East Village and prepared breakfast for her each morning before Gladys arrived. On Tuesdays she also picked up her father in Greenwich, Connecticut, and drove him into the city to visit his sister.

Hildegarde called long-distance from Rochester several times a day. During Marianne's second winter at West Ninth Street, Hildegarde became alarmed one evening by Marianne's condition and called Louise Crane to check on her. Louise saved Marianne's life, according to Warner, by getting Anny Baumann, Louise's friend and personal physician, to take charge of Marianne. Louise also hired a day nurse and a night nurse to care for Marianne twenty-four hours a day.

Marianne nevertheless continued to make as many public appearances as Dr. Baumann would allow. She appeared on *The Tonight Show* in February 1968, threw out the ball at Yankee Stadium in April, and in May flew to Austin to give a reading and to discuss selling her papers to the University of Texas.

Marianne never outgrew her poor appetite or disability with numbers. Since she did not like to spend money on food, Hildegarde often inquired what Marianne was eating and, if she thought it not enough, would order cartons of food from the Woman's Exchange, a charity organization that paid indigent women to prepare food. And while Marianne had several hundred thousand dollars from prizes, gifts, and investments by the time she moved to West Ninth Street, she feared that she could not afford the increase in monthly rent from $69 to $350. She sometimes alarmed her impecunious friends by letting them believe she lived hand to mouth on the checks she received from magazines, and she sometimes accepted checks of $10 to $15 from such friends. Marianne was "a child about money," according to Ethel Taylor, her nurse. She sometimes snuck off to the bank by herself and then stood on the street corner to count the cash she withdrew.

Louise Crane got her own attorney, Lawrence E. Brinn, to manage Marianne's investments. Marianne told Brinn that she had sufficient money for food and rent but that she wanted "pocket money." Marianne gave Louise power of attorney and made Brinn and Louise executors of her estate (worth $450,000 at her death). To reimburse Warner for his many years of support, Marianne had some years earlier opened a joint account in Brooklyn where she deposited $150 monthly and sometimes larger sums she received from magazines. This account, kept secret from Constance, had more than $6,000 in it when he closed it in 1969. At Marianne's request, Louise Crane continued to send Warner the monthly checks.

None of Marianne's friends and acquaintances could worry about her financial situation after word got out that she had sold her archive for $100,000. Competition for her books and papers had become fierce. She originally promised them to Bryn Mawr, but its space was limited. Andreas Brown of the Gotham Book Mart convinced her to expect at least $100,000 from the sale and got the University of Texas to offer her that amount. But she did not like the thought of her things being in Texas with James Michener's. Robert Wilson of the Phoenix Bookstore had meanwhile introduced her to Clive Driver, director of the Rosenbach Museum & Library in Philadelphia. Long an admirer of the poet and her work, Driver quickly won his way into her affections. He brought a lamb from his family farm for her to hold while they negotiated terms of the sale.

While in the hospital during the summer of 1968, Marianne read a biography of A. S. W. Rosenbach, the famous rare book dealer who left his nineteenth-century row house and possessions to form the Rosenbach Museum & Library. Rosenbach's New York shop had thrilled her when she visited it in 1951. She admired "the electrically-lighted, suspended magnifying glass," various examples of the art of bookbinding, and a first folio of *Othello*—"The Moores Tragedy," she noted with pleasure.

The Rosenbach contained a room that exactly matched the dimensions of Marianne's West Ninth Street living room, including the placement of its two windows and fireplace. In December 1968 she sold her books and papers to the Rosenbach and bequeathed her furniture and personal possessions for a Marianne Moore Room. Driver, whom she named her literary executor, thereafter spent a couple of days a week at her apartment, organizing her papers and answering her mail.

Due to repeated small strokes during the spring of 1969, Marianne lost much physical strength. But she continued to write and to make appearances. In February she earned $5,000 for appearing in Braniff Airways' historic "When you got it, flaunt it" advertising campaign that paired unlikely celebrities such as Andy Warhol and Sonny Liston in adjacent airline seats. Warhol explains the significance of soup cans to Liston, and the pulp fiction author Mickey Spillane explains the power of words to Marianne. "Tough Mickey Spillane and gentle Marianne Moore always fly Braniff," said the voice over.

Marianne accepted the Senior Citizen of the Year Award, attended Elizabeth Bishop's reading at the Guggenheim Museum, and traveled to Bryn Mawr for her sixtieth class reunion in May. In June she saw Ezra Pound briefly at the New York Public Library and traveled to Harvard to accept her sixteenth honorary degree. The degree meant a great deal to her, and Dr. Baumann allowed her to go on the condition that she not speak publicly, that she remain in her wheelchair, and that Ethel Taylor accompany her. It was her last public appearance.

A massive stroke in July almost killed her. She nevertheless retained her spirit and sense of humor. Louise Crane hosted a musicale for Marianne's eighty-second birthday. The baritone Arthur Thompson, Ethel Taylor's nephew, provided the entertainment. Thinking of her elderly patient, Dr. Baumann announced at the end of the evening that it had been a lovely party but it was time for everyone to go home. Marianne called out from her wheelchair: "Goodbye, Anny Baumann!" The room burst into laughter. During the last two years of her life, Marianne rarely left the hospital bed in her bedroom and, though she received occasional visitors, her speech was so slurred that few could understand her. Her nurses served as translators.

Warner was both a comfort and a trial to his sister in her final years. She could not bear the thought that he might die before she did—they both prayed that she would go first—and yet his presence often distressed her. "You know, your father tries to arrange things to please her," Ethel Taylor told Sallie, "and she tries to do things to please him, and they don't tell each other the truth. I just listen to them and say to myself, 'Two old babies living in a fairy tale.' It just makes an awful mess, and frankly, it puts her into a tizzy when he's here."

While Warner tried to be gracious to Louise Crane and Clive Driver and thanked them profusely for the good they did, he had difficulty accepting that two outsiders had as great a claim to his sister as he did. While Marianne was in the hospital, he had the locks to her apartment changed to keep Driver out. The next time she went to the hospital, Driver had the locks changed to keep Warner out.

Warner and Constance traveled to Florida for a couple of months each winter. But as Marianne approached her end, Warner could not bring himself to tell her he was leaving. In January 1971 he kept saying that he was not going, that he could not afford to go, right up to the day before he left. His profuse apologies on the phone and in letters afterward only upset her the more. The next January he could not bear to tell her at all and left without saying goodbye. He never saw her alive again.

On February 5, 1972, Marianne died in her sleep at 2:55 in the afternoon. She was eighty-four. Her dear Gladys was with her, and the attendant nurse, Jeannette Edwards, phoned Ethel Taylor and Anny Baumann. Louise Crane arrived at the apartment with Dr. Baumann and made all the necessary arrangements before calling Warner at about six in the evening.

The next day, a Sunday, President Nixon issued a statement mourning the death of "one of our most distinguished poets," and the headline "Marianne Moore Dies" ran above the fold on page one of *The New York Times*. Her obituary and three of her poems filled a full page inside.

The First Presbyterian Church at Fifth Avenue and Eleventh Street opened its doors for a few hours Monday evening so that mourners in Manhattan could pay their respects before Marianne's closed casket. Warner delivered a prayer he had written for the occasion. And on Tuesday Dr. George Knight, Marianne's beloved minister at the Lafayette Avenue Presbyterian Church in Brooklyn, conducted two

services. Several dozen close friends and family members attended the
first one at noon. Warner invited Gladys and the two nurses to sit with
the family. Among others in attendance were Monroe Wheeler, Hildegarde Watson (Sibley was ill), Louise Crane, Clive Driver, Lincoln
Kirstein, and Elizabeth Bishop. A few cousins from the Moore side
came as well.

At one o'clock, Dr. Knight conducted a public memorial service.
Despite the bitter cold, nearly three hundred friends and neighbors attended. Others watched highlights on the *CBS Evening News.* Marianne had instructed Dr. Knight about each detail of the service down
to the color of the program: morning-glory blue. Two violins, a cello, a
harp, and eight voices provided music from the church balcony. The
forty-five-minute service concluded with the "Hallelujah Chorus"
from Handel's *Messiah* as the casket was carried down the aisle into
the stark, snowy afternoon.

In Venice, Ezra Pound broke his self-imposed silence to read
"What Are Years" at a memorial service he arranged. The last of the
major Modernists, he died the next November.

Sallie retrieved Marianne's ashes from Lawrence Brinn's safe in
the spring. Warner's family then held a small service of its own at the
Marsh Creek Church near Gettysburg and buried Marianne's remains
with her mother's. Warner declined quickly after his sister's death. He
died in February 1974.

Like the first two stanzas of "Blue Bug," Marianne Moore's late poems show her ambivalence about her own fame. She wanted anonymity
at the same time she craved the adoration of her public. In "O to Be a
Dragon," she writes that, like a dragon, she wants to be "of silkworm /
size or immense; at times invisible." At the height of her fame in 1957, she
added to her oeuvre a poem she had first published in her senior year at
Bryn Mawr, a poem that now seems prophetic of a career in which she
would enjoy silkworm-size obscurity, dragon-size visibility, and—
abruptly after the appearance of her full-page obituary—near invisibility.

A JELLY-FISH

Visible, invisible,
    a fluctuating charm

an amber-tinctured amethyst
    inhabits it, your arm
approaches and it opens
      and it closes; you had meant
to catch it and it quivers;
    you abandon your intent.

Notes

DH65	Interview with Donald Hall, 1965. *Their Ancient Glittering Eyes.* 297–315.
EB	Elizabeth Bishop, 1911–1979.
EP	Ezra Pound, 1885–1972.
GS	George Saintsbury, 1845–1933.
GW	Glenway Wescott, 1901–1987.
HD	Hilda Doolittle, 1886–1961.
HW	Hildegarde Lasell Watson, 1888–1976.
JMM	John Milton Moore, 1858–1925.
JRW	John Riddle Warner, 1827–1894.
JSW	James Sibley Watson, 1894–1982.
JWM	John Warner Moore, 1886–1974.
KJ	Kathrine Jones, 1883–1952.
MC	Marcia King Chamberlain, 1880–1955.
MCM	Marianne Craig Moore (MM's niece), b. 1923.
MCS	Mary Craig Shoemaker, 1862–1955.
MFC	Moore Family Collection, West Hartford, CT.
MH	Marcet Haldeman, 1887–1941.
MM	Marianne Moore, 1887–1972.
MMN	*Marianne Moore Newsletter*, 1977–1983.
MN	Mary Jackson Norcross, 1875–1938.
MW	Monroe Wheeler, 1899–1988.
MWM	Mary Warner Moore, 1862–1947.
NYPL	Berg Collection of English and American Literature, New York Public Library, New York.
OA	Elizabeth Bishop. *One Art: Letters*, ed. Robert Giroux. New York: Farrar, Straus and Giroux, 1994.
Prose	*The Complete Prose of Marianne Moore*, ed. Patricia C. Willis. New York: Viking, 1986.
RML	Marianne Moore Papers, Rosenbach Museum & Library, Philadelphia.
SEM	Sarah Eustis Moore, 1921–2007.
SL	*The Selected Letters of Marianne Moore*, ed. Bonnie Costello with Celeste Goodridge and Cristanne Miller. New York: Knopf, 1997.
ST	Scofield Thayer, 1889–1982.
TSE	T. S. Eliot, 1888–1965.
TWWLN	"The Way We Live Now." Unpublished novel, 1939. RML.
VCL	Vassar College Libraries, Poughkeepsie, NY.
WCW	William Carlos Williams, 1883–1963.
WHA	W. H. Auden, 1907–1973.
WS	Wallace Stevens, 1879–1955.
YCAL	Yale Collection of American Literature, Beinecke Rare Book & Manuscript Library, New Haven.
YW	Yvor Winters, 1900–1968.

Unless otherwise noted, quotations from poems in chapters 1–16 are from *BMM*, quotations from poems in chapters 17–19 are from *AQS*, and quotations from poems in the preface and chapters 20–24 are from *CP*. Spelling and punctuation have been modernized, and errors made in haste silently corrected.

PREFACE
xi   "No poet has been so chaste": *CCE*, 85.
xi   Van Doren, Untermeyer, et al.: *CRMM*, 32–50.
xii   "With Miss Moore": *CRMM*, 72.
xii   "insufferable high brows": *CRMM*, 34.
xii   "too good": *CRMM*, 46.
xiii "Moore's poems are famously": Brad Leithauser, "Digesting Hard Iron," *New York Times Book Review* (January 4, 2004), nytimes.com.
xiii "Feeling at its deepest": *Prose*, 396.
xiv   "the least possessive": Kathleen Cannell, "Colloquies with a Sibyl," ts., 1957, RML.
xiv   "a case of arrested": DH65, 298.
xiv   "Politically I cannot": MM to Stanley Kunitz, carbon, August 25, 1939, RML.
xv   "We'd have arguments": WCW, *The Autobiography of William Carlos Williams* (New York: New Directions, 1951), 136.
xvi   "Sometimes I think": MWM to JWM, September 27, 1918, RML.
xvi   "external facts": Charles Molesworth, *Marianne Moore: A Literary Life* (New York: Atheneum, 1990), xxii.
xvii "little narrow white face": MWM to JWM, October 27, 1919, RML.
xviii "incapable of a shut door": Henry James quoted in *Prose*, 322.

FAMILY TREE
xix   Genealogical information supplied by Randy Campbell, Willard Greene, MCM, and Jennifer Urick; also the following sources: W. G. Moore, "The Moores of Portsmouth, Ohio," MFC; MCS, *Five Typical Scotch Irish Families of the Cumberland Valley* (Albany, NY: 1922); Henry Warner, "The Autobiography of Henry Warner," RML; Urick Family Web Site, www.uricks.com; and the Moore family correspondence, RML.

1. SOJOURN IN THE WHALE
3   "Sojourn in the Whale": MM to JWM, December 19, 1915, *SL* 107.
4   *honesty . . . spirit*: "What 291 Means to Me" in *Camera Work* (July 1914).
5   "Mr. Stieglitz": MM to JWM, December 12, 1915, *SL*, 103.
6   "an amazing output": quoted in MM to JWM, October 3, 1915, *SL*, 100.

6   "literary monstrosities": MM to JWM, December 19, 1915, *SL*, 110.

6   "I was never": MM to JWM, December 12, 1915, *SL*, 104.

6   "an astonishing person": Alfred Kreymborg, *Troubadour: An Autobiography* (New York: Boni and Liveright, 1925), 238–39.

6   "couldn't live . . . poetry": quoted in MM to JWM, December 12, 1915, *SL*, 104.

7   *Others*: Suzanne W. Churchill, *The Little Magazine* Others *and the Renovation of Modern American Poetry* (Aldershot, UK: Ashgate, 2006).

7   "blouse . . . wit": MM to JWM, December 12, 1915, *SL*, 105.

7   "bohemian fierceness": MM to MWM, December 2, 1915, RML.

7   "impossible . . . ever seen": MM to JWM, December 12, 1915, *SL*, 106–107.

8   "silver spoons . . . Shelley": MM to JWM, December 12, 1915, *SL*, 106.

8   "mark of the elect": MM to JWM, December 26, 1915, RML.

9   "had diverged": Ibid.

9   "You know": Ibid.

9   "revolutionary . . . form": J. B. Kerfoot, "The Latest Books," *Life* (September 23, 1915), 568.

9   "light, airy": MM to JWM, December 26, 1915, RML.

10   "a positive dogmatist": MM to JWM, December 19, 1915, *SL*, 108.

10   "light flashed": *CRMM*, 20.

11   "the unbridled leap": *CRMM*, 73.

2. A GENIUS FOR DISUNION

12   "pathological . . . mentioned": WCW to Ronald Lane Latimer, December 20, 1934, Paul Mariani, *William Carlos Williams: A New World Naked* (New York: Norton, 1981), 394.

12   "Spenser's Ireland": *CP*, 112–13.

13   Mary Riddle Warner: CEM's notes in MCS, *Five Typical Scotch-Irish Families*, MFC.

13   Henry Warner: "The Autobiography of Henry Warner—Commenced Nov. 30th 1870, Re-written 1875–76," transcribed by MM in 1920, RML.

14   "nothing will": MM to Sue Craig Stauffer, [Fall] 1954, RML.

14   "strenuous . . . God": George Norcross, Speech to the Scotch-Irish Congress in Harrisburg, June 4–6, 1896, in "Scrapbook compiled for 39th anniversary of George Norcross DD in the Second Presbyterian Church Carlisle, PA Jan 5, 1908," CCHS.

14   "I am Irish": MM to EP, January 9, 1919, *SL*, 122.

14   MM's Irish identity: Laura O'Connor, *Haunted English: The Celtic Fringe, the British Empire, and De-Anglicization* (Baltimore: Johns Hopkins University Press, 2006), 154–57.

15   "whistling around": Hugh Boyd Craig to Jennie Craig Warner, July 13, 1863, RML.

16   "Our ancestry": MWM to JWM, December 6, 1936, RML.

17 "bring out": Henry Warner to JRW, December 21, 1864, RML.

17 "My own sad": MWM to JWM, October 31, 1919, RML.

18 Mary Institute: Edmund H. Sears, "The Mary Institute 1859–1934" (St. Louis, 1934).

18 meeting of MWM and JMM: MWM to unspecified recipient, August 19, 1941, RML.

19 "deaf and mute": MWM to Moorhead B. Holland, draft, November 6, 1937, RML.

19 William Moore: William G. Moore, "The Moores of Portsmouth, Ohio" (1951), MFC and www.uricks.com.

20 "take a struggling": Mrs. Harold O. [Margaret Peebles] Hunt to MM, October 27, 1954, RML.

20 JMM at Stevens Institute: Stevens Alumni Association records and the yearbook *Eccentric*, May 1879, Stevens Institute, 77–78, 79.

21 "I am utterly . . . conceive of": MWM to JRW, October 3, 1885, MFC.

21 "a mechanical *genius*": MWM to JRW, December 31, 1885, MFC.

22 "untiring zeal," MWM to JRW, March 5, 1886, MFC.

22 "the question . . . confused": MWM to JRW, January 24, 1887, MFC.

22 "He is kind": MWM to JRW, March 7, 1887, MFC.

23 "how silent": MWM to JRW, June 29, 1887, MFC.

23 "vague, random thoughts": MWM to JRW, June 29, 1887, MFC.

23 "I certainly": MWM to JRW, August 27, 1887, MFC.

24 "real crazy": JMM to MWM, November 19, 1887, MFC.

24 "delusional monomania": Lunacy case #1630, Scioto County Probate Court, Portsmouth, OH.

25 "He does not deplore": A. B. Richardson to JRW, October 7, 1889, MFC.

25 November 1896: Lunacy case #1630, Scioto County Probate Court.

25 "remembrance . . . matters": Lunacy case #9523, Scioto County Probate Court.

25 JWM meeting Enos Moore: MCM and SEM in conversation with the author, August 23, 1999.

25 MM told nieces: MCM and SEM in conversation with the author, August 25, 1999.

26 Some critics: For example, Jeanne Heuving, *Gender in the Art of Marianne Moore: Omissions Are Not Accidents* (Detroit: Wayne State University Press, 1992), 117–20.

3. DESIGNING HEAVEN

27 designing heaven: James Dickey, "What the Angels Missed," review of *Tell Me, Tell Me: Granite, Steel, and Other Topics* by Marianne Moore, *New York Times Book Review* (December 25, 1966), 1; www.nytimes.com.

27 "unconquerable country": *CP*, 144.

28 "picturesque . . . lizards": CA, 7.

28 Kirkwood: June Wilkinson Dahl, *A History of Kirkwood Missouri 1851–65* (Kirkwood: Kirkwood Historical Society, 1965); and John Lindenbusch, "Four Walking Tours of Historic Kirkwood Missouri," Kirkwood Historical Society, 1981, accessed online: www.kirkwooddesperes.com/walking-tours.asp.

28 "high location": Dahl, 67.

29 "Mrs. Moore . . . with joy": "Twentieth Anniversary, An Interesting Event in the Presbyterian Church," unidentified newspaper clipping, RML.

29 "the most gentle . . . joy": MWM to AWA, August 25, 1893, RML.

29 "The solemnest baby": MWM to JWM, May 5, 1921, RML.

30 "One day Warner": MWM to AWA, November 24, 1893, RML.

30 "Every time I go": MM to JWM, January 25, 1945, RML.

31 "Marianne is very": JRW to Henry Warner Armstrong, July 8, 1889, RML.

31 "funny mixture . . . *water*": MWM to AWA, October 18, 1892, RML.

31 flash of red: MCM and SEM in conversation with the author, August 25, 1999.

31 "demanded perfect": MWM to JWM, April 8, 1924, RML.

31 "filled my life": MWM to JWM, September 25, 1921, RML.

32 "be a little child": MWM to MM, January 14, 1907, RML.

32 "Remember how": MWM to JWM, March 17, 1909, RML.

32 "ennobling purpose": MWM to JWM, January 10, 1924, RML.

32 "abhorrent . . . elephant": CA, 3–4.

33 *The Century*: Talcott Williams, "The Kindergarten Movement," *The Century Magazine* (January 1893), 369–78.

33 "All / external": *CP*, 32–33.

33 "parabolic"; "pyramids"; "close-laid": *CP*, 143, 103, 122.

34 Kandinsky and kindergarten: Norman Brosterman, *Inventing Kindergarten* (New York: Harry N. Abrams, 1997).

34 "The children": MWM to JWM, February 23, 1916, RML.

36 "the pleasure of": CA, 14

36 "You would laugh . . . body": MWM to MCS, March 12, 1895, RML.

36 "possessed . . . poetess": Ibid.

37 "ever strove": JRW, *Sermons*, 32–33.

37 "look away": Ibid., 59.

37 "as verity itself": CA, 15.

37 "that most shaped": *Prose*, 670–71.

4. A PECULIAR PEOPLE

39 "love and intensity . . . morning": MWM to JWM, October 26, 1919, RML.

39 "the clannish feeling": MWM to JWM, February 27, 1910, RML; see 1 Peter 2:9.

40 "Carlisle, the site": Metzger College Circular of Information, 1895, Dickinson College Archives, Carlisle, PA.

40 "Mother, don't you . . . woman": quoted in MWM to Mrs. Dings, July 17, 1921, RML.

41   "You would have . . . praises": MWM to MCS, December 28, 1896, RML.
41   "Strike the tent": DH65, 297.
42   "English aspect": MWM to B, September 21, 1921, YCAL.
42   "storybook people . . . success": Laura Benét, *When William Rose, Stephen Vincent, and I Were Young* (New York: Dodd, Mead, 1976), 61.
42   "a quiet child": Ibid., 13.
42   community leaders: Jeff Wood, e-mail to the author, December 4, 2008.
42   temperance movement . . . "white man": G. Norcross, Scrapbook, CCHS.
43   "Blake, Rembrandt": *Prose*, 571–72.
43   "Derogation"; "tolerance": CA, 30, 29.
44   "hand reared": DH65, 300.
44   "experienced society . . . invitations": *Prose*, 502.
45   "made us think": DH65, 300.
45   "not because I": *Prose*, 662.
45   "felt considerable antipathy": CA, 25.
45   "Will you laugh": MWM to MCS, October 17, 1900, RML.
45   "*indulge* me": MWM to MCS, November 7, 1901, RML.
46   "I fear": MN to MWM, March 24, 1901, RML.
46   "Think of having": MN to MWM, February 15, 1904, RML.
46   "To think of": MN to MWM, February 19, 1904, RML.
46   "be good when": MN to MWM, Saturday afternoon, [March 1904], RML.
47   "a strange and appealing": EB, *The Collected Prose* (New York: Farrar, Straus and Giroux, 1984), 45.
47   "her pugnacious": MWM to MCS, July 2, 1902, RML.
47   "sweeping down": MM quoted in Ira Berkow, "Famed Poetess Warms Up for Yankee Opener," *NEA Sports Green* (March 21, 1968), clipping in RML.
48   "tennis": *Prose*, 684.
48   "Once in *ante-luvian*": quoted in MWM to MCS, March 19, 1897, RML.
48   "Cousin Annie and I": MM to MCS, July 23, 1901, RML.
49   "Your hero-worshipper": MWM to MCS, July 24, 1899, RML.
51   "Endless delight": CA, 34
51   "the kind of tame": *Prose*, 547.
52   "It is sad": MWM to JWM, September 16, 1904, RML.
52   "O I wish": MWM to JWM, October 17, 1904, RML.
52   "It's hard to resist": MWM to JWM, October 20, 1904, RML.
53   "Perhaps you get": MWM to JWM, October 8, 1904, RML.
53   "is seeing girls": MN to JWM, n.d., RML.
54   "highly opprobrious": JWM to MWM and MM, February 12, 1905, RML.
55   "I greatly regret": MM to JWM, May 1, 1905, RML.
55   "When I want": MWM to JWM, April 20, 1905, RML.
55   "If we had not": MWM to JWM, March 31, 1911, RML.
55   "If you had a family": quoted in MWM to JWM, November 7, 1904, RML.
56   "were to real letters": quoted in MWM to JWM, May 4, 1905, RML.

5. THE EDGE OF A PRECIPICE

57 Low Buildings: Helen Lefkowitz Horowitz, *Alma Mater: Design and Experience in the Women's Colleges from Their Nineteenth-Century Beginnings to the 1930s* (New York: Knopf, 1984), 185–86.

58 "do something": MN to MWM, February 13, 1904, RML.

59 "over-anxious": *Prose*, 662.

59 "very talented and unusual": *Prose*, 663.

60 "the popular belief": "A College Girl's Experience as a Wife as Told by Herself," *Ladies' Home Journal* (October 1905), 42.

60 "that the average": Mrs. S. T. Rorer, "What College Girls Eat," *Ladies' Home Journal* (November 1905), 13–14.

60 "The celibate influences": Caroline McCook [Morgan] to MM, July 24, [1908], RML.

61 "most heavenly": MM to MWM and JWM, November 12, 1905, RML.

61 "very much opposed . . . breaking down": MM to MWM and JWM, November 5, 1905, RML.

61 "Won't they all": Elizabeth Rose, quoted in MWM to MM, September 25, 1905, RML.

61 "alternately a mountain": MM to JWM, August 30, 1905, RML.

62 "It would do your heart": MN to MWM, September 24 and 25, 1905, RML.

62 "The paper is dark green": MM to MWM and JWM, September 25, 1905, RML.

62 "as well fixed . . . world": MM to MWM and JWM, October 1, 1905, RML.

63 "I have never": MM to MWM and JWM, October 4, 1905, RML.

63 "The work is enormous": MM to MN, October 6, 1905, RML.

63 "Don't imagine": MM to MN, October 8, 1905, *SL*, 11–12.

63 "occasionally indescribably horrible": Ibid., 12.

63 "satanic malady": MM to MN, October 9, 1905, RML.

63 "sick, vibrating, . . . burden": MM to MN, October 10, 1905, RML.

63 "hungry for their meals": MM to MN, October 9, 1905, RML.

63 "I suddenly feel . . . give up": Ibid.

64 "physically all right": MM to MN, October 11, 1905, RML.

64 "Soon after Rustles left": MM to MWM and JWM, October 15, 1905, RML.

64 "If anyone was ever homesick": DH65, 300.

64 "I seemed to need": Ibid., 301.

64 "One of my small troubles": MM to MWM and JWM, October 22, 1905, RML.

65 "most newsworthy event": MM to MWM and JWM, October 29, 1905, RML.

65 "every stone": quoted in MM to JWM, November 4, 1904, RML.

65 Carey Thomas: Helen Lefkowitz Horowitz, *The Power and Passion of M. Carey Thomas* (New York: Knopf, 1994); and Edith Finch, *Carey Thomas of Bryn Mawr* (New York: Harper's, 1947).

65 curricular innovations: Cornelia Meigs, *What Makes a College? A History of Bryn Mawr* (New York: Macmillan, 1956), 41–42.

66 "When she isn't": MM to MWM and JWM, April 2, 1906, RML.

66 "the Dean said pronounce": MM to MWM and JWM, October 20, 1906, RML.

66 "The students are requested": CA, 42.

66 "an impassioned emancipator": *Prose*, 419.

66 "I was appalled": CA, 38.

67 "corrected, phrase by phrase": DH65, 300.

67 "private reading" list: *Bryn Mawr College Program*, 1905–1906, BMC.

67 "My English Comp.": MM to MWM and JWM, November 26, 1905, RML.

67 "a network of quotations": MM to MWM and JWM, January 17, 1906, RML.

67 "a vast reputation": MM to MWM and JWM, November 26, 1905, RML.

67 "made biology and its toil": *Prose*, 572.

68 60 percent: Hilda W. Smith and Helen Kirk Welsh, *Constance M. K. Applebee and the Story of Hockey*, privately published [1975], 17.

68 "You want all these students": quoted in Rebecca Raham, "Hockey is a R-R-R-Running Game," *Bryn Mawr Now* 8.3 (February 1981), 5.

68 "There had to be": Ibid.

68 "ring high": MM to MWM and JWM, January 21, 1906, RML.

68 "I am puny": MM to MWM and JWM, January 26, 1906, RML.

68 "suspended from a pulley": MM to MWM and JWM, February 6, 1906, RML.

69 "extra large lung": MM to MWM and JWM, October 15, 1906, RML.

69 "Am I myself? . . . misdemeanors": MM to MWM and JWM, February 25, 1906, RML.

70 "I cannot conceive": MM to MWM and JWM, November 26, 1905, RML.

70 "simply can't help writing": MM to MWM and JWM, November 2, 1905, RML.

70 "a feeling like": MWM to JWM and MM, February 12, 1907, RML.

71 "medieval lady": HD to MM, August 21, 1915, RML.

71 "I have what sad to say": MM to MWM and JWM, February 11, 1906, RML.

71 "I have liked her": MM to MWM and JWM, July 1, 1906, RML.

6. POSSESSED TO WRITE

72 "Really college": MM to MWM and JWM, October 28, 1906, RML.

72 "English makes me rant": MM to MWM and JWM, January 23, 1907, RML.

73 "as willing as can be": MWM to JWM and MM, November 16, 1906, RML.

73 "white and drawn": MM to MWM and JWM, November 27, 1906, RML.

73 "Then, *in truth*": JWM to MWM and MM, November 24, 1906, RML.

74 "always acquiring": MWM to MM, December 3, 1906, RML.

74 "own far-off self . . . by you": MWM to MM, February 8, 1907, RML.

74 "a militant Blue Stocking": Lucy Martin Donnelly, "The Heart of a Blue Stocking," *The Atlantic Monthly* (October 1908), 536–39.

75 "ostentatious": MM to MWM and JWM, February 19, 1907, *SL*, 25.

75 "mooning": MM to MWM and JWM, October 28, 1906, RML.

75 "mostly a joke": MM to MWM and JWM, March 7, 1907, RML.

75   "Dante-and-Beatrice": MM to MWM and JWM, October 28, 1906, RML.
75   "Byronesque": MM to MWM and JWM, January 29, 1907, RML.
75   "I'd give anything . . . your story": MM to MWM and JWM, November 13, 1906, RML.
76   Terry "knows": MM to MWM and JWM, October 13, 1907, RML.
76   "My story": MM to MWM and JWM, February 10, 1907, RML.
76   "possessed to write": MM to MWM and JWM, February 19, 1907, SL, 25.
76   "He loved color . . . nauseous": Prose, 3–6.
77   "seized with": MM to MWM and JWM, December 16, 1906, RML.
77   "perfectly carried away": MM to MWM and JWM, April 15, 1907, RML.
77   "Noon": MM to MWM and JWM, May 17, 1907, RML.
78   "all Margaret Morison's . . . James": MM to MWM and JWM, April 22, 1907, RML.
78   MM's college transcript: Emily Mitchell Wallace, "Athene's Owl," Poesis 6.3/4 (1985), 98–123.
78   "very handsome": MM to MWM and JWM, March 17, 1907, RML.
78   "She is tall": MM to MWM and JWM, March 18, 1907, RML.
78   "had a real sound": MM to MWM and JWM, March 18, 1907, RML.
79   "Bird News": MM to MWM and JWM, May 9, 1907, SL, 27.
79   "wildly excited . . . in her hair": MM to MWM and JWM, October 17, 1907, RML.
79   "Peggy is the staff": MM to MWM and JWM, October 9, 1907, RML.
79   "Peggy irritates me": MM to MWM and JWM, October 13, 1907, RML.
79   "She is no devotee": MM to MWM and JWM, October 20, 1907, RML.
79   "brotherly": MM to MWM and JWM, October 30, 1907, RML.
79   "She largely overestimates": MM to MWM and JWM, November 2, 1907, RML.
80   "that it is normal": MM to B, August 31, 1921, SL, 177.
80   "Peggy's friendship": MWM to JWM and MM, October 13, 1907, RML.
80   "little heart . . . temperament": Ibid.
81   "As bad old Cassius": MWM to JWM, November 18, 1907, RML.
81   "Peggy likes the Mouse": MM to JWM, November 18, 1907, RML.
81   "portrait in green": MM to MWM and JWM, October 30, 1907, RML.
81   A Quiet Hour: [Patricia C. Willis], "MM on the Literary Life, 1907," MMN 5 (Spring 1981), 4–13.
81   "a series of individual": MM to MWM and JWM, October 24, 1907, SL, 28.
82   "big aggressive brute . . . actual experience": Prose, 12–16.
82   "Marianna, your ears": quoted in MM to MWM and JWM, January 26, 1908, RML.
82   "perfectly rotten": MM to MH, January 26, [1908], SL, 35.
83   "love college madly . . . doing it": MM to MH, February 9, 1908, SL, 35–36.
83   "Trust yourself . . . Try poetry": MH to MM, February 24, 1908, RML.
83   "Why is it": MH to MM, March 3, 1908, RML.
83   "the artistic point of view": MM to MH, March 15, 1908, SL, 41.

83 "godly parentage": MWM to JWM and MM, March 15, 1908, RML.

83 "I am sorry": MM to MWM and JWM, March 18, 1908, RML.

84 "takes off Peggy": MM to MH, February 18, 1908, BMC.

84 "Love is the thing": *Prose*, 321.

84 "like all wild Wales": MM to MH, March 15, 1908, *SL*, 41.

84 "a demon needing": MM to MH, February 7, 1908, BMC.

85 "Writing is all": MM to MWM and JWM, April 5, 1908, *SL*, 45.

85 "sacrifice for the people": Ibid., 46.

85 "I shall never forget it": MM to MWM and JWM, April 14, 1908, RML.

85 "an unseen spiritual": William James, "Is Life Worth Living?," *William James: Writings 1878–1899* (New York: The Library of America, 1992), 495.

85 "Be not afraid": Ibid., 503.

85 "that the thing to do": MM to MWM and JWM, April 26, 1908, RML.

85 "a fair wave": MM to MWM and JWM, April 28, 1908, RML.

85 "were on excellent terms": MM to MH, May 17, 1908, *SL*, 49.

86 Bruce Porter: R. W. B. Lewis, *The Jameses: A Family Narrative* (New York: Farrar, Straus and Giroux, 1991), 623–25.

86 "about six lines long": MM to MWM and JWM, April 2, 1908, RML.

86 "drifting to biology": MM to MWM and JWM, April 14, 1908, RML.

86 "ridiculous to outsiders": MM to MH, May 17, 1908, *SL*, 48.

86 "I admire the Dean": MM to MWM and JWM, April 14, 1908, RML.

7. APPROPRIATING

87 "a perfect corker": quoted in MM to MWM and JWM, March 18, 1908, RML.

87 "I love to 'talk'": MM to MH, May 17, 1908, *SL*, 49.

87 "The net result": MM to B, August 31, 1921, *SL*, 178.

88 "You have an immense": George A. Barton, comments on MM, "Babylonian Poetry," January 18, 1909, RML.

88 Georgiana Goddard King: Susanna Terrell Saunders, "Georgiana Goddard King (1871–1939): Educator and Pioneer in Medieval Spanish Art," in *Women as Interpreters of the Visual Arts, 1820–1979*, ed. Claire Richter Sherman (Westport, CT: Greenwood Press, 1981), 209–38.

88 "relinquish [her] own": MM to MWM and JWM, February 9, 1909, RML.

88 "is the best teacher": MM to MWM and JWM, February 25, 1909, RML.

89 "No decent, half-kind": MM to MWM and JWM, February 14, 1909, *SL*, 63.

89 "the indecency": MM to MWM and JWM, May 16, 1909, RML.

89 "Many of the class": MM to MWM and JWM, March 20, 1909, RML.

89 "He is kind": MM to MWM and JWM, December 17, 1908, RML.

89 "the most pursued": MM to MWM and JWM, March 20, 1909, RML.

89 "an invaluable ability": Agnes Kirsopp Lake, an appreciation of Henry Sanders on the occasion of his retirement, *Bryn Mawr Alumnae Bulletin* 15 (July 1935), 19, BMC.

90 "I pretended": MM to MWM and JWM, March 15, 1909, RML.

90 "The Bored Lady": MM, Notebook for General Philosophy, RML.

91 "pious women . . . Janus-headed man": *Prose*, 26–30.

91 "Shirley is prejudiced": MM to MWM and JWM, February 22, 1909, RML.

91 "very popular": A Bryn Mawr freshman quoted in MWM to JWM and MM, February 18, 1909, RML.

91 "supposed to be a 'mecca' ": MM to MWM and JWM, March 10, 1908, RML.

92 *"aghast"*: MWM to MM, February 5, 1909, RML.

92 "careful not to": MM to MWM and JWM, February 2, 1909, RML.

93 "the most interesting man": MM to MWM and JWM, February 1, 1909, *SL*, 55.

93 "fatal way of losing": MM to MWM and JWM, May 26, 1909, RML.

93 "like unsettled coffee": George A. Barton, quoted in MWM to JWM, February 5, 1909, RML.

93 "a certain captious . . . decadent": MM to MWM and JWM, February 28, 1909, RML.

94 "the collision of truths": Vernon Watkins to MM, July 4, 1965, RML.

94 "a bird from Heaven": MM to MWM and JWM, April 4, 1909, RML.

94 "I was taken by storm": Ibid.

94 "I rush home": Margaret Ayer [Barnes] to MM, November 14, 1907, RML.

95 "teaching and living narrowly": MM to MWM and JWM, April 5, 1908, *SL*, 45.

95 "I grieve to think": MWM to JWM and MM, February 25, 1909, RML.

95 "Basilisk": JWM to MWM and MM, March 14, 1909, RML.

95 "About next year": MM to MWM and JWM, March 21, 1909, RML.

95 "As I've said before": MWM to JWM and MM, March 23, 1909, RML.

96 "I want no work": MM to MWM and JWM, April 18, 1909, RML.

96 "a long and salutary": MM to MWM and JWM, May 2, 1909, *SL*, 69.

96 "Listen!": MM to MWM and JWM, May 16, 1909, RML.

96 "You know it isn't easy": MWM to JWM and MM, May 17, 1909, RML.

96 "Please do find out": MM to MWM and JWM, May 17, 1909, RML.

97 "Baltimore is a sleepy town!": MWM to JWM and MM, May 19, 1909, RML.

97 "Baltimore may be": JWM to MWM and MM, May 21, 1909, RML.

97 "your daughter has": CA, 41–42.

8. WILD AND GLORIOUS

99 "She is one of": Ellinor Hays to MWM, [June 30, 1909], RML.

99 "amazed and delighted looks . . . wilder": MM to MWM, draft, June 28, 1909, RML.

100 "The youngster talks": MWM to JWM, July 12, 1909, RML.

100 "The next time": Mabel [Mary Isabel] O'Sullivan to MM, February 18, 1910, RML.

100 "I am having": MM to JWM, November 26, 1909, RML.

101 "He misses you": MWM to JWM, January 7, 1910, RML.

101 "great marvel": quoted in MWM to JWM, June 7, 1909, RML.

101 "sling[ing] doctrine": MM to JWM, May 15, 1910, RML.

102 "Are you very sad": Mabel [Mary Isabel] O'Sullivan to MM, June 12, 1909, RML.

102 "To counteract melancholy": MM to Catherine Flagg, carbon, n.d. [early 1930s], RML.

103 "and talks as if": MWM to JWM, December 1, 1909, RML.

103 "highest standards": *Lake Placid Club Handbook* (Essex Co., NY: Forest Press, 1914), 5, 9.

103 "snout out": JWM to MWM and MM, May 2, 1910, RML.

103 "She is so 'young' ": MWM to JWM, May 6, 1910, RML.

104 "He looks worse": MWM to JWM, June 26, 1910, RML.

104 "vile treachery": MM to MWM and JWM, July 31, 1910, *SL*, 80.

104 "fidget and gnash": Ibid.

104 "The 'help' ": MM to MWM and JWM, July 10, 1910, RML.

104 "all splendid": MM to MWM and JWM, July 7, 1910, RML.

104 golf caddies: Wayne A. Wiegand, *Irrepressible Reformer: A Biography of Melvil Dewey* (Chicago: American Library Association, 1996), 318.

104 "I have seven suitors": MM to MWM and JWM, August 21, 1910, *SL*, 82.

105 "Fangs, what means": MWM to JWM and MM, September 1, 1910, RML.

105 "are has beens": MM to MWM and JWM, September 11, 1910, RML.

105 "I am spending": MM to MWM and JWM, July 31, 1919, *SL*, 80.

105 "The Steeple-Jack": *CP*, 6.

106 "an HM . . . liberalizing": MM to MWM and JWM, July 10, 1910, RML.

106 "Pressure of business": *Prose*, 178.

106 "They are very liberal": MM to MWM and JWM, July 10, 1910, RML.

106 "refund my permit": MM to MWM and JWM, August 18, 1910, *SL*, 82.

106 "For heaven's sake": MN to MM, July 15, 1910, RML.

106 "razor expression": MWM to JWM and MM, July 17, 1910, RML.

107 "For the comparative inexpense": MM to MWM and JWM, [September 17, 1910], RML.

107 "fashion plate": MM to JWM, September 25, 1910, RML.

108 "How do you think": MWM to MM, September 27, 1910, RML.

108 "I couldn't bear": MN to MM, September 23, 1910, RML.

108 "is self possessed": MM to MWM, September 27, 1910, RML.

109 "Don't turn away": MWM to MM, September 30, 1910, RML.

109 "Sissy feels her home life": MWM to JWM, October 23, 1910, RML.

109 "The Gator": quoted in MWM to JWM and MM, October 10, 1910, RML.

109 "a little rest": MCS to JWM, October 20, 1910, RML.

109 "I don't know that I": MM to JWM, November 13, 1910, *SL*, 86.

110 "seemed to hate everything": MWM to JWM, December 5, 1910, RML.

9. AN INTRAMURAL RAT

112 "very sad-eyed": MWM to JWM, March 29, 1911, RML.

112 "honest penny": MM and MWM to JWM, February 6, 1911, RML.

112 "Gnashings and knottings": MM to JWM, April 2, 1911, RML.

113 "I *must do it*": MWM to JWM, April 6, 1911, RML.

113 "pleasant": quoted in MWM to JWM, July 7, 1911, RML.

114 "Life is so exciting": MM to JWM, June 11, 1911, RML.

114 "I shan't be satisfied": MM to JWM, July 5, 1911, *SL*, 89.

114 "wee folk . . . bells": MWM to JWM, July 14, 1911, RML.

114 "personal Waterloo": MWM to JWM, July 16, 1911, RML.

114 "be patient with anything": MWM to JWM, June 15, 1911, RML.

114 "appreciation bag": MM to JWM, July 11, 1911, RML.

114 "separated an instant": MM to JWM, May 30, 1911, RML.

115 "a coachdriver": MM to JWM, June 11, 1911, RML.

115 "Having once seen London": MM to JWM, July 9, 1911, *SL*, 91.

115 "happy hours": MM to JWM, July 13, 1911, RML.

115 "Ezra Pound and Ernest Dowson": MM, Notebook 1250/1 (1907–15), RML, 20.

115 Elkin Mathews: James G. Nelson, *Elkin Mathews: Publisher to Yeats, Joyce, Pound* (Madison: University of Wisconsin Press, 1989), 131–47.

115 MM's purchases: [Patricia C. Willis], "Marianne Moore on Ezra Pound, 1909–1915," *MMN* 3.2 (Fall 1979), 5–8.

116 "great outbreak": MM to JWM, July 13, 1911, RML.

116 "beautifully placed": MM to JWM, July 16, 1911, RML.

116 "atrocities": MM to JWM, August 13, 1911, RML.

116 "Karl Baedeker's": *Prose*, 215.

116 "something more mellow": "Museums," *MMN* 1.1 (Spring 1977), 8–9.

117 "very substantial and imposing": quoted in Robert Cantwell, "The Poet, the Bums and the Legendary Red Men," *Sports Illustrated* (February 15, 1960), 77.

117 "some neurotic": Ibid., 76.

117 "were an ideal . . . intelligent": CA, 43.

118 "a little laborious . . . reserve": *Prose*, 682.

118 "I felt myself": quoted in Cantwell, 82.

118 "You mustn't hold me": MM and MWM to JWM, January 15, 1914, RML.

119 "Sissy has avoided . . . cases": MWM to JWM, February 14, 1914, RML.

119 "Rat is the cheerfulest": MWM to JWM, September 25, 1914, RML.

119 "It would never do": MWM to MCS, February 15, 1913, RML.

120 "paraded with": EB, *Complete Prose*, 55. EB assumed the march took place in New York.

121 "I've never seen": Milton Flower quoted, October 1, 1915, Notebook 1250/23, RML, 16.

121 notes on Old Testament poetry: Notebook 1252/25 (1914), RML.

121 "drop into poetry": MWM to JWM, March 15, 1914, RML.

122 "Instead of shaking him": MM to JWM, January 30, 1914, RML.

122 "Seen altogether": Floyd Dell to MM, March 21, 1914, RML.
122 "Bah!": MM to JWM, March 26, 1914, RML.
122 "Whatever you do": JWM to MM [July 27, 1913], RML.
122 "Togo dear": MWM to JWM, February 2, 1914, RML.
123 "a distinguished poem": MWM to MM, November 30, 1915, RML.
123 sonnetlike revision: *BMM*, 187.
123 "the shining jewel": MWM to MM, July 6, 1914, RML.
123 "like a cloudburst": MWM to JWM, June 25, 1912, RML.
124 "I find myself wishing": MWM to JWM, July 6, 1912, RML.
124 "mother joy": MWM to MCS, February 15, 1913, RML.
124 "thrilled to the soul": JWM to MWM and MM, May 24, 1915, RML.
124 "Well, there's no girl": JWM to MWM and MM, October 21, 1912, RML.
124 "She sends us wonderful": MWM to JWM, December 9, 1913, RML.
125 "You know in all the years": MWM to JWM, January 5, 1914, RML.
125 "definite move": JWM to MWM, January 6, 1914, RML.
125 "out of a clear sky": MWM to JWM, January 8, 1914, RML.
125 "You and [Marianne]": MWM to JWM, January 27, 1914, RML.
125 "I'm done with": JWM to MWM, March 25, 1914, RML.
126 "antiquated rabbit": Alice Benjamin Mackenzie to MWM, April 19, 1914, RML.
127 "He doesn't know": MM to JWM, September 24, 1914, RML.
127 "To an Intra Mural Rat": MM to JWM, May 27, 1914, RML.

10. A FINE STEEL BLADE
128 "gorgeous bathrobe": MM to JWM, October 15, 1914, RML.
128 "Rat hates his": MWM to JWM, October 18, 1914, RML.
129 "Rat has been": MWM to JWM, October 11, 1914, RML.
130 "No masters . . . continuity": MM quoted in Louise Bogan, "A Poet is Questioned," *P.E.N. News* 8.2 (January 1962), 1. Glenway Wescott and Monroe Wheeler Collection of Marianne Moore, YCAL.
130 "My war poem": MM to JWM, October 10, 1914, RML.
130 "tic-tic-ing": MWM to JWM, February 19, 1915, RML.
131 "*Poetry* is a respectable": MM to MWM, July 7, 1914, RML.
131 One review in her scrapbook: GS, "Des Imagistes: The Latest School of Modern English Poetry," unidentified clipping in Scrapbook, 1914, RML.
131 "eight or nine magazines . . . buy me": MM to MWM, March 2, 1915, RML.
131 "Both are worth . . . hade": MM to MWM, March 3, 1915, RML.
132 "No money however": MM to JWM, March 15, 1915, RML.
132 "R. has spoken often": HD to MM, August 21, 1915, RML.
132 "I'll have to tell Billy": MM to JWM, May 9, 1915, RML.
133 "an outsider": MM to William Rose Benét, carbon, February 4, 1916, RML.
133 "Disappointment makes wreckage . . . with you": MM to JWM, March 21, 1915, RML.

134 "Mole can't be taken . . . life to Mole": MM to JWM, March 21, 1915, RML.

134 "our circling ways": MWM to JWM, May 9, 1921, RML.

134 "He is a *good* rat": MWM to JWM, April 16, 1915, RML.

135 "Now with what poems . . . ephemeral": MM to JWM, October 3, 1915, *SL*, 100.

135 "I'm so proud": JWM to MM, October 7, 1915, RML.

135 "confederates . . . full of life": MM to JWM, October 10, 1915, *SL*, 101.

136 "Ratty looks almost": MWM to JWM, October 29, 1915, RML.

136 "extreme and fantastic": MM, October 21, 1915, Notebook 1250/23 (1915–1919), RML.

136 "to find something": MM to JWM, October 21, 1915, RML.

136 "Congress of Gospelated Wigeons": MM to JWM, "The File," November 7, 1915, RML.

136 "a wealthy, rotundly proportioned": MM to JWM, November 7, 1915, RML.

137 "I do not wish to cast": MWM to JWM, November 6, 1915, RML.

137 "*He did see her*": MWM to JWM, November 12, 1915, RML.

137 "Ratty has came": MWM to JWM, December 10, 1915, RML.

138 "Rats need room": MM to JWM, January 24, 1916, RML.

138 "I am just as sure": MM to JWM, December 16, 1915, RML.

138 "always on the watch": Mr. McGowan, quoted in MWM to JWM, January 17, 1916, RML.

139 "Was there ever anything": Ibid.

139 "first the Buldy": MM to JWM, January 24, 1916, RML.

139 TSE on "A Talisman": *CRMM*, 106.

140 "curiously wrought patterns": *CRMM*, 19–21.

140 "fighting spirit . . . compromise": MM to HD, August 9, 1916, *SL*, 113.

140 "too compact and keen": *CRMM*, 22.

140 "something you are willing": WCW to MM, May 9, 1916, RML.

140 "Ambition without understanding": MM, April 29, 1916, Notebook 1250/24, RML.

142 "persist, no matter": *Prose*, 32.

143 "knows the ground": MM to JWM, December 19, 1915, *SL*, 108.

143 "What is all that": quoted in WCW, *Autobiography*, 240.

143 "architecture" and "tune": DH60, 287.

143 "I believe in": MM to Isabel Lachaise, April 13, 1946, quoted in Carolyn Kinder Carr and Margaret C. S. Christman, *Gaston Lachaise: Portrait Sculpture* (Washington, DC: National Portrait Gallery, 1985), 84.

144 "the waste of time": *Prose*, 319.

144 "to waste effort": DH60, 295.

11. DEFIANT EDIFICE

145 "She has a mind": JWM to MWM and MM, June 20, 1915, RML.

146 "Miss White was taken": MWM to JWM, July 9, 1915, RML.

146 "Mole wins": JWM to MWM and MM, September 17, 1915, RML.

146 "*Times* and *times* a day": MWM to JWM, October 29, 1915, RML.

146 "a new era . . . follow": JWM to MWM and MM, January 3 and February 24, 1916, RML.

147 "Ratty is full of joy": MWM to JWM, June 22, 1916, RML.

147 "When we went": MWM to MCS, June 8, 1934, RML.

147 "less and less interest": MM, October 12, 1916, Notebook 1250/24, RML.

147 "repellent larvae": MWM to JWM, July 17, 1917, RML.

147 "a slender woman": Julie Hutchinson, "They Remembered Marianne Moore," *Chatham Courier*, February 10, 1972, RML.

147 "an astonishing person": Kreymborg, 238–39.

147 "I'm so glad . . . like him": MM, November 11, 1916, Notebook 1250/23, RML.

148 "gold slippers . . . life": MM to HD, January 11, 1921, *SL*, 140.

148 "coiled around . . . Niagara": WCW, "Marianne Moore" (1948), in WCW, *Selected Essays* (New York: Random House, 1954), 292.

148 "You interest me": MM, December 27, 1916, Notebook 1250/23, RML.

149 "descent into . . . his theories": Kreymborg, 244–45.

150 "Middle Pullman Period . . . sidewalk": MM, December 1916, Notebook 1250/23, RML.

150 "Many of these things": MM, April 9, 1917, Notebook 1250/23, RML.

152 "like corn silk": MM, October 21, 1915, Notebook 1250/23, RML.

153 "the perfect swordsman": *CRMM*, 20.

153 "Oh! I wish": quoted in JWM to MWM and MM, January 7, 1918, MFC.

154 Constance Eustis: MCM and SEM in conversation with the author, February 18, 2000.

154 Warner and Constance courtship: MCM and SEM in conversation with the author, August 23, 1999.

154 "the hideous attack": JWM to MWM and MM, June 8, 1918, MFC.

154 "When I set upon Ben": Ibid.

155 "I don't think you would": quoted in JWM to MWM, November 14, 1919, RML.

155 "Sixty or a hundred years from now": quoted in JWM to MWM and MM, September 12, 1918, MFC.

155 "My crime": JWM to MWM and MM, August 6, 1918, MFC.

155 "wonderful event": J. Dey Conover to JWM, November 22, 1917, RML.

155 May's trip to Athens, OH: MCM and SEM in conversation with the author, June 17, 2000. JMM likely did work for the institution, as most patients did, but court records show that he was a patient from 1909 until his death in 1925.

155 Johns Hopkins expert: JWM to CEM, January 10, 1918, MFC.

156 "feverishly": MWM to JWM, November 6, 1919, RML.

156 "prose work": MM, "Miscellaneous Notes," 1937, RML.

156 "It was an hour": MWM to JWM, May 31, 1919, RML.

156 "the marriage ought not": MWM to CEM, undated draft, [July 1918], RML.

157 "a sick, sick boy": JWM to MWM and MM, August 12, 1918, MFC.

157 "Now I think": JWM to MWM and MM, August 29, 1918, RML.

157 "The Fish": *"Others" for 1919: An Anthology of the New Verse*, ed. Alfred
     Kreymborg (New York: Nicholas L. Brown, 1920), 125–27.
159 "beauty / intertwined": Margaret Holley, *The Poetry of Marianne Moore: A
     Study in Voice and Value* (Cambridge: Cambridge University Press, 1987), 62.
159 "mystery of emotion": Donald Hall, *Marianne Moore: The Cage and the Animal*
     (New York: Pegasus, 1970), 47.
160 "Life is a good deal": MM to JWM, September 14, 1918, MFC.

12. THE SECRET OF EXPANSION

161 "14 St. Luke's Place": MM to JWM, [September 30, 1918], RML.
162 "Well, there are reasons": MM, summer 1918, Notebook 1250/23, RML.
162 "Ratty . . . *too little*": MWM to JWM, September 22, 1920, RML.
162 "Her deepest feelings": MWM to JWM, October 27, 1919, RML.
162 "the only thing in life": MWM to JWM, April 23, 1919, RML.
163 "is as shy today": MWM to Mr. and Mrs. Dings, draft, September 23, 1920,
     RML.
163 "dependent": 1929 income tax statement, RML.
163 "with hat and coat on": MWM to JWM, June 5, 1921, RML.
163 "wisplike": Robert McAlmon, *Post-Adolescence: A Selection of Short Fiction
     1923* (Albuquerque: University of New Mexico Press, 1991), 75.
163 "a stick of a woman": WCW quoted in Mariani, 394.
163 "the frailest bit o' bones": MWM to JWM, May 19, 1921, RML.
163 "literary guys": WCW quoted in Mariani, 394.
163 "no man-instincts": MWM to JWM, April 17, 1921, RML.
163 "a case of arrested": DH65, 298.
164 "all day remunerative": MM to JWM, September 7, 1919, RML.
164 "Our wildest extravagance": MWM to JWM, October 27, 1919, RML.
164 "DOANT": MM quoted in MWM to JWM, November 11, 1920, RML.
164 "My stomach has been": MM to JWM, October 17, 1920, RML.
164 anorexia nervosa: Salvatore Minuchin's concept of the "enmeshed family"
     helps to explain MM's eating disorder. Boundaries between an enmeshed
     family and the outside world are strongly defined, he says, but within the
     family there is little regard for autonomy or privacy. Not only are the parents
     overprotective of the children, fearing outside influences, but the children
     themselves can become unreasonably fearful for the family's safety. En-
     meshed families resist change, they refuse to accept conflict, and they have
     no means for resolving it. Any change, such as the children's growing up,
     seems to threaten the family's survival. Girls can minimize the physical
     changes associated with puberty by refusing to eat. See Salvatore Minuchin,
     Bernice L. Rosman, Lester Baker, *Psychosomatic Families: Anorexia Nervosa
     in Context* (Cambridge, MA: Harvard University Press, 1978), 30–31 and
     passim.

165 "high-flying fashion plate": MM to JWM, September 25, 1910, RML.
165 androgyny and the New Woman: Cristanne Miller, *Marianne Moore: Questions of Authority* (Cambridge, MA: Harvard University Press, 1995), 93–100.
165 "Starve it down": *Prose*, 572.
165 "passion for the particular": *CP*, 231.
167 "the only person": quoted in MM, summer or fall 1919, Notebook 1250/24, RML.
167 "astonishingly improved": MWM to JWM, July 1, 1919, RML.
168 "diamond hard": McAlmon, 75.
168 "I think I'd be": Ibid., 70.
168 "a rafter holding up": WCW, *Autobiography*, 146.
168 "the first adequate presentation . . . characters": *CRMM*, 22.
169 "write living English": Ibid., 23.
169 "traces of emotion": Ibid., 22.
169 "fusion of thought": Ibid., 24.
169 "Your stuff holds my eye": EP to MM, December 16, 1918, *CRMM*, 28.
169 "The resemblance . . . produce": MM to EP, January 9, 1919, *SL*, 122–23.
170 "Definiteness of your delineations": EP to MM, February 1, 1919, RML.
170 "lechery": Ibid.
171 "wholly dissatisfied": MM to EP, January 9, 1919, *SL*, 123.
171 "*Poetry*'s approach": MM to Harriet Monroe, May 10, 1918, *SL*, 115.
171 "Miss Monroe": quoted in MWM to JWM, February 7, 1919, RML.
171 "The frailest of humans": Kreymborg, 330–31.
172 "Reading aloud": Kreymborg, 332–33. The party where ST first approached MM occurred in late February or early March 1920. She mentions him in a letter dated January 1920 (*SL*, 127–28) but actually written in January 1921. This is a common error in her January letters.
172 "By all means": quoted in MM to JWM, September 19, 1920, *SL*, 133.
172 "infinitely poetic": MM to Gilbert Seldes, March 27, 1920, RML.
173 "spiritual home": EP to ST, January 25, 1920, *Pound, Thayer, Watson, and* The Dial: *A Story in Letters*, ed. Walter Sutton (Gainesville: University of Florida Press, 1994), 11.
173 "most everything": ST to EP, March 8, 1920, Ibid., 12–13.
173 "the type of magazine": JSW to EP, July 28, 1920, Ibid., 92.
173 "Yes . . . I do": MWM to JWM, October 27, 1919, RML.
174 "to put my hands": MWM to JWM, October 1, 1918, RML.
174 "Doubtless it is here": MWM to JWM, September 27, 1918, RML.
174 "passion loose": MWM to JWM, April 8, 1919, RML.
174 "It is touching": MWM to MM, September 14, 1919, RML.
174 "I never tell stories": Ibid.
175 "a churchgoing, cerebralizing": McAlmon, 68.
175 "Marianne said one day": MWM to JWM, April 23, 1919, RML.
175 "a sense of human": *CP*, 9.
175 "minor prophets": MM to EP, January 9, 1919, *SL*, 123.

175   "prose with a sort": *BMM*, 74. See Cristanne Miller, "Marianne Moore and a Poetry of Hebrew (Protestant) Prophecy," *Sources* 12 (Spring 2002), 29–47.

176   "the mysterious inner world": William Zorach, *Art Is My Life: The Autobiography of William Zorach* (Cleveland: World Publishing Company, 1967), 65.

176   "I have never seen": MM, spring 1919, Notebook 1250/24, RML.

176   "democratic respect": William James, *Talks to Teachers on Psychology and to Students on Some of Life's Ideals*, in *William James: Writings 1878–1899* (New York: Library of America, 1992), 708.

176   "fine distinctions": MM to JWM, October 5, 1919, RML.

176   "Those 'few strong wrinkles' ": JWM to MWM and MM, September 30, 1919, RML.

177   "our own special 'language' ": JWM to MWM and MM, May 1, 1920, RML.

177   "The most interesting thing": MM to JWM, June 8, 1920, RML.

178   "the old family one-ness": MWM to JWM, November 8, 1920, RML.

178   "cried and couldn't": JWM to MWM and MM, November 17, 1920, RML.

178   "When we got here": MWM to JWM, August 12, 1920, RML.

178   "Miss Leonard was enthusiasm": MM to JWM, August 10, 1920, RML.

178   "lived like anchorites": quoted in McAlmon, 75.

13. BLUEBEARD'S TOWER

179   "composure and look": MM to HD, draft [c. January 23, 1921], RML.

180   "sat back in her chair": B, *West* (London: Jonathan Cape, 1925), 37.

180   "austere boyish head": Ibid., 35.

180   "greatly superior": MWM to JWM, September 13, 1920, RML.

181   ten poems: MWM told JWM (September 13, 1920, RML) that MM took "a lot of mss." to HD. She took "Black Earth," "Roses Only," "In This Age of Hard Trying Nonchalance Is Good, And," "The Fish," "My Apish Cousins," "Picking and Choosing," "England," "Dock-Rats," "Radical," and "Poetry." According to Robin Schulze's notes in *BMM*, MM revised each of these in at least minor ways before she gave them to HD.

181   "we are so different": B to MM, September 24, 1920, RML.

181   "your interest": MM to B, October 15, 1920, *SL*, 133.

182   "I shall like any name": MM to B, December 13, 1920, *SL*, 137.

182   "I like what you say": MM to B, November 29, 1920, *SL*, 135–36.

182   "some heraldic version": B, *West*, 39.

182   "extended on the point . . . hatching": MM to JWM, January 23, 1921, *SL*, 141.

182   "a great deal of happiness": MM to B, January 23, 1921, *SL*, 141–42.

182   "eager to repeat": B, *West*, 190.

183   "get some of your prose": ST to MM, September 12, 1920, RML.

183   "Sweet Ratty": MWM to JWM, September 16, 1920, RML.

183   "Nunkey says": Ibid.

183   "very terrifying": MM to JWM, September 29, 1920, *SL*, 133.

183 "His wife has an apartment . . . harmless": MWM to JWM, September 16, 1920, RML.

183 "Mr. Thayer's sense": MM quoted in MWM to JWM, September 23, 1920, RML.

184 "rather knocked . . . that is all": MM to JWM, October 17, 1920, *SL*, 135.

184 "I'm not snuggling . . . *two*": MM, early draft of "If I Were Sixteen Today" sent to Henrietta Holland, n.d., RML.

184 "a poem, a prose article": MWM to JWM, November 27, 1920, RML.

184 "Did you remind him": MWM to JWM, January 16, 1921, RML.

185 "M. Moore has managed": EP to ST, March 23, 1921, *Pound, Thayer, Watson*, 215.

185 "Ratty has been far . . . price we pay": MWM to JWM, February 1, 1921, RML.

185 "We have grown to love": MWM to JWM, February 20, 1921, RML.

186 "tried most of one . . . I like you": MM to JWM, February 13, 1921, *SL*, 144.

186 "I don't suppose": Ibid.

186 "Were Rat staying": MWM to JWM, March 17, 1921, RML.

187 "very silent . . . entertained": MM to JWM, February 20, 1921, *SL*, 144–45.

187 "Wouldn't you like . . . I know": quoted in MWM to JWM, February 28, 1921, RML.

187 "true ladyhood . . . part of London": MWM to JWM, February 20, 1921, RML.

188 "He can write": quoted in MWM to JWM, February 20, 1921, RML.

188 "What I miss": MM to HD, March 27, 1921, *SL*, 149.

188 "a little cheque": B to MWM, February 25, 1921, RML.

188 "Your check is here": MM to B, March 3, 1921, YCAL.

188 "float her across": MWM to B, May 9, 1921, YCAL.

188 "like[d] to talk . . . fooled": MWM to JWM, April 17, 1921, RML.

189 "as it turned out": Ibid.

189 "It was of ivory . . . take this": TWWLN, 248–49.

189 "Mr. Cummings": ST to MM, draft, July 11, 1921, YCAL.

190 "T. S. Eliot has asked": Robert McAlmon to MM, April 12, 1921, RML.

190 "I wish that you would": TSE to MM, April 11, 1921, RML.

190 "Were I to publish": MM to TSE, April 17, 1921, *SL*, 152.

190 "You say I am stubborn . . . Dactyl": MM to B, July 7, 1921, *SL*, 164–67.

191 "The poems ought not": MM to McAlmon, July 8, 1921, *SL*, 168.

191 "everything about": MM to HD, July 26, 1921, *SL*, 172.

191 "among the two or three": JWM to MWM and MM, July 28, 1921, RML.

191 "a half dozen": MWM to JWM, August 1, 1921, RML.

192 "eccentricities of spacing": Frederick T. Dalton, *CRMM*, 32–33.

192 "stiffly geometrical intellectuality": *CRMM*, 35–40.

192 "because I can only": *CRMM*, 44–46.

193 "the very great importance": EP to MM, December 16, 1918, *CRMM*, 28.

193 "air of condescension": Richard Aldington, "Marianne Moore's Poetry," *Literary Review, New York Evening Post* (October 14, 1922).

193 "among the most interesting": *CRMM*, 35.

193 "forms which impose": *CRMM*, 39.

193 "the greatest living master": *CRMM*, 108.

194 "If an ingeniously constructed": Emmy Veronica Sanders, quoted in *BMM*, 385.

194 "Emotion in her": M[atthew] J[osephson], *CRMM*, 40.

14. LIBERTY AND UNION

195 "I never knew anyone": DH60, 283.

195 "pull and tug": MWM to JWM, March 21, 1921, RML.

195 "There are things": spring 1919, Notebook 1250/25, RML.

196 "a veiled Mohammedan woman": quoted in MM to HD, July 26, 1921, *SL*, 172.

196 "collateral reading": MWM to JWM, October 24, 1920, RML.

196 "privately, sniffed": MWM to JWM, October 3, 1919, RML.

196 "Last evening my hair": MWM to JWM, June 18, 1921, RML.

196 "I was determined": MM to JWM, June 19, 1921, RML.

197 "stinging greatness": MWM to JWM, July 20, 1921, RML.

197 "blessed of God": MWM to JWM, March 21, 1921, RML.

197 "*his true religion*": MWM to JWM, April 19, 1921, RML.

197 "He is a . . . quiet": MM to JWM, July 17, 1921, RML.

197 "Mr. Watson liked them": MM to JWM, October 17, 1920, RML.

199 "Mere mysteriousness": *Prose*, 328.

199 "I have finished": MM to JWM, November 5, 1921, RML.

199 "the terrific experience": MM to B, April 14, 1922, YCAL.

200 "the mean trick": JWM to MWM and MM, February 6, 1922, RML.

200 "A jewel of mechanism . . . romance": MM to B, July 18, 1922, YCAL.

200 "We had a glorious . . . back": MM to B, July 28, 1922, YCAL.

200 "men have power . . . an ear": Notebook 1251/17, RML.

201 "He is a lovely fellow": MM to JWM, October 9, 1921, RML.

201 "supremely fine . . . ten years ago!": quoted in MWM to JWM, October 9, 1921, RML.

201 Glenway Wescott and Monroe Wheeler: Jerry Rosco, *Glenway Wescott Personally* (Madison: University of Wisconsin Press, 2002); and Anatole Pohorilenko, "The Expatriate Years, 1925–34," in *When We Were Three* (Santa Fe, NM: Arena Editions, 1998).

202 "No one ever has come": MWM to JWM, January 18, 1923, RML.

202 "Glenway's fund of conversation": MWM to JWM, January 31, 1923, RML.

202 "We all chat": MWM to JWM, May 6, 1923, RML.

202 "The impulse of the mind": *CRMM*, 42.

203 "the most scholarly": MM to JWM, January 21, 1923, RML.

203 "Scofield turned white": MWM to JWM, October 28, 1923, RML.

203 considerable sum: $180, according to Schulze, *BMM*, 459.

203 "I am so thankful": MWM to JWM, October 28, 1923, RML.

204 "veil anything personal": *Prose*, 551.

204 Bryher and McAlmon's: Two of MM's best critics have read "Marriage" as a response to the Bryher-McAlmon marriage. See Schulze, *BMM*, 458–65; and Patricia C. Willis, "A Modernist Epithalamium: Marianne Moore's 'Marriage,'" *Paideuma* 32:1–3 (2003), 265–99.

204 "young couple": For example, MWM to JWM, December 5, 1920, RML.

205 "Love is more important": *Prose*, 284.

205 "upon a fellow creature's": *CP*, 9.

205 "intensively / watched eggs": *CP*, 121.

205 "the least possessive": Kathleen Cannell, "Colloquies with a Sibyl," ts., 1957, RML.

206 "little narrow white": MWM to JWM, October 27, 1919, RML.

206 "life has come": MWM to JWM, April 23, 1919, RML.

206 "Buffalo is developing": MM to JWM, March 25, 1923, *SL*, 194.

207 "Mole got chloroform": MM to JWM, March 29, 1923, RML.

207 "I never speak of Buffy": MWM to JWM, April 29, 1923, RML.

207 "one of the memorable": MWM to JWM, May 8, 1923, RML.

208 "a person of undoubted talent": Ibid.

208 "a real carnage": MM to JWM, May 10, 1923, *SL*, 199.

208 "loathed and abhorred": MWM to JWM, May 8, 1923, RML.

208 "*Excrement*": Ibid.

208 "What do you think": Ibid.

208 "a purple red fight": Ibid.

208 "Shakespeare exhilarates me": MM to JWM, May 10, 1923, *SL*, 198–99.

208 "All my stinging legs": quoted in MWM to JWM, May 8, 1923, RML.

209 "cruelty": *Prose*, 35.

209 "I could not be amused": quoted in MWM to JWM, May 8, 1923, RML.

209 "Rat [rise] like": Ibid.

15. THE UNBRIDLED LEAP

210 "an old-fashioned house": MM to JWM, December 19, 1923, RML.

210 "The word *office*": AG, *The Day Is Gone* (New York: E. P. Dutton, 1948), 208.

211 "at once adventurous": Ibid., 202.

212 "How wonderfully": AG to MM, July 17, 1924, YCAL.

212 "It is impossible": *Prose*, 85.

213 "picks over an ash-heap": YW to MM, January 12, 1926, RML.

213 "We would want it": WCW to MM, February 10, 1924, RML.

214 "under oath to myself": MM to ST, September 2, [1924], YCAL.

214 "the great catastrophe": WCW, *Autobiography*, 146.

214 "macabre": MM to YW, December 20, 1922, *SL*, 191.

215 "off and on": MM to B, September 9, 1924, *SL*, 208.

215 "Am I right": ST to MM, carbon, September 12, 1924, YCAL.

215 "Thank you for": ST to MM, September 22, 1924, RML.

216 "laboriousness . . . short poems": MM to ST, September 25, 1924, YCAL.

216 Dante and Milton: Patricia C. Willis, "The Road to Paradise: First Notes on Marianne Moore's 'An Octopus,'" *Twentieth Century Literature* 30 (Summer/Fall 1984), 260–64.

216 Shelley: Robin G. Schulze, *The Web of Friendship: Marianne Moore and Wallace Stevens* (Ann Arbor: University of Michigan Press, 1995), 48–51.

217 "an enormous frozen": Robert Sterling Yard, *The National Parks Portfolio*, third edition (Washington, DC: Government Printing Office, 1921), 85.

218 "a poet bristling": *CCE*, 79.

218 "content with smallness": Ibid., 84.

219 the greatest of Moore's poems: John Ashbery, *Selected Prose*, ed. Eugene Richie (Ann Arbor: University of Michigan Press, 2005), 111.

219 "self-portrait of a mind": *CRMM*, 52.

220 "It can be done": Lincoln MacVeagh to ST, September 2, 1924, quoted in *BMM*, 34.

220 "bets are going": MWM to JWM, December 19, 1923, RML.

221 "Dare I permit": MM to ST, draft, November 13, 1924, RML.

221 "the practical and moral": ST to JSW, carbon, November 3, 1924, YCAL.

221 "some reliable person . . . noo no!": JSW to ST, November 7, 1924, YCAL.

221 "Mr. Wescott": ST to JSW, carbon, November 12, 1924, YCAL.

221 "It *must* go": ST to Sophia Wittenberg, November 25, 1924, YCAL.

221 "so incomparably": *CRMM*, 53.

221 "the beauty of": MM to ST, JSW, and AG, December 23, 1924, *SL*, 216.

221 "the Renaissance tombstones . . . confusion": MM to B, December 22, 1924, YCAL.

222 "Imaginative Individual . . . to judge": *CRMM*, 53.

222 "mastery of phrase": *CRMM*, 67.

222 "passages of pure": *CRMM*, 51.

222 "long since overgrown": Herbert S. Gorman, "Miss Moore's Art Is Not a Democratic One," Book Review, *New York Times* (February 1, 1925), BR5.

223 "Only a person": AG to ST, October 8–9, 1921, YCAL.

223 "I know why": February 17, 1925, Notebook 1250/25, RML.

223 "Very elegant": MM to HD, July 26, 1921, *SL*, 172.

224 "stubbornness and naturalness": *Prose*, 362.

224 "to keep alight . . . seduction": *CRMM*, 54–55.

224 "youth and sex": *CRMM*, 62.

225 "friendly raillery": MM to MW, April 19, 1925, *SL*, 218.

225 "Everything is worthless . . . unbridled leap": *CRMM*, 67–73.

16. PICKING AND CHOOSING

227 "We could not but": MM to Hart Crane, August 13, 1925, YCAL.

228 "It is so much": MM to Hart Crane, November 10, 1925, YCAL.

228 "the sensibility and skill": Hart Crane to MM, November 10, 1925, YCAL.

228 "the Rt. Rev. Miss Mountjoy": *The Letters of Hart Crane 1916–1932,* ed. Brom
     Weber (New York: Hermitage House, 1952), 218.
228 "vapid and pretentious": MM to JSW, March 9, 1927, YCAL.
228 "denunciatory": MM to JSW, February 3, 1927, YCAL.
229 "irreparable loss": AG to MM, March 13, 1925, YCAL.
229 "I am busy": MM to B, June 22, 1925, YCAL.
229 "enthralling": MM to B, November 29, 1925, YCAL.
229 "my entire life": MM to B, November 2, 1925, YCAL.
229 "The Palm Tree's the thing": MWM to JWM, December 1, 1927, RML.
230 "I so firmly believe . . . I shall": MM to B, December 4, 1926, YCAL.
231 "ruins and museums": MWM to MW, June 2, 1927, RML.
231 "many unjustifiable calls": MM to TSE, August 10, 1927, *SL*, 234.
231 "the embodiment": MM to JWM, July 31, [1927], *SL*, 232.
231 "in a caper": MWM to JWM, August 14, 1927, RML.
231 "I know well": MM to GW, carbon, June 26, 1925, YCAL.
231 "God, how I hate you": Maxwell Bodenheim to MM, January 20, [1926], YCAL.
232 "hated": MWM to JWM, February 21, 1927, RML.
232 "an aesthetic Gibraltar": MM, advertisement, August 1927, RML.
232 "individuality": DH60, 289.
232 "a kind of eagle's perch": *Prose*, 646.
232 "art of educating": *Prose*, 215.
233 "Academic feeling . . . unintentional portrait": *Prose*, 182–83.
233 "to get just": MWM to JWM, September 12, 1927, RML.
234 "ingenuity and scrupulosity": Kenneth Burke, "She Taught Me to Blush,"
     Festschrift for Marianne Moore's Seventy Seventh Birthday, ed. Tambimuttu
     (New York: Tambimuttu & Mass, 1964), 61.
234 "Your resignation": JSW to MM, November 30, 1925, YCAL.
234 "I cannot bear": MM to ST, carbon, January 16, 1926, RML.
235 "The disarticulated limbs": ST, "Dawn from a Railway Day-Coach," *The Dial*
     79 (August 1925), 117.
235 "O wry": ST, "The Poet Takes Leave," *The Dial* 79 (December 1925), 467.
235 "Cannot publish": MM to ST, April 23, 1926, YCAL.
235 "self-command": MM to JWM and CEM, undated carbon or draft on verso of
     letter dated October 19, 1948, RML.
235 "the new name . . . express any": JSW to MM, January 29, 1927, RML.
235 "my strong dependence": MM to MW, June 28, 1925, NYPL.
235 "a disembodied spirit": MWM to JWM, February 25, 1928, RML.
236 "The first time": MM to HW, November 1, 1929, BMC.
236 "master . . . the art": *Prose*, 161.
236 *"Who Look on Beauty"*: MM to Laura Benét, June 16, 1926, RML.
236 "I tend to be": MM to B, March 27, 1926, YCAL.
236 "I have read Mr. Hemingway's": MM to Elise DePollier, March 7, 1925, YCAL.
237 "Your opinion": MM to TSE, draft, after May 28, 1925, RML.

237 sequence of Yeats's poems: Parts VI, VII, VIII, and X of "A Man Young and Old," *The Variorum Edition of the Poems of W. B. Yeats*, eds. Peter Allt and Russell K. Alspach (New York: Macmillan, 1957), 454–59.

237 "my unwavering assent . . . pleasure": MM to W. B. Yeats, carbon, May 7, 1926, YCAL.

237 "Your review occupies . . . piece": Sylvia Beach to MM, July 12, 1926, YCAL.

238 "acquiesce": JSW to MM, cable, September 16, 1926, YCAL.

238 "reducing it by": MM to Sylvia Beach, carbon, September 17, 1926, YCAL.

238 "speaking emphatically . . . letter": MM to JSW, September 22, 1926, YCAL.

238 "bad . . . intrinsically": MM to JSW, March 3, 1927, YCAL.

238 "We have elected": MM to JSW, March 10, 1927, YCAL.

239 "sacrilege to change": MM to GS, draft in MWM's hand, September 20, 1927, RML.

239 "One of the stories": MM to JWM, October 2, 1927, RML.

239 "Please do review": JSW to MM, [December 3, 1925], RML.

239 "It was a most": MWM to MW, January 3, 1926, YCAL.

239 "was one of the most": MM to Gertrude Stein, carbon, July 13, 1926, YCAL.

239 "has previously been slighted": JSW to MM, [February 1926], RML.

240 "It is a happiness": MM to Gertrude Stein, carbon, April 5, 1927, YCAL.

240 "I do appreciate": Gertrude Stein to MM, [April 1927], YCAL. "A Long Gay Book" would not be published in its entirety until 1933.

240 "Your equipoise": JSW to MM, November 16, [1925], RML.

240 "that publishing Pound's poetry": quoted in *Pound, Thayer, Watson*, 261.

241 "Have you ANY knowledge": EP to MM, February 9, 1927, YCAL.

241 "independently advocating": MM to JSW, February 25, 1927, YCAL.

241 "With regard to Ezra Pound": JSW to MM, on verso of MM to JSW, February 25, 1927, YCAL.

241 "Perhaps I am criminal": MM to EP, April 26, 1927, YCAL.

241 "Dear Miss Moore": JSW to MM, November 11, 1927, YCAL.

241 "It is I who": MM to JSW, November 14, 1927, YCAL.

242 "there is a baby": WS to MM, November 19, 1925, YCAL.

242 "Have you any": JSW to MM, July 10, 1928, YCAL.

242 "You are very good": MM to JSW, July 18, 1928, YCAL.

243 histories of *The Dial* that dismiss MM's editorial effectiveness: Nicholas Joost, *Scofield Thayer and* The Dial: *An Illustrated History* (Carbondale: Southern Illinois University Press, 1964); and *Pound, Thayer, Watson*. More sympathetic treatments of MM include chapter 5 of Jayne E. Marek, *Women Editing Modernism: "Little" Magazines & Literary History* (Lexington: University Press of Kentucky, 1995); and chapter 3 of Taffy Martin, *Marianne Moore: Subversive Modernist* (Austin: University of Texas Press, 1986).

244 "any interesting new": quoted in Joost, 246.

244 "squeezing the already dry orange": EP to MM, January 5, 1928, YCAL.

244 "criticized about town": WCW to MM, February 20, 1927, RML.

245 "cavalierly": ST to MM, December 6, [1925], RML.

245 "interweaving of the aesthetic": Burke, 61.

246 "much battered": MWM to JWM, January 26, 1929, RML.

246 "bright wild circus flesh": D. H. Lawrence, "When I Went to the Circus," *The Dial* (May 1929), 383–84.

246 "so full of vinegar": MM, addition to MWM to JWM, May 16, 1929, RML.

246 "In person you could": MM to D. H. Lawrence, June 22, 1929, *SL*, 249–50.

247 "deep, indeed reverent": MM to GS, draft, March 31, 1930, RML.

247 "I suppose a magazine": MM to GS, draft, August 28, 1929, RML.

247 "It is *this I care for*": MWM to JWM, April 4, 1929, RML.

247 "I still have myself": MM to JWM, May 20, 1929, RML.

247 "We have monopolized": JSW to MM, July 10, 1929, RML.

247 "too beautiful a thing": MM to JSW, July 12, 1929, *SL*, 250.

17. WHERE ONE DOES NOT WISH TO GO

249 "so evidently better . . . grief": MM to JWM, August 1, 1929, RML.

250 "It is not primarily": MWM to JWM, [August 10, 1928], RML.

250 "I never felt anything": MM to JWM, August 10, 1928, RML.

250 "oppressive": MCM to the author, October 28, 2009.

250 "I really should lose": MWM to JWM, September 26, 1920, RML.

250 "that there are a lot": JWM to MWM and MM, August 1, 1929, RML.

251 "indolent . . . can be done": MM to JWM, August 1, 1929, RML.

251 "Brace your paws!": JWM to MWM and MM, August 13, 1929, RML.

252 "every room": MM to GS, copy, December 25, 1930, RML.

252 "maid with starched cap": *Prose*, 540.

253 "so outraged": MM to B, February 22, 1933, *SL*, 296.

254 "the most remarkable": Notes for CA, October 18, 1969, MFC.

254 "a staff on which": MM to B, June 20, 1932, YCAL.

254 "extreme damsel in distress": MM to JWM, October 21, 1934, RML.

254 "like a mother animal": MWM to MCS, March 19, 1931, RML.

254 "a cloud of fiery": EB, "Invitation to Miss Marianne Moore," *The Complete Poems, 1927–1979* (New York: Farrar, Straus and Giroux, 1983), 82.

255 "what I am calling": MM to MW, March 26, 1934, YCAL.

255 "[Marianne] and I": MWM to EP, draft, February 1932, RML.

255 "I have been demolished": MM to EP, carbon, February 25, 1932, RML.

255 "This is about": MM to MW, March 26, 1934, YCAL.

256 "I hope, my dear Marianne": AG to MM, July 17, 1930, RML.

256 "Mon dieu!": AG to ST, October 8–9, 1921, YCAL.

256 "It is most beautiful": MM to AG, draft, July 29, 1930, RML.

256 "A great deliverance . . . thanksgiving!!": MWM, May 26, 1931, "Perry's Beauty Salon" Notebook, RML.

257 "be omitted": MM to YW, carbon, January 29, 1925, RML.

257 unrhymed version of "Poetry": *The New Poetry: An Anthology of Twentieth-Century Verse in English*, ed. Harriet Monroe and Alice Corbin Henderson (New York: Macmillan, 1932), 414–15.

257 "forcing her pattern": *CRMM*, 38, 39.

257 "unemphasized rhymes": *Prose*, 265.

257 "embedded rhyme": *Prose*, 267.

258 "I have about two or three thousand": MM to JWM, July 29, 1931, RML.

258 "unprudery . . . yesterday": *Prose*, 268–77.

259 "good for another ten . . . respectability": EP to Harriet Monroe, October 6, 1931, *Dear Editor: A History of* Poetry *in Letters, The First Fifty Years: 1912–1962*, ed. Joseph Parisi and Stephen Young (New York: Norton, 2002), 295.

259 "Her praise and enjoyment": MM to JWM, November 6, 1932, RML.

259 "One goes into . . . Lord Balfour": *Prose*, 283–84.

260 "it is by far": Lincoln Kirstein to MM, November 9, 1931, RML.

260 "frail for a long time": MWM to MCS, September 25, 1931, RML.

260 "My 'writing'": MM to B, April 4, 1932, *SL*, 264.

261 "both Brooklyn": MM to Barbara Kurz, April 25, 1961, *MMN* 1.2 (Fall 1977), 7.

261 "Rat's noble work": JWM to MWM and MM, August 9, 1932, RML.

18. DEBTS OF GRATITUDE

263 "felt down a little": MWM to MCS, May 29, 1932, RML.

263 "Why should I not speak": WCW to MM, June 2, 1932, RML.

264 "very very deep . . . family": MWM to JWM, July 2–20, 1932, RML. Since a mail steamer traveled to Samoa only once a month, MWM added to her monthly letter until it was time to mail it.

264 "cookie dust . . . *like*": Ibid.

264 "working like a demon": MM to JWM, June 24, [1932], *SL*, 257.

264 "to say what is boiling": MM to JWM, June 25, 1932, *SL*, 265.

264 "maybe the one": Ibid.

265 model stanza: Margaret Holley, "The Model Stanza: The Organic Origin of Moore's Syllabic Verse," *Twentieth-Century Literature* 30.2–3 (Summer/Fall 1984), 186.

265 "chock full": MWM to JWM, November 7, 1928, RML.

266 "the possibility of having": MM to GS, typed copy, November 27, 1928, RML.

267 "Mr. Kirstein": MM to JWM, December 12, 1932, RML.

267 "Yeats made": MM to JWM, December 18, 1932, *SL*, 286.

267 "with daring and ease": MM to EP, carbon, December 19, 1932, RML.

267 "and made some remark": MM to JWM, December 18, 1932, *SL*, 287.

267 "the starlings that form . . . sincerity": MM to JWM, January 29, 1933, RML.

268 "Come out here" . . . escorted away: Ibid.

269 "rush and spontaneity": MM to JWM, December 12, 1932, RML.

269 review of Dickinson's letters: See the author's "Marianne Moore's Emily Dickinson," *Emily Dickinson Journal* 12.2 (2003), 1–20.

270 "witnessed": MM to HD, draft answering HD to MM, March 2, 1935, RML.

270 "So are yours": MM to JWM, June 11, 1933, *SL*, 308.

270 "Deraly Beloved . . . Home Town": EP to MM, February 3, 1934, RML.

271 "she preceded the successes": EP, "Notes on Particular Details," *Active Anthology*, ed. EP (London: Faber and Faber, 1933), 254.

271 "terrific shove": MM to JWM, March 1, 1934, *SL*, 319.

271 "a complete volume": TSE to MM, February 27, 1934, RML.

271 "a kind of companion": TSE to MM, June 20, 1934, RML.

272 "At your simplest": Ibid.

272 "deplored a great deal": MM to JWM, May 5, 1934, RML.

272 "synonym books . . . bad poem": MWM to JWM, June 1, [1932], RML.

273 "diffident and miserable": TSE to MM, October 5, 1934, RML.

273 "tidal wave": MM to TSE, carbon, October 23, 1934, RML.

273 "We have had a violent": MM to WCW, May 12, 1934, RML.

274 "nicer than ever": MWM to JWM, April 27–May 19, 1933, RML.

274 "Would you accept": MWM to JWM, June 2–20, 1933, RML.

275 "Rat's chief joy": Ibid.

275 "supernatural . . . agent": MM to B, January 18, 1936, *SL*, 359–60.

275 MM's identification with Henry James: See the author's "Marianne Moore, the James Family, and the Politics of Celibacy," *Twentieth-Century Literature* 49.2 (2003), 219–45.

276 "Be thankful": MM to JWM, March 1, 1934, *SL*, 320.

276 "respectful humility . . . direction": *Prose*, 321–22.

276 "outlook on life": MM to Dorothea Gray, draft, November 5, 1935, RML.

276 "One's debts of gratitude": MM to B, January 18, 1936, *SL*, 360.

277 "the old story": MM to HW, June 24, 1934, BMC.

277 "ought to be guiding": EP to MM, July 9, 1932, RML.

277 "three pupils": MM to JWM, March 5, 1933, RML.

277 "full of born": MM to JWM, March 26, 1933, RML.

277 "the pride that refuses": MWM to B, February 5, 1934, Yale.

277 "interested in college boys": MM to Fanny Borden, March 8, 1934, VCL.

278 "quaint": EB, *Collected Prose*, 124.

278 "simply amazing": EB to Frani Blough, April 1, 1934, *OA*, 21.

278 "my Vassar friend": MM to HW, transcription, March 18, 1934, BMC.

278 "two huge brown": EB, *Collected Prose*, 125.

278 "Miss Bishop fed . . . sense": MM to JWM, April 26, 1934, RML.

279 "Miss Bishop is 'older' ": MM to JWM, February 18, 1935, RML.

279 "is her strongest": T. C. Wilson to MM, November 5, 1934, RML.

279 "I felt her ability": MM to T. C. Wilson, draft, November 5, 1934, RML.

280 "an eye-opener": EB, *Collected Prose*, 123.

280 minor changes: Joelle Biele, e-mail to the author, November 2, 2011.

280 "unwordiness": *Prose*, 328.

281 "I have given myself": EB to MM, August 21, 1936, *OA*, 45.

281 "Interesting as medicine": MM to EB, August 28, 1936, *SL*, 363.

281 "a half-dozen *phrases*": EB to MM, September 11, 1940, *OA*, 94.

281 MM's response to "Roosters": David Kalstone, *Becoming a Poet: Elizabeth Bishop with Marianne Moore and Robert Lowell* (New York: Noonday Press, 1989), 78–85.

282 "docile and respectful": MM to JWM, September 6, 1940, RML.

282 "What I'm about to say": EB to MM, October 17–20, 1940, *OA*, 96–97.

282 "tender and solicitous": MWM to JWM, November 1, 1940, RML.

282 EB's dislike of MWM: Chester Page in conversation with the author, January 20, 2010.

282 "You have done so much": MM to EB, June 1, 1945, VCL.

19. THE SEA IN A CHASM

283 "It certainly looks": MM and MWM to JWM, June 20, 1934, RML.

283 "like a demon": MM to JWM, June 1, 1934, RML.

283 "nutritious summer": MM to JWM, January 23, 1935, RML.

284 "the size of bats . . . asleep": MM to B, August 9, 1934, YCAL.

284 "These colonial grandeurs": MM to B, August 27, 1934, *SL*, 329.

284 "we have given away . . . *wrote*": MM to JWM, September 18, 1934, RML.

285 "hundreds of apartments": MWM to MCS, October 4, 1935, RML.

286 "I am now preparing": MM to JWM, August 6, 1933, RML.

287 "strict attention": MM to EP, March 4, 1935, *SL*, 343.

288 "Miss Moore is": *CRMM*, 106.

288 "that Miss Moore's poems": Ibid., 109.

288 "The moderately intellectual": Ibid., 106–107.

288 "very much less": *CRMM*, 110.

289 "Unless one is that": *CRMM*, 113–18.

289 "lovers of poetry": *CRMM*, 106.

291 "idiosyncrasies of technique": MM to Alice Bartlett, carbon, April 20, 1935, RML.

292 "a most romantic place": MM to EB, July 28, 1935, VCL.

292 "a chameleon attempt": MM to B, August 9, 1935, *SL*, 350–51.

293 "a task of a non-general kind": MM to Morton Dauwen Zabel, March 19, 1937, RML.

293 "over decorated": MM [c. 24 July 1935], Notebook 1250/29, RML.

294 "Once upon a time": TWWLN, 1.

294 "modern Audubon . . . cogitating": Ibid., 19.

294 "orphan": MM to JWM, October 11, 1939, RML.

295 "a minnow trapped": TWWLN, 249.

295 "Hand it to them": JWM to MM, December 13, 1939, RML.

295 "brisk with people": TWWLN, 109–10.

295 "a partial lake": Ibid., 257.

296 "dashing toward the house . . . white heels": Ibid., 6.

296 "Our mariner becalmed?": Ibid.

296 "As their Victoria": Ibid., 252.

296 "We simply do not": Harold S. Latham to MM, January 15, 1940, RML.

297 "internal quicksilver orangutan": MM to HW, transcription, June 6, 1938, BMC.

297 "Resistance must give place": MM to JWM, May 14, 1938, RML.

297 "Solicitude for others": MM to Bennett Cerf, December 6, 1938, RML.

298 "My mother has been ill": MM to EP, draft, April 21, 1939, RML.

298 "read nothing": MM to EP, carbon, December 10, 1939, RML.

298 "Yes. Ezra P.": JWM to MWM and MM, May 4, 1939, RML. MM's own letter about the meeting does not survive.

299 "things like the amount": TWWLN, 221.

299 "What Are Years?": Ibid., 226

299 "the long foot . . . straight up": Ibid., 228.

300 "Sojourn in the Whale": *CP*, 90.

20. HINDERED TO SUCCEED

301 "What I think about": EB to MM, February 19, 1940, *OA*, 87.

301 "Technical virtuosity": MM to JWM, March 20, 1940, RML.

302 "stinging greatness": MWM to JWM, July 20, 1921, RML.

302 "very abundant head": MWM to JWM, March 7, 1921, RML.

302 "wrought up or excited": MWM to JWM, April 8, 1940.

302 "'Welcome difficulty'": MM to MW, July 15, 1939, YCAL.

303 "victory by surrender": chapter title in David Seabury, *Help Yourself to Happiness* (New York: McGraw-Hill, 1937).

303 "refusing compromise": chapter in Seabury, *How to Worry Successfully* (Boston: Little, Brown, 1936).

304 "We are out of humor": MM to MCS, [March 18, 1941], RML.

304 "obduracy . . . I'm Irish": *Adversity & Grace: Marianne Moore, 1936–1941*, ed. Heather Cass White (Victoria, BC: ELS Editions, 2012), 48–50.

306 "still-life parables": [Schuyler Jackson], "Books: Poetry," *Time* (March 9, 1942), www.time.com/time/magazine/article/0,9171,885975,00.html.

306 "The bits about you . . . themselves": KJ to MM, March 5, 1942, RML.

307 "What elfin": MM to KJ, draft, March 9, 1942, RML.

307 "difficult" and "restricted": KJ to MM, September 9, 1942, RML.

308 "adores *getting things*": EB to MM, March 20, 1939, RML.

308 "reverence for people's": MM to LC, February 4, [1939], RML.

308 "the terrible kitten": MM to HW, September 29, 1933, BMC.

308 "an incubus": MM to MW, October 9, 1943, *SL*, 440.

308 "Now what do you think?": KJ to MM, May 20, 1942, RML.

308 "best friend . . . business woman": KJ to MM, March 13, 1942, RML.

308 Kathrine Jones and Marcia Chamberlain: [Patricia C. Willis], moore123
.wordpress.com/book-of-days/.

309 "I want to . . . exhausted": KJ to MM, May 24, 1942, RML.

309 "In addition to": KJ to MM, June 1, 1942, RML.

309 "Oh Marianne . . . with you": KJ to MM, June 10, 1942, RML.

309 "No hotels": quoted in KJ to MM, June 4, 1942, RML.

309 "gravely . . . *sulk*": KJ to MM, June 19, 1942, RML.

310 "By all means": DeWitt B. Lucas to MM, April 26, 1915, RML.

310 "highly intelligent": DeWitt B. Lucas to MM, January 23, 1943, RML.

310 "Kathrine has gotta": MM to JWM, October 13, 1944, RML.

311 "BEAUTIFUL! . . . this or that": WCW to MM, December 7, 1936, RML.

311 "baffled with admiration": EB to MM, December 5, 1936, *OA*, 47.

311 "I seemed 'entirely natural'": MM to JWM, May 2, 1940, RML.

311 "Your talk won": MM to JWM, May 2, 1940, RML.

311 "I am sure that": Henry Ware Eliot to MM, December 19, 1941, RML.

312 "Are you working": KJ to MM, June 24, 1942, RML.

312 "the Printing-Shop": MM to MCS, August 22, 1942, RML.

312 "was that instead of ": MM to B, October 4, 1942, YCAL.

313 "just a protest": DH60, 285.

314 "Oh Marianne": EB to MM, July 15, 1943, *OA*, 113.

314 "the only war poem": WHA to MM, April 7, 1944, RML.

314 "We wage . . . Iceland": *Prose*, 364.

314 "The crowning ornament": Ibid., 366.

314 "We are . . . double": Epigraph to W. H. Auden, *The Double Man* (New York:
Random House, 1941), title page.

314 "Precision is both . . . arrogant": *Prose*, 396.

315 "concealed rhyme": Ibid., 399.

315 "It seems so idle": MM to MCS, September 10, 1943, RML.

315 "these days of homelessness": MM to MCS, April 2, 1944, RML.

315 "attended lectures . . . a blessing": MM to MCS, August 20, 1943, RML.

315 "Wallace Stevens is beyond": MM to WCW, November 12, 1944, *SL*, 453–56.

316 "friendly and ready": MM to Lloyd Frankenberg, September 19, 1943, *SL*, 437.

316 "a moral force": Barbara Church to MM, May 1, 1951, RML.

316 "genius": MM to JWM, April 21, 1944, *SL*, 447.

316 "bound to Mr. Auden": MM to EB, November 16, 1943, *SL*, 442.

317 "hordes & hordes . . . shoes": MM to JWM, April 21, 1944, *SL*, 449.

317 "glowing with freedom": MWM to JWM, April 19, 1944, RML.

317 "I don't see how": MM to MW, September 29, 1943, YCAL.

318 "strong adherent": MM to MW [September 1943], YCAL.

318 "impeccable prose": quoted in MM to Cynthia S. Walsh, carbon, July 22, 1944,
RML.

318 "Never hold back": quoted in MM to JWM, May 14, 1944, RML.

318 "We are going to give . . . met": MM to JWM, May 14, 1944, RML.

318 "generous, quiet": MM to JWM, July 7, 1944, RML.

318 "kindred artists": MW interviewed in "Marianne Moore: In Her Own Image," *Voices & Visions*, video series from Annenberg Media, www.learner.org/catalog/extras/vvspot/Moore.html.

319 "almost silent way": quoted in MM to JWM, July 9, 1944, RML.

319 "I *refuse* to lend": MM to MCS, October 3, 1943, RML.

320 Cristanne Miller: *Cultures of Modernism: Marianne Moore, Mina Loy, and Elsa Lasker-Schüler* (Ann Arbor: University of Michigan Press, 2005), 182.

320 "One doesn't get through": MM to Kamon Friar, carbon, June 12, 1947, RML.

320 "neat and businesslike": MM to JWM, October 7, 1944, RML.

320 "There is certainly no poet": *CRMM*, 136–38.

321 "Congratulations": Henry McBride to MM, January 1, 1945, RML.

21. PERSEVERANCE

322 "twinkling lights": MM to MCS, June 10, 1943, RML.

322 "Scotty and Tommy": MM to MCS, May 31, 1944, RML.

323 "with all his pugnacious": MM to MCS, August 30, 1944, RML.

323 "insulting didacticism": MM to JWM, January 21, 1941, *SL*, 410.

323 "religious alligator": MM to JWM, March 19, 1944, RML.

324 "fire-breathing Catholic C.O.": Robert Lowell, *Collected Poems*, ed. Frank Bidart and David Gewanter (New York: Farrar, Straus and Giroux, 2003), 187.

324 "the only 'minister' ": EB to MM, February 4, 1937, RML.

324 "Twenty-seven people": MM to EB, carbon, May 15, 1938, RML.

325 "I believe in prayer": MM to Samuel McDuff McCoy, February 3, 1951, RML.

325 "plenty of 'rhymes' ": MM to JWM, November 5, 1944, RML.

325 "What enticed me": MM to Stephen Stepanchev, carbon, January 8, 1957, RML.

325 "I have respected": Robert Motherwell to MM, November 29, 1945, RML.

326 "your violets and crimsons": MM to Motherwell, carbon, December 1, 1945, RML.

326 "I wish I had": Motherwell to MM, January 23, 1946, RML.

326 "her poems" and "creative work": MM to JWM, April 26, 1945 [misdated 1944], RML.

326 "a masterpiece . . . here": Harry Levin to Walter H. Pistole, Jr., April 15, 1945, passage transcribed by Pistole and sent to MM, RML.

327 "heartier": MM to Eleanor Glenn Wallis, November 30, 1945, RML.

327 "quite easy and true": Pistole to MM, September 4, 1945, RML.

328 "I am belly deep . . . things": MM to JWM, August 25, 1944, RML.

328 "It will take me": MM to MCS, October 28, 1946, RML.

329 "after supper": MM to MCS, January 5, 1947, RML.

329 "inaccuracies": MM to Chester Kerr, carbon, June 20, 1947, RML.

329 "You must not be scared": MM to MCS, July 9, 1947, RML.

330 "We were helped": MM to MCS, July 9, 1947, RML.

330 "I kept her": JWM to KJ and MC, carbon, October 30, 1947, RML.

331 "*ill* in certain . . . *alcoholic*": JWM to MM, September 29, 1948, RML.

331 "Ulysses among the sirens": MM to LC, August 28, 1947, RML.

331 "been the cause of strain": MM to CEM and JWM, undated draft on verso of letter dated October 19, 1949, RML.

332 "I lost my grip a little": MM to MCS, April 27, 1948, RML.

332 "Terrible as it is": JWM to MM, September 29, 1948, RML.

332 happy marriage: MCM and SEM in conversation with the author, September 15, 2007.

333 "The household": MM to HW, August 4, 1947, BMC.

333 "I am much improved . . . *kind*": MM to MCS, August 13, 1947, RML.

334 "We do live": MM to LC, September 19, 1947, RML.

335 "Now, my boy": JWM to MM, July 31, 1947, RML.

335 "So must we now": JWM to MM, August 1, 1947, RML.

335 "A Face": *Collected Poems*, by MM (New York: Macmillan, 1951), 141.

335 "I don't seem to": MM to MCS, April 27, 1948, RML.

336 "Can you conceive . . . B-29": MM to Fanny Borden, December 2, 1946, VCL.

336 "that they really": MM, postscript to MWM to JWM, November 27, 1945, RML.

336 "doubtful sales risk": Chester Kerr to MM, December 22, 1947, RML.

337 "I marvel": Harry Levin to MM, January 16, 1948, RML.

337 "deep satisfaction": quoted in MM, addition to MWM to JWM, November 27, 1945, RML.

337 "condemnation was so thorough-going": MM to EP and Dorothy Pound, carbon, June 3, 1948, RML.

338 "encouraging energetic enthusiasm": MM to MCS, June 8, 1948, RML.

338 "My fables are": MM to MCS, August 13, 1949, RML.

339 "confirmation of one's freedom": MM to Laura Metzger, carbon, February 26, 1947, RML.

339 "Perseverance": MM to Eleanor Glenn Wallis, carbon, January 25, 1950, RML.

339 "very severe . . . words": MM to Levin, photocopy, July 17, 1949, RML.

339 "arbitrary . . . authority": MM to JWM, February 6, 1952, RML.

339 "There is no one": MM to YW, January 29, 1925, RML.

340 "'absolutely faithful'": MM to Barbara Church, June 18, 1953, RML.

340 "labored and uneuphonious": MM to Barbara Church, July 20, [1953], RML.

340 "fanatical": MM to HW, May 21, 1954, BMC.

22. A LUMINESCENT PAUL REVERE

341 "an uncommon *sweetness*": MM to JWM, February 28, [1950], RML.

342 "*a great flat foot*": quoted in Ibid., RML.

342 "wry gusto": MM to James Laughlin, carbon, May 15, 1950, RML.

342 "Mount Rushmores": Donald Hall, *Their Ancient Glittering Eyes: Remembering Poets and More Poets* (New York: Ticknor & Fields, 1992), 154.

343 "evanescent firefly quality": Henrietta Fort Holland, "Poet-Recluse," *Park East* (February 1951), 50.

343 "the fiercest": Ibid.

343 "above the accidents": EB, *Complete Poems*, 82–83.

343 "an astonishing person": Kreymborg, *Troubadour*, 238–39.

343 "I never saw a more": Kenneth Burke interviewed in "Marianne Moore," *Voices & Visions*.

343 "Everyone loved her": WCW, *Autobiography*, 146.

344 "apparently effortless": Joseph Roach, *It* (Ann Arbor: University of Michigan Press, 2007), 8.

344 "my 'cats and dogs'": MM to MCS, December 3, 1951, RML.

345 "the war poems": MM to B, January 20, 1952, Yale. The reviewer is the English poet Roy B. Fuller.

346 "warmly human": Wallace Fowlie, Review of *Collected Poems* by Marianne Moore, *Sewanee Review* 60:3 (July–September 1952), 543.

347 "I think you": "Jones, Miss Carson Get Book Awards," *New York Times* (January 30, 1952), nytimes.com.

347 "see no reason for calling . . . without": *Prose*, 648–49.

347 "I could live to ninety . . . wrinkled": JWM to MM, February 3, 1952, RML.

348 "I like you in the *cape*": quoted in MM to HW, August 6, 1953, BMC.

348 "heroically diligent": MM to MCS, May 26, 1953, RML.

348 "suppressed": MM to HW, September 19, 1953, BMC.

349 "famous . . . American poet": "Life Goes on a Zoo Tour with a Famous Poet," *Life* (September 21, 1953), 202.

349 "hideous": MM to MCS, September 22, 1953, RML.

349 "like a feminine": EB to MM, July 16, 1954, RML.

349 "I am wild": MM to MWM and JWM, November 13, 1906, RML.

350 "Could you get me . . . velvet": quoted in Eileen Foley, "Genius at Work: 'I Write Because I Can't Help It,'" *The* [Philadelphia] *Evening Bulletin*, October 26, 1965, RML.

350 "The hat did it!": JWM to MM, February 3, 1952, RML.

351 "discussed the ethics": MM to MCS, March 25, 1954, RML.

351 "like a construction worker": MM to MCS, May 18, 1954, RML.

351 "as poems to be read": *CCE*, 134.

351 "preoccupied . . . thrive": *CCE*, 143.

352 "Ah Marianne!": EB to MM, January 19, 1957, *OA*, 335.

352 "repairs": MM to Barbara Church, September 9, 1957, RML.

353 "champions of harmonious speed": MM to LC, August 2, 1952, *SL*, 504.

353 "What would trust": MM to MCS, January 25, 1952, RML.

354 "in misery": MM to MCS, December 28, 1952, RML.

354 "How magnificently . . . electric touch": HW to MM, August 23, 1953, RML.

355 "a subterranean career": MM to Sue Craig Stauffer, June 7, 1949, RML.

355 "Courage": MM to E. McKnight Kauffer, January 27, 1952, RML.

355 "my chief aid": MM to MCS, April 29, 1954, RML.

355 "My dear Marianne": TSE to MM, April 27, 1956, RML.

356 "To Miss Marianne Moore": [TSE] to MM, May 8, 1956, RML.

356 heartbroken: Gladys Berry interviewed in "Marianne Moore," *Voices & Visions*.

356 "honest, auspicious": MM to Margaret Marshall, February 19, 1953, YCAL.

356 "Well, I'm sure Eisenhower": EB to MM, December 3, 1956, RML.

356 "our most distinguished": Louise Bogan, "Verse," *New Yorker* (November 11, 1944), 96.

357 "should be a source": Louise Bogan, "Books," *New Yorker* (August 2, 1952), 65.

357 "feel very badly": EB to MM, August 24, 1952, RML.

23. CONEY ISLAND FUN FAIR VICTIM

358 "a quite outrageous": Winthrop Sargeant, "Profiles: Humility, Concentration, and Gusto," *New Yorker* (February 16, 1957), 38.

358 "bric-a-brac . . . snugness": Ibid., 42.

358 "The connoisseurs . . . herself": Ibid.

359 "I take it very hard": MM to Chester Page, photocopy, February 15, 1957, gift to author.

359 "tall, spare . . . association": Sargeant, 56.

359 "some visceral feeling": "Department of Amplification," *New Yorker* (April 13, 1957), 140–41.

359 "removes the blur": MM to Bon Ami Company, carbon, April 15, 1936, RML.

359 "educating visualization": *Prose*, 215.

360 "To our favorite Turtletopper": "Department of Amplification," 146.

360 "a genius": MM to B, December 16, 1921, YCAL.

361 "encouraging James Merrill . . . compliment": MM to HW, October 4, 1957, BMC.

361 "with much zeal": MM to Lota Soarez, August 16, 1958, VCL.

361 "We are overjoyed": Howard Moss to MM, September 30, 1958, RML.

361 "Whether you can use": MM to Moss, carbon, October 15, 1958, RML.

362 "phenomenally liberal . . . writing-world": MM to Rachel MacKenzie, carbon, July 1, 1959, RML.

362 "It has taken *The New Yorker*": EB to MM, January 5, 1961, RML.

362 "half a grapefruit": *Prose*, 661.

362 "I do for the most part": MM to Grace Schulman, April 26, 1969, RML.

362 "desperate": MM to Karen Aptakin, December 13, 1968, RML.

362 "FREEDOM for press . . . freedom": MM to Charles H. Percy, carbon, May 13, 1959, RML.

363 "My anonymous mail": MM to Barbara Church, August 13, 1957, RML.

363 "Careful typing": MM to Arno Bader, carbon, May 9, 1958, RML.

363 "I think you write": quoted in MM to Frances and Norvelle Browne, August 5, 1960, RML.

363 "a kind of Coney Island": MM to HW, August 19, 1957, BMC.

363 "I am being obliterated": MM to Richard Avedon, carbon, October 17, 1959, RML.

363 "I beg to be neglected": DH65, 314.

363 "Dear Miss Elizabeth": MM to Elizabeth Coffrey, draft, May 12, 1969, RML.

364 "Dear Marianne": Beatrice Roethke to MM, February 22, 1962, RML.

364 potted plant: Hall, *Ancient Glittering Eyes*, 162.

364 "Try to be": Valerie Eliot to MM, January 29, 1969, RML.

364 "They say time heals grief": MM to Thomas Guinzberg, carbon, October 22, 1961, RML.

364 "My writing suffers": MM to Stephan Stepanchev, carbon, January 8, 1957, RML.

365 "My reading was": MM to JWM, October 11, 1957, RML.

365 "Every college": MM to HW, May 7, 1957, BMC.

365 "emergency underwear": MM to JWM, October 11, 1957, RML.

365 "Malvina is a rare companion": MM to Barbara Church, August 13, 1957, RML.

365 "We grew up": "Malvina Hoffman Honored at Rites," *New York Times* (July 14, 1966), nytimes.com.

366 "as if I were": MM to JWM, August 17, 1962, RML.

366 "veil anything personal": *Prose*, 551.

369 "a master of hyperbole": *Prose*, 660.

369 "This book is more": MM to J. Randall Williams, carbon, October 10, 1959, RML.

369 "a fine youth": MM to MCS, January 27, 1954, RML.

370 "the best woman poet": quoted in Harry Gilroy, "Marianne Moore Wins Gold Medal," *New York Times* (April 14, 1967), nytimes.com.

370 "Lincoln's assassination . . . reasons": SEM, Notes, MFC.

24. SENIOR CITIZEN OF THE YEAR

373 "at a measured": Adrienne Rich, *Poetry and Prose*, eds. Barbara Charlesworth Gelpi and Albert Gelpi (New York: Norton, 1993), 168.

373 "one of Mr. Johnson's": MM to Lyndon B. Johnson, draft for telegram, January 15, 1965, RML.

373 "a stately and grave": MM to Jeff Kindley, June 14, 1965, RML.

373 "truly the poet laureate": Harry Gilroy, "Marianne Moore Wins Gold Medal."

374 "an award to tenacity": MM to Nelson A. Rockefeller, carbon, February 22, 1969, RML.

374 "that whines and wanders": *Prose*, 630.

374 "She must be": Sylvia Plath to Aurelia Plath, April 16, 1955, *Letters Home by Sylvia Plath*, ed. Aurelia Schober Plath (New York: Harper & Row, 1975), 168.

374 "more patient": MM to Joseph M. Bottkol, carbon, April 18, 1955, RML.

375 "ageing giantesses": Sylvia Plath, *The Unabridged Journals, 1950–1962*, ed. Karin V. Kukil (New York: Anchor, 2000), 360.

375 "a blue streak": Sylvia Plath to Warren Plath, June 10, 1958, *Letters Home*, 340.

375 "warmly . . . copy": MM to Sylvia Plath, July 13–14, 1958, facsimile in Vivian R. Pollak, "Moore, Plath, Hughes, and 'The Literary Life,'" *American Literary History* 17:1 (Spring 2005), 105.

375 "I thought and think": MM to Henry Allen Moe, carbon, November 1961, RML.

376 "Talent, knowledge": *Prose*, 571.

377 "Now that you are": Pascal Covici to MM, May 25, 1956, RML.

378 "the finest": Dickey, "What the Angels Missed."

378 "her least good": Ashbery, *Selected Prose*, 83.

378 "Forced to avoid . . . poet": Ibid., 85–86.

380 "the greatest living poet . . . poet": Ibid., 108.

380 "farcical": CRMM, 230.

381 "This medal and gift": MM, December 10, 1968, notes for National Medal of Literature acceptance speech, RML.

383 "a child about money": quoted in SEM, March 1, 1968, Notes, MFC.

383 "pocket money": quoted in SEM, October 27, 1967, Notes, MFC.

383 Clive Driver's lamb: Grace Schulman, in conversation with the author, 1999.

383 "the electrically-lighted, suspended": MM to LC, July 7, 1951, RML.

384 "Goodbye, Anny Baumann!": quoted in SEM, November 16, 1969, Notes, MFC.

385 "You know, your father": quoted in SEM, May 5, 1969, Notes, MFC.

385 events of MM's death and funeral: SEM to John Warner Moore III, photocopy, February 13–April 17, 1972, MFC.

385 "one of our most": Richard Nixon: "Statement About the Death of Marianne Moore," February 6, 1972, accessed online at the American Presidency Project, www.presidency.ucsb.edu/ws/?pid=3723.

Acknowledgments

Among my greatest pleasures in writing this biography have been the people I have met and the encouragement I have received from friends and family. For convincing me that I would like to attempt a biography of Marianne Moore, I am indebted to N. John Hall and to the members of his National Endowment for the Humanities Summer Seminar on literary biography. For giving me permission to proceed and for their kindness and generosity throughout the years I have known them, I thank the members of Moore's family: Marianne Craig Moore, John Warner Moore, Jr., David Markwick Moore, John Stauffer, Martha Stauffer, and the late Sarah Eustis Moore and Mary Moore Reeves.

I will refrain from naming the many teachers who have fostered my writing except to acknowledge my most demanding one: Susan Rabiner, my agent, who made me rewrite my book proposal over and over until I found the story in my facts.

Never have I doubted my good fortune in garnering the support of Jonathan Galassi, my editor. His encouragement, courtesy, and promptness are a marvel. This book owes much to the resourceful expertise of Miranda Popkey, Christopher Richards, and other members of the editorial staff at Farrar, Straus and Giroux. My thanks go also to the publicity department and especially to Lottchen Shivers.

The archival research for this biography would not have been possible without a sabbatical fellowship from the American Philosophical Society, a travel grant from the National Endowment for the Humanities, and a sabbatical from Oklahoma State University. The National Endowment for the Humanities supported the writing of the book with a yearlong fellowship. The Center for the Humanities at Oregon State University provided a five-month fellowship and an ideal setting in which to work. A second sabbatical from Oklahoma State University granted me another year in which to write. Two research grants from the Oklahoma Humanities Council and a summer stipend from the College of Arts and Sciences at Oklahoma State University also aided my research and writing.

Proceedings of the American Philosophical Society, Twentieth-Century Literature, Journal of Modern Literature, South Central Review, and Bucknell University Press have published portions of this book in different form.

The staff at the Rosenbach Museum & Library in Philadelphia endured my daily presence for more than a year. They could not have been kinder or more accommodating. I would like to name in particular Catherine Hitchens, the late Evelyn Feldman, Michael Barsanti, Elizabeth Fuller, Bill Adair, Derick Dreher, Joan Watson, and Najia Khan. Katherine Haas and Patrick Rodgers have also helped me with various matters since that year.

Fruitful conversations that began in the Rosenbach's reading room have contributed to my understanding of Moore and of biography, especially those with Grace Schulman, Ellen Levy, Vivian Pollak, Lisa Cohen, Luke Carson, Roberta Tarbell, and Karin Roffman. Equal gratitude goes to Allen Hibbard, Susan Balée, Teresa Jaynes, Daniel Hoffman, Elizabeth McFarland, Terry Daugherty, Marjorie Sandor, Susan McCabe, and Joelle Biele for enlightening conversations at various stages of the project.

I thank the staff at the Beinecke Rare Book Room and Library. Patricia Willis has facilitated my understanding of Marianne Moore since I began researching Moore many years ago. Nancy Kuhl and

Ingrid Lennon-Pressey have gone out of their way to help me with Beinecke resources.

My appreciation also goes to David Robinson and Wendy Madar at the Center for the Humanities at Oregon State University; Eric Pumroy, Lorett Treese, and Marianne Hansen of the Bryn Mawr College Library; David Smith of the Cumberland County (Pennsylvania) Historical Society; Jeffrey Wood of the Whistlestop Bookshop; Dean M. Rogers of the Vassar College Library; Jim Gerencser and Jane Schroeder of the Dickinson College Library; Loretta Brissette of the Stevens Alumni Association; Carolyn Cottrell of the Portsmouth (Ohio) Public Library; Debbie Schuler and the Honorable James W. Kirsch of the Scioto County (Ohio) Probate Court; Carolyn Elwess of Park University; and the Interlibrary Services librarians at Oklahoma State University.

The exceptionally generous community of Moore scholars has aided this project in countless ways. Cristanne Miller and I have been talking about Moore for twenty-five years. Robin Schulze has often been part of that conversation. Charles Molesworth shared with me the materials he gathered for Moore's first biography. I owe more than my brief citations indicate to the scholarship of Patricia Willis, Bonnie Costello, Cristanne Miller, Robin Schulze, Heather White, Elizabeth Gregory, Jeanne Heuving, Cynthia Hogue, Stacy Hubbard, Jennifer Leader, Margaret Holley, and Laurence Stapleton. The work of the cultural historians Norman Brosterman and Helen Lefkowitz Horowitz and of the psychologist Salvadore Minuchin also provided important contexts for my understanding of Moore's life.

All Moore scholars are in debt to Melanie Fortunato for restoring a cache of letters to the Moore archive. My thanks to Marsha Recknagel and Richard Howard for opening important doors to me early on. Mr. and Mrs. Samuel J. Bernard of Carlisle, Pennsylvania, literally opened their front door to me when I asked to see the house where Moore lived for twenty years. Edward Moran escorted me through Moore's Brooklyn neighborhood and introduced me to Moore's friend Chester Page, who has become my friend, too. Willard Greene, Jennifer Uricks, and Randy Campbell assisted me in piecing together the Moore family tree.

Good friends have helped me revise the book during its long

progress. Margaret Ewing read every chapter as I drafted it, and asked astute, clarifying questions about matters large and small. Patricia Willis read the whole manuscript at a late stage and suggested a few salient corrections. Friends who provided insights and correctives to individual chapters include Linda and Leonard Leff, Terry Zambon, Susan Balée, Stephanie Ross, Duke Pesta, Toni Graham, Michael Gilmore, and Susie Rosenberg.

Writing groups in Northwest Arkansas have offered excellent advice on several chapters in the book. I appreciate in particular Ann Teague, Susan Raymond, Mary Jean Place, Lee Guthrie, June Jefferson, Pamela Lee Hill, Mary Charlton, Peggy Konert, Jan Larkey, Barbara Youree, Marilyn Collins, Maeve Maddox, Robin Mero, Pat Prinsloo, Raymona Anderson, Marilyn Lanford, Nancy Hartney, and Velda Brotherton.

All of my friends of recent years have had to befriend Marianne Moore, too. For their ongoing encouragement, I thank Beth Collins, Leonard and Linda Leff, Gretchen Schwarz, Mike and Ellen Sowell, Margaret and Sidney Ewing, D. Dutt and Jean D'Offay, Sandy Cohlmia, Pat Darlington, Mary Ellen Holley, Kay Heath, Jan Bartels, Susie Rosenberg, Darlene Moore, Sue Ross, Liz Wagner, Carol Luszcz, Ninette Euler, Mardi Dunkley, Deb Kosnett, Margie Segal, Marsha Recknagel, Patti Simmons, John and Connie Catsis, Jeff Walker, Bill Decker, Linda Austin, Belinda Bruner, Joyce Bender, Linda Hager, Fran Taylor, Jim and Julie Jensen, Donna Dover, Kathy Siegfried, Lois Haase, Janet Poole, Rebecca Newth, and others already named above. Within my family, Marjory and Paul Cretien, Neal and Cherie Leavell, Martha and Stan Shimkus, Frank and Kim Newport, John Paul Newport and Polly King, Carolyn and Don Towles, Ava Leavell Haymon, and Libby Bennett have been especially supportive. Among several coffee shops that have fueled my writing, I note especially The Daily Grind in Stillwater, Oklahoma, and its morning regulars.

I dedicate this book to Brooks Garner, who has accepted Marianne Moore's presence in our lives since the day we married.

Index